John Warwick Montgomery

**The Libraries of France
at the Ascendancy of Mazarin**

Geschichte – Kirchengeschichte – Reformation

Volume 28

Vol 21: Friedrich Wilhelm Schirrmacher. Briefe und Akten zum Marburger Religionsgespräch (1529) und zum Augsburger Reichstag (1530). 2003.

Vol 22: Friedrich Wilhelm Schirrmacher. Die Entstehung des Kurfürstenkollegiums. 2003.

Vol 23: John Warwick Montgomery. Heraldic Aspects of the German Reformation. 2003.

Vol 24: Thomas Schirrmacher. Indulgences: A History of Theology and Reality of Indulgences and Purgatory: A Protestant Evaluation. 2011.

Vol 25: Christina v. Torklus. Die Formierung der mittelalterlichen Kirche Livlands: Strukturen, Träger und Inhalte der kirchlichen Nacharbeit (13.-16. Jahrhundert). 2012. 3 Bände.

Vol 26: Amelie Kruse-Regnard. Am Rande des Grabes spazieren gehen: Johannes Calvins Theologie des Leidens. 2013.

Vol 27: Manfred Stedtler. Baptisten in der Weimarer Republik. 2015

John Warwick Montgomery

The Libraries of France at the Ascendancy of Mazarin

Louis Jacob's
Traicté des plus Belles Bibliotheques

Part Two in English Translation,
with Introduction and Notes

Verlag für Kultur und Wissenschaft
Culture and Science Publ.
Dr. Thomas Schirrmacher
Bonn 2015

THE LIBRARIES OF FRANCE AT THE ASCENDANCY OF MAZARIN
Louis Jacob's Traicté des plus Belles Bibliotheques, Part Two in English Translation, with Introduction and Notes

Copyright © 2016 John Warwick Montgomery. All rights reserved. Except for brief quotations in critical publications or reviews, no part of this book may be reproduced in any manner without prior written permission from the publisher. Write: Permissions, Wipf and Stock Publishers, 199 W. 8th Ave., Suite 3, Eugene, OR 97401.

This edition published by Wipf and Stock Publishers in cooperation with Verlag für Kultur und Wissenschaft.

Wipf & Stock
An Imprint of Wipf and Stock Publishers
199 W. 8th Ave., Suite 3
Eugene, OR 97401

www.wipfandstock.com

PAPERBACK ISBN: 978-1-4982-6897-4
HARDCOVER ISBN: 978-1-4982-8991-7

Manufactured in the U.S.A.

For

W. Howard Hoffman, M.D.

and

Kurt & Debra Winrich

who rightly believe that the Word has been made flesh

ACKNOWLEDGMENTS

A number of institutions and individuals have put me in their debt in the course of the present study. Assistance with particularly difficult editorial and translational problems was received from Ian R. Willison, Assistant Keeper, Department of Printed Books, British Museum; P. Josserand, Conservateur en chef, Départment des Imprimés, Bibliothèque Nationale; E. Brin, Conservateur, Réserve des Imprimés, Bibliothèque Nationale; J. Porcher, Conservateur en chef, Cabinet des Manuscrits, Bibliothèque Nationale; F. Dousset, Adjoint au Directeur Général Archives de France; Martin Wittek, Bibliothécaire, Bibliothèque Royale de Belgique; Frederick R. Goff, Chief, Rare Books Division, Reference Department, Library of Congress; J. M. Edelstein, Reference Librarian, Rare Books Division, Reference Department, Library of Congress; Robert Rosenthal, Head, Department of Special Collections, University of Chicago Library; and Robert W. Wadsworth, Head, Acquisitions Department, University of Chicago Library.

Inter-library loans and photoreproductions were supplied by the Bibliothèque Nationale, Paris; Rare Books Department, Boston Public Library; Department of Printed Books, British Museum; University of California Library, Berkeley; University of Chicago Library; Cornell University Library; Friedrich-Alexander Universität Library, Erlangen, Germany; Harvard University Library; University of Illinois Library; Library of Congress; University of Michigan Library; National Library of Canada, Ottawa; Newberry Library, Chicago; University of Pennsylvania Library; Princeton University Library; Union Theological Seminary Library, New York; History of Medicine Division, U.S. National Library of Medicine, Cleveland, Ohio; University of Virginia Library; University of Washington Library; and Yale University Library.

The National Lutheran Educational Conference, Washington, D.C. (executive director, Gould Wickey) presented me with two of its Martin Luther graduate fellowships to assist in carrying out the study. The University of Toronto Library kindly provided me with an extra-mural readership, which made it possible for me to do a large part of my basic research work in their fine book collection; appreciation is particularly due to R. Brian Land, Assistant Chief Librarian, in this regard.

Finally, I wish to acknowledge the guidance received from Howard Winger, Ruth French Strout, and Donald Lach of the University of Chicago's Graduate Library School; the assistance obtained in matters of interlibrary loan from Mrs. A. Margaret Evans, Reference Librarian, Waterloo Lutheran University (now, Wilfrid Laurier University); and the excellent typing of successive drafts of the manuscript by Mrs. Carmen Lipp of Thornhill, Ontario.

CONTENTS

	Page
ACKNOWLEDGMENTS	vii
INTRODUCTION	1

TREATISE ON THE FINEST LIBRARIES, PUBLIC AND PRIVATE,
WHICH HAVE EXISTED AND WHICH EXIST TODAY IN THE WORLD
PART TWO

Chapter

			Page
I.	(LXXXII.)	THE KINGDOM OF FRANCE	57
II.	(LXXXIII.)	THE CITY OF PARIS	58
III.	(LXXXIV.)	LIBRARIES OF PARIS WHICH HAVE BEEN DISPERSED	191
IV.	(LXXXV.)	LIBRARIES IN THE VICINITY OF PARIS . . .	207
V.	(LXXXVI.)	ANJOU	209
VI.	(LXXXVII.)	AVIGNON AND THE COMTAT VENAISSIN	211
VII.	(LXXXVIII.)	AUVERGNE	219
VIII.	(LXXXIX.)	BÉARN	221
IX.	(XC.)	BERRY	225
X.	(XCI.)	THE DUCHY AND COUNTY OF BURGUNDY	227
XI.	(XCII.)	BRITTANY	238
XII.	(XCIII.)	CHAMPAGNE	240
XIII.	(XCIV.)	DAUPHINÉ	243
XIV.	(XCV.)	GUIENNE	248

CONTENTS--Continued

Chapter			Page
XV.	(XCVI.)	LANGUEDOC	250
XVI.	(XCVII.)	LORRAINE	262
XVII.	(XCVIII.)	LYONNAIS, FOREZ, AND BEAUJOLAIS	264
XVIII.	(XCIX.)	LIMOUSIN	272
XIX.	(C.)	MAINE	273
XX.	(CI.)	MARCHE	276
XXI.	(CII.)	METZ, TOUL, AND VERDUN	278
XXII.	(CIII.)	NORMANDY	280
XXIII.	(CIV.)	THE PRINCIPALITY OF ORANGE	286
XXIV.	(CV.)	THE REGIONS ABOUT ORLÉANS, CHARTRES, BLOIS, VENDÔME, ETC.	287
XXV.	(CVI.)	PICARDY	295
XXVI.	(CVII.)	POITOU	297
XXVII.	(CVIII.)	PROVENCE	300
XXVIII.	(CIX.)	TOURAINE	313
XXIX.	(CX.)	SAVOY	316
SELECTED BIBLIOGRAPHY			318

INTRODUCTION

INTRODUCTION

France in 1644

Louis Jacob begins Part Two of his <u>Traicté des plus belles bibliothèques publiques et particulières, qui ont esté & qui sont à present dans le monde</u> with the striking assertion: "France today surpasses all other realms in learned men and in libraries." What in fact was the condition of France and of the other major powers of Europe at the time the first book-length universal survey of libraries was written?

In 1644, the Thirty Years' War was drawing to a close; in four years the treaties of Westphalia would provide the first all-European peace settlement for the first all-European war. This exceedingly long conflict, involving both North and South European powers, had been fought on the soil of the German territorial principalities, and the result of the continual crossing and re-crossing of mercenary armies over the German lands was a frightfully weakened Germany.[1] The Thirty Years' War increased

---

[1] Grimmelshausen, in his horrifying novel based in part upon his personal experiences in the Thirty Years' War, describes the soldiery engaged in such activities as forcing peasants to drink liquid filth, blowing off their thumbs by sticking them in the barrels of their pistols, and betting on the number of people who could be killed by one shot when placed one behind the other (<u>Simplicissimus</u>, chaps. i, iv, xiv). The recent attempts to present a mild view of the effects of the War on Germany (e.g., S. H. Steinberg, "The Thirty Years' War: A New Interpretation," in Herman Ausubel [ed.], <u>The Making of Modern Europe</u> [2 vols.;

the momentum of German territorialism and political fragmentation which had received its charter in the Golden Bull of 1356; now a bewilderingly divided Germany and a hopelessly decentralized Holy Roman Empire of the German Nation would offer little competition for a France which, under powerful leadership, was beginning to realize the ideal of the national state.[2]

Significantly, Henri Hauser titles his survey of the European scene from 1559 to 1660, La prépondérance espagnole.[3] But by 1644 unfortunate economic policies[4] and weak occupants of the throne[5] had clearly marked the downward path which Spain

---

New York: Dryden Press, (1951)], I, 207-21) have not successfully countered C. V. Wedgwood's balanced interpretation (The Thirty Years War [2d ed.; Harmondsworth, Middlesex: Penguin Books, 1957]).

[2] This point has been well made by G. Barraclough, The Origins of Modern Germany (Oxford: Blackwell, 1952).

[3] Henri Hauser, La prépondérance espagnole (1559-1660) (3d ed.; "Peuples et Civilisations"; Paris: Presses Universitaires de France, 1948). The next volume in the "Peuples et Civilisations" series is Philippe Sagnac and A. de Saint-Léger's appropriately titled, La prépondérance française: Louis XIV (1661-1715).

[4] One can mention in this connection not only the much-discussed expulsions of the Jews (1492) and Moriscos (1609) from Spain (cf. Rafael Altamira, A History of Spain, tr. Muna Lee [New York: Van Nostrand, 1949], pp. 286-89, 391), and the questionable treatment of gold bullion obtained from the New World (cf. Myron P. Gilmore, The World of Humanism, 1453-1517 [New York: Harper, 1952], pp. 45-47), but also and especially the crown's promotion of the Mesta, a guild of migratory Castilian sheep-growers, which reduced radically the amount of land in Castile under cultivation (see Julius Klein, The Mesta: a Study in Spanish Economic History, 1273-1836 [Cambridge: Harvard University Press, 1920]).

[5] The deterioration of the Spanish Hapsburgs after Philip II has been frequently pointed out, and can even be detected in the portraits of these sovereigns. Philip III (reigned 1598-1621) was melancholy and introspective; Philip IV (ruled 1621-1665) was an amiable non-entity; and Charles II, the last of the Spanish

would take over the next centuries. Indeed, the Thirty Years' War "assured the replacement of Spain by France as the dominating power in Western Europe."[6] As for France's traditional third rival, England, the internal constitutional struggles which characterized the reign of Charles I occupied the nation's attention when Louis Jacob wrote his *Traicté*;[7] though in England "déjà se prépare une autre hégémonie qui supplantera, le jour venu, l'hégémonie française,"[8] that day is not yet contemplated by Jacob's contemporaries.

Mid-seventeenth century France differed little in territorial extent from France today, but enjoyed a great population advantage relative to the other countries of Europe. In 1650, some 20,000,000 out of the 100,000,000 inhabitants of Europe were Frenchmen; in 1950, only 42,000,000 of the 540,000,000 people in Europe lived in France.[9] Thus, whereas today only one out of twelve Europeans is a Frenchman, at the time Jacob wrote his *Traicté*, one out of five was his countryman. Although it is exceedingly difficult to obtain satisfactory

---

Hapsburgs (reigned 1665-1700), was "regarded by contemporaries as a medical curiosity" (David Ogg, *Europe in the Seventeenth Century* [8th ed.; London: Adam & Charles Black, 1960], p. 6).

[6]Wedgwood, *The Thirty Years War*, p. 10 (Introduction to the revised ed.).

[7]See G. W. Prothero's articles in *The Cambridge Modern History*, IV (New York: Macmillan, 1906), 256-355.

[8]Hauser, *La prépondérance espagnole*, p. 534.

[9]Data from Michel Huber, Henri Bunle, and Fernand Boverat, *La population de la France, son évolution et ses perspectives* (3d ed.; Paris: Hachette, [1950]), pp. 22-23.

statistics on the population of Paris in the seventeenth century, it appears that only Constantinople and Naples among European cities surpassed in size the chief city of France.[10] Moreover, France held a position of pre-eminence in natural resources, for she benefited from varied climate and very fertile soil. It was not mere rhetorical obsequiousness, but accurate powers of description, which led Montchrestien to write thus to Louis XIII and his mother the Regent in 1615: "Vos Majestés possèdent un grand état, agréable en assiette, abondant en richesses, fleurissant en peuples, puissant en bonnes et fortes villes, invincible en armes, triomphat en gloire."[11]

When Jacob's Traicté appeared, three decades had passed since the presageful year 1614--the year of the last Estates-General until the Revolution, and a year marked by Richelieu's emergence into the political scene.[12] These decades immediately

---

[10] For comparative figures, see Roger Mols, Introduction a la démographie historique des villes d'Europe du XIVe au XVIIIe siecle (3 vols.; Gembloux: J. Duculot, 1954-1956), Vol. II. Josiah Cox Russell (Late Ancient and Medieval Population [Philadelphia: American Philosophical Society, 1958], p. 130) believes that the high population figure (300,000) for Constantinople, which is derived from the report of a Venetian ambassador in 1573, is greatly exaggerated. Between 1656 and 1688 the population of Naples declined from 300,000 to 186,354; Paris during the same period was growing rapidly (at the beginning of the seventeenth century she had only some 200,000 inhabitants; by 1700, the number had increased to about 350,000, and by the Revolution 600,000 people were living there). London, by contrast, had but 70,000 inhabitants in its old city (excluding suburbs) in 1600.

[11] Antoine de Montchrestien, L'économie politique patronale, ed. Th. Funck-Brentano (Paris: E. Plon, 1889), p. 23.

[12] Cf. Gabriel Hanotaux, La jeunesse de Richelieu (1585-1614), la France en 1614 (new ed.; Paris: Societe de l'histoire nationale, Librairie Plon, [1932]); this work comprises Vol. I of the author's Histoire du cardinal de Richelieu.

preceding the publication of Jacob's book were dominated by the inflexible will of Richelieu. Guérard tells us that "every child in France learns by heart, like a magic formula, the three points of Richelieu's policy: to surpress the political privileges of the Protestants, to reduce the nobles to strict obedience, to humble the House of Austria."[13] These three policies were but applications of Richelieu's governing life-principle: to make France the unquestioned leader among European powers by unifying the French state in unquestioned obedience to its sovereign's will.[14] One cannot fairly say that Richelieu achieved absolutism in France, for he did not alter such existing decentralized structures as the provincial governorships (when, for example, Montmorency revolted in Languedoc, he merely replaced him), but "if he did not establish a strongly centralized government, his ruthless policy so cowed the aristocracy and all the other sections opposed to absolutism that, although during the minority which followed they were to

---

[13] Albert Guérard, *France, A Modern History* (Ann Arbor: University of Michigan Press, 1959), p. 166. In his *Testament politique*, written in his later years, Richelieu summed up his efforts in behalf of his King thus: "ruiner le parti huguenot, rabaisser l'orgueil des grands, réduire tous ses sujets en leur devoir et relever son nom dans les nations étrangères au point où il devait être" (Richelieu, *Testament politique*, ed. Louis André [Paris: Laffont, 1948], p. 95).

[14] Wedgwood effectively points up the prophetic character of Richelieu's christening motto: *Regi Armandus*, "Armand for the King" (C. V. Wedgwood, *Richelieu and the French Monarchy* [London: English Universities Press, 1949], p. 7). Richelieu's inflexible determination to elevate king and country is best seen in the monumental biography begun by Gabriel Hanotaux and completed with the assistance of the Duc de la Force, *Histoire du cardinal de Richelieu* (6 vols., new ed.; Paris: Societe de l'histoire nationale, Librairie Plon, [1932]-1947).

make one last attempt to arrest the progress of the monarchy towards absolutism, he had laid the foundations of the unchallenged power which Louis XIV was to wield."[15] Richelieu died in 1642; in 1643 Enghien, his last appointment, crushed the Spanish army at Rocroi, a blow from which Spanish prestige never recovered. In the same year Louis XIII passed away, but not before appointing Mazarin as first minister to succeed Richelieu. In this choice, as in practically all others, the King followed Richelieu's personal recommendation, and it was to prove a typically wise decision. By the time Jacob's Traicté appeared in 1644, Mazarin, as first minister of the regency, had begun to demonstrate the astuteness with which he would shortly put down civil strife (both the so-called parlementary and princely Frondes), and ultimately carry out such successful diplomatic operations that "from 1648 to 1660, every great international agreement was a triumph for Mazarin and for France."[16]

The social structure in France at the time Jacob wrote his Traicté can be most conveniently described in terms of the

---

[15] John Lough, An Introduction to Seventeenth Century France (London: Longmans, Green, 1954), p. 126.

[16] W. F. Reddaway, A History of Europe from 1610 to 1715 (London: Methuen, 1959), p. 235. The severely critical and manifestly unfair evaluation of Mazarin by Michelet (which is unfortunately still reflected in such modern works as Guérard, pp. 170-72) has been effectively refuted by Adolphe Chéruel's Histoire de France pendant la minorité de Louis XIV (4 vols.; Paris: Hachette, 1879-1880) and Histoire de France sous le ministère de Mazarin (3 vols.; Paris: Hachette, 1882). Cf. also my review of Mazarin, homme d'état et collectionneur (Paris: Bibliothèque Nationale, 1961), in the Library Quarterly, XXXII (April, 1962).

traditional divisions recognized by the Estates-General: the
First Estate (clergy), Second Estate (nobility), and Third
Estate (the other inhabitants of the realm, both bourgeoisie
and peasants).[17] The First Estate, comprising all the clergy,
regular and secular, from individual parish priests and monks
to powerful abbots and archbishops, was supported by rents,
feudal dues, and (especially) tithes. This income, "considering
the small proportion of the population which it [the clergy] represented, made it the wealthiest body in France."[18] However,
great economic inequalities existed; the regular clergy was in
general in a better financial position than the secular clergy,
and the parish priests and other lower clergy frequently found
themselves in severe straits. Although commendable examples
of piety and reform can be mentioned (e.g., Francis de Sales;
Vincent de Paul; Pierre Bérulle of the Oratory), the French
ecclesiastical situation in the seventeenth century was far
from ideal. The ghastly case of the possessed nuns of Loudun
has often been cited as reflecting the superstitious and malevolent tendencies of the age;[19] but a more basic difficulty was

---

[17] Aynard correctly points out that these divisions were <u>classes</u>, not <u>castes</u>, i.e., that they did not constitute an absolute barrier to social mobility; continual movement (both up and down) from Estate to Estate was in fact going on in the seventeenth century (Joseph Aynard, <u>La bourgeoisie française</u> [Paris: Perrin, 1934], pp. 313-17).

[18] Lough, p. 90.

[19] See Aldous Huxley, <u>The Devils of Loudun</u> (New York: Harper, 1959). It is of interest that a few years before this incident, King James I of England wrote his work, <u>Daemonologie</u>. The religious intolerance which prevailed in Louis Jacob's France has been well described and analyzed in W. J. Stankiewicz, <u>Politics & Religion in Seventeenth-Century France</u> (Berkeley: University of California Press, 1960).

the secularistic atmosphere which prevailed in the higher church offices. Since the Concordat of 1516 the Crown had had the right to appoint to all the higher church positions; the resulting appointments reflected the King's desire to control the great bishoprics and archbishoprics, and his willingness to reward the loyalty of the great noble families by providing their younger sons with valuable church posts. Those who received such appointments often left much to be desired in the way of spirituality. No better example exists than the notorious Cardinal de Retz, whom Louis Jacob served as librarian for a time; as Retz himself tells us, he entered on his church career--in spite of a predilection for duelings and love-affairs--because he was a younger son and because his family had held the archbishopric of Paris for three generations.[20] Though such ecclesiastics often displayed commendable literary interests, their lack of true vocation must be regarded as a powerful contributory element in the eventual dissolution of the ancien régime.

The Second Estate was well on its way to becoming a feudal anachronism by 1644. Technically, the nobility consisted only of noblesse d'épée--of nobility who inherited the title by birth and lineage--but, as we shall see, a newer nobility of office-holders (noblesse de robe) who purchased their patents was now coming to the fore. The hereditary nobility was not a homogeneous group, for a considerable distinction in

---

[20]Cardinal de Retz, Oeuvres, ed. Alphonse Feillet, et al. (11 vols.; Paris: Hachette, 1870-1920), I, 89-90.

status existed between the <u>noblesse de cour</u> (who frequented the court) and the <u>noblesse de province</u> (who remained on their estates);[21] indeed, the small provincial nobleman, or <u>hobereau</u>, was the subject of lampooning in Paris and at court.[22] But all the older nobility were united in their common misery: the lack of money. Their fixed incomes suffered catastrophically from the sixteenth-century rise in prices, and by the middle of the seventeenth century their condition can best be described as impoverished.

> It is this impoverishment of all sections of the French aristocracy in the seventeenth century, revealed in innumerable documents of the period, which accounts in a large measure for the failure of the last efforts of the great noblemen under Richelieu and Mazarin to put the clock back and to regain some of the power which the gradual development of the Monarchy towards absolutism had taken from them. Living from hand to mouth, crushed by their debts and by an extravagant mode of living, compelled very often to swallow their pride and save their family from ruin by a <u>mésalliance</u> with a wealthy bourgeois heiress, the great noblemen were in no position to offer effective resistance to the growth of the royal power. . . . When the government was in firm hands, as it was under Richelieu, and still more under Louis XIV, only obedience to the Crown could allow them to keep up the costly mode of life to which they were accustomed. . . . In the last resort it is economic reasons which explain how in the course of the seventeenth century the turbulent great noblemen, still close in outlook to their ancestors of feudal times, were gradually transformed into the lackeys and flatterers whose presence added to the splendour of the court of Louis XIV.[23]

---

[21] This distinction is far more important than the traditional distinctions of title (<u>comte</u>, <u>marquis</u>, <u>baron</u>, etc.), for these titles were attached to estates and devolved upon their owners; thus by purchasing an estate one could readily obtain a title or add to the titles already held.

[22] Cf. Molière's <u>Georges Dandin</u>.

[23] Lough, pp. 86-87.

The misery of the <u>noblesse d'épée</u> was compounded by the growth of a new aristocracy based on wealth. The latter, called the <u>noblesse de robe</u>, included those who acquired their noble rank by purchase or by the possession of an official post, rather than by ancient pedigree.[24] The most attractive posts which carried hereditary nobility with them were the parlementary offices. Since these judicial positions were very costly to obtain, and could be passed on in one's family by the payment of an annual tax, they readily became a stronghold of the <u>nouveaux riches</u>. Not infrequently, the result was gross ineptitude and inefficiency. Tallement describes one candidate's admission to a councillorship in the Paris Parlement thus:

> La Barroire ... était fils d'un riche marchand de la Rochelle. Il épousa ici la fille de M. l'Hoste, beau-frère de l'intendant Arnaut. Après il acheta un office de conseiller au Parlement qui lui coûta onze mille écus. Il se présenta pour être reçu, c'était une grosse bête; mais son beau-père avait du crédit; on le reçut à cause de lui. On disait: "C'est M. l'Hoste, et non son gendre, qu'on reçoit." Cumont fut examiné en même temps, et fit fort bien. "Il les faut recevoir, dit-on, l'un portant l'autre."[25]

It was not mere political vindictiveness that produced the following definitions in the anonymous Mazarinade entitled, "Catéchisme des courtisans de la cour de Mazarin" (1649):

---

[24] The <u>noblesse de robe</u> of course argued that there was no distinction between themselves and the <u>noblesse d'épée</u> (cf. the arguments of [Président de Novion], "Requêts anonyme de Messieurs du Parlement à S.A.R.M. le duc d'Orléans, Régent," <u>Revue rétrospective</u>, 2e série, VI [1836], 107). During the eighteenth century the two groups did in fact almost completely fuse.

[25] Gédéon Tallemant des Réaux, <u>Les historiettes</u>, ed. Georges Mongrédien (8 vols.; Paris: Garnier, 1932-1934), VI, 348.

> Qu'est-ce qu'un Président? -- Un homme d'apparence grave, dont la parole fait quelquefois tort aux innocens et souvent peur aux coupables.
> Qu'est-ce qu'un ieune Conseiller? -- Un homme qui chastie en autruy ce qu'il commet luy mesme, et qui parle plus de bouche que d'effet.[26]

On the cultural side, however, the wealthy and influential Parlementaires tended to be avid amateurs, and one finds many of their number among the library owners described in Jacob's pages.

The Third Estate included the vast gamut of Frenchmen who were neither clergy nor members of the nobility; it thus encompassed both the uneducated, ominously silent peasantry, and the rising, vocal bourgeoisie. From the upper and middle bourgeoisie came not a few of Jacob's book collectors; we conclude our brief survey with a description of this variegated and increasingly important element in mid-seventeenth century French society:

> In the seventeenth century, after the nobility of the robe became a recognized class including the members of the Parlements and other sovereign courts, the high bourgeoisie consisted of the officers of bailiwicks, seneschals' courts, presidials, and provostships, and the bankers and other financiers; below them were the avocats, notaries, registrars, procureurs, and other lawyers. Most of the lawyers of the lower rank might be considered as belonging to the middle bourgeoisie, a group which sought honor and position rather than wealth. It also included the physicians, and especially the professors of medicine in the Universities of

---

[26] C. Moreau (ed.), Choix de Mazarinades (2 vols.; Paris: Jules Renouard, 1853), II, 7 (this Mazarinade is No. 651 in Moreau's standard Bibliographie des Mazarinades). Numerous criticisms of the Parlements can be found in the contemporary materials listed in Doris Varner Welsh (ed.), A Checklist of French Political Pamphlets, 1560-1644, in the Newberry Library (Chicago: Newberry Library, 1950), and in her Second Checklist of French Political Pamphlets, 1560-1653 (Chicago: Newberry Library, 1955).

Paris and Montpellier, with the surgeons and apothecaries far behind. Here too we should place the University professors, wealthy printers and publishers, architects, and artists. In the petty bourgeoisie were the heads of the six powerful merchant guilds of Paris and other cities and the masters of various crafts in a rigidly defined scale of dignity. The "high" group was rather a minority; the "petty," though made up of greater numbers, was rich, intelligent, and scornful of the artisans, the small shopkeepers, and the peasants so far beneath them in prestige. The distinguishing mark of all grades was that the members did not work with their hands; they enjoyed an income from their investments or they managed a business organization or they were engaged in a profession. And of the professions, the law was the most highly regarded.[27]

Louis Jacob de Saint-Charles

To provide adequate biographical treatment of the author of the Traicté des plus belles bibliothèques is an exceedingly difficult task. Louise-Noëlle Malclès states the basic problem in the most recent article to appear on Jacob:

> Unfortunately, very little is known about that innovator, for apparently our unique source of information on him is a study written, if not published, by the Carmelite Cosme De Villiers de Saint-Étienne (born in 1683). The Barnabite J.-P. Niceron relied heavily on this sketch in the Mémoires pour servir a l'histoire des hommes illustres (1739), and it was reproduced in Latin in 1752 by the same Cosme De Villiers, in his Bibliotheca Carmelitana. . . . One looks in vain for an original study better illuminating the personality of Father Jacob or specifying the progress of his learned activity and the circumstances in which it was carried on.[28]

---

[27] David T. Pottinger, The French Book Trade in the "Ancien Régime," 1500-1791 (Cambridge, Mass.: Harvard University Press, 1958), pp. 7-8. Cf. Charles Normand, La bourgeoisie française au XVIIe siecle (Paris: F. Alcan, 1908), pp. 211-32.

[28] Louise-Noëlle Malclès, "Le fondateur de la bibliographie nationale en France, le R. P. Louis Jacob de Saint-Charles (1608-1670)," Mélanges d'histoire du livre et des bibliothèques, offerts à Monsieur Frantz Calot (Paris: Librairie d'Argences, 1960), p. 245.

The known facts of Jacob's life are few and can be stated very briefly; our main concern will be to "illumine his personality" and describe "the circumstances in which his learned activity was carried on."

Louis Jacob was born in the town of Chalon-sur-Saône in Burgundy[29] on August 20, 1608 and was baptized in the bishop's chapel there four days later.[30] His baptismal name was Charles, which he afterwards changed (as was customary) on entering the Carmelite order. His father, Jean Jacob, came originally from Siena in Tuscany; his mother, Claudine Mareschal, was a native of Auxonne, a Burgundian town on the Saône. Louis Jacob donned the Carmelite habit at Chalon on June 8, 1625, and made his profession a year later, on June 11, 1626. In 1639 he journeyed to Italy, and lived for some time at Rome, where he had the misfortune of losing in the catacombs a collection of epitaphs which he had copied on his travels. It was apparently

---

[29] He himself states this in the Traicté (see below, the text at n. 371).

[30] Unless otherwise stated, subsequent biographical particulars on Jacob are derived from Jean-Pierre Niceron, Mémoires pour servir à l'histoire des hommes illustres dans la république des lettres (43 vols.; Paris: Briasson, 1727-1745), XL, 87-102; and Cosme de Villiers de Saint-Étienne, Bibliotheca carmelitana (2 vols.; Aurelianis, 1752), II, 272-88. Niceron states that the data on Jacob in his article (and in that by Villiers) were in large part taken from Jacob's own "Bibliotheca carmelitana," the manuscript of which was acquired by the Carmelite monastery of Les Billettes along with his books after his death. Manuscript additions and corrections to Villiers' work were made by one Norbertus a S. Juliana and are preserved in the Royal Library at Brussels (ms. 16491); however, a letter of August 17, 1961 from Martin Wittek, Bibliothécaire of the Bibliothèque Royale de Belgique, assures me that these corrections and additions refer only to Belgian Carmelites, and offer no further information on Jacob.

in Rome that he met and began his lifelong friendship with Gabriel Naudé, the "living library" and author of the Avis pour dresser une bibliothèque (1627), correctly described by Shera as "the first formal treatise on library organization and administration."[31] While in Rome, Jacob was persuaded by Naudé to undertake a valuable theological subject-bibliography, the Bibliotheca Pontificia ... cui adjungitur catalogus haereticorum qui adversus Romanos Pontifices aliquid ediderunt (Lugduni: Boissat & Anisson, 1643). We know that Jacob had returned to France by 1643, for he supervised the publication of the Bibliotheca Pontificia at Lyons.

Jacob himself tells us that by October, 1643 he had taken up residence in Paris.[32] There he received the title of royal councillor and chaplain, and was soon at work on his Traicté, which was completed by July 16, 1644[33] and was available to the public by August of that same year.[34] Jacob

---

[31] Jesse H. Shera, Historians, Books, and Libraries (Cleveland: Western Reserve University Press, 1953), p. 43, n. 8. On the close relations between Naudé and Jacob, see below, n. 229 to the text of the Traicté. Jacob and his Bibliographia Parisina are mentioned in Naudé's Jugement de tout ce qui a esté imprimé contre le cardinal Mazarin (Mascurat) ([2d ed.; Paris, 1650]), pp. 45, 237.

[32] Jacob, Traicté des plus belles bibliothèques (Paris: Rolet Le Duc, 1644), Preface to the Reader (unpaged).

[33] The dedicatory epistle is so dated.

[34] This is evident from the fact that Gui Patin had obtained his copy by August 8; in a letter of that date he writes: "We have here a new book which is very interesting--an octavo treatise in two parts on all the libraries of the world, and especially the libraries of France, where there are some great private collections" (Gui Patin, Lettres, ed. J.-H. Reveillé-Parise [3 vols.; Paris: J.-B. Baillière, 1846], I, 116). This

dedicated it to Jean-Paul-François de Gondi, then coadjutor of Paris, later cardinal de Retz. This dedication probably contributed to Jacob's entrance into the future cardinal's service as his librarian in 1652. During the years 1645-1654, Jacob produced the series of nine bibliographies of books published in France and in Paris (<u>Bibliographia Parisina</u> and <u>Bibliographia Gallica universalis</u>) on which his later fame has chiefly rested; these works, undertaken with the assistance of booksellers and fellow clerics both in Paris and in the provinces, have earned for Jacob the title of "founder of French national bibliography."[35] This same period witnessed the appearance of Jacob's bibliography of his native town of Chalon --a work which Besterman considers his "most valuable bibliog-

---

is, as far as I can determine, the first published reference to the <u>Traicté</u>, and it is especially significant as coming from the influential physician Patin (on Patin, his circle, and his library, see below, n. 233 to the text of the <u>Traicté</u>).

[35]Indeed, Schneider asserts that "the term 'bibliography' was first used by Louis Jacob de Saint Charles in his <u>Bibliographia Parisiana</u>" (Georg Schneider, <u>Theory and History of Bibliography</u>, tr. Ralph Robert Shaw [New York: Columbia University Press, 1934], p. 39). Bob L. Mowery quite correctly argues in his "Gabriel Naudé, Librarian" (unpublished Master's thesis, University of Chicago, 1951), p. 47, that Naudé (in his <u>Bibliographia politica</u> of 1633) was actually the first to use the term "bibliography" for a study of the books pertinent to a given subject. However, when Besterman states that none of Naudé's works, "not even the <u>Bibliographia politica</u> ... are strictly bibliographies" (Theodore Besterman, <u>The Beginnings of Systematic Bibliography</u> [London: Oxford University Press, 1935], p. 37), he is pointing up the fact that Naudé's <u>Bibliographia politica</u> is really a bibliographical essay rather than an annotated list of books. Malclès conclusively shows (<u>Mélanges ...</u>, pp. 243-44) that it was Jacob who "modified a two-century old conception" of bibliography ("the deciphering and study of ancient manuscripts") to the modern, broad definition ("the knowledge of the books published on such-and-such a subject, their editions, their value, their rarity").

raphy."[36] To Malclès, "it seems clear that it was his new responsibilities in the service of the future Archbishop of Paris [Retz]--responsibilities which began in 1652--that abruptly interrupted" his "great work as a modern bibliographer."[37] The death of Naudé in 1653[38] may also have had a deleterious effect on Jacob's bibliographical productivity.[39]

---

[36] "The *De claris scriptoribus Cabilonensibus* was published by Cramoisy in 1652 and extends to 180 quarto pages, in which Jacob sets out in chronological order, with an alphabetical index, the writings of about a hundred writers of or on Chalon" (Besterman, p. 41).

[37] Malclès, *Mélanges ...*, p. 245. The following cryptic remarks appear in a letter written from Paris by Gui Patin on November 16, 1652: "I am very pleased that at Troyes you have seen the chaplain to the Bishop of Autun; he is a defrocked Carmelite [carme défroqué] whom we here called Father Louis Jacob. He's a good fellow; I doubt that he will continue any longer to give us bibliographies every year" (Patin, *Lettres*, ed. Reveillé-Parise, I, 185). It is difficult to know what construction to place on these statements. On the one hand, there is no corroborating evidence that Jacob was ever chaplain to the Bishop of Autun or defrocked; on the other hand, Patin had contact with Jacob in the Dupuy cabinet and Colletet's circle (see n. 233 to the text of the *Traicté*), and his remarks are clearly intended to refer to our Jacob (by "bibliographies" Patin of course means the successively-appearing *Bibliographia Gallica universalis* and *Bibliographia Parisina*, which ceased in 1654). If Jacob did in fact suffer a "fall from grace," it was not long before he was restored, for in 1657 Patin refers to him as a Carmelite (*Lettres*, ed. Reveillé-Parise, II, 329), and in 1659, on the title page of the *V. cl. Gabrielis Naudaei tumulus*, Jacob describes himself as a member of the Carmelite order.

[38] It was Jacob who edited the memorial volume for Naudé, which is regarded as one of the basic primary-source accounts for Naudé's life. This work (*V. cl. Gabrielis Naudaei tumulus* [Parisiis: C. Cramoisy, 1659]) includes Jacob's epitaph for Naudé, which concludes with the words: "Amico singulari amicus singularis posuit monumentum aere perennius" (p. 35). Cf. James V. Rice, *Gabriel Naudé, 1600-1653* ("Johns Hopkins Studies in Romance Literatures and Languages," No. 35; Baltimore: Johns Hopkins Press, 1939), p. 44.

[39] Jacob did not terminate all writing in 1654, but the works he produced after that date are mostly of a brief, ephemeral, and non-bibliographical character (e.g., pamphlet eulogies);

18

Jacob's last years were spent as librarian to Achille (III) de Harlay, first president of the Paris Parlement. The date at which Jacob left Retz's employment is not known, but "doubtless it was in 1662, when the Cardinal resigned his office"[40] as archbishop of Paris. Considering the Cardinal's chaotic manner of life and his alienation from the Crown as a result of the prominent role he played in the Fronde (he was imprisoned in December, 1652, and after his escape two years later he wandered about in various countries),[41] one can hardly assume that Jacob's time in his employ had been fully satisfying; unfortunately, his experiences in Harlay's service do not seem to have met his expectations either. Ménage, who considered Jacob "one of his friends,"[42] tells us that Jacob "had lodgings with M. Achille de Harlay, but he was not happy there and he complained that he was treated with contempt, though

---

for a list of these works, see Jean-Pierre Nicéron, XL, 87-102, and Villiers, II, 272-88. Cf. also Pierre Clauer [Carlos Sommervogel], "Une poignée de pseudonymes français recueillis dans le Bibliotheca personata de P. Louis Jacob de Saint-Charles," Études: revue fondée en 1856 par des pères de la Compagnie de Jésus, 5ᵉ série, XII (1877), 74-89. J. Porcher, Conservateur en chef, Cabinet des Manuscrits, Bibliothèque Nationale, informed me by letter of February 23, 1959, that B. N. ms. fr. 24521 contains on leaves 42-50 an extract from a bibliographical work by Jacob entitled, "Bibliotheca illustrium foeminarum quae scriptis claruerunt."

[40]Malclès, Mélanges ..., p. 245.

[41]Ménage reports a very appropriate epitaph composed for Retz: "Ille inquietus hic quiescit Gondus" (Gilles Ménage, Ménagiana [Amsterdam: A. Braakman, 1693], p. 172).

[42]Ménage, Ménagiana (4 vols., new ed.; Paris: Delaulne, 1729), II, 405 (item supplied by M. Pinsson).

he ate at M. de Harlay's table."[43] Harlay's library was undoubtedly a source of great satisfaction to him however, for it was one of the finest private book collections in Paris at that time.[44] On May 10, 1670, in his sixty-second year, Jacob died at President de Harlay's home. "His body was placed in a coach, together with his books, for transfer to his monastery of Les Billettes," where interment took place.[45]

Such are the fragmentary biographical details of Jacob's life. Is it possible from these facts, taken in conjunction with his Traicté and his known contacts with the

---

[43] Ibid., p. 407 (item supplied by M. Galland).

[44] Jacob himself had praised it in 1644 in his Traicté (see below, the text at n. 156). The library was a Harlay family heritage. It had been passed on to Achille (III) de Harlay (1639-1712) by his great-grandfather Achille (I), likewise a first president of the Paris Parlement; by his grandfather, Christophe (II), ambassador to England; and by his father, Achille (II), attorney general in Parlement. Achille (II) had had as librarian of the collection the famous Denys Godefroy. However, of all the members of the family, it was Achille (III) who did most to enlarge and organize the library. He bought some of the ancient manuscripts of Alexandre Pétau (cf. the text of the Traicté at nn. 234-40), and, utilizing his position as keeper of the Treasury of Deeds, he had a great number of its historic documents transcribed for his own library. The great Mabillon did a partial catalog of Harlay's library, which especially excelled in manuscripts concerned with the public law of France. The Harlay library eventually entered Saint-Germain-des-Prés, and thus ultimately became incorporated into the Bibliothèque Nationale; for further information on it, see Léopold Delisle, Le cabinet des manuscrits de la Bibliothèque Impériale (3 vols.; Paris: Imprimerie Impériale, 1868-1881), II, 100-103. Edmond Bonnaffé, in his Dictionnaire des amateurs français au XVIIe siècle (Paris: A. Quantin, 1884), pp. 134-35, emphasizes the wide collecting interests of Achille (III), and notes that many of his antiquities and medals came originally from the outstanding cabinet of Nicolas-Claude Fabri de Peiresc (cf. the text of Jacob's Traicté at nn. 507-517).

[45] Ménage, Ménagiana, 1729 ed., II, 407 (item supplied by M. Galland).

scholarly life of his day, to reconstruct his personality--his interests, goals, and personal Weltanschauung?

In her valuable Erlangen doctoral dissertation on Naudé's Avis pour dresser une bibliothèque, Eva Albrich effectively shows that "living contact with contemporaries" was Naudé's most basic source of information for the Avis, and that he considered such contact the most fruitful avenue to library development.[46] Thus it does not strike us as strange that Naudé was a member of a number of the Parisian literary societies of his time, and indeed maintained a discussion circle of his own.[47] This same emphasis on participation in communities of learning characterizes Jacob's scholarly approach. He is known to have been a member of three mid-seventeenth century cabinets--the Académie de Retz, Colletet's circle, and the great Dupuy cabinet. The Retz "Academy" existed for a shorter time and was less influential than the other two, but it had an especially important place in Jacob's life, for out of it, by way of Ménage's recommendation, came his appointment as the future Cardinal's librarian.[48] This circle, which met from about 1640 until Retz was imprisoned in 1652, began in Gondi's attempt to rehabilitate himself in the public eye by exemplary

---

[46] Eva Albrich, "Der Avis pour dresser une bibliothèque von Gabriel Naudé" (unpublished Ph.D. dissertation, Friedrich-Alexander Universität, Erlangen, Germany, 1949), pp. 13, 37.

[47] See below, n. 229 to the text of Jacob's Traicté.

[48] "I had him [Jacob] accepted as librarian to the Cardinal de Retz" (Ménage, Ménagiana, 1693 ed., p. 177 [item supplied by M. Galland]). Ménage describes Jacob as a "grand Bibliothécaire" (ibid., p. 343 [item supplied by M. Pinsson]).

association with learned men.[49] The atmosphere, however, was by no means coldly formalistic; here one encountered "une académie d'aussi joyeuse humeur que de bon appetit," where Chapelain and Sarasin on one occasion successfully debated _pro_ the thesis that worthy love is necessary to a young man's social charm, valor, and literary success.[50] The circle met in Retz's archiepiscopal palace in winter, and at his beautiful estate at Saint-Cloud in summer. Here Jacob engaged in discussion with such diverse intellects as Ménage, Saint-Amant, Gassendi, and Marolles. Indicative of the spirit of the group was their debate on the value of Old French romances; "of greatest interest to us is the pride of these men in their own cultivated society, urbane conversation, and the good sense, order, and reason, which characterized their opinions and actions in contrast to the emotionally inspired valor, love, and piety of feudal France."[51]

The erudite circle of Guillaume Colletet, the leading literary historian of mid-seventeenth century France, has been described in detail below.[52] This influential cabinet, which

---

[49] Retz, I, 331-46; cf. Joseph Michon, _Étude littéraire sur le génie et les écrits du cardinal de Retz_ (Paris, 1863), p. 17.

[50] The title of the debate was "S'Il Faut qu'un Jeune Homme soit Amoureux"; the _pro_ argument appears in Jean-François Sarasin, _Oeuvres_, ed. Paul Festugière (2 vols.; Paris: É. Champion, 1926), II, 146-232. Ménage took the negative side.

[51] Josephine de Boer, "Men's Literary Circles in Paris 1610-1660," _Publications of the Modern Language Association of America_, LIII (September, 1938), 757.

[52] See n. 136 to the text of the _Traicté_. Since Jacob added his paragraph concerning Colletet's library at the very end of his book (it really forms a second addendum), we may

in winter met in Colletet's excellent library, discussed such a wide variety of intellectual topics and engaged in such varied literary productivity that a contemporary wrote of it: "Dont le travail plaisant, utile et raisonnable,/Se rend sur tous sujets aux doctes agréables."[53] The significance of Jacob's contact with this *cabinet* stems from the fact that "in the course of its long existence, this circle attracted, as regular or occasional visitors, almost all writers and many of the scholars of the time."[54] That Jacob was an active participant in the life of this circle is emphasized by his close contact with Colletet; the latter's respect for our author is evident in the following epigram written for the publication of Jacob's Bibliographia Parisina of 1645:

> Puisque ce livre seul en faict voir plus de mille,
> Nostre siècle a-t-il fait un livre plus utile,
> Ny plus digne des yeux de la postérité?
> Jacob, fameux autheur de ce fameux ouvrage,
> Si la France défère à mon juste suffrage
> Tu recevras l'honneur que mille ont mérité.[55]

Jacob was a member not only of the Académie de Retz and of Colletet's circle, but also of the scholarly circle which was "by far the most varied in scope and far reaching in influence of any seventeenth-century group"[56]--the Dupuy cabinet.

---

conclude that he did not participate in Colletet's circle until July, 1644, the month of the Traicté's completion.

[53] Jacques du Lorens, "Satyre contre les Demy-Sçavans" (1654), in Ed. Tricotel, Variétés bibliographiques (Paris: Gay, 1868), pp. 290-95.

[54] De Boer, PMLA, LIII, 752.

[55] Quoted in Malclès, Mélanges ..., p. 255.

[56] De Boer, PMLA, LIII, 730.

So influential was this society of the learned that Nicaise could write as late as 1691:

> For more than a century this illustrious Paris assembly, which is called "le cabinet," has continued with the same brilliance it had at its commencement. It has always been composed of a great number of gentlemen--the most able in Paris and the provinces--the most renowned representatives of the sword and of the robe. Even ambassadors and envoys of foreign princes have been seen there, who have honored the cabinet by their presence. Such was once that famous cabinet in Alexandria, of which Strabo gives us such a fine and agreeable description.[57]

The history of the Dupuy cabinet, a list of its most prominent members in Jacob's time, and its connection with the de Thou library, the library of the brothers Dupuy, and the Bibliothèque royale have been given below[58] and need not be repeated here; what does deserve underscoring is that Jacob's connection with this cabinet provides the best evidence of his participation in the central stream of mid-seventeenth century scholarly life.[59] A remark such as the following from Gui Patin, who was

---

[57] Claude Nicaise, Les sirenes, ou discours sur leur forme et figure (Paris: Jean Anisson, 1691), p. 4; on p. 11 the rhetorical question appears: "Do I need to add that the meetings of the cabinet have served as a model for many others which are held in various parts of Paris?" Nicaise (1623-1701) corresponded extensively with Leibnitz, and "became the chief propagator of Leibnitz's fame in France"; Nicaise's importance rests chiefly on the fact that he "spent his entire time communicating the latest scientific and learned news to scholars all over Europe" through "a kind of central press-agency in which he copied out and redistributed extracts from all the letters that reached him" (R. W. Meyer, Leibnitz and the Seventeenth-Century Revolution, tr. J. P. Stern [Cambridge, England: Bowes & Bowes, 1952], p. 107).

[58] See n. 244 to the text of the Traicté.

[59] The importance of the seventeenth-century French scholarly circles has nowhere been better shown than in René Pintard's masterly work, Le libertinage érudit dans la première moitié du XVIIe siècle (Paris: Boivin, 1943).

active with Jacob both in the cabinet Dupuy and in Colletet's circle, will serve as a concrete, concluding illustration of our author's intense awareness of the pulse of erudite activity in his day: "I once heard Father Louis Jacob, the Burgundian Carmelite, say that a certain M. de Tavannes had had printed on the sly in a château a volume of Mémoires historiques in folio, which he hadn't dared to publish on account of the many extraordinary things he had said in it against the great--among others, Catherine de Médicis--and that he had only given out a few copies of the book to close friends."[60]

The three literary circles of which Jacob was a member were by no means the only such gatherings which took place in Paris in the mid-seventeenth century, and our author's non-participation in a certain type of group tells us something significant about his personal Weltanschauung. Jacob's intimate friend Naudé had a small literary circle of his own, called the "Tétrade" because of its four principal members (Naudé, Gassendi, Deodati, and La Mothe le Vayer),[61] but there is no indication that Jacob participated in it. The same is true of La Mothe le Vayer's circle,[62] and the circle of Gui Patin.[63] These three cabinets had a common element which undoubtedly explains Jacob's absence from them: they were all avant-garde in emphasis--the "Tétrade" reflecting Naudé's

---

[60] Patin, Lettres, ed. Reveillé-Parise, II, 329-30 (letter of July 13, 1657).

[61] See n. 229 to the text of the Traicté.

[62] See n. 98 to the text of the Traicté.

[63] See n. 233 to the text of the Traicté.

religious liberalism,[64] La Mothe's circle reflecting its leader's ethical liberalism,[65] and Patin's circle reflecting that physician's political liberalism.[66] It is obvious to any reader of Jacob's Traicté that he was a man of conservative rather than liberal temperament, and this is in all probability the reason why he did not involve himself in the three circles just mentioned, though he did have close scholarly ties with their individual members. The circles to which he did belong concentrated on scholarly and literary subjects per se, and, although avant-garde discussions took place in

---

[64] "He [Naudé] is a skeptic and a rationalist. The shape of Naudé's skepticism is determined, however, by conditions peculiar to his age. . . . In religious questions he preserves the appearance, at least, of orthodoxy. The time is not yet ripe for wholesale and unveiled opposition to the established order. . . . The most significant net result of the Italian influence on Naudé's thought was the support it offered to skepticism, veiled in orthodoxy" (Rice, pp. 112, 118; see also Pintard, pp. 156-78).

[65] Pintard, not without reason, calls La Mothe "un voluptueux incrédule" (ibid., pp. 131-47, 756). It is of interest that La Mothe addressed a literary epistle to Jacob in which he listed some one hundred "best" books that could satisfy the intellectual needs of a gentleman of the time; this letter, included in La Mothe's Oeuvres (2 vols., 3d ed.; Paris: A. Courbé, 1662), II, 454-58, and republished several times, caused much discussion and controversy, and is of value today as an indicator of the reading of seventeenth-century savants.

[66] Patin hated both Richelieu and Mazarin with a vengeance, and though he took no active part in the Fronde, he sympathized with those who did. Speaking of an opiate which he thought a surgeon had given to Richelieu shortly before his death to hasten the end, Patin said, "Would to God he had given it to him twenty years sooner." He habitually referred to Mazarin as "the Pantaloon in a long robe" or "the Pantaloon with a red hat." (See Francis R. Packard, Guy Patin and the Medical Profession in Paris in the XVIIth Century [New York: Hoeber, 1925], pp. 258-65).

them, such discussions were not their raison d'être.[67]
Jacob's conservatism of course has both an attractive and an unattractive side. Negatively, one may legitimately complain of his almost eager subservience to those in authority,[68] his religious intolerance,[69] and the naiveté which seems to

---

[67]This is true even of the Académie de Retz, which, though a high-spirited group, was organized by the future Cardinal to give his life an air of academic and social respectability.

[68]A particularly unfortunate example in the Traicté is Jacob's mention of François-Auguste de Thou without any reference to his death at Richelieu's hands (see n. 65 to the Traicté and the text corresponding). De Thou had not participated in the Cinq-Mars' conspiracy against Richelieu, but had known of it; Richelieu had this young master of the royal library beheaded because he would not betray his friends. This act of the dying Richelieu horrified the learned of Paris (e.g., Patin); but Jacob says nothing of it, and when speaking of Richelieu never breathes a word of criticism of him. Since Richelieu had been dead for two years at the time Jacob wrote of de Thou, our author cannot very well be excused for keeping silent because of fear of Richelieu's wrath.

[69]In the Traicté Calvinists are regularly treated in summary fashion or simply ignored. Thus the great Huguenot statesman, scholar, and bibliophile Philippe du Plessis Mornay is dispensed in a single sentence (see the text of the Traicté at n. 328); and in discussing the Geneva library Jacob makes no mention of Calvin, whose personal library was one of its foundation-collections (see n. 543 to the text of the Traicté). When our author speaks of the tragic death of Pierre Ramus, he neglects to inform his readers that as a Protestant Ramus was one of the victims of the terrible St. Bartholomew massacre in 1572 (see n. 311 to the Traicté and the corresponding text). In actuality, Jacob and his Catholic confrères owed far more to French Protestant scholarship than they realized; Karl Holl is quite correct when he writes: "Whoever has learned the intellectual history of seventeenth-century France not only from the manuals, but also senses something of the connection of scientific work with the ecclesiastical questions that were prominent at the time, will also know that only the aggravation of opposition, the necessity of discussion with equal--or victorious--Reformed adversaries, coerced the Catholic side also into a strictness of procedure, which, taking its beginning from theology, became a part of a common intellectual possession" (Karl Holl, The Cultural Significance of the Reformation, tr. Hertz and Lichtblau [New York: Meridian Living Age Books,

flourish in a personality which allows itself to believe too much.[70] On the other hand, conservatism and deep respect for tradition can be advantageous in bibliographical work, for they lead to careful recording of the efforts of the past rather than rejection of them; and it is very doubtful that a way of life such as that of La Mothe would have resulted in the production of the first universal, book-length description of libraries.

Louis Jacob's clearest, most well-defined personality trait is his love for books--exemplified in his lifelong devotion to them as bibliographer, librarian, and historian of libraries. Ménage captures the essence of the man when he writes of him: "He could not put up with the contempt people show toward these old books [incunabula]--out of which, he said, they make fuses and with which butchers enbellish their shops, when in

---

1959], pp. 120-21). It is of more than routine interest that the second universal description of libraries--the De bibliothecis (1st ed., 1669; 2d ed., 1680) of Johannes Lomeier, a Dutch Calvinist--is much fairer to Roman Catholic libraries and library owners than Jacob is to Protestant bibliophiles and their collections.

[70]For example, Jacob has no difficulty in believing that "St. Peter, the immediate successor of the Redeemer of the world, was the first to establish a library in the Church of Rome" (Traicté, p. 82). The following remarks of Patin well illustrate Jacob's credulity: "I think that that Gaza-Christ who was here called the King of Ethiopia was another imposter. He died at Ruel, near Cardinal Richelieu's mansion, in 1638. I find nothing better in the whole story of this man than the four lines composed on his death: 'Cy gît le Roy d'Ethiopie,/Soit original ou copie;/La mort a vuidé les debats,/S'il fut Roy ou ne le fut pas.' Father Louis Jacob, who saw him at Rome and had intimate contact with him, has assured me that he was truly Prince of Ethiopia" (Gabriel Naudé and Gui Patin, Naudaeana et Patiniana [2d ed.; Amsterdam: F. vander Plaats, 1703], sec. "Patiniana," pp. 84-85).

actuality people ought to value them as if they were original manuscripts."⁷¹ But Jacob's bibliophilism was not a subjectively-based bibliomania which revels in the odor of musty tomes; his love of books was founded on both functional and theoretical considerations. Practically, he believed that reading was essential for any one holding a position of responsibility in the increasingly complex mid-seventeenth century civilization. To the future Cardinal de Retz he wrote:

> The formation of a library is not merely useful but absolutely essential to a great prelate such as yourself, since through good books he must learn everything others know, together with the things they do not. Building a library is the most irreproachable and praiseworthy avocation of all. It is the true way of serving the living and the dead equally, for thereby remembrance of the latter is awakened and the minds of the former are educated.⁷²

Jacob's theoretical argument for the importance of books and libraries is set forth in the opening paragraph of Part One of the *Traicté*; here we see an attempt, via Aristotle, to ground the quest for knowledge (and thus its preservation) in the very psychological nature of man:

> It is not without reason that Aristotle teaches us in the first book of his *Metaphysics* that man has a natural desire to know, for he is born with a capacity to learn, and knowledge serves as a divine nourishment for his spirit. In fact, man's spirit desires more than anything else to become personally acquainted with good, useful, and delightful things. When the learned man has attained that joyous state, he can be among human beings

---

[71] Ménage, *Ménagiana*, 1693 ed., p. 343 (item supplied by M. Pinsson).

[72] Jacob, *Traicté*, Dedicatory Epistle (unpaged). Jacob's failure to move Retz to become a paragon of learning should not be charged too heavily against him; St. Vincent de Paul was tutor to Retz, and the latter's spiritual and moral state was far more reprehensible than his intellectual life.

> what the sun is among the stars; for that prince of
> stars is not satisfied in merely directing his bright
> rays to us, but also produces a number of marvellous
> effects in our midst through the heat which he imparts
> to us in the terrestrial sphere. Thus the mind of the
> man who is versed in the sciences both sheds rays of
> light upon us, in that he has a perfect acquaintance
> with all essential matters, and also communicates to us
> the means of preserving them. It follows that the man
> endowed with maximum natural ability not only is at
> great pains to learn all the branches of knowledge
> through continual study, but also assumes the task of
> preserving this knowledge for himself through a great
> multitude of books. He takes care to collect his books
> from all parts of the world, in order thereby to estab-
> lish monuments for all posterity.73

This argument, based not on special revelation but on natural reason,[74] and utilizing Aristotle, as seventeenth-century Roman Catholics so often did, as a bridge from Thomistic-Aristotelian philosophical theology to natural philosophy, places Jacob squarely in the cultural stream flowing toward the eighteenth-century Enlightenment. Since the advent of depth psychology few would attempt to defend the importance of books and libraries in these terms, but it should be remembered, in fairness to our author, how long such argumentation persisted and how many have been enamored of it.[75] And regardless of the ultimate truth-value of this line of reasoning, the very fact that

---

[73]Ibid., p. 1.

[74]It is instructive to contrast Martin Luther's revelationally-based arguments for library development; see my article, "Luther and Libraries," Library Quarterly, XXXII (April, 1962), 133-47.

[75]Cf. the influence on American social-library development (1790-1850) of the Unitarian natural-theology dogma that "man is by nature good and intelligent" (Jesse H. Shera, Foundations of the Public Library; the Origins of the Public Library Movement in New England 1629-1855 [Chicago: University of Chicago Press, 1949], p. 87; cf. pp. 216-28, 238-39).

Jacob rooted library promotion in the nature of man indicates how central such activity was to his own experience and how basic it was to his personal world-view.

The "Traicté des plus belles bibliotheques"

Its Origin, Character, and Value

The best introduction to Jacob's Traicté--both as to circumstances of origin, scope, method, and sources--is provided by the author himself in his Preface to the Reader. We therefore quote in extenso from this Preface:

> Various well-known authors have published rather brief works describing the finest libraries of the world; their purpose, however, has been to stress ancient rather than modern libraries. Such authors are Theodor Zwinger, who wrote the Theater of Human Life;[76] Fulvio Orsini, a Roman canon, who published a certain treatise on the subject;[77] and Justus Lipsius, who imitated the latter work in his Syntagma, or Book, of Libraries, printed in 1602 and 1607.[78]

---

[76]Theodor Zwinger, the elder (1533-1588), a Swiss physician, humanist, and professor at the University of Basel, wrote a much-admired universal encyclopedia containing an article on libraries; this encyclopedia appeared in several editions, e.g., Theatrum humanae vitae ... tertiatione novem voluminibus locupletatum ... Jacobi Zvingeri fil. recognitione ... ampliatum (29 vols.; Basileae: Sebastianus Henricpetri, [1604]). On Zwinger, see the Allgemeine deutsche Biographie [hereafter cited as ADB] (56 vols.; Leipzig: Duncker, 1875-1912), XLV, 543-44.

[77]Jacob refers to Orsini's De bibliothecis commentatio, which can be most readily consulted in Joachim Johann Mader and Johann Andreas Schmidt (eds.), De bibliothecis atque archivis (3 vols.; Helm[e]stadi[i]: G. W. Hammius, 1702-1702). Orsini (1529-1600) an archaeologist, historian, and humanist, was the owner of the greatest private collection of manuscripts in the sixteenth century; he bequeathed to the Vatican library a total of 413 manuscripts (270 Latin, 113 Greek, and 30 Italian), as well as a number of printed books (see Pierre de Nolhac, La bibliothèque de Fulvio Orsini [Paris: Bouillon & Vieweg, 1887]).

[78]Justus Lipsius (1547-1606), the famous classical

Onofrio Panvinio, an Augustinian, composed a volume on libraries which is still in manuscript.[79] Angelo Rocca, a member of the same religious order, has left us source material in his description of the Vatican Library;[80] Claude Clément, a Jesuit, has done likewise in his work on the Escorial[81]--as has Anton Sander in his Advisory Essay for the establish-

---

historian and editor of Tacitus, demonstrated his interest in books and libraries both by his activities in behalf of the great Plantin publishing house at Antwerp, and by his De bibliothecis syntagma. This short treatise deals only with libraries in classical times; it was reprinted in the Mader collection, and appears in English under the title, A Brief Outline of the History of Libraries, tr. John Cotton Dana ("Literature of Libraries in the Seventeenth and Eighteenth Centuries," Vol. V; Chicago: A. C. McClurg, 1907).

[79] Panvinio (1529-1568), an Italian antiquarian and historian, was nicknamed "the devourer of antiquity" (helluo antiquitatis) by Paulus Manutius the printer; his studies were eagerly sponsored by such sovereigns as King Philip II of Spain and Holy Roman Emperors Ferdinand I and Maximilian II. A number of Panvinio's works still remain in manuscript today in German and Italian libraries; a treatise of his entitled De Bibliotheca Vaticana was published posthumously by Juan Bautista Cardona as part of the latter's De Regia S. Laurentii Bibliotheca (Tarracone: P. Mey, 1587), and is included in Mader's reprint collection.

[80] Angelo Rocca (1545-1620) was a prominent sixteenth-century bibliophile. In 1585, he assumed direction of the Tipografia Vaticana (the Vatican Printing Plant) by request of Pope Sixtus V, and he was made bishop of Tagaste in 1605. He is known principally for founding a rich library in Rome which he called the "Bibliotheca Angelica." (See Carlo Frati, Dizionario bio-bibliografico dei bibliotecari e bibliofili italiani [Firenze: Olschki, 1933], p. 499.) Jacob refers to Rocca's Bibliotheca Apostolica Vaticana a Sixto V (Romae: ex typogr. Apostolica Vaticana, 1591).

[81] Reference is here made to Claude Clément's Musei sive bibliothecae tam privatae quam publicae extructio, instructio, cura, usus (Lugduni: J. Prost, 1635), in which the description of the Escorial is based in part upon José de Sigüenza's Historia de la Orden de San Jerónimo, Vol. II, and Juan de Mariana's De rege et regis institutione. On Clément, his book, and its relation to these other works, see my Seventeenth-Century View of European Libraries. Lomeier's De bibliothecis, Chapter X, Translated with an Introduction and Notes (Berkeley: University of California Press, 1962, sec. "Spain."

ment of the library at Ghent.[82] Francis Sweerts has given a rather extensive enumeration of libraries at the beginning of his Belgian Athens.[83] In his Monument of Italy Lorenz Schrader, a jurist, speaks of those libraries he observed there.[84] François de La Croix du Maine, in the catalogue of his writings, promised a treatise on the finest libraries of the French kingdom; but death prevented that work from seeing the light.[85] Andreas Schott, a Jesuit, has written briefly on the libraries of Spain.[86] Lastly,

---

[82] Anton Sander (1586-1664), a Flemish historian and bibliographer, published his Dissertatio paraenetica pro instituto bibliothecae publicae Gandavensis at Brussels in 1633; Jacob quotes at length from this essay in his Chapter LXXIV, dealing with libraries in the county of Flanders. On Sander, see ADB, XXX, 345-47, and the text of the Traicté at n. 383.

[83] (Peter) Francis Sweerts (1567-1629) was a learned Dutch merchant who corresponded frequently with Lipsius, Scaliger, Casaubon, Heinsius, and other distinguished scholars of his day; see Jean-Pierre Nicéron, XXVII, 262-67. Jacob cites Sweert's Athenae Belgicae, sive nomenclator Infer. Germaniae scriptorum qui disciplinas philologicas, philosophicas ... illustrarunt. ... Accessit eodem auct. succinta XVII ejusdem Inf. Germ. provinciar. nec non praecipuarum orbis bibliothecarum et academiarum ... descriptio (Antverpiae: apud Gulielmum a Tungris, 1628). This Belgian biobibliographical dictionary was used extensively by Jean François Foppens in preparing his very important Bibliotheca Belgica (2 vols.; Bruxellis: P. Foppens, 1739); and it contains "the first classified bibliography of bibliographies" (Archer Taylor, A History of Bibliographies of Bibliographies [New Brunswick, N.J.: Scarecrow Press 1955], p. 18).

[84] Lorenz Schrader (ca. 1530-1606) was a philologist and councillor in Osnabrück, Germany. Jacob refers to his Monumentorum Italiae, quae hoc nostro saeculo et a Christianis posita sunt, libri quatuor (Helmaestadii: J. L. Transylvanus, 1592). Schrader's interest in libraries is shown by the fact that "he gave his own not insignificant book collection to the city of Osnabrück as a basis for a city library; later it was combined with the book collection of the Council-Gymnasium" (ADB, LIV, 179).

[85] Jacob devotes Chapter c of his Traicté to La Croix du Maine; see the text of the Traicté at n. 454 for the title of La Croix's proposed work on the libraries of France.

[86] Andreas Schott (1552-1629), a celebrated Flemish philologist and book collector, published under the pseudonym "A.S. Peregrinus" the work to which Jacob refers here: Hispaniae bibliotheca, seu de academiis et bibliothecis;

we have the most recent author in this field, and
the one who, I imagine, has done the most work in it:
Jodocus à Dudinck, who published an octavo Latin treatise on the subject at Cologne in the year 1643. The
printer was Jodocus Kalcoven, and the title is:
Palatium Apollinis & Palladis, hoc est, designatio
praecipuarum bibliothecarum mundi veteris nouique
saeculi. This book, however, has not yet fallen into
my hands, although I made every effort to obtain it
and had written to Flanders to secure it.[87] But the
lack of communication at present, due to war,[88] has
kept me from reading this work which might have further enriched my research on the private libraries of
Germany with which I have had no acquaintance except
through books.

Since all these authors had written only briefly
on the subject of libraries, I became convinced that
the public would gain some benefit from the appearance
of the present treatise--which was born as soon as it
was conceived. For I arrived in Paris last October
with the intention of devoting myself to a great work,
as useful to the French nation as it is eagerly desired
by foreigners; namely, La Bibliothèque Vniuerselle de
tous les Autheurs de France, qui ont escrits en quelque
sorte de sciences & de langues que ce soit, which I hope
(depending on the grace of God) to set forth in four
folio volumes, two in Latin and two in French. But this
work takes much time; although it was begun in 1638, the

---

item elogia et nomenclator clarorum Hispaniae scriptorum,
qui latine disciplinas omnes illustrarunt (Francofurti:
C. Marnius & haeredes J. Aubrii, 1608). Authorship identification is confirmed in Michael Holzmann and Hans Bohatta,
Deutsches Pseudonymen-Lexikon (Wien: Akad. Verlag, 1906),
p. 211. Graesse considered the book "rarissime" (Johann
George Theodor Graesse, Trésor de livres rares et précieux
[7 vols.; Dresden: Kuntze, 1859-1869], VI, Pt. 1, 314).
Colomiès, after revealing the author of the Hispaniae
bibliotheca, says: "I have been apprised of this by the
Rev. Father Jacob de Saint-Charles, Carmelite monk and royal
chaplain, to whom I am obliged for numerous other points of
information" (Paul Colomiès, Bibliothèque choisie [2d ed.;
Amsterdam: G. Gallet, 1699], p. 198).

[87] Jacob's inability to find this work was due to the
fact that it (like Dudinck's Bibliothecariographia) is a
bibliographical ghost; for the powerful reasons against its
ever having existed, see Taylor, A history of Bibliographies
of Bibliographies, pp. 21-23.

[88] I.e., the Thirty Years' War.

great number of our authors will necessitate a delay of some years more to perfect it before the public can enjoy it.[89] However, at the request of M. Naudé, librarian of His Eminence, Cardinal Mazarin (I can refuse Naudé nothing, so close is our friendship), I diverted myself from that labor to provide some Additions for his Avis pour dresser une bibliothèque, a second printing of which was desired.[90] Naude's constant efforts to increase that incomparable library of His Eminence allowed him little freedom to reread his book for the purpose of making some additions worthy of his rare and outstanding spirit. For this reason, when he saw that he could not work at that task, he asked me to try to take the responsibility for it and to make some appropriate contributions to his project. At first it was very difficult for me to bring myself to do it, for I recognized my great deficiency of scholarship and dreaded that through the weakness of my pen I might obscure that work rather than illuminate it. Indeed, the accolades which its author obtained throughout Europe, because of his surpassing knowledge of the humanities, indicated that it deserved the pen of one of the most able men of France, not that of one who goes beyond his depth (seeing that my capacities are very remote from his). Nevertheless, I was obliged by his orders to undertake this labor; I therefore tried in every way to carry out his wishes and to put myself in line with his feelings, instead of continuing to resist him as I had intended.

---

[89]This work was never published; probably Jacob's series of bibliographies of current French publication (Bibliographia Gallica universalis and Bibliographia Parisina) represented a modification of his original plan. A misreading of the above passage from Jacob's Preface led Dibdin to write erroneously: "La Bibliothèque universelle de tous les Autheurs de France ... was completed in 1638: but, on the death of the author it does not appear what became of it" (Thomas Frognall Dibdin, Bibliomania; or Book-Madness [new ed.; London: Chatto & Windus, 1876], Pt. 2, p. 39).

[90]Naudé's Avis first appeared in 1627. The second edition was published under Jacob's supervision by Rolet Le Duc along with the Traicté in 1644 (see the "Catalogus omnium operum Gabrielis Naudaei," in the Naudaeana et Patiniana, sec. "Naudaeana," pp. 237-38; and Albrich, p. 10). The appearance of the Traicté and the second edition of the Avis under identical imprints and in the same format led the generally reliable bibliographer Peter Lambeck to the fallacious conclusion that Naudé wrote both books (Peter Lambeck, Commentariorum de Augustissima Bibliotheca Caesarea Vindobonensi liber primus [-octavus] [8 vols.; Vindobonae: typis Matthaei Cosmerovii, 1665-1679], I, 115).

Now at the time that second edition of the Avis was begun, I planned to add only five or six leaves to the book. For that purpose I tried to see all the authors who had written on the subject, and I gathered together into my notes everything I had observed concerning the libraries of Rome during my stay of a year and a half there, as well as observations on libraries throughout Italy and in some provinces of France where I had travelled. But my work grew so successfully through the material sent me by my friends that it reached a length of more than fifty leaves.[91]

I trust that the public will find use for this book, since it will be of value to all interested persons, and especially to those who would journey anywhere in the world, for it will acquaint them with those rich treasuries of the Muses where they will find unparalleled satisfactions. My book will above all serve as a guide to libraries here in the French kingdom, where there are more today than in all the other kingdoms of the world. Why, I am able to state that the city of Paris alone has many more libraries than the whole of Germany and Spain, as one can see for himself by the enumeration I have made.

If, however, a few libraries have been omitted here, due to my not having received accounts of them until after the main part of this book had been printed, they will be placed in their proper order in a second edition;[92] I refer to libraries which shall come to

---

[91] In its small octavo format, the Traicté consists of 18 preliminary pages (6-page Dedication; 12-page Preface), 717 text pages, a 35-page appendix, and an alphabetical index of libraries discussed in the book. The work contains some 84,175 words, exclusive of its index.

[92] The Traicté never appeared in a second edition, if we mean by new edition--and here we use the most generally acceptable bibliographical definition--that "the type of the whole book, or at any rate of the text as distinguished from the preliminary matter, has been set up afresh" (Ronald B. McKerrow, An Introduction to Bibliography for Literary Students [Oxford: Clarendon Press, 1928], p. 176). Two new issues of the book did appear, however ("when we speak of a new issue, we mean that what were left of the old sheets of the text have been bound up with a new title-page or with new preliminary matter" [ibid.]). The first of these new issues appeared in 1655, under the same imprint (Paris: Rolet Le Duc) as the original issue in 1644; the British Museum's Catalogue of Printed Books states that the 1655 issue differs from the original issue only in that the latter has with it the second edition of Naudé's Avis, while the 1655 issue does not (I have not personally

my attention both in the French provinces and in all
other realms. For this reason I beg those who own
notable book collections to direct accounts of them
to M. Rolet Le Duc, bookseller, who is located in the
rue Saint-Jacques near the Posting-House, and who
financed the printing of this work. But to be included
libraries must contain at least 3000 to 4000 volumes,
arranged in some way; this is the minimum size to which
I have bound myself. The owners may note down the
quality of the books, viz., whether the library excels
in either theology, history, law, medicine, philosophy,
poetry, or other subjects; also, whether it contains a
variety of manuscripts; and, particularly, whether they
bought some important book collection which had belonged
to distinguished scholars. This should be done in order
that these libraries may not be forgotten; for it is not
reasonable that fine book collections which have been
brought together with such great care and which at one
time deserved high commendation should remain in oblivion
at the homes of their owners.

---

seen a copy of the 1655 issue). The second issue of the Traicté
carried the title Le bibliothequaire universel, and appeared in
1668 at Paris under the imprint of Sebastien and François
Eschart. A comparison of the 1644 and 1688 issues at the Newberry Library has shown that the latter was in fact prepared
from old sheets of the former (even the same cancels are used
--note especially pp. 90, 128); the only changes in the 1668
issue are the new title pages of Parts One and Two, and the
omission of the prefatory matter (signatures ã [8 leaves] and
ē [2 leaves]) and of the "Extraict du Privilege du Roy" (final
leaf) of the 1644 issue. The appearance of two later issues,
but no new editions, of the Traicté seems to indicate that the
book was not especially successful. The size of a typical French
scholarly edition of the time is thought to have been 600-800
copies (Pottinger, p. 202); on seventeenth-century issuing practice, cf. William B. Todd, "The Issues and States of the Second
Folio and Milton's Epitaph on Shakespeare," Studies in Bibliogra-
phy: Papers of the Bibliographical Society of the University of
Virginia, V (1952-1953), 81-108. For data on Le Duc and the
Escharts (who were related, for Rolet Le Duc's mother was an
Eschart), see Philippe Renouard, Imprimeurs parisiens (Paris:
A. Claudin, 1898), pp. 120-21, 228; and [Jean de la Caille],
Histoire de l'imprimerie et de la librairie (Paris: Jean de la
Caille, 1689), pp. 165, 181, 303. It is very significant that
Caille concludes his work with data on the publication of Jacob's
Traicté and of the second edition of Naudé's Avis in 1644;
Caille writes: "I cannot better close this history than with
these two last books. The one acquaints you with the finest
and most interesting libraries of Europe, and the other gives
principles for choosing the most essential books to form a
library" (p. 303).

It is evident from these remarks by our author that he intended in his <u>Traicté</u> to provide the first book-length, universal description of libraries, with special emphasis on the libraries of France; and that he utilized both written sources, personal observation, and correspondence with others in the collection of his data. What valuation should be placed upon his resultant work?

From the historiographical standpoint, there can be no doubt of the significance of Jacob's <u>Traicté</u>, for it is in fact the first book attempting to describe libraries of all places and all times.[93] Dibdin does not exaggerate when he writes: "The splendour of almost every preceding bibliographer's reputation was eclipsed by that arising from the extensive and excellent publications of Louis Jacob; a name at which, if we except those of Fabricius and Muratori, diligence itself stands amazed."[94] Jacob will always remain a landmark in bibliographical history; but how important is his <u>Traicté</u> as a work of historical scholarship?

Early critics were severe on the <u>Traicté</u>. Morhof, in comparing Jacob's <u>Traicté</u> with Lomeier's <u>De bibliothecis</u> (the

---

[93]Evidence in support of this statement appears in the Introduction to my edition of Lomeier's <u>De bibliothecis</u>, Chapter X.

[94]Dibdin, Pt. 2, p. 39. Dibdin notes that in the <u>Traicté</u> Jacob "first brought together the scattered notices relating to libraries, especially to modern ones," and adds: "His work is well worth consultation. . . . It must be remembered that this was published as an unfinished production: as such, the author's curiosity and research are highly to be commended. I have read the greater part of it with considerable satisfaction."

second major universal history of libraries to be published), stated that Jacob had more information on modern libraries, especially monastic collections, than Lomeier did, but omitted many celebrated collections, such as the Augustan library at Wolfenbüttel and the Hamburg library; Morhof was especially disturbed over the fact that Jacob compared Morhof's Germany unfavorably with France with regard to number and importance of libraries, and yet admitted that he had never visited German libraries and referred his readers to Dudinck's work for them --a work he had not himself seen.[95] Baillet said that Jacob's Traicté suffered from "a bit too much diligence and a bit too little discernment."[96] And Jean-Pierre Nicéron presented the following harsh evaluation of the book:

> This huge work is full of useless and incorrect information. Because the author was by nature good and credulous, he found it easy to believe everything people said and wrote to him, and he relied too much on the good faith of others. This is what led him to magnify so excessively the number of "excellent libraries," among which he has often included very mediocre collections.[97]

One must certainly agree that there is an element of truth in these criticisms. Jacob employed no rigorously systematic method of collecting his data, so the omission of some libraries

---

[95] Daniel Georg Morhof (d. 1691), Polyhistor literarius, philosophicus et practicus (3 vols., 4th ed.; Lubecae, 1747), I, sec. 17, pars. 14-16, 190-91.

[96] Adrien Baillet (d. 1706), Jugemens des savans sur les principaux ouvrages des auteurs, ed. M. de la Monnoye (8 vols.; Paris: C. Moette, et al., 1722-1730), II, 149-52 (entry 229).

[97] Jean-Pierre Nicéron, XL, 93.

was inevitable;[98] and we have already spoken of our author's penchant for naïveté. But when Morhof condemns Jacob for his neglect of German libraries, we must remember that the Thirty Years' War had been raging in the German lands for over a quarter of a century when Jacob wrote the Traicté, and thus there may well be real preciseness in his prefatory assertion that "the city of Paris alone has many more libraries than the whole of Germany." And as to Nicéron's argument that too many libraries are included in the Traicté, we today, at a distance of three hundred years from the libraries described in it, are thankful for every scrap of bibliothecal information included by its author.[99]

---

[98]Bonnaffé, in his Dictionnaire des amateurs français au XVIIe siècle (Paris: A. Quantin, 1884), includes a number of private book collectors omitted by Jacob (and, as a matter of fact, passes over a number of library owners whom Jacob does discuss). Such strange institutional omissions as the library of Saint-Martial at Limoges (which receives no mention in chap. xcix) and the archiepiscopal library at Toul (which one expects to find in chap. cii) are unquestionably the result of our author's lack of system in obtaining his data. He depended for his material upon his extensive but desultory reading, his personal observation, and the communications of his friends and acquaintances, and where these sources happened to be silent about a library, the result was its omission from the Traicté. Thus one cannot conclude from the absence of a library in the Traicté that it could not have existed in Jacob's time; the value of the Traicté lies rather in the information it gives on the libraries which are included.

[99]In fairness to our author, we should recognize that he could not possibly have known with precision which libraries of his day would be considered of greatest historical significance centuries later. The concept of "significance" involves value-judgment, and is thus always conditioned by the historical perspective (or lack of it) possessed by the one making the value-judgment. This is especially evident in the changing interpretations placed upon historical epochs (cf. Wallace K. Ferguson's The Renaissance in Historical Thought; Five Centuries of Interpretation), but it is equally true of the valuations

40

Nicéron's claim that much of the information in the Traicté is unreliable simply cannot be sustained. It is true that Part Two of the work has much greater primary-source value than Part One, for in the second part Jacob writes of the libraries of his own country and his own time; but the quality of written sources employed throughout the work is very high,[100] and the frequent citation of works published in

---

placed upon individual historical phenomena. Jacob had no way of knowing that the high opinion of, say, Colletet as a poet in his own time would not persist in our time--and that therefore his library would not have the same interest for the twentieth century as it had for the seventeenth-century. But at the same time, we have no assurance that Colletet's reputation (and thus historical interest in his library) will be the same a century from now as it is today. In Carl Becker's words, "If the modern historian exhibits detachment, certainly it is not from the dominant ideas of his own age" (Carl L. Becker, Detachment and the Writing of History, ed. Phil L. Snyder [Ithaca, N.Y.: Cornell University Press, 1958], p. 25). This serious historiographical problem (which creates particular difficulties for historians in the positivist tradition) should give us pause when about to criticize Jacob for discussing too many libraries of his day or for considering too many of them "plus belles." In this connection, the following statement of John Hill Burton is well worth pondering: "Whoever desires to be really acquainted with the condition of a nation at any particular time . . . will not attain his object by merely reading the most approved histories of the period. He must endeavour as far as he can to live back into the times, and to do this most effectually he had better saturate himself to the utmost with its fugitive literature, reading every scrap he may lay hand on until he can find no more" (John Hill Burton, The Book-Hunter [new ed.; Edinburgh: William Blackwood, 1885], p. 323).

[100]For example, in his chapters on Greek and Roman libraries in classical times, Jacob relies heavily on Justus Lipsius' Syntagma - the best seventeenth-century work on the subject, and a book to which Naudé is heavily indebted in his Avis (see Albrich, p. 41). The high quality of the sources for Part Two of the Traicté can best be seen by a perusal of the notes to the text, for there Jacob's individual sources are evaluated in the context of their use. It is instructive to see how our author handles the problem of conflicting sources; when faced by two contradictory views as to the existence of a library in Ethiopia, he presents both positions by means of exact quotations, and comments thus: "Personally, I leave the resolution of this argument

1644--the very year of the Traicté's appearance--shows how concerned its author was to utilize the latest fruits of scholarship.[101] In our notes to text of the Traicté, we have attempted to identify all errors of fact, and the reader is thus in a position to see for himself how few these are relative to the size of Part Two as a whole. Indeed, bibliographical history stands in debt to Louis Jacob for providing not merely the first universal description of libraries, but a description which will remain the chief source of reliable information on many of the private, and not a few of the institutional, libraries of his day.

The Plan of the Present Edition

The historical and historiographical significance of Jacob's Traicté makes virtually self-evident the need for a modern scholarly edition of the book. The present edition-translation, limited to Part Two of the total work because of the special importance of France in the seventeenth-century

---

to those who go to Ethiopia, and content myself merely in reporting the views of the parties. The reader will thus see that I am scrupulous in clarifying truth; that I certainly do not embrace the opinions of individuals unless they are manifestly probable; and that where questionable views are concerned, I leave the judgment to the reader" (Traicté, Appendix [unpaged]).

[101]Two random examples of 1644 publications used by Jacob are Auberoche's Eminentissimo principi Julio cardinali Mazarino (see the text of the Traicte at nn. 95, 102) and Anton Sander's Bibliotheca belgica manuscripta, Vol. II (see Jacob's text at n. 383). The recency of information obtained from correspondents is another evidence that Jacob made a serious effort to produce an up-to-date description of libraries; see, for example, the data supplied by Suarès in chap. lxxxvii.

scene and the particular primary-source value of Jacob's description of the libraries in his own land, attempts to fulfil the four requirements of a scholarly edition as set forth by Chauncey Sanders:

> First, it should provide a correct text, representing as exactly as possible the author's final intention, with all errors eliminated. Second, it should explain any allusions or other readings that are likely to prove difficult for the sort of person who may be expected to use the work. Third, it should furnish a commentary that will serve to fit the work into its setting so that the reader may be able to appreciate its literary and historical significance. Fourth, it should, as Professor Morize wrote, "be easy to handle and convenient, arranged and printed in such a way as to afford instruction and pleasure, with notes that elucidate and do not submerge the text."[102]

In line with the basic objective of providing a text which "represents as exactly as possible the author's final intention," the material in the appendix to the Traicté--material added after the body of the Traicté had gone to press--has been integrated into the text at appropriate places in accord with Jacob's specific instructions concerning it. Such integrated material has been enclosed in triangular brackets (<,>) for easy recognition. The only other special sign employed in the text is the L in square brackets ([L]), which follows all translations from the Latin, to distinguish them from matter appearing in French in the original text. Jacob's text has been followed as closely as possible in the translation, and even his marginal rubrics have been retained; a single concession to modernity will be observed in the case of the orthography of proper nouns, for in the translation we have con-

---

[102] Chauncey Sanders, An Introduction to Research in English Literary History (New York: Macmillan, 1952), p. 97.

sistently employed recognized modern spellings both for place names and for personal names.

Some remarks are in order here concerning the sources employed in the notes. Contemporary materials of general value for corroborating Jacob's text included histories of the time (such as Jacques-Auguste de Thou's Historia sui temporis), critical bibliographies of seventeenth-century publications (e.g., Colomiès' Bibliothèque choisie), correspondence of noted scholars and bibliophiles (Peiresc, Patin, Mersenne, etc.), diaries and travel accounts by those with bibliothecal interests (John Evelyn, Martène and Durand, etc.), "ana" (Ménagiana, Naudaeana, Patiniana), and even poetry (e.g., the works of Dorat and Auberoche). The great dictionaries of Moréri and Bayle were also helpful at many points, though as always they had to be used with caution. Among modern works, the most generally useful were Delisle's great Cabinet des manuscrits, and the Bourgeois and Hauser volumes evaluating French historical sources (Les sources de l'histoire de France).

Collateral information on private libraries, whether in Paris or in the provinces, was often provided by such contemporary collective biography as Jean-Pierre Nicéron's Mémoires, Bates' Vitae selectorum aliquot virorum, La Croix du Maine's Bibliothèque françoise, Scévole (I) de Sainte-Marthe's Gallorum doctrina illustrium ... elogia, Borel's Antiquitez de Castres (containing a list of the most prominent French owners of cabinets in 1649), François Duchesne's Histoire de tous les cardinaux françois, and de Coste's eulogies of the

French royal house. Contemporary individual biographies--
including eulogies and funeral orations--were of the greatest
usefulness; an excellent example is Gassendi's Life of Peiresc.
The search for additional data on private libraries and their
owners often led to such modern works as the unfinished
Dictionnaire de biographie française, Sandys' History of
Classical Scholarship, Bonnaffé's Dictionnaire des amateurs
français au XVIIe siècle, the Backer-Sommervogel bio-bibliography of Jesuits (and similar works for other orders),
Hirsch's Biographisches Lexikon der hervorragenden Aerzte (and
similar works for other disciplines), individual biographies
of the quality of Espiner-Scott's Claude Fauchet and Mark
Pattison's Isaac Casaubon, and studies of personal libraries
(such as Le Roux de Lincy's Researches concerning Jean Grolier,
His Life and His Library). Contemporary histories of institutions (e.g., Héméré's De Academia Parisiensi) were often useful
for the further study of institutional libraries mentioned by
Jacob; data on institutional libraries were also provided by
modern works such as Milkau and Leyh's Handbuch der Bibliothekswissenschaft, Niepce's Bibliothèques anciennes et modernes de
Lyon, Fouqueray's Histoire de la Compagnie de Jésus en France
(and histories of other orders), and histories and catalogs of
particular libraries (e.g., Herbet's article on the Fontainebleau library, and Delandine's catalog of the manuscripts in
the Lyon city library).

In annotating Jacob's lengthy chapter on the libraries
of Paris, use was made of such contemporary sources as Du Breul

and Malingre's Antiquitez de Paris, and Blanchard's biographical listings of presidents and councillors of the Paris Parlement; two modern works which were invaluable in corroborating Jacob's Paris material were Franklin's Anciennes bibliothèques de Paris and Maugis' Histoire du Parlement de Paris. The libraries of the provinces posed greater bibliographical problems than the libraries of Paris, for no modern treatment of them has been done on the scale of Franklin's work. The most generally useful modern sources were the fifty-volume Catalogue général des manuscrits des bibliothèques publiques de France. Départements; and Vogel's Literatur früherer und noch bestehender europäischer öffentlicher und Corporations-Bibliotheken. General histories of a region (e.g., Vic's history of Languedoc) or of a city (e.g., Phister's history of Nancy) were sometimes helpful. Biographical dictionaries of an area frequently aided in the research task; here one thinks especially of Papillon's Bibliothèque des auteurs de Bourgogne and Levot's Biographie Bretonne. Information on provincial monasteries and their libraries came in many cases from Montfaucon's Bibliotheca bibliothecarum manuscriptorum nova, and from the multivolume Abbayes et prieurés de l'ancienne France. For episcopal and archiepiscopal book collections in the provinces, and for biographical data on their owners, the Gallia Christiana of Scévole (II) de Sainte-Marthe, et al. was of course indispensable.[103]

---

[103]Full bibliographical information on the foregoing publications can be found in the Selected Bibliography (for all works cited in two or more non-consecutive notes) and in the

The French Bibliothecal Situation in 1644

Unquestionably the most striking characteristic of the mid-seventeenth century French library situation, as revealed by Part Two of Jacob's _Traicté_, is the extent to which book collecting was carried on. Clergy, from the cardinal statesmen--who virtually determined the fate of the country--to the humble monks in the monasteries; nobility, from the king to the marquis, whether of the sword or of the robe, both in Paris and in the provinces; bourgeoisie, not only _avocats_ and physicians but even the lower echelons of the class;--all are found in Jacob's pages. True, the majority of libraries are owned by royalty, _noblesse de robe_, Parlementaires, higher clergy, and upper bourgeoisie at Paris; but it is equally clear that library ownership was not restricted to these more privileged and economically-fortunate Parisians.[104]

---

notes (complete bibliographical data are given at the first citation of all works). It will be seen from the text that Jacob used as sources many of the contemporary (sixteenth-seventeenth century) publications in this list--or employed works of similar scope (e.g., in place of Sainte-Marthe's _Gallia Christiana_, published in 1656, Jacob uses Jean Chenu's _Archiepiscoporum et episcoporum Galliae chronologia historia_, Claude Robert's _Gallia Christiana_, and Pierre Frizon's _Gallia purpurata_).

[104] That private libraries of consequence were not all to be found at Paris is evident especially from Jacob's account of Peiresc's book collection at Aix (see the _Traicté_, chap. cviii). That even the petty bourgeoisie were interested in book collecting is suggested by Jacob's mention of the library of Rasse des Neuds, a barber-surgeon (see the text at n. 307). Studies of sixteenth-century notarial inventories just in the last few years seem to point to an even greater concern for book collecting among petty bourgeoisie than Jacob indicates; see Alexander H. Schutz, _Vernacular Books in Parisian Private Libraries of the Sixteenth Century according to the Notarial Inventories_ ("University of

But the degree of bibliothecal interest goes far beyond library ownership per se. In the few instances where private libraries were opened to the "public" (i.e., to any one with the qualifications for using them), the response was tremendous.[105] As early as 1588, in his Le diverse et artificiose machine published at Paris, Ramelli had pictured a "reading machine"--a five-foot, gear-operated wheel permitting one to work with twelve books simultaneously without moving from one's chair. The year 1627 saw the appearance of Naudé's Avis, the first systematic treatise on library administration. In 1635, Blanchot published his proposal for a universal library, and the idea was warmly received by Descartes.[106] When Jacob produced his Traicté, he noted that at least two other Frenchmen of the period had thought of doing a similar project,[107] and one other compatriot was

---

North Carolina Studies in the Romance Languages and Literatures," No. 25; Chapel Hill: University of North Carolina Press, [1955]), and R. Doucet, Les bibliothèques parisiennes au XVIe siècle Paris: A. & J. Picard, 1956). It is hoped that similar studies will soon be made of later notarial records. With the concentration of French libraries in Paris in the seventeenth century, cf. Louis R. Wilson's classic, The Geography of Reading (Chicago: American Library Association and University of Chicago Press, 1938), where it is shown that also for the United States today "the regions which rank high in per cent of urban population also rank high in library service" (p. 344 and passim).

[105] See n. 92 to the text of the Traicté, where response to the public opening of Mazarin's library is discussed; and cf. nn. 463-64 on the public use of the Rouen Cathedral library.

[106] See n. 153 to the text of the Traicté.

[107] They were La Croix du Maine (see above, the Introduction at n. 85) and Joseph-Marie Suarès (see below, the text at nn. 342-45). The urge to produce a universal guidebook to libraries may well have been influenced and conditioned by the numerous "geographical" and travel books published from 1480 to

writing a book along the lines of Naudé's Avis.[108] Book collecting had such an important place in the mid-seventeenth century French scene that one of the Mazarinades composed at the time of the Fronde was actually devoted to private libraries--thus showing the inextricable involvement of political history with library history during the period.[109] And the French bibliothecal activity as described by Jacob had by no means reached a peak. During the latter half of the seventeenth century the French royal library, as a result of "the intelligence and energy of Colbert (who as Surintendant des Batiments du Roi was practically all-powerful) and the glory of the Grand Monarch, his master" attained a splendor second only to that of its formative period under Louis XII and Francis I;[110] and a year before Colbert's death, Richard Simon,

---

1609; five hundred and twenty four of these have been analyzed by Atkinson, who shows by means of them that at the beginning of the seventeenth century French scholarship had developed a real critical ability to describe the world at large (Geoffroy Atkinson, Les nouveaux horizons de la Renaissance française [Paris: E. Droz, 1935], pp. 253-97, 402-429, and passim).

[108]This was Jean Macé (in religion: Léon de Saint-Jean); see the text of the Traicté at n. 220.

[109]Reference is here made to No. 3550 in Moreau's Bibliographie des Mazarinades. The tract is available in a modern edition: Rymaille sur les plus célèbres bibliotières de Paris en 1649, ed. Albert de la Fizelière (Paris: A. Aubry, 1868). This four-page anonymous poem mentions sixty-six noteworthy institutional and private libraries of Paris. The following lines in the concluding section of the poem show the prominent place Jacob held in Parisian society at the time: "Dom Jacob Bibliotier/Et Naudé Grand Ramassier,/Pourront faire un Dictionnaire/Pour les Docteurs de Grammaire." The intimate connection between political and bibliothecal life in mid-seventeenth century France is also reflected in the numerous Mazarinades which made a point of mentioning Mazarin's rich library.

[110]Arundell Esdaile, National Libraries of the World, ed. F. J. Hill (2d ed.; London: The Library Association, 1957), pp. 50-51.

the great Old Testament scholar and Hebraist, could say in comparing the libraries of France and England, "In short, it is only at Paris that a man of letters can carry on substantial studies."[111] Although the fact does not seem to be sufficiently recognized in general historical studies or even in the field of bibliographical history, the seventeenth century in Europe--and particularly in France--was the incunabular period of modern librarianship, even as the fifteenth century--especially in Germany--had been the cradle period of modern printing.[112] What in the seventeenth-century situation, particularly in France, led to the bibliothecal concern which Jacob depicts with such heavy strokes?

Certainly for France the economic strength of the

---

[111] Richard Simon, Lettres choisies (Amsterdam: Louis de Lorme, 1700), p. 64 (letter of March 20, 1682).

[112] Probably the best survey of the seventeenth century in English, G. N. Clark's The Seventeenth Century (2d ed.; Oxford: Clarendon Press, 1947), says nothing whatever about the growth of libraries during the period; the only general work to do even partial justice to this aspect of seventeenth-century civilization is Preserved Smith's A History of Modern Culture, I (New York: Henry Holt, 1930), 351-55. The importance of the seventeenth century as the formative period of modern librarianship is not brought out in the commonly-used texts on the history of libraries (e.g., Hessel's History of Libraries and Vorstius' Grundzüge der Bibliotheksgeschichte, where the sixteenth and seventeenth centuries are treated together); among modern bibliographical historians, only Archer Taylor seems to recognize clearly the significance of the seventeenth-century in the rise of modern librarianship and bibliography (cf. his History of Bibliographies of Bibliographies, Chapter II). That library concern was an all-European (not just a French) phenomenon in the seventeenth-century is demonstrated in my edition-translation of Lomeier's De bibliothecis, Chapter X; cf. also Gladys Scott Thomson, Life in a Noble Household, 1641-1700 (reprint ed.; Ann Arbor: University of Michigan Press, 1959), Chapter XIV ("The Library"), pp. 262-79, which suggests a close parallel between English and French private book collecting during the period.

nation must be considered a primary factor in the establishment and augmentation of libraries. At the outset of this Introduction we underscored the advantages France possessed both in population and economic power relative to Europe as a whole in the seventeenth century. Just as the Renaissance in Italy from about 1350 to 1525 was related to the strength of Italian commerce in the Mediterranean prior to the Turkish advance,[113] so the economic power of France in the seventeenth century made possible the diverting of money to book-collecting, and provided the time and leisure for such an avocation. But the economic argument is in this case ultimately a <u>petitio principii</u>; for the question still remains as to why book collecting and library organization should have been the avocational choice of men with money and leisure, rather than any number of other possible activities. Moreover, why should there have been great interest in bibliography throughout Europe during the seventeenth century--even in areas such as Germany where the economic situation was dreadful? Economic strength can explain why France succeeded in building more library collections than other European countries, but it does not explain why so many in France--and in Europe generally--considered a bibliothecal interest "the most irreproachable and praiseworthy avocation of all" (to use Jacob's expression). Bonnaffé argued that "the passion to conserve was developed in

---

[113] See Armando Sapori, <u>Studi di storia economica (secoli XIII-XIV-XV)</u> (2 vols., 3d ed.; Firenze: G. C. Sansoni, [1955]), I, 619 ff.; Gino Luzzatto, <u>Studi di storia economica veneziana</u> (Padova: Cedam, 1954), pp. 5-16; and Luzzatto's <u>Storia economica d'Italia</u>, I (Roma: Edizioni Leonardo, 1949), 209 ff.

direct proportion to the mania to destroy"--that in a century colored by the horrors of the Thirty Years' War, Frenchmen in particular wanted to compensate for their participation in war and personally forget their involvement in it; and bibliophilistic and collecting interests satisfied this need in a real way.[114] Unquestionably there is truth in this interpretation; but is it possible to cut deeper?

In his recent study of Leibnitz, R. W. Meyer writes:

> The most characteristic trait of the age following upon the Thirty Years' War was its attempt to overcome all conflicts by an exertion of the will. And this exertion was to be found not only in the systematic constructions of philosophy, but also in a practical, quasi-stoic attitude towards the will. In philosophy itself the rational will carried with it the impetus towards the construction of systems.[115]

It is highly suggestive that Leibnitz himself, who sought so desperately for a harmonia universalis, served with destinction as a librarian, and was interested in problems of library classification.[116] The desire for system, order, and control of knowledge inevitably led the great philosopher to problems of collecting and organizing books as the chief carriers of human

---

[114]Bonnaffé, Dictionnaire ..., p. ii. On the place of war in seventeenth-century civilization, see Sir George Clark's War and Society in the Seventeenth Century (Cambridge: Cambridge University Press, 1958).

[115]Meyer, p. 16.

[116]See the Handbuch der Bibliothekswissenschaft, ed. Fritz Milkau and Georg Leyh (2d ed.; Wiesbaden: Harrassowitz, 1952-), III, 612-21, and the literature there cited. It does not seem possible that Meyer, in his otherwise excellent study of Leibnitz, makes no reference to the philosopher's bibliothecal concerns--which relate so basically to his quest for a "manysided order" as reflected in his early maxim, "We can only rejoice in variety when it is reduced to unity" (cf. Meyer, pp. 94, 111).

experience. But why the passion for system in the seventeenth century? Reynold touches the heart of the matter in his analysis of the French Zeitgeist:

> The seventeenth century had to recapture--to reconfirm--all the values accumulated by the Renaissance, to submit them to screening, and above all to give them thorough study, for the Renaissance in its youth and enthusiasm had been in too much of a hurry to make contact with everything, and had manifested too great superficiality. To do this required a method, and the seventeenth century was the century of method. It had a method in political life which allowed it to build the most solid system of government and of administration that the kingdom had to that day known. Sully, Richelieu, Colbert, Louis XIV himself, <u>le roi travailleur</u>, were great men of method. . . . It had a method in religion: the works of all the great theologians and all the great mystics--Francis de Sales, Olier, Bérulle, Bossuet-- demonstrate this; the apologetic for which Pascal has left us only the unfinished but immortal notes is a method. . . . The "gentleman" of the seventeenth century is an ideal type, the result of a method applied to create a society, to train an elite. The greatest philosopher of the time, Descartes, has given us, significantly, a <u>Discourse on Method</u>. In all the literature, the regard for method is evident: <u>Pratique du theatre</u>, <u>Discours sur les unités</u>, <u>Art poétique</u>; indeed, the "doctrine classique," with its precepts and its rules, is a method. In the works both of the savants and of the artists one finds the same preoccupation with formulating and pondering rules. The seventeenth century is a steady reaction to the improvizing spirit that characterizes the Renaissance.117

117Gonzague de Reynold, <u>Le XVIIe siècle, le classique et le baroque</u> (Montréal: Éditions de l'Arbre, 1944), pp. 29-30. The author of this penetrating and exceedingly important work was professor at the University of Fribourg and a correspondant de l'Institut de France; on him see Otto Forst de Battaglia, "Gonzague de Reynolds 75 Jahre," <u>Neue Deutsche Hefte</u>, XIV (1955), 296-301. In connection with the systematization motif, one should note Cassirer's distinction between the seventeenth-century "<u>esprit de système</u>" (the love of system for its own sake) and the eighteenth century "<u>esprit systématique</u>" (inductive, rational search for system); see Ernst Cassirer, <u>The Philosophy of the Enlightenment</u> tr. Fritz C. A. Koelln and James P. Pettegrove (Princeton: Princeton University Press, 1951), <u>passim</u>. Though some of Jacob's friends (e.g. La Mothe le Vayer) were precursors of the "Systematic spirit" of the Enlightenment, Jacob himself--a conservative by temperament and interests--must be associated chiefly with the seventeenth-century "spirit of systems."

Just as the thirteenth and early fourteenth centuries in many respects constituted a period of systematization following the innovations of the twelfth century, so the seventeenth century may be viewed as the era of systematization following the Renaissance and Reformation.[118] It is unfortunate that the seventeenth century has so seldom been treated as an era with an "anatomy" of its own--that it is so often viewed as but a somewhat uninteresting halfway-house between the exciting eras of Renaissance-Reformation and Enlightenment-Revolution. The spirit of systematization appears more effectively to capture the actual seventeenth-century Zeitgeist than Toynbee's stress on growing self-determination, tolerance, and scientific research as precursors of an "oecumenical civilization;"[119] indeed, it may be that the systematization motif has the potential of illuminating the seventeenth century as effectively as Burckhardt's individualism motif has illumined the Italian Renaissance.[120]

---

[118]In the period following what Charles Homer Haskins has called "the renaissance of the twelfth century" came the great systematizations of scholastic theology (Thomas Aquinas' Summa theologiae, etc.). Hard on the heels of the early sixteenth-century Reformation in Germany came the late sixteenth and seventeenth century Protestant theological syntheses (e.g., the remarkable Loci theologici of Martin Chemnitz and Johann Gerhard).

[119]See Arnold J. Toynbee, A Study of History, XII ("Reconsiderations") (London: Royal Institute of International Affairs and Oxford University Press, 1961), 528-30. Closer to our view is Thompson's designation of the period as "The Age of Erudition" (James Westfall Thompson, A History of Historical Writing [2 vols.; New York: Macmillan, 1942], II, Chapter XXXVII and passim).

[120]With regard to Burckhardt's classic Civilization of the Renaissance in Italy, Catherine E. Boyd correctly says:

If the urge to systematize was basic in seventeenth-century European civilization, then it is not strange that bibliographical and bibliothecal concerns played so large a part in the life of the day, or that in France, where the economy permitted, a very large number of libraries were established. During periods of systematization following epochs of innovation, libraries have more than once played a strong role.[121] Societies as well as individuals seem to need "plateau" periods after times of exhilerating and yet exhausting discovery and innovation.[122] Louis Jacob has described the efforts of the greatest nation of his day to bring order out of the fascinating chaos of the Renaissance via libraries; and it should be recognized that an effort such as this, though not possessing the *prima facie* dynamic of a renaissance, had a vital importance of its own, for on the basis of such periods of system new renaissances arise. A recent study of seventeenth-century autobiographies is titled,

---

"Author's interpretations have been repeatedly challenged and in part overthrown, but no comparable synthesis has taken its place" (American Historical Association, Guide to Historical Literature [New York: Macmillan, 1961], p. 530). Probably it is Burckhardt's individualism motif which has stood up best against the criticisms of Thode, Burdach, etc.

[121] Note that the Philobiblon of Richard de Bury (1287-1345) appeared during the period of synthesis following the twelfth century "renaissance"; and that the rise of the professional library movement in the United States in the last quarter of the nineteenth century occurred after America had passed through its formative period politically and ideologically.

[122] Cf. James Deese, The Psychology of Learning (2d ed.; New York: McGraw-Hill, 1958), pp. 184-87.

Every Man a Phoenix;[123] the title could well apply to the age as a whole, and to Jacob's France in particular: in expending itself to collect and organize the fruits of the past it gave birth to a new age. Perhaps, indeed, the phoenix symbol deserves to be applied to the book collector and to the librarian in every age.

Bibliographical Addendum

Little has been written on Louis Jacob de Saint-Charles. The most recent treatment, focusing not on his *Traicté* but on his contributions to national bibliography, is the thoroughly researched essay by Oxford Professor Ian Maclean, "Louis Jacob de Saint-Charles (1608 - 1670) and the Development of Specialist Bibliography," in his *Learning and the Market Place: Essays in Early Modern Book History* (Leiden: Brill, 2009), pp. 403-445. Maclean notes the importance of the French section (Part Two) of the *Traicté* — the subject of our translation here — when he observes that Jacob's "desire to achieve accuracy" was focused on "the French and Italian spheres of which he had direct knowledge and to which he felt strong loyalty" (p. 438).

---

[123] Margaret Bottrall, Every Man a Phoenix; Studies in Seventeenth-Century Autobiography (London: John Murray, 1958).

TREATISE

ON THE FINEST

LIBRARIES,

PUBLIC AND PRIVATE,

WHICH HAVE EXISTED AND

WHICH EXIST TODAY

IN THE WORLD

Divided into Two Parts

Written by Father Louis Jacob
of Chalons, a Carmelite Monk

PART TWO

PARIS
Rolet Le Duc,
Rue Saint-Jacques, near the Posting-House

1644

With the King's Privilege

TREATISE ON LIBRARIES

PART TWO [: FRENCH LIBRARIES]

CHAPTER I (LXXXII)

THE KINGDOM OF FRANCE [: INTRODUCTION]

France today surpasses all other realms in learned men and in libraries.[1] As for men of letters, this will be easy to see in our <u>Bibliothèque universelle des autheurs françois</u>, covering French authors who have honored their country by their writings.[2] And with regard to libraries, the enumeration to follow will make quite clear that our France excels all the other nations.

I shall begin with the libraries of Paris, and with the royal library there. But in dealing with the rest of the provinces, I will employ alphabetical order.

---

[1] This "proud" (<u>stolz</u>) assertion by Jacob is quoted by Ludwig Klaiber and Albert Kolb in their general overview of French libraries from the Renaissance to the Revolution (<u>Handbuch der Bibliothekswissenschaft</u> [hereafter cited as <u>HB</u>] ed. Fritz Milkau and George Leyh [2d ed.; Wiesbaden: Harrassowitz, 1952--], III, 686). They note that the courtly-aristocratic cultural life of the baroque era in France was characterized by a flowering of the book arts and book collecting, and that a definite connection between political power and library development was here manifested (cf. Richelieu, Mazarin, and Colbert). On the comparison between French libraries and those of other European countries in the middle of the seventeenth century, see above, editor's Introduction.

[2] See above, editor's Introduction at n. 89.

CHAPTER II (LXXIII)

THE PROVINCE OF FRANCE. THE CITY OF PARIS

Although Emperor Charlemagne was the first of our monarchs to establish libraries, I discover that they were not located at Paris at all, but at Aix-la-Chapelle (as I have noted on page 201 [Pt. I]) and at Lyon (as will be seen when we discuss that place). Consequently I find that it was King Charles V who first, at Fontainebleau, laid the foundations of the magnificent royal library.[3] Indeed, to enrich it he had

---

[3]Alfred Franklin begins his tabular summary of the history of the royal library with King John (1350-1364), Charles V's immediate predecessor (Les anciennes bibliothèques de Paris [3 vols.; Paris: Imprimerie Imperiale, 1867-1873], II, 210). However, since John possessed only a dozen books at the time of his death (ibid., p. 110), Charles V may rightly be considered the founder of the royal library at Paris. Léopold Delisle, before giving a brief summary of royal book collecting from Charlemagne to Charles V, states that the latter was the first French monarch to have established on a solid foundation a library "not just to satisfy his personal tastes and those of his family or of high court officials, but also to facilitate the studies of scholars whose work he encouraged" (Le cabinet des manuscrits de la Bibliothèque Impériale [3 vols.; Paris: Imprimerie Imperiale, 1868-1881], I, 1). For the content of Charles V's library, see Arthur Tilley, The Dawn of the French Renaissance (Cambridge: University Press, 1918), pp. 57-58. The location of Charles' library was not at Fontainebleau, as Jacob asserts following Gabriel Naudé (Addition à l'histoire de Louys XI [Paris: F. Targa, 1630], pp. 79, 362) and Jacques Du Breul (see below, n. 13), but in his palace in the Cité at Paris until 1367, and after that in the Louvre palace. That the library was not first placed in the Louvre by Charles VI (as Du Breul, Naudé, and Jacob claim) is proven by the inventories of 1373 and 1380, both of which indicate the location of the library with the words "en son chastel du Louvre" in their titles (Franklin, II,

very careful searches made for the best books available in his time. And though that monarch did not know the Latin language,[4] he was naturally inclined to learning, and employed a marvellous eloquence in his discourses. This is attested by the orations which he delivered to pacify the Parisian rebels and to answer the abuse of Charles, called the Bad, king of Navarre; we are told this by Hilarion de Coste, the Minimite, in his Eloges des dauphins de France, p. 223.[5] Charles the Wise bore a great love

---

114, 120). The belief that Charles V kept the library at Fontainebleau and his son moved it into the Louvre has been a persistent one, however; the error appears, for example, in the manuscript outline of the history of the royal library which Franklin transcribes in full (ibid., pp. 214-18) and considers "the first attempt at a methodical summary of the royal library's history" (a strange evaluation, it should be noted, since the outline postdates Jacob's Traicté, and very obviously relies heavily upon it). All arguments in support of a Fontainebleau location for Charles V's library have been effectively refuted by Félix Herbet, "La librairie royale de Fontainebleau," Bibliographe moderne, XXIV (1928-1929), 141-43. For a very full discussion of the contents of Charles V's library in the Louvre, see Delisle, I, 18-38; and for a valuable contemporary physical description of the library, see John Willis Clark, The Care of Books (2d ed.; Cambridge: University Press, 1902), pp. 293-94.

[4]An assertion made by Robert Gaguin (see below, n. 19), and afterwards by César Égasse Du Boulay as well as by Jacob. That Charles V did in fact know Latin is evident from Christine de Pisan, Le livre des fais et bonnes meurs du sage roi Charles V, chaps. iii, xii; cf. Jean Lebeuf, Dissertations sur l'histoire ecclésiastique et civile de Paris (3 vols.; Paris: Lambert et Durand, 1739-1743), III, 390.

[5]The fame of Olivier (Brother Hilarion) de Coste (1595-1661) rests chiefly upon his numerous biographical productions; he is known particularly as the biographer of Mersenne. De Coste and Jacob were members of Colletet's literary circle at Paris during the 1640's (see below, n. 136). Jacob here cites de Coste's Les éloges de nos rois, et des enfans de France, qui ont esté daufins de Viennois (Paris: S. Cramoisy, 1643), p. 223. The continuing value of de Coste's work for historical investigations is made clear by the various references to his writings given in Émile Bourgeois and Louis André, Les sources de l'histoire de France: XVIIe siècle (1610-1715) (8 vols.; Paris: A. Picard, 1913-1935), entries 1295-96, 1337, 1573, 1803.

for men of letters, and employed them to make a variety of translations. He commanded Nicolas Oresme, doctor of the Faculty, grand master of the Collège de Navarre, canon of Sainte-Chapelle, and afterwards twenty-eighth bishop of Lisieux, a man well versed in theology and philosophy, to translate the Bible, Aristotle's Ethics, Politics, and On the Heavens and On the Universe, together with Francesco Petrarcha's Dialogues on Good and Evil Fortune.[6] By order of this king, Jean Golain, doctor of Paris and provincial of the Carmelites in France, translated the Rationale of the Divine Offices or Ceremonies of the Church, and the Collations of the Holy Fathers which Cassiodorus had translated from Greek into Latin.[7] Jean Corbichon, doctor of

---

[6] On Oresme and his translations done under royal commission, see César Égasse Du Boulay, Historia Universitatis Parisiensis (6 vols.; Parisiis: Noel & de Bresche, 1665-1673), IV, 977; Jean-Baptiste-Louis Crevier, Histoire de l'Université de Paris, depuis son origine jusqu'en l'annee 1600 (7 vols.; Paris: Desaint et Saillant, 1761), II, 427; and Gilles Mallet, Inventaire, ou catalogue des livres de l'ancienne bibliothèque du Louvre, fait en l'annee 1373, ed. J. B. B. van Praet (Paris: de Bure, 1836), p. 46. Eduard Zeller, W. D. Ross, and others consider the De mundo ("On the Universe") to be of non-Aristotelian authorship; Zeller views it as a Stoic production and places it in the latter half of the first century B.C. The exact title of Petrarch's work is De remediis utriusque fortunae. Delisle, in his section entitled, "Translations Done for Charles V" (I, 38-43), discusses Oresme and the other translators about to be mentioned by Jacob, and correctly attributes the Petrarch translation not to Oresme, but to Jean Daudin or Doudin (like Oresme a canon of Sainte-Chapelle), and the Bible translation to Raoul de Presles.

[7] Golain's name appears also as Goulain and Golein. The Rational (Latin title, Rationale divinorum officiorum) was one of the chief productions of the French liturgiologist Guillaume Durand (Durandus; Duranti), who wrote it not later than 1286; it was immensely popular (its first printing was by Fust and Schoeffer as early as 1459), and it is still a basic authority on Western liturgies. The author of the Collations translated by Golain was in fact Johannes Cassianus (ca. 350--ca. 433), the French hermit and theological writer (Franklin, II, 111); in referring to Cassiodorus, Jacob follows Naudé, Addition..., p. 358 (de Coste, p. 224, commits the same error by following Naudé).

the Augustinian order, performed the same service for Bartholomew Anglicus' Great Proprietor of All Things.[8] Simon de Hesdin, also a doctor, made a translation of Valerius Maximus;[9] and Raoul de Presles did the same for Saint Augustine's City of God.[10] A number of other learned men presented various works to the king, and he received them with great pleasure, as a testimony to his literary interests.

Charles V's son and successor, King Charles VI, was versed in the sciences, as is noted by Charles de Louviers in his Le songe du vergier[11] and by many others. These writers

---

[8] The author of the Great Proprietor (actually, De proprietatibus rerum), a very popular encyclopedic compilation, was the English (Anglicus) Franciscan Bartholomew de Glanville, who wrote it about 1360. There were numerous editions in Latin, English, French, Dutch, and Spanish; Corbichon's translation itself was printed fourteen times from 1482 to 1556. Corbichon (or Corbechon) apparently had a noteworthy library in his own right (Franklin, II, 112).

[9] Hesdin did the first seven books of the translation; the work was completed in 1401 by Nicolas de Gonesse (ibid.).

[10] The first French translation of the City of God. Presles began the translation in 1371 and finished it in 1375; it was printed at Abbeville in 1486 in two folio volumes.

[11] The reference to Le songe du vergier (Somnium viridarii) and its attribution to Charles de Louviers derive from Naudé, Addition ..., pp. 361-62, which Jacob here follows. Naudé writes: "Charles VI was quite carefully educated in his youth, as Charles de Louviers notes in his Songe du vergier." Louviers is but one possible candidate for the authorship of this anonymous work which reflects the political ideas of Charles V and his advisors; some have attributed it to Raoul de Presles. Naudé apparently confuses the Songe du vergier, which relates to Charles V, with another, almost contemporary Songe (Le songe du vieil pélerin by Philippe de Mézières, to whom Charles V entrusted his son's education). Mézières wrote his Songe for the instruction of the young King Charles VI, and Bk. II, Chapter XXIV specifically speaks of Charles VI's tutors. The frequent confusion of the two Songes is discussed and the points of difference between them are set forth by Bernard de La Monnoye, the eighteenth-century philologist, in the prefatory dissertation to the text of the Songe du

assure us that Charles VI had a great affection for mathematicians, and that he possessed at the Louvre a
<u>Charles VI</u>   fine library with which he combined his father's
book collection, formerly at Fontainebleau.[12] He
put Antoine des Essars in charge of it, and later Garnier de
Saint Yon, who was then municipal magistrate of the city of
Paris; we have this on the authority of Jacques Du Breul, the
Benedictine, in the third book of his <u>Antiquitez de Paris</u>,
p. 1049,[13] where he provides an extract from the eighth book
of the <u>Mémoriaux</u> of the Chamber of Accounts (section H,P,S).
I shall include the extract here as an authentic testimony to
the antiquity of our royal library.[14]

<u>vergier</u> printed in Vol. II of <u>Traitez des droits et libertez de
l'Eglise gallicane</u> ([Paris], 1731). Philippe de Mezières' <u>Songe
du vieil pelerin</u> (Bibliothèque Nationale, ms. fr. 22542) is
reproduced on film at the Library of Congress (Pho M 30-153).
Naudé rather apologetically states that he has been unable to
find many testimonies to the learning and scholarly interests of
Charles VI (the fact is that Charles suffered from periodic at-
tacks of madness and from increasing feeblemindedness during his
life). Jacob's mention of Charles' affection for "mathematicians"
also derives from Naudé, and the latter suggests that they were
of a particular variety--namely, astrologers.

[12] An erroneous assertion, following Naudé. See above, n. 3.

[13] Jacques Du Breul, <u>Le théâtre des antiquitez de Paris</u>
Paris: C. de La Tour, 1612), pp. 1048-49. In this brief section
entitled, "Of the Library of the King Which was Formerly at the
Louvre", Du Breul makes the erroneous, but frequently encountered,
assertion that Charles V's library had been at Fontainebleau and
that Charles VI moved it to the Louvre where his own book collection was situated (see above, n. 3). The <u>Antiquitez</u> of Du Breul
(1528-1624), a monk of the abbey of Saint-Germain-des-Prés, is
cited in Bourgeois, I, entry 277; Bourgeois quotes approvingly
Piganiol de la Force's statement that the book is "one of the
best which has appeared on the subject." Cf. n. 149 below.

[14] The <u>Mémoriaux</u> were destroyed in the Chamber of Accounts
fire which occurred in 1737 (see Joseph Petit, <u>Essai de restitution
des plus anciens Mémoriaux de la Chambre des comptes de Paris</u>

"Garnier de Saint Yon, municipal magistrate of the city of Paris, is placed in charge of the royal library in the Louvre, and also of other royal books wherever located, to replace Antoine des Essars, who, for certain reasons deemed important by the king himself, has been relieved of the post; by this royal edict handed down on May 8, 1412, and so signed" [L]--by the king, in the presence of Master Gerard de Graneval and others, and by the hand of Calot. "And on the 12th of the same month he executed the customary oath" [L]. And a little farther on: "The king, by edict handed down at Paris on July 21, 1418, and so signed" (by the king, in the presence of Master Jacques Denté and others, and by the hand of J. Milet), "committed to Garnier de Saint Yon the care of his books in the Louvre, and at the request of the said Garnier, commissioned certain persons from the Chamber of Accounts to inventory the collection. The inventory has today been delivered to this office by the said commissioners and a second copy of it made, and Garnier has sworn well and faithfully to care for the said books and to disclose to no one the special treasures of this library. His oath having been executed, Garnier has again[5] been invested with the key to the said library (the other key remaining in the possession of the Chamber), and has been presented with the inventory, whose duplicate, signed with his own hand, he committed to the Chamber with other like papers" [L].

See how concerned these monarchs were to build and maintain this library!

[Paris: F. Alcan, 1899], and Henri Jassemin, La Chambre des comptes de Paris au XVe siècle [Paris: A. Picard, 1933]). In the eighteenth century, a "Reconstitution officielle des Mémoriaux" was made, but it is by no means complete, and I am informed that the Reconstitution does not include the passages quoted here by Jacob (letter from F. Dousset, adjoint au directeur général des Archives de France, Paris, November 18, 1960). However, before the 1737 fire, Boivin transcribed the pertinent passages, and they are given in Delisle, I, 46-47.

[15]In 1413, less than a year after his first appointment, Saint Yon was discharged (as was Des Essars, his predecessor) for taking sides against the house of Orléans (Franklin, II, 126). Jacob does not mention the name of the librarian who served from 1413 to 1418 (Jean Maulin, who in fact continued as co-librarian with Saint Yon from 1418 to 1425). Nor does Jacob mention Des Essars' predecessor, who served as garde de la librairie under both Charles V and Charles VI--namely, Gilles Malet or Mallet, who probably became librarian as early as 1368, and who accomplished much in the position (ibid., pp. 114-22, 210). Arundell Esdaile states that Malet's inventory of 1373, "with the supplements by Jean le Begue of 1411 and 1424, forms the foundation-

Afterwards Louis XI came to the throne.[16] According to his faithful chronicler Philippe de Commines, lord of Argenton, he had a perfect knowledge of political science; Commines calls him "the master in statecraft; the wisest person I ever knew for getting himself out of a bad situation, and the most expert in the art of distinguishing people's characters."[17] But even though he applied himself so assiduously to political philosophy, he did not neglect the other branches of learning; for Jean Bouchet, the author of the Annales d'Aquitaine, says of him: "He acquired as much historical as legal knowledge--more than the kings of France ordinarily

Louis XI

---

stone of French bibliography" (National Libraries of the World [2d ed. revised by F. J. Hill; London: The Library Association, 1957], p. 49).

[16]Charles VII (reigned 1422-1461) held the throne after Charles VI and before Louis XI. He contributed virtually nothing to the royal library; in fact, he "did not dream of restoring" the loss which the library suffered in 1429 (Franklin, II, 130). In that year--the year of Charles' coronation following Jeanne d'Arc's success at Orléans--the Duke of Bedford, regent for Henry VI of England (who was recognized as king of France in the north and was supported by the Burgundians), bought and took to England what remained of the royal library in the Louvre. In the inventory of 1373 the collection had numbered 973 volumes, and in that of 1423, 853 volumes; it was now necessary for Louis XI to start afresh in building the royal library (see Delisle, I, 51-54, 72-79).

[17]Commines, Mémoires, Bk. I, Chapter X; cf. Bk. III, Chapter XII. Commines "was a Belgian by birth and long in the service of both Charles the Bold and Louis XI. He wrote these reminiscences of the year 1464 to 1498 late in life. His work is primary for the history of the times. He is the first French writer who manifests a marked influence of the Italian Renaissance. He is sometimes called the French Machiavelli, and in many ways he is a counterpart of the Florentine" (G. M. Dutcher et al., Guide to Historical Literature [New York: Macmillan, 1931], p. 582); see also Tilley, pp. 352-64.

obtained."[18] This is confirmed by his chronicler and librarian Robert Gaguin, who writes in the tenth book of his History of France: "He was well versed in literature, and more erudite than sovereigns usually are" [L].[19] Now his knowledge of books

---

[18][Jean Bouchet], Les annales d'Aquitaine (Poictiers: E. de Marnef, 1557), folio 154 v. The 1557 edition of this work was the last to be revised and corrected by the author himself; it seems to have been issued shortly after his death. A record of editions of this important work is provided by Auguste Hamon, Jean Bouchet (Paris: H. Oudin, 1901), pp. 404-405; cf. pp. 185-86. Hamon says of the work: "Its prime merit lies in the great number of documents which its author assembled by patient research; it is an inexhaustible mine . . . and represents a unique labor which it is impossible to repeat today, due to the disappearance of many of the original materials" (ibid., p. 201). Bouchet was a friend of Rabelais, and a poet and literary writer of original genius as well as a noteworthy historian.

Of Louis XI's intellectual interests and attainments his modern biographer Pierre Champion writes: "The king was well educated--he knew Latin and Italian. Commines described him as assez lettré. . . . The ambassador Cagnola wrote of him in 1479: 'Sometimes he engages in study and he often cites the best authorities.' Louis read the duke of Milan's letters as easily as a native Italian. . . . But his was the learning of a prince rather than of a scholar. His favorite subject, and the one he knew best, was the history of France" (Louis XI [2 vols.; Paris: H. Champion, 1927], II, 188). Tilley says: "Louis XI had not the time, even if he had had the inclination, to play the part of art-patron. He did not care to spend money on illuminated manuscripts, and when he confiscated the possessions of rebels and traitors, he seems to have spared their libraries. But he was far from unlettered; he was, indeed, fond of literature, and, like his friend Francesco Sforza, he was too shrewd and intelligent not to encourage learning and art. He founded . . . a new University at Bourges, and he gave his support to the new art of printing" (Tilley, p. 78).

[19]Robert Gaguin, Annales (Lugduni: J. Osmont, 1524), folio 108 v. Gaguin (1433-1501) was one of the foremost French humanists of the late fifteenth century. At the University of Paris he was an intimate of Guillaume Fichet. In 1473 he was elevated to minister general of the Trinitarian order. As a result of a failure in a diplomatic mission for Louis XI, he was in disfavor from 1477 until Louis' death; under Charles VIII he served as an ambassador. (For a work containing a remarkable wealth of biographical detail on Gaguin, see Louis Thuasne (ed.), Roberti Gaguini epistolae et orationes [2 vols.; Paris: E. Bouillc 1903]; and see also the fine sketch in Tilley, pp. 185-214). Some

was as valuable to him as his knowledge of the sciences. Because he applied himself only to important matters in the interest both of governing his kingdom and also of advancing and extending the liberal arts, it was natural that he should have improved the royal library by adding to it the greatest number of books he could find. To this end he employed Robert Gaguin, a member of the Trinitarian order and a man of great learning in his time, who later--under Charles VIII--earned the position of ambassador, and ultimately became minister general of his order. Gaguin's wide acquaintance with good books merited

---

have claimed that Gaguin did not hold the librarian's office. However, such a view is indefensible; his grave inscription, preserved for a long period at the convent of the Mathurins in Paris, describes him as "selectae Ludovici XI bibliothecae authoris et praefecti" (Franklin, II, 131). His principal writing is the Annales (i.e., Compendium de origine et gestis Francorum), first published in 1495. Auguste Molinier evaluates the work as follows: "The material pertaining to the reigns of Louis XI and Charles VIII constitutes an interesting chronicle. The author is not very favorably disposed toward Louis XI, but he does not demonstrate an exaggerated aversion. The entire work is useful even today, and seems to have been too long disdained. It is only a summary, but one written by a generally well-informed contemporary of judicious spirit" (Les sources de l'histoire de France dès origines aux guerres d'Italie (1494) [6 vols.; Paris: A. Picard, 1901-1906], V, 26-28). A bibliophilistic contribution on Gaguin's part which Jacob fails to mention is described as follows by Tilley: "Among the services which Gaguin rendered to his Order and at the same time to the cause of Humanism in Paris was the construction of a library over the cloister of the Mathurin monastery with money which he had obtained by subscription from the Sorbonne and other bodies. The collection of manuscripts and books grew to considerable proportions, and was extremely useful to Paris students. As General of the Order Gaguin seems to have had power to lend the books at his pleasure. We have two letters from Erasmus, written in March 1500, just before he brought out the first edition of his Adagia, in one of which he asks for the loan of a Macrobius, and in the other for a Quintilian and a treatise on rhetoric by George of Trebizond. 'I do not ask,' he says, 'whether you have the book, as I know that no good authors are absent from your shelves'" (Tilley, pp. 195-96).

for him the high rank of librarian to King Louis XI. (He was
not librarian to Louis XII, as Aubert Le Mire mistakenly says
in his eulogy to Gaguin:

> Since Gaguin was extraordinarily gifted in eloquence
> and common sense, he often engaged in diplomatic mis-
> sions for the French kings in Italy, Germany, and Eng-
> land. He was especially esteemed by Louis XII (sic, XI)
> who, in his zeal for book collecting, provided him with
> vast sums of money for that purpose and put him in
> charge of his royal library [L].[20]

Now it is well established that Gaguin died at the beginning
of the reign of Louis XII, who had his library at Blois--as
M. Naudé has judiciously remarked in the fourth chapter of his
Addition à l'histoire de Louys XI.[21] Naudé there sets forth
arguments to prove that Le Mire is in error, and I refer the
reader to his book.) Many have thought strange what they read
in the Registers of Louis' Medical Schools--that he gave his

---

[20]Aubert Le Mire, Elogia belgica (Antverpiae: D. Mar-
tinius, 1609), pp. 176-77. Le Mire or Miraeus (1573-1640) is
best known for his excellent biographical funeral oration for
his close friend Justus Lipsius (Biographie nationale de Belgique
[hereafter cited as BNB], ed. Academie Royale des Sciences, des
Lettres, et des Beaux-arts de Belgique [28 vols.; Bruxelles:
Bruylant-Christophe, 1866-1944], XIV 894). Canon Le Mire is
remembered in library history as the founder and first librarian
of the town library in Antwerp (Edward Edwards, Memoirs of
Libraries [2 vols.; London: Trübner, 1859], II, 513).

[21]Naudé, Addition ..., pp. 80-81. Naudé here provides a
fine example of historical criticism. In proving his point he
utilizes three arguments: the first based on rational considerations (under Charles VIII Gaguin had served as an ambassador and
had been minister general of his order; these are positions of
much greater eminence than that of librarian, so it is highly
questionable that Louis XII would have given him the latter post),
the second based on external evidence (Louis XII's library was
at Blois, but Gaguin, as minister general of the Trinitarians,
did not reside there), and the third employing internal evidence
(in another place Le Mire substitutes Louis XI for Louis XII, so
it would not be strange if he made the opposite error in writing
of Gaguin).

silver plate to these Schools as security for a copy of Rhazes which was in their library and which he requested through Master Jean de la Driesche. But those who have read what the aforementioned Gabriel Naudé says on the matter in his Addition a l'histoire of the king will recognize and understand this prince's love of books.[22]

King Louis XII[23] earned the distinction of being unanimously proclaimed "father of his people" not only because of the kindness and affection which he bore toward his subjects, but also for his great interest in literature. Indeed, a learned historian calls him the "Ptolemy of his time," on account of his extensive and costly search for books to enrich the library which he maintained at Blois. This historian is Symphorien Champier

---

[22] Ibid., pp. 81-84, where the beginning portion of the letter to Louis from the Faculty of Medicine, containing the borrowing conditions, was published for the first time. This celebrated incident is described in detail in Franklin, II, 22-23, and a facsimile reproduction of the Faculty's letter, together with an accurate transcription, is also provided. Louis, always concerned about his health, wanted the Rhazes in order to have it copied for his own library; the Faculty, which freely loaned its books to professors and scholars, demanded the high security in this case because (1) the complete works of Rhazes, the great tenth-century Arab physician, were not available anywhere else in Paris, and (2) the Faculty realized that without such security it might not be easy to retrieve the volume once it was in royal hands. Louis gave the required security, and returned the Rhazes on January 24, 1472. Jean de la Driesche acted as the king's agent in the transaction because of his position as president of the Chamber of Accounts and treasurer of France. Cf. the text at n. 304 below.

[23] Charles VIII (ruled 1484-1498) followed Louis XI and preceded Louis XII. During his Italian expedition Charles appropriated part of the valuable royal library at Naples which had been collected by Robert of Anjou, patron of Petrarcha and Boccaccio, and by Alfonso I and Ferdinand of Aragon. Robert Gaguin effected the integration of these books with the collection built up by Louis XI at the Louvre (ibid., p. 131; see also Delisle, I, 94-98 [with revision of viewpoint on p. 233]).

of Lyon, physician to the duke of Lorraine, and author of a life of the king under whom he lived. The biography appears in the third book of his Trophies of the French, and there one will see with what love Louis XII cherished the Muses. Champier writes:

> His wisdom, understanding, and other virtues are admired by all; so much so that it is very hard to determine which is preeminent or deserves the greater praise. Indeed, in his great love of literature, his powerful interest in learned men, and his deep affection for books, he stands with Ptolemy Philadelphus, who put Demetrius Phalerius in charge of his library and placed much money in his hands so that by purchase or transcription he would bring books together from far and wide for the king's library. And when Ptolemy asked him how many books were now in the collection, he replied that there were more than 200,000--but in a short time he thought he could reach 500,000. So likewise our most Christian King Louis, with no less diligence, orders books to be collected from everywhere; and the library which he has built is as sumptuous as that of Philadelphus himself, who certainly was a very wise man and most worthy of his great kingdom--a man who, from the time he took the royal diadem, managed with greatest skill all things he considered pertinent to the welfare of the state. [L][24]

---

[24]Champier (ca. 1472--ca. 1539/40) was a physician and writer of high reputation in his own time. He received a doctor of medicine degree at age twenty; he was personal physician to Antoine de Lorraine; and he attended the coronation of Francis I at Reims in 1515. He was one of the most influential citizens of Lyons in his later years, and propagated there the ideas of Ficino's Platonic Academy in Florence (Frances A. Yates, The French Academies of the Sixteenth Century [London: Warburg Institute of the University of London, 1947], p. 3). He wrote extensively on medicine, magic, philosophy, and history (for a complete listing, see Paul Allut, Étude biographique et bibliographique sur Symphorien Champier [Lyon: Scheuring, 1859]); his historical works, though on the whole of little present-day value, can still be useful for material on contemporary events and persons, as Roman d'Amat notes (Dictionnaire de biographie française [hereafter designated DBF], ed. J. Balteau et al. [Paris: Letouzey, 1933--], VIII, 325). Champier's Tropheum Gallorum, here cited, is published as Pt. II of his Liber de quadruplici vita. Theologia Asclepij (Colophon: Lugduni: Gueynardus & Huguetanus, 1507); the quotation given by Jacob appears on leaf B 7, recto and verso, of the Tropheum.

How can Greece any longer boast a unique reputation because of Ptolemy's splendid library? She should remind herself that France has been her sister with regard to libraries as well as letters, and that our monarchs have been the true imitators of hers in the establishment of their library.

One of the principal additions to this library under Louis XII consisted of the acquisition of a large number of legal classics, which were seized at Milan and brought here from there.[25] The library was so famous that an ambassador named Bolognini, on seeing it at Blois, considered it one of the marvels of his time; one can read this in his Book of Wonders, which describes the four most remarkable things he saw in France--and he does not hesitate to give the library first place among these.[26]

The great King Francis I was in his time "the Parnassus

---

[25] Jacob here refers to Louis XII's expropriation, during his conquest of Milan in 1499, of the Visconti-Sforza library at Pavia; it consisted of at least 1,000 Greek, Latin, Italian, and French manuscripts. On this collection and other acquisitions incorporated into Louis' library at Blois, see Tilley, pp. 148-49; Delisle, I, 121-40; and Johannes Lomeier, A Seventeenth-Century View of European Libraries, tr. and ed. John Warwick Montgomery (Berkeley: University of California Press, 1962), sec. "Italy," n. 80.

[26] Lodovico Bolognini, a doctor of civil and canon law, came from Bologna as an ambassador to Louis XII; after seeing his library at Blois he treated it as the first of "the four marvels of France" discussed in his pamphlet, De quattuor singularibus in Gallia repertis. He addressed the work to Symphorien Champier, and the latter included it in his De triplici disciplina (Colophon: Lugduni: S. Vincent, 1508), leaves eee ij--[eee vi]. The other three marvels, in Bolognini's opinion, were the happy and stable condition of the French kingdom, due to its monarchs, and especially to Louis XII; the city of Lyons (Champier's residence); and the city of Blois (the king's residence). Bolognini, using the famous line from Vergil, says that the royal library should be extolled "as a cypress among trailing hedge-row shoots" (Eclogues i. 25; Mackail's rendering).

of the Muses and a library of learning." For though the liberal arts had been flourishing under his predecessors, his care and diligence adorned their perfections. In the year 1527 he ordered the relocation of the royal library at Fontainebleau.[27] (It had been moved from there in Charles VI's time, as has been noted above.)[28] This action of his was based on the counsel and advice of Janus Lascaris, a Greek by nationality, and Guillaume Budé.[29] And wishing to augment and

---

[27] The date is wrong. The official transfer from Blois to Fontainebleau was effected by letters patent dated May 22, 1544 (Franklin, II, 136; Delisle, I, 178). Francis had, however, begun a library at Fontainebleau considerably before the transfer--perhaps as early as 1522-1523 (Herbet, Bibliographe moderne, XXIV, 143-44, 147). On these collections, see also Henri-Victor Michelant, Catalogue de la bibliothèque de François Ier à Blois en 1518 (Paris: A. Franck, 1863), and Ernest-Quentin Bauchart, La bibliothèque de Fontainebleau et les livres des derniers Valois (1515-1589) (Paris: E. Paul, 1891).

[28] See nn. 3 and 12 and the text corresponding.

[29] Janus Lascaris (1445-1535), a famous Renaissance Greek scholar, emigrated to Italy after the fall of Constantinople, and returned twice to the East to collect manuscripts for Lorenzo de' Medici before entering French service; on him, see Börje Knös, Un ambassadeur de l'hellénisme--Janus Lascaris--et la tradition greco-byzantine dans l'humanisme français (Uppsala: Almquist & Wiksells, 1945). His aid to Francis I in establishing the Fontainebleau library was considerable, as we see from Henri Omont, Catalogues des manuscrits grecs de Fontainebleau sous François Ier et Henri II (Paris: Imprimerie Nationale, 1889), pp. iv f. "In this work he was associated with Budaeus, who, as an occasional pupil of his colleague, learnt more Greek from Lascaris than from his former teacher, Hermonymus of Sparta" (John Edwin Sandys, A History of Classical Scholarship [3 vols.; Cambridge: University Press, 1903-1908], II, 78). On Budé, see below, n. 56. Jacob's statement concerning Lascaris and Budé is derived from Pierre Dan (see below, n. 33), and Dan in turn bases his assertion on the Chronographia of Gilbert Genebrard (1537-1597), the French theologian and archbishop of Aix (on the Chronographia, see Henri Hauser, Les sources de l'histoire de France, XVIe siècle (1494-1610) [4 vols.; Paris: A. Picard, 1906-1915], entry 25).

improve the library, he sent Juste Tenelle, Guillaume Postel, and Pierre Gilles to the East to engage in a careful search for rare books in Eastern tongues for the enrichment of that magnificent collection.[30] So that these languages might be taught publicly, in the year 1531 he appointed twelve royal lecturers --lecturers in Latin, Greek, and Hebrew, and in mathematics, philosophy, rhetoric, and medicine as well.[31] It is noteworthy

---

[30] Jacob's source here is Naudé, Addition ..., pp. 368-69. Herbet (Bibliographe moderne, XXIV, 151) notes that while such other early authorities as Thevet, Abel de Sainte-Marthe, La Croix du Maine, and de Thou likewise claim that the royal library at Fontainebleau acquired precious manuscripts from royally-sponsored Eastern expeditions by Tenelle, Postel, and Gilles, the evidence for the claim is actually very weak. Delisle, I, 157-61 (following Boivin) points out that no surviving manuscripts in the collection carry the signatures of the three men, and the list of donors of Greek manuscripts drawn up by Angelus Vergetius in 1545 does not include their names. Moreover: (1) Corroborating biographical material on Tenelle cannot be found (Delisle, in making this telling point, unfortunately does not realize that Jacob relied upon Naudé for the name and therefore was not responsible for its introduction). (2) Postel made two sojourns in the East, one before and one after the death of Francis I; the first was a diplomatic mission, and there is no evidence that Postel brought back manuscripts for the royal library. On both journeys he collected books for his own use, but beyond this the historical data do not permit us to go (see William J. Bouwsma, Concordia Mundi: The Career and Thought of Guillaume Postel, 1510-1581 [Cambridge, Mass.: Harvard University Press, 1957], pp. 5-6, 16; and cf. n. 542 below). (3) As Boivin clearly shows, several contradictions surround the Eastern activities of Gilles, and there is no proof that he actually supplied manuscripts to the royal library. It is true that he was sent with the French ambassador to the Turks, d'Aramon, to collect manuscripts for the king (Jean Chesneau, Le voyage de Monsieur d'Aramon, ed. Ch. Schefer [Paris: E. Leroux, 1887], pp. 138-39); but his treasures (if they actually existed) never reached the Bibliothèque royale.

[31] Jacob refers to the establishment of the Collège royal, which would eventually become the Collège de France. The professors were titled "lecteurs royaux" or "liseurs du Roi en l'Université de Paris", or sometimes simply "professeurs en l'Université", and experienced considerable opposition from the hyperorthodox and reactionary Sorbonne. Chief credit for the founding of the Collège should undoubtedly be given to Budé. See Abel Lefranc, Histoire du Collège de France (Paris: Hachette, 1893).

that the books which entered this library were all very well bound; for in that period bindings began to be very handsomely executed.[32]

Before going on, I shall quote the description of the library which is found in the Trésor des merveilles de Fontainebleau, printed shortly after the events just mentioned. Pierre Dan, a Redemptionist and superior of their monastery at Fontainebleau, writes (in Bk. II, Chapter VII, sec. 4; pp. 98-99):[33]

> I proceed now to the top floor of this establishment, where the gallery is located which formerly served as the library. The great King Francis, with much effort and enthusiasm, set up this library in the royal residence, and put the learned Pierre Gilles in charge of it. The most one can say about it now is that to prevent its being dispersed in our tragic civil wars, its books were moved to Paris, where one still finds them today. This library was indeed one of the most significant attractions of Fontainebleau, for Francis spared no effort to collect all the rarest and most interesting books and manuscripts available. To

---

[32]Roger Devauchelle, La reliure en France, de ses origines à nos jours (Paris: J. Rousseau-Girard, 1959--), I, 87, while noting that the bindings executed for Francis are "on the whole rather simple", states that his reign marked the "beginning and flowering of decorative binding" in France. To this period of course belongs Jean Grolier. For magnificent illustrations both of bindings in Francis' library and of Grolier bindings, see ibid., plates 32-38.

[33]Concerning the historical value of Le trésor des merveilles de la maison royale de Fontainebleau (Paris: S. Cramoisy, 1642) by Pierre Dan (d. 1649), Bourgeois writes: "His description is precise and almost exclusively technical; the author, because he himself had been the architect of the monument, pays particular attention to giving exact measurements. . . . In spite of its defects, this work must still be consulted" (Bourgeois, entry 284). As Herbet notes, Dan is apparently the only early writer who asserts that Pierre Gilles was a garde of the library at Fontainebleau (Bibliographe moderne, XXIV, 147-48); the assertion is not on that account necessarily false, but should probably be accepted with some caution. Gilles' librarianship, if it did take place, must have been in the earliest period of the Fontainebleau library's history--from, say, 1522 to 1538 (cf. n. 27 above).

find such treasures, he sent Gilles and numerous other
distinguished persons to Asia, Greece, and other parts
of the world, and if they could not obtain the manuscripts themselves, he saw to it that by his favor
copies were made. (Belleforest, Cosmographie, p. 333.)[34]
One reads that when some foreign princes and lords
visited France, they were ever so much more eager to
come to Fontainebleau and view this treasure house of
books than to see anything worthy of admiration elsewhere.

See what glory this great monarch obtained by returning the sciences to that splendor which they had originally possessed and from which they had fallen through the barbarism that crept over our French people; his work insures that his name will be forever blessed among the nations--and especially among men of letters, whose Maecenas he was, and whom he so tenderly loved that he called scholars his children.

We pass on from this king to his beautiful daughter-in-law, Catherine de Médicis, who married Henry II, his successor to the crown. At an early age she survived the 1529 rebellion of the Florentines against the house of Medici, when the latter were driven from Florence.[35]

Catherine de Médicis

---

[34]Pierre Dan's reference (given as a marginal rubric in his Trésor) is to Sebastian Münster's La cosmographie universelle de tout le monde ... beaucoup plus augmentée, ornée et enrichie, par François de Belle-Forest (2 vols.; Paris: M. Sonnius, 1575), I, Pt. I, 333. This passage describing the magnificence of the Fontainebleau library is quoted in full in Franklin, II, 139-40, and in Herbet, Bibliographe moderne, XXIV, 145. On Belleforest (1530-1583), who held the coveted title of royal historiographer, see Hauser, entry 20; and cf. Belleforest, L'ancienne et grande cité de Paris, ed. Valentin Dufour (Paris: Quantin, 1882), pp. i-xxxvi. Münster (1489-1552) was the greatest geographer of the German Reformation period; his Cosmographia, in which he was assisted by over one hundred collaborators, is his most important work (see Viktor Hantzsch, Sebastian Münster, Leben, Werk, wissenschaftliche Bedeutung [Leipzig: Teubner, 1898]).

[35]The rebellion broke out in 1527 and was successful chiefly because of Clement VII's inability to maintain Medicean power and prestige at Rome in the face of the imperial sack of

Then later she wed our Henry II, and brought to him, among other things, the manuscripts of the famous Medicean library;[36] these were placed in the royal library, where they remain to the present day. Learning owes this queen perpetual remembrance, for she brought about its great advancement. This is asserted by Father Hilarion de Coste in his eulogy, from which I shall borrow the testimony as an embellishment for my presen-

---

the city in that year. Catherine was held as hostage in Florence by the citizenry during the difficult period 1527-30 (Paul Van Dyke, <u>Catherine de Médicis</u> [2 vols.; London: John Murray, 1923], I, 10-14).

[36] Jacob here refers to the nine hundred manuscripts which Catherine obtained from Marshal Strozzi's estate in 1558; many of these manuscripts had been acquired by Catherine's father, Lorenzo de' Medici, in the wake of Muhammed II's capture of Constantinople. "All her life she collected books and at her death her library consisted of 4,550 volumes. Her beautiful collection of nine hundred manuscripts in Greek and Latin theology and philosophy, Greek and Hebrew literature, canon and civil law, she had gotten from the estate of her cousin, Marshal Strozzi, at his death in 1558, with a promise to his son to pay for them. She never did so, but the family of Strozzi, advanced and enriched in France by Catherine's influence, had no reason to complain of her. At her death these manuscripts were in the house of her first chaplain, the Abbé of Bellebranche, where they remained until the close of the century, when the repeated order of Henry IV compelled him to turn them into the royal library; whence they passed into the Bibliothèque Nationale. . . . The indications are that, although she kept up the traditions of her house in collecting a library she cared very much more for people than for books and preferred the talk of a live poet to the page of a dead one" (<u>ibid</u>., II, 40-41). On Catherine's library, see especially Delisle, I, 207-12, and Antoine-Jean-Victor Le Roux de Lincy, <u>Notice sur la bibliothèque de Catherine de Médicis avec des extraits de l'inventaire de cette bibliothèque</u> (Paris: J. Techener, 1859). Catherine's husband, King Henry II, is important bibliophilistically for the magnificent Renaissance bindings executed for his royal library and for his favorite, Diane de Poitiers (see Devauchelle, I, 98-100, and plates 46-48, 50; cf. Delisle, I, 187-89). Henry did not, however, supply much money for increasing the size of the royal book collection; in Naudé, <u>Addition ...</u>, pp. 372-73, we read: "Henry II, though well educated in his youth, was so distracted by the wars which he carried on with Charles V that he scarcely had the means to embrace and foster the Muses."

tation:[37]

> During peace time, Queen Catherine encouraged a flowering of literature, mechanical arts, architecture, painting, and sculpture. One is at a loss to praise her enough for having supported learned and erudite men (in doing so she followed the example of those princes of her house who gave refuge to the Greek Muses when they were expelled from Constantinople and the East by the barbarous Ottomans)--and for having expended a royal amount, worthy of the beautiful daughter of that "father and restorer of letters," the great King Francis, in financing the search through Greece and the whole Levant for the rarest manuscripts in all languages. Such treasures were above and beyond those of the Medicean library which she brought from Italy and which now serve to adorn the royal library of our sovereigns.

That noble Queen of the Medici family
Has, like Calliope, produced an offspring.
In order not to fall short of her greatest forbears,
She has devoted herself to searching out the
          oldest books--
Ronsard   Books in Hebrew, Greek, and Latin--translated and
          still to be translated.
And at lordly cost she has refurbished for them
The lofty palace of the Louvre,[38] so that
          Frenchmen may
Without jeopardy become conquerors of foreign
          knowledge.

It is not unreasonable that this great poet Pierre Ronsard, gentleman of the Vendôme region, has praised this queen in such dignified terms for her part in advancing knowledge; as a matter of fact, she deserves eternal glory from those who are nursed by

---

[37] De Coste's eulogy for Catherine is included in his *Les eloges et les vies des reynes, des princesses, et des dames illustres* (2 vols.; Paris: Cramoisy, 1647); the quoted passage (which includes the lines from Ronsard) is found at I, 240. On de Coste, see above, n. 5.

[38] In the 1584 and 1587 editions of Ronsard's poetry, the phrase "Her château of St. Maur" appears instead of "The lofty palace of the Louvre." The queen built St. Maur in 1563 and had her library moved there; this country house was located five miles from the city gates of Paris. Ronsard's lines here quoted are taken from his poem entitled "Compleinte a la Royne mere du Roy," whose incipit is "Royne, qui de vertus passes Artemesie," and which was first published in 1564; see Pierre de Ronsard, *Oeuvres complètes*, ed. Paul Laumonier (Paris: Hachette, et al., 1914--), XII, 188, ll. 333-40.

the Muses.[39]

For some years after the death of that princess these books were in the keeping of Jean Baptiste Benciregni, abbot of Bellebranche.[40] Then King Henry IV, by letters patent of June 14, 1594, commanded that all the ancient volumes--Hebrew, Greek, Latin, Arabic, French, Italian, etc.--which were a part of the personal estate of the deceased queen, should be incorporated into the royal library; and Abbé Benciregni was ordered to place all of the aforesaid books into the hands of the late Jacques-Auguste de Thou, at that time librarian to his majesty,[41] in order that the personal property of the French crown might forever be preserved from dispersal. It is noteworthy that the majority of these books are bound in rose-

---

[39] "Many poets and literary men found her sympathetic; for we find in her patronage of literature, the same vivid interest in personality--in people--which can be traced through all her patronage of art. Of five great masters of the French tongue in her day, Amyot, Calvin, Montaigne, Rabelais and Ronsard, Rabelais died before she had any real power of patronage, and Calvin lived an exile bitterly hostile to the Crown of France, but with Amyot, Montaigne and Ronsard she had intimate relations. It does not mean much that they put compliments on her wisdom and taste into their works--men of letters sent eulogies to patrons or powerful friends much as men of society now send bouquets to their hostesses--but there seems to be an unusual note of sincerity in some of the things they said of her. It is plain that she wished to be a patron of literature" (Van Dyke, II, 39-40). Catherine's encouragement of learning is pointed up with the aid of contemporary testimonies by Yates, pp. 20-21, 29, 30, 60-61, 182, 202-203, 319, 323.

[40] The abbot's name is variously spelled; Parlement referred to him as "Bencheviny"; Félibien, "Benemouy"; Maichelius, "Beneiregnius"; Hauréau, "Bencivenny"; and Franklin, "Benciveni." See Franklin, II, 153-55, and our n. 36 above.

[41] On de Thou, see below, nn. 64 and 256 ff.

colored morocco,[42] and the money for doing this was obtained from certain revenues which belonged to the Jesuits but which the king enjoyed during the period of their expulsion from the kingdom.[43]

Charles IX, son of Henry II and Catherine de Médicis, received a liberal education, as can be seen by the books De la venerie and De la chasse which he wrote; though unfinished, they were printed in 1625.[44] This monarch augmented the royal library considerably by adding to it some of the very excellent Latin manuscripts previously owned by President de Ranconnet, who died in the Bastille while Charles was in power.[45]

Charles IX

---

[42]On discussing the bindings executed for Henry IV, Devauchelle, I, 118, writes: "The dominant color of the morocco was antique red"; his plates 59 and 61 provide good illustrations of such bindings.

[43]The Jesuits were expelled in 1594 and recalled in 1603; Henry IV ruled from 1589 to 1610.

[44]A single work, published under the title, La chasse royale, ed. N. de Neufville, sieur de Villeroy (Paris: Rousset & Alliot, 1625). Jacob's reference to Charles IX's literary activity derives from Naudé, Addition ..., p. 374. Contemporary opinions of Charles' book are collected in Paul Colomiès, Bibliothèque choisie (2d ed.; Amsterdam: G. Gallet, 1699), pp. 26-29.

[45]An error of chronology; Aimar (or Emard) de Ranconnet was thrown into the Bastille under pretext of religion by the cardinal of Lorraine during the one-year reign of Francis II, and died there that same year (1559). Decrees of January 8 and February 27, 1560 prescribed that his fine library be in part sold and the proceeds given to his widow and to his children who had not yet reached majority, and in part transferred to the royal library at Fontainebleau; since the royal portion was chosen first, the most valuable items in the library were preserved from dispersal (Édouard Maugis, Histoire du Parlement de Paris de l'avènement des rois Valois à la mort d'henri IV [3 vols.; Paris: Picard, 1914-1916], III, 191-92; Franklin, II, 143; Delisle, I, 190). This was the only addition to the royal library during Francis II's brief and unhappy reign. Under Charles IX the situation was similar "at the coronation of Charles, who was Ronsard's patron and a poet in his own right, one would have expected an era favorable to

‹Jean Dorat of Limoges, an outstanding poet of his time, wrote an epigram for King Charles on the subject of his library, and this poem will serve to ornament my presentation. The epigram appears in Bk. I, on p. 6, of the octavo edition of Dorat's poetry issued at Paris by Guillaume Linocier in 1586, and carries the title, "To Charles IX, King of France; concerning the Royal Library" [L]:

> Illustrious were the palaces of the Ptolemies
>   and renowned the shores of the Ptolomean Pharos:
> Because of the blazing flame these shores could be clearly seen
>   afar off through the waves at night;
> For sailors unsure of their course Pharos would be like a constellation,
>   and with its welcome torch it would orient the seafaring sails.
> But in olden time that fire was not a more gracious guide
>   to sailors in wandering courses on the unknown sea
> Than that other Pharos--that illustrious library--was to men of learning,
>   for it continually shed forth light from Apollo's citadel;
> Thence its volumes, their knowledge disseminated through countless lands,
>   thrust forth shining torches to men of genius.
> But just as other human works have died natural deaths,
>   so those ancient gifts of royalty pass from the scene;
> Now Pharos is no more: the high tower has been cast down,
>   the fires are extinguished and die, and light is gone;
> No less is true of that which was called the Museum--
>   the library with its books descends to oblivion.
> But, O Charles, the pious labor of thy grandfather King Francis
>   brought together again the scattered stones of the academic Pharos;
> Thus he consecrated a new Museum to the Muses,
>   and to them properly dedicated the fountains of Fontainebleau.

---

letters, but the religious struggles determined otherwise" (Franklin, II, 145). The same unfavorable conditions were present during Henry III's reign (1574-1589); and the library had all it could do merely to survive in the midst of the League conflicts (ibid., pp. 149-52). The only bibliophilistic importance attached to the activities of Francis II, Charles IX, and Henry III lies in the bindings executed for them (cf. Delisle, I, 190-93); but even here there is definite deterioration as compared with the reigns of Francis I and Henry II.

Let the renowned Alexandrian Pharos yield to the Pharos
                                                of France;
  let they power, O Ptolemy, yield to Francis.
Thy halls contained no more books of learning than ours,
  and our halls attract more men of learning than
                                                thine.⁴⁶[L]

    With the reign of Henry IV this library was transferred to Paris.⁴⁷ It was placed in the Collège de Clermont during the exile of the Jesuits from France (this occurred in 1595),

<u>Henry IV</u> but after their restoration it was moved to a great room in the residence of the Cordeliers by order and through the care of President de Thou. There it remained for some years, and then was relocated in a particular house which the king rented from the Cordeliers for that purpose.⁴⁸ The keeper of the library had his lodging there also.

---

⁴⁶These elegiac stanzas are quoted <u>ibid.</u>, p. 190, to prove that the royal library managed to retain its reputation during Charles IX's time. In line 15, the reading <u>terris</u> has been corrected to <u>turris</u> on the basis of the Linocier, 1586 text of Dorat's <u>Poematia</u>, which Jacob used. Jean Dorat or Daurat (1508-1588) is remembered today chiefly for his Greek learning, and for the fact that he was the teacher of Ronsard, Du Bellay, and Baïf, and spiritual father of La Pléiade (Yates, pp. 14-16). His poetical production was enormous (15,000 of his Greek and Latin verses have survived), but its quality seems to have been overestimated by his contemporaries. He was given the title of <u>poeta regius</u> by Charles IX (Sandys, II, 186-88).

⁴⁷Franklin, II, 145, has effectively demonstrated, in spite of almost universal testimony to the contrary, that the transfer occurred during the reign of Charles IX. Henry IV moved the library from its former Paris location to the College de Clermont (<u>ibid.</u>, p. 152; cf. Herbet, <u>Bibliographe moderne</u>, XXIV, 145-47, and see Delisle, I, 194-200). The only important addition to the library under Henry IV was the incorporation of Catherine de Médicis' manuscripts, discussed previously.

⁴⁸The Jesuits returned to France in 1603. The royal library was moved from the Collège de Clermont to the monastery of the Cordeliers in 1614. It remained there until 1622, when, as Jacob says, it was moved to another house of the Cordeliers; this was situated on the rue de la Harpe. No further move took place prior to the publication of Jacob's book in 1644. In

M. Rigault negotiated that arrangement through his friends.⁴⁹

Louis XIII, that just king of blessed memory, yielded to none of his predecessors in the enrichment of this treasury of the Muses.⁵⁰ During his reign he was told that among the books of the late Philippe Hurault, 108th bishop of Chartres and son of Philippe, count of Chiverny and chancellor of France, there was a great number of ancient Greek and Latin manuscripts which had been carefully brought together by M. de Boistaillé Hurault, king's ambassador to Venice. A decree was handed down at Council on March 8, 1622 appointing MM. Pierre Dupuy and Nicolas Rigault to reach an agreement with two other persons (specifically, the heirs and creditors of the bishop) as to the value of the books; and this they did. MM. Olivier de Fontenay and Henri de Sponde (afterwards bishop of Pamiers), together with the above-mentioned Dupuy and Rigault, appraised the books at 12,000 francs;⁵¹ this

<u>Louis XIII</u>

1642, when Louis XIV came to the throne, the library had attained a size of only 6,000 volumes; by the end of his reign in 1715, however, it had reached 70,000 volumes (Franklin, II, 211, 162-63).

⁴⁹Rigault was keeper of the library from 1615 to 1645, and resided there until 1635. See below, n. 71.

⁵⁰The Hurault manuscripts, which Jacob will now discuss, constituted the only significant addition to the royal library during Louis XIII's reign. The reasons for this relative lack of progress (as compared with the great periods of past splendor under Louis XII and Francis I, and future splendor under Louis XIV) were the king's personal lethargy in this area as well as in most others, and the fact that his minister, Richelieu, was far more interested in his own library than in the royal collection.

⁵¹I.e., livres; the two terms were used synonymously at this time (Gaston Cayrou, <u>Le Français classique: lexique de la langue du XVIIe siècle</u> [Paris: Didier, 1948], p. 525). Although it is always dangerous practice to attempt to translate currency

amount was banked and the volumes were moved to the royal library.[52]

If under Louis XII this library was compared to Ptolemy's, in what regard must it be held today, now that it has received such notable additions through the liberality of our invincible monarchs! Who is unaware that all nations hold this incomparable library in great esteem for its rare and ancient manuscripts in languages of every variety? And as for printed books, it is easy to see how well furnished it must be from the fact that two copies of every book printed under royal licence in France are deposited there[53]--not to mention the keepers'

---

values when wide time differences exist, we may tentatively consider 12,000 livres/francs to equal $17,250. This figure is based on the value given for the livre tournois in 1614, namely 5/9 in English money immediately prior to World War I (John S. C. Bridge, A History of France from the Death of Louis XI [5 vols.; Oxford: Clarendon Press, 1921-1936], I, 257). At that time the English pound was equivalent roughly to five dollars in American money.

[52]This collection is described in detail in Delisle, I, 213-14; it consisted of a little over four hundred volumes, of which about one hundred and fifty were in Greek. On Philippe Hurault, count of Chiverny (d. 1599), see Maugis, III, 203; on Jean (II) Hurault, lord of Boistaillé (d. 1572), see ibid., p. 207. Dupuy, Rigault, Fontenay, and Sponde are dealt with elsewhere in the present work.

[53]"France was the first country to have a system of legally enforced deposit of new books. As early as December 28, 1537, by the Ordonnance de Montpellier, François I ordered that one copy of every book printed in France should be deposited in his library at Blois, and that a copy of every book printed abroad and sold in France should be offered to the Library for purchase. In 1617 an edict ordered the deposit of two copies, as a condition of privilege, whereas the element of trade privilege, like that of censorship, was entirely lacking from the ordinance of 1537. Throughout the seventeenth and eighteenth centuries there were constant complaints by the Royal Librarians, and constant and unsuccessful attempts to enforce the statutory delivery of copies" (Esdaile, p. 56; cf. James Breck Perkins, France under Mazarin [2 vols.; New York: G. P. Putnam, 1886], II, 437). See Henri Lemaître, Histoire du dépôt légal: 1re partie (France) (Paris: A. Picard, 1910).

diligence in buying all the best books printed in Europe. For
these reasons the royal library has the reputation of being one
of the most splendid and famous book collections in the world.

Now that I have noted all the strides made by this library up to the present day, I shall provide a catalog of the masters of the royal library from the time of Francis I to that of our young sovereign Louis XIV. This list has been given to me

<u>Masters of the</u>
<u>royal library</u>

by M. Dupuy, councillor of state, a man whose integrity and learning are well known throughout Europe. The expression "master of the library" will be employed rather than "librarian."[54] Although I have mentioned as masters of the royal library Antoine des Essars and Garnier de Saint Yon in discussing Charles VI, and Robert Gaguin, member of the Trinitarian order, in dealing with Louis XI, I shall restrict myself in the present catalog to the period following the relocation of the library under Francis I.

Guillaume Budé, a Parisian and a master of requests,[55]

---

[54]Until 1522 the personnel of the royal library consisted of a "librarian" (<u>bibliothécaire</u>) and several copyists. Francis I created an office above these, the <u>Maître de la Librairie du Roi</u> ("master of the royal library"), primarily as a means of recognizing high literary merit and scholarship. From the outset this office was considered one of the most honorable and distinguished in the state. The first incumbent, as Jacob notes, was Guillaume Budé. The position of "librarian" or "keeper of the library" (<u>garde de la librairie</u>) continued, and sometimes more than one person held the title at a single time (e.g., Pierre and Jacques Dupuy) and served in the capacity of assistant to the master of the royal library. A complete list of masters and keepers is given in Franklin, II, 210-11.

[55]An office mentioned frequently in the Paris section of Jacob's presentation. "The jurisdiction of the Court of Requests of the Hôtel originated in the custom of an earlier age, when the

was appointed to the office of master of the library by King

G. Budé
Francis I. Francis gave him this position because of his abilities, and especially on account of his great learning, attested by publications such as his

De asse. Budé died at Paris on August 22, 1540, at the age of seventy-three.[56]

---

sovereign had been wont to administer justice in person, and had deemed it part of his kingly duty to be accessible to every subject who might desire to approach him with his suit or his plea. When the patriarchal practice of a simpler age was abandoned, and the King no longer had time or inclination to 'sit in the gate,' his place was taken by certain legal members of his entourage, who came to be known as Masters of Requests. To this tribunal came suitors desirous that the decision of some supreme court should be reviewed, and all the privileged persons, such as Household officers and civil servants, whom letters of <u>committimus</u> exempted from amenability to the common-law jurisdiction" (Bridge, V, 74-75, discussing political conditions at the time of Francis I); cf. n. 202 below. The term "master of requests" sometimes refers, it should be noted, to members of the Chamber of Requests, one of the minor courts of the Paris Parlement. The duty of these latter "Maîtres des Requêtes of the Palais de Justice" was "to examine the humble petitions of those who addressed themselves to the sovereign as the fountain of justice, to hear the suits of persons and corporations whom the privilege of <u>committimus</u> made specially amenable to the jurisdiction of the Parlement, and to issue the <u>lettres de justice</u> which every would-be litigant must obtain" (<u>ibid</u>., p. 88). All the decisions of the Chamber of Requests were subject to review by the Grand Chamber of the Parlement.

[56] Of Budé, Sandys writes: "Under Francis I and Henry II his fame as a Greek scholar was one of the glories of his country. . . . In 1515 (N.S.), he broke fresh ground as the first serious student of the Roman coinage in his treatise <u>De Asse</u>. It was the ripe result of no less than nine years of research, and in twenty years passed through ten editions. . . . Perhaps his most important, certainly his most permanent, service to the cause of scholarship was his prompting Francis I to found in 1530 the Corporation of Royal Readers. . . . It was mainly owing to Budaeus that the primacy in scholarship had passed from Italy to France" (Sandys, II, 170-73). (On the royal lecturers, see above, n. 31.) A basic, primary-source biography of Budé is that by Louis Le Roy (Regius), <u>Vita Gul. Budaei</u> (1540), reprinted in [William Bates (ed.)], <u>Vitae selectorum aliquot virorum</u> (Londini: George Wells, 1681), pp. 215-39; see also Jean Plattard, <u>Guillaume Budé (1468-1540) et les origines de l'humanisme français</u> (Paris: Société d'edition "Les belles lettres," 1923), and Tilley, pp. 269-87. Budé's personal library receives mention later (see the text at n. 172).

Pierre du Chastel, or Chastelain, of Langres, succeeded Budé by Francis' appointment.[57] The king had been employing him to discuss the various fields of knowledge with him in personal conversation, for du Chastel was a man of wide learning;

<u>P. du Chastel or Castellanus</u> thus he acquired that prince's favor and was honored with the position of master of the library. Also the king gave him the bishopric

of Tulle, then that of Mâcon, and finally the see of Orléans--where, according to the epitaph composed for him by Michel de L'Hospital, chancellor of France, he died in 1558 while preaching.[58]

---

[57] Du Chastel (or Duchâtel) "was not only erudite, but his organising powers were unequalled, and in his day the library flourished exceedingly. . . . Duchâtel had travelled in the East and added 400 volumes of Oriental manuscripts. He also persuaded the King to unite the Library of Blois with the books newly collected at Fontainebleau, and it was during his régime that the unification took place and formed the beginnings of the national collection. . . . At the death of François I. in 1547, Duchâtel offered to retire, but Henri II. loaded him with fresh honours and made him Grand Almoner of France. He retained his post as Librarian until his death in 1552, but finding Henri II. less generously disposed towards the arts than his father, he did not add to the number of volumes during that time, but turned his attention to the care and preservation of those already in his charge" (Frank Hamel, "The Librarians of the Royal Library at Fontainebleau," <u>The Library</u>, 3d series, I, No. 2 [April, 1910], 194-95 [note that this article, though very useful, must be used with caution, since in several instances it has kept alive traditions whose falsity had already been demonstrated by other writers]); cf. Pierre Bayle, <u>Dictionnaire historique et critique</u> (8 vols., 5th ed. with supplement by de Chauffepie; Amsterdam: Brunel, <u>et al</u>., 1740-1756), art. "Chastel [du]."

[58] Jacob is mistaken with regard to the year of du Chastel's death; du Chastel died on February 2, 1552. His epitaph by the famous French statesman Michel de L'Hospital or L'Hôpital is found in the latter's <u>Oeuvres complètes</u>, ed. P. J. S. Duféy (5 vols.; Paris: Boulland, 1824-1826), III, 517; the epitaph title states that he died "inter concionandum." On L'Hospital, see below, n. 162.

The next incumbent of the office was Pierre de Montdoré, or Montaureus, a native of Orléans, a master of requests, and a man of great abilities,[59] as we learn from the just-mentioned Chancellor de L'Hospital:

P. de Montdoré

> He was all gold within—
> Golden in his character and learning, a man of golden habits.
> Moreover, he knew all languages and all liberal arts,
> And he composed worthy lines by your power, O Muses, and
> by thine, O Apollo.
> Had Rome borne a man of such greatness and quality as
> Montaureus,
> His golden statue would have stood on the pinnacle of the
> Capitoline hill:
> Golden effigies on the Rostra in the Forum, and throughout
> the city.[60][L]

Jacques Amyot of Melun was so learned that he earned the position of tutor to Kings Charles IX and Henry III. The same Charles provided him with the office of master of the library after the death of Montdoré.[61] He also became bishop of Auxerre and grand almoner of France; his death occurred on February 7, 1593, at the age of

Jacques Amyot

---

[59]Mon(t)doré "was a Member of the Grand Council and a celebrated mathematician. His first care on taking the post of Librarian was to make an examination of all the books in the collection, checking them from two catalogues of the Greek manuscripts, one in alphabetical order and one arranged by subjects, compiled by Constantine Palaeocappus and copied by Vergetius. Montdoré marked each entry with an arrow to show that the book was present, noting the absence of others in the margin. He also entered some new manuscripts on the list and added a note concerning his investigations. In 1567, Montdoré was accused of heresy and went into hiding at Sancerre" (Hamel, The Library, 3d series, I, No. 2, 195-96).

[60]Lines 5b-11 of the 30-line epitaph in dactylic hexameters found in L'Hospital, III, 521-22. The force of these lines depends on an untranslatable play-on-words involving the name "Montdoré" (Latin, "Montaureus"), meaning "golden mount/mount of gold."

[61]Strictly speaking, Amyot succeeded to the mastership after Montdoré had to flee to Sancerre because he was suspected

seventy-nine. His erudite translations of Plutarch have sufficiently demonstrated his background in Greek language and culture.[62]

That learned historian Jacques-Auguste de Thou, president of the Parlement of Paris, succeeded Amyot as master of the royal library. He exercised great care with regard to the library, not only by having it moved to Paris,[63]

J.-A. de Thou   but also by enriching it with the best books to be found at that time. He died at Paris in May of 1617.[64] The reader will find more information on J.-A. de Thou when I discuss below the library of the de Thou

---

of Calvinism. Thus Amyot became master of the royal library in 1567, three years before Montdoré's death in 1570.

[62] On Amyot, the "prince of translators," who, in Montaigne's words, made Plutarch speak the French tongue, see René Sturel, *Jacques Amyot, traducteur des Vies parallèles de Plutarque* (Paris: Honoré Champion, 1908), and Alexandre Cioranescu, *Vie de Jacques Amyot d'apres des documents inédits* (Paris: E. Droz, 1941).

[63] He was responsible not for moving the library to Paris, but for transferring it to a new Paris location at the Collège de Clermont in 1594-1595; see above, n. 47.

[64] Collinson presents in translation the following extract concerning de Thou's librarianship from *Les hommes illustres qui ont paru en France pendant ce siècle* (1696) by Charles Perrault: "This famous library [the royal library], the finest in the world, after that of the Vatican, was never committed to the care of a more worthy person: and on this occasion it both received and conferred honor. This repository of literature became more than ever the rendez-vous of the most conspicuous characters, who united science and learning with virtue; and under his management afforded particular gratification, as well by concentrating the society of scholars, who came thither to confer on every branch of knowledge, as by the opportunity it supplied of consulting the best dead authors" (J. Collinson, *The Life of Thuanus* [London: Longman et al., 1807], p. 239). On the succeeding two pages Collinson gives several condensed extracts from the present section of Jacob's *Traicté*, in order to provide a "short account" of the royal library's history which will be "acceptable to the reader." On de Thou's personal library, see below, the text at nn. 256 ff.

family; we now move on to his successor as master of the royal library, namely his son François-Auguste de Thou, councillor of state, who possessed a very fine mind.⁶⁵

F.-A. de Thou

The talents of Jérôme Bignon, councillor of state, caused the late King Louis XIII to bestow the master's office on him in 1642. He is carrying out the functions of the post with marvellous conscientiousness.⁶⁶

J. Bignon

I shall note that the salary of the master of the royal library is 1200 livres, and that there are keepers under him who have their lodging near the library and receive a salary of 400 livres.⁶⁷ I will provide here a list of those keepers whose

---

⁶⁵F.-A. de Thou held the mastership from 1617 until his death at age thirty-six in 1642. He was beheaded because he had known of Cinq-Mars' conspiracy against the state (and especially against the dying Richelieu) but had not revealed it. Collinson, after quoting Voltaire's condemnation of the execution, reproduces Constantine Huygen's distich on the subject: "'O legum subtile nefas, quibus inter amicos/Nolle fidem frustra prodere, proditio est.' The play of words is not translatable, but the thought is: 'How unjust is the subtilty of those laws, which make it treason in a man, not to commit a useless breach of faith towards his friend'" (ibid., pp. 264-65). F.-A. de Thou's portrait had a prominent place in Gui Patin's library (see below, n. 233).

⁶⁶On Jérôme Bignon (1589-1656), the founder of a virtual family dynasty of masters of the royal library, and a juridical scholar and writer of high reputation in his own time, see Johann Albrecht Portner, Elogium seu breviarium vitae Hieronymi Bignonii (Parisiis: Cramosius, 1657), Gabriel-Louis Perau, Vie de Jérôme Bignon (Paris: Hérissant, 1757), and René Kerviler, "Les Bignons, grands maîtres de la bibliothèque du Roi," Bibliophile français, VI (1872), 275-83, 300-312, 322-42. Bignon and Jacob were fellow members of "le cabinet Dupuy" (see below, n. 244).

⁶⁷At the time Jacob wrote this (1644), a master's salary of 1200 livres was probably equivalent to $1440, and a keeper's salary of 400 livres to $480. Our computation is based upon Perkins, II, 371, where the French livre from 1640 to 1660 is considered to have a relative value equal to "nearly one dollar and twenty cents of American money"; one should of course realize that Perkins' work was published in 1886 and that he was thinking

89

names have been communicated to me:[68]

1. Jean Gosselin was given the post because of his great knowledge of books. He died at Paris at an advanced age.[69]

2. Isaac Casaubon, a native of Geneva, is known to all men of letters for his erudition.[70] His learning provided him

---

in terms of the buying power of the dollar at that time. (Cf. n. 51 above.) Of the keeper's salary, Mark Pattison writes: "It was the pay of a professor in a provincial university--a classical, not a law professor, these got much higher stipends,--or a principal regent in a provincial college" (Isaac Casaubon [London: Longmans, Green, 1875], p. 200).

[68]The three keepers listed by Jacob span the period 1560-1644. Since the position of master of the library was chiefly a post of dignity in recognition of literary scholarship, the tasks of administering and attending the collection devolved upon the keeper.

[69]Gosselin held the keeper's position for forty-four years, from 1560 to 1604, and served under three masters of the library (Montdoré, Amyot, and J.-A. de Thou). His greatest service to the royal library lay in his partially successful efforts to preserve its volumes from being carried off during the League conflicts which ended with the surrender of Paris to Henry IV in 1594; his own narrative concerning this was discovered on the first page of a manuscript ("La Marguerite" of Jean Massue) and was printed in the Bulletin du bibliophile, 1871, p. 415, and in Franklin, II, 150-51. However, little else can be said in a commendatory way concerning Gosselin's librarianship. Though he had been a mathematician of note, he was no longer young when appointed to the post, and he deteriorated into a senile state before death removed him from the position when he was almost one hundred years old. In 1605 Scaliger wrote of him: "I knew his way forty-four years ago; too ignorant to use the library himself, too jealous to allow others to use it" (Joseph Juste Scaliger, Epistolae [Lugduni Batavorum: Elzevir, 1627], p. 273).

[70]The librarianship of Casaubon, one of the greatest classical scholars of the seventeenth century, is described in much detail in Pattison, pp. 194-209. He held the position of garde from 1604 until his death in 1614, though his last four years were, because of his Protestant faith, spent in England. During his six-year period of actual library service, he contributed greatly to the scholarly activity of the time. "He supplied materials to Scaliger and Heinsius at Leyden, Gruter at Heidelberg, Hoeschel at Augsburg, and Saville at Eton, while his own works prove how eagerly he ransacked the Royal MSS." (Sandys, II, 207). However, Casaubon spent most of his time reading, and apparently carried on no cataloging or arranging of materials. Pattison writes: "When

with this position for some years; but on his moving to England, a successor was appointed, namely

3. Nicolas Rigault, councillor in the Parlement of Metz, who published with annotations the works of Tertullian and of Greek authors. These books will not gain more glory for him than his efforts to augment the library of our monarchs with the best books to be found and his labors to establish an accurate catalog of this collection.[71] In this he has been assisted by MM. Hautin and Claude de Saumaise, specialists in Greek and Latin manuscripts.[72]

---

any correspondent asked for any book, he tried to find it, but he never made any thorough and complete investigation, once for all, of what was there, much less a catalogue. In 1608 Hoeschel applied to him for MSS. of Arrianus. Though Casaubon had then been nearly four years in full possession of the library, he did not know if there were any MSS. of Arrianus, but would look. He found, on searching, at least two" (Pattison, p. 207). In this connection Pattison makes his famous statement, so frequently quoted out of context: "The librarian who reads is lost"; Casaubon's fault was of course not that he was an avaricious reader and fine scholar, but that he frequently engaged in reading instead of in cataloging and administering the library during the time of his employment.

[71]Rigault (1577-1654) is cited in Sandys, II, 283, for his editions of Tertullian and Cyprian. During the period of his librarianship (1615-1645), his great accomplishment, as Jacob notes, was the production of a complete catalog of the collection--a task which neither of the previous <u>gardes</u> (Gosselin and Casaubon) had even attempted. This catalog is described in Franklin, II, 163-65, and in Delisle, I, 198-200. It carries the date 1622, and consists of five folio volumes in manuscript. The first two volumes list the manuscripts and older printed works in the library, and the remaining three volumes list the more recent printed works in the collection. Jacob had contact with Rigault in "le cabinet Dupuy" (see below, n. 244), and he discusses his personal library later on in this chapter (see the text at n. 248).

[72]On Claude de Saumaise (Salmasius), 1588-1653, who was considered by Grotius to be "the best interpreter of classical times," but was regarded as a pedant by others, and who engaged in literary controversy with Milton, see Sandys, II, 285-86. Saumaise and Jacob were both members of "le cabinet Dupuy" (see below n. 244). Jean-Baptiste Hautin maintained a noteworthy library of his own, which Jacob discusses below (cf. n. 157).

Although our sovereigns possess that rich and opulent public library which we have been discussing, they also maintain for their use a private library in the Louvre.

<u>The library at the Louvre</u>   There numerous good books are kept, among which are all the volumes presented to them as gifts. M. Chaumont, councillor of state, is in charge of this library at the present time.[73]

There is another small library at Fontainebleau, the purpose of which is to provide diversion for our monarchs when they stay there. Its librarian, by authorization of the late King Louis XIII, is Abel de Sainte-Marthe, councillor of state, son of Scévole, and elder brother of Louis and Scévole, historians of France.[74]

---

[73]Jean de Chaumont-Quitry (<u>ca</u>. 1583-1667), lord of Boisgarnier, by title lord of Chaumont, had been personal librarian to Henry IV. He wrote numerous anti-Calvinist polemics, and was himself a convert from Calvinism to the Roman faith (see Roman d'Amat, in <u>DBF</u>, VIII, 876). On the king's private library at the Louvre, see Edme-Jacques-Benoît Rathery, <u>Notice historique sur l'ancien cabinet du roi et sur la bibliothèque impériale du Louvre</u> (Paris: J. Techener, 1858). The most important book collection incorporated into this "cabinet" was that of Cardinal Georges (I) d'Amboise, who, in the first decade of the sixteenth century, had purchased the most valuable part of the library of the Aragonese kings of Naples. Sometime between 1593 and 1610 this collection entered the Louvre cabinet, and remained there until the beginning of Louis XV's reign, when it became a part of the Bibliothèque royale (see Delisle, I, 217-60).

[74]Abel (I) de Sainte-Marthe (1566-1652) was an important historian in his own right; he has provided later generations with three publications dealing with significant events during the Louis XIII-Richelieu period, and these works, though suffering from the usual faults of "official histories," are of great value for the detailed and comprehensive accounts they present. (See Bourgeois, entries 3525, 3568, and 3690 for evaluations.) His son, Abel II (d. 1706), succeeded him as librarian at Fontainebleau in 1646, and attempted through a treatise entitled <u>Discours au Roy sur le rétablissement de la Bibliothèque royale de Fontainebleau</u>

The museum of our sovereigns is considered a wonder of the world because of the rarities and antiquities--not to mention the precious stones--in it. Indeed, I find

<u>The royal</u> that on a single occasion it received by purchase
<u>museum</u>   the museum of Jean Grolier, native of Lyon, knight, viscount of Aiguisy, treasurer of Milan and of
<u>J. Grolier</u> France, a credit to the literary life of his time, and the most indefatigable antiquary to have appeared in the realm for a long time.[75] After his death, his collection of antiquities was carried to Marseilles in order to be transported to Rome for sale. King Charles IX was informed of this, and he ordered it to be brought back to be combined with

---

(1648) to persuade the king to make the post more than a sinecure; in this he was unsuccessful, and no one was appointed to the position after his death (see Franklin, II, 160-61; Herbet, <u>Bibliographe moderne</u>, XXIV, 148-49). The father of Abel I was Gaucher (II) de Sainte-Marthe, who took the classical name Scévole, and is generally known as Scévole (I) de Sainte-Marthe; he is the author of a book of biographical sketches (<u>Lucubrationum pars altera, qua continentur, Gallorum doctrina illustrium, qui nostra patrumque memoria floruerunt, elogia</u> [Lutetiae: P. Durand, 1616]), which Jacob uses elsewhere in his <u>Traicté</u> (on Scévole I, see Léon Fougère, <u>Essai sur ... Henri Estienne, suivi d'une étude sur Scévole de Sainte-Marthe</u> [Paris: Delalain, 1853], pp. 265-371). As Jacob states, Abel I was Scévole I's eldest son; Scévole II (1572-1650) and Louis (1572-1656) were Abel's twin brothers. Abel and Louis were associated with Jacob in "le cabinet Dupuy" (see n. 244 below). The twins prepared genealogical publications, and a four-volume work listing all French abbots, bishops, and archbishops through French history (the famous <u>Gallia Christiana</u> of 1656); this book, which underwent later editions and expansions, is considered "the principal source" in its field by Bourgeois (entries 4336; cf. 1403, 1409, 1431). On the Sainte-Marthe family library, see below, the text at n. 250.

[75]Jacob here refers to that famous patron of the bookbinder's art, Jean Grolier (1479-1565). See Antoine-Jean-Victor Le Roux de Lincy, <u>Researches concerning Jean Grolier, His Life and his Library, with a Partial Catalogue of His Books</u>, trans. and rev. Carolyn Shipman (New York: Grolier Club, 1907); and cf. the text at nn. 298-300 below.

his own; and he paid Grolier's heirs the value of the collection. These facts are given by the learned President de Thou when he praises Grolier in Bk. XXXVIII of his *History* (for the year 1565): "His copper medals, which are of the best quality, were taken from Paris to Provence for export to Italy, but our most Christian king, by his diligence, kept France from being deprived of such a treasure by redeeming them at great cost and having them added to his own museum to take their place with the other relics of antiquity there" [L].[76] M. de Chaumont is also supervisor of this royal museum.[77]

His Royal Highness Jean-Baptiste Gaston, duke of Orléans and of Chartres, son of Henry the Great, brother of Luis the Just, uncle of Louis XIV, lieutenant general of France, and governor of Languedoc, causes admiration and amazement throughout Europe because of his complete knowledge of ancient medals. I can without flattery say of this prince that neither the Roman Emperor Alexander Severus, nor Cicero's great friend Atticus,

The duke of Orléans

---

[76] Jacques-Auguste de Thou, *Historia sui temporis* (7 vols.; Londini: Buckley, 1733), II, 469. The *Historia sui temporis*, which de Thou endeavored to make a truly objective and impartial work, has been considered an historical classic, and has been praised in the highest terms by the learned from his own day to the present. Samuel Johnson thought seriously of translating the gigantic work into English; Voltaire placed its author on the same level with Hume and Guicciardini; and the twentieth-century French historian Charles Bémont has asserted that de Thou's "history is a model of exact research, drawn from the best sources, and presented in a style both elegant and animated." A catalog of testimonies to the work is given in Collinson, pp. v-xx, and that author also provides an English translation of the preface to the *Historia*, together with detailed background information on the work and a summary of its contents (*ibid.*, pp. 279-443).

[77] Jacob has noted earlier that Chaumont served as librarian of the king's personal book collection in the Louvre (see n. 73).

nor the very learned Varro had a knowledge of medals comparable to his. And his intellectual curiosity does not end with them, but also devotes itself to book collecting. His good books adorn the rich and splendid library which he has recently established in his Luxembourg mansion.[78] The library is situated at the end of that admirable gallery where one sees the whole life of the late Queen Marie de Médicis depicted by that fine artist Rubens.[79] This library is remarkable for its ornamented bookshelves, which are all lined with green velvet, and with bands of the same material, decorated with gold braiding and fringes; and all the visible woodwork is embellished with gold and rich paintings. But the library is remarkable not only for its bookcases, its collection consists of

---

[78] I.e., the Luxembourg palace in Paris. This library is discussed in Delisle, I, 265-66, and the present passage in Jacob's Traicté is there quoted in full. Gaston's cultural interests are evidenced by the "academy" or discussion circle which he established in his home during 1626-1627; this is described by Josephine de Boer, "Men's Literary Circles in Paris 1610-1660," PMLA, LIII (September, 1938), 745-46. With our author's laudatory remarks concerning Gaston's book collecting should be contrasted Aldous Huxley's sound evaluation of the moral character of this cowardly conspirator; "worthless" and "despicable" are the two terms he applies to him (Grey Eminence [New York: Meridian Books, 1959 (c 1941)], pp. 186, 328).

[79] Of Rubens' assignment, Magurn writes: "This assignment--the decoration of the two great galleries in Marie de' Medici's new Palace of the Luxembourg--was the noblest Rubens had yet received [1622], and the most coveted commission in all Europe. His first visit to Paris for this purpose brought the artist into contact with many eminent personalities, among them Nicolas-Claude Fabri de Peiresc, with whom he formed a friendship that produced a fruitful correspondence lasting many years. The French scholar was very helpful in smoothing Rubens' path in his preliminary dealings with Marie de' Medici, and acted as intermediary between Rubens and the Queen Mother's adviser, the Abbé de St. Ambroise. It required both tact and ingenuity to weave the inglorious episodes of Marie's life into a pictorial cycle" (Peter Paul Rubens, Letters, tr. and ed. Ruth Saunders Magurn [Cambridge, Mass.: Harvard University Press, 1955], p. 6).

all the best editions available, and the books are all bound uniformly and display the monogram of his royal highness. This prince continually engages in an intensive search for the best books to be found in Europe, and issues written requests to that end. In this activity he is given great encouragement by M. Bruneau, his librarian, who labors constantly to perfect his treasury of books and medals.[80]

<u>M. Bruneau</u>

His late Eminence Cardinal Duke Armand Jean du Plessis de Richelieu received a thorough literary education; this is evident from his published works. Here we have the reason why he always loved and honored books, and why he established for them those superb monuments which (along with his governing of the state under our most pious King Louis XIII) will immortalize his memory. The sumptuous Collège de Sorbonne provides irreproachable testimony to this,[81] and along with it I shall add the magnificent library which he built at great expense.[82] Indeed, he spared nothing that could contribute to the enlarging or embellishing of the library. He sent the

<u>Cardinal Richelieu's library</u>

---

[80] On Bénigne Bruneau, see Anatole Chabouillet, <u>Recherches sur les origines du Cabinet des médailles et particulièrement sur le legs des collections de Gaston, duc d'Orleans, au roi Louis XIV</u> (Paris: Nouvelles Archives de l'art français, 1874). Cf. also Franklin, II, 173-75.

[81] Richelieu's activities in behalf of the Sorbonne were considerable; he planned a complete architectural reconstruction of the Collège at his own expense (<u>ibid</u>., I, 265).

[82] On this library, see Edmond Bonnaffé, <u>Recherches sur les collections des Richelieu</u> (Paris: E. Plon, 1883); Franklin, I, 271 ff.; Delisle, II, 204-206; and Lomeier, sec. "France," n. 21.

learned Jacques Gaffarel to Italy and the erudite Jean Tilleman Stella to Germany to collect the best available manuscripts and printed books,[83] and so successfully did they execute this task that the library has been esteemed by all who know good books. When our invincible monarch of blessed memory, Louis XIII, subdued heresy by the capture of La Rochelle in 1628, he granted

The library of La Rochelle to the cardinal the public library of that city.[84] Richelieu had it transported to Paris and combined with his own for preservation there. At the close of his life, this great cardinal and protector of the Muses did not want to allow his library to fall into decline, and therefore willed it to the Duke of Richelieu, the chief bearer of his name and coat of arms. Although the cardinal's testament has appeared in print, I shall not forgo quoting from it those clauses which pertain to

---

[83] Gaffarel (1601-1681), an astrologer and linguist, was the cardinal's librarian (see Le mercure galant, January, 1682, p. 159), and a close friend of Gabriel Naudé (see n. 227); his own library is treated in the text at n. 523. Stella receives further mention later in this chapter, where his personal library is discussed (see the text at n. 254).

[84] On the siege of La Rochelle, Huxley writes: "With the fall of La Rochelle, the political power of the Huguenots in France was at an end. . . . At the beginning of the siege, La Rochelle had counted twenty-five thousand inhabitants; five thousand remained alive, when the city was surrendered. Such, however, was the violence of theological hatred that there were many among the Catholic party who clamoured for further and yet more frightful punishment. To his everlasting credit, the Cardinal would not hear of reprisals. The surviving Rochellois were pardoned, confirmed in the enjoyment of their property and granted freedom of worship. His reward was the Protestants' unswerving loyalty to the crown. Half a century later, Louis XIV reversed the Cardinal's policy, persecuted the Huguenots and finally revoked the Edict of Nantes. His reward was the loss to France by emigration, of a large number of its most productive citizens" (Huxley, p. 202).

the library:[85]

> Item, I grant to the said Armand de Vignerot, my grand-nephew, according to the clauses and conditions of the institutions and substitutions which shall be hereafter appended, my library, not only as it is at present, but as it shall be at the time of my decease, declaring that I desire it to be installed in the Hôtel de Richelieu which I have begun to build, adjoining the Palais Cardinal; and, my design being to have the said library as complete as possible, so that it shall serve not only my family, but the public as well, I desire and ordain that, at the time of my death, a general inventory shall be made by such persons as my testamentary executors may judge proper, by calling in two doctors of the Sorbonne, who shall be deputed by their colleagues to be present at the making of the said inventory; the which being made, I desire that it shall be placed, one copy in my library, signed by my testamentary executors and the said doctors of the Sorbonne, and another copy likewise placed in the said house of the Sorbonne, signed as above. And, so that the said library may be conserved in its entirety, I desire and ordain that the said inventory shall be amended and verified every year by two doctors who shall be deputed by the Sorbonne, and that a librarian shall be placed in charge, at a salary of 1000 livres per year,[86] whose salary and emoluments I desire to be in preference to every other charge, from quarter to quarter and in advance, on the revenue of the rentals of the houses built or to be built around the Palais Cardinal, but not forming part of the palace; and I desire and intend that in consideration of the said 1000 livres of emoluments he shall maintain the said

---

[85] Our English translation of the clauses from Richelieu's testament generally follows that given in Auguste Bailly, The Cardinal Dictator : A Portrait of Richelieu, tr. Hamish Miles (London: J. Cape, 1936), pp. 292-94. The will was dictated on May 23, 1642, and Richelieu died on December 4. The cardinal's great administrative abilities, which made him the virtual ruler of France in his day, are evidenced by the precise and efficient rulings here given concerning the disposition of his library. Three points are especially worth noting: book selection is placed in the hands of Sorbonne faculty; professional library activity is explicitly separated from non-professional duties through the requirement that a janitor as well as a librarian be appointed, the functions of each being set forth in detail; strong interest in personnel is shown by the requirement that salaries be paid before any other financial obligations are discharged--even including book-budget obligations.

[86] Probably equivalent to $1200. On the equivalents of this and the other monetary amounts mentioned in the will, see above, n. 67.

library, keep it in good condition, and allow admission, at certain hours of the day, to men of letters and erudition, to see the books and to study them in the library, without taking the books elsewhere; and should it not have a librarian at the time of my death, I desire and ordain that the Sorbonne shall name three to the said Armand de Vignerot and his successors, who shall be dukes of Richelieu, in order to choose whichever of the three they may judge to be the most suitable; that this procedure shall always be observed when it is necessary to appoint a new librarian.

And, moreover, for the preservation of the interior of the said library, it will have need of frequent cleaning, and there shall be chosen, by my said nephew, a man suitable for the purpose, who shall be obliged to sweep out the said library once a day, and to dust the books or the presses in which they are kept; and, in order to maintain him, and to furnish the brooms and other things necessary for cleaning, I desire that his wages shall be 400 livres per year, on the same basis as those of the librarian, and in the same form, to be paid, like those of the librarian, under the management and authority of my said nephew and his successors in possession of the said Hotel de Richelieu.

And inasmuch as it is necessary to maintain a library in its completeness, to add to it from time to time good books newly printed or old ones that it may lack, I desire and ordain that the sum of 1000 livres per year shall be employed in the purchase of books, on the advice of the doctors who will be deputed every year by the Sorbonne to make an inventory of the said library, the which sum of 1000 livres shall be likewise taken, in preference to all other charges except those specified in the above two articles, from the revenue of the said rentals of the houses which have been or will be built around the park of the Palais Cardinal.

From this testament one sees the great care exercised by the cardinal to preserve his library. Shortly before his death he placed M. Claude Héméré, a doctor of the Sorbonne, in charge of the library; now, however, the librarian's office is held by M. Geoffroy.[87] The cardinal's death occurred at Paris in his

---

[87]Héméré (ca. 1580-1650), the learned historian of the University of Paris, had been librarian of the Sorbonne from 1638 to 1643; in 1645 he was commissioned, along with Valérien de Flavigny, a fellow doctor of the Sorbonne, to inventory the cardinal's library according to the directive in his will (Franklin, I, 264, 273, 296). Jacques Geoffroy, in his capacity as librarian of the cardinal's personal library in 1643, prepared a two-volume folio inventory of the collection, with the assistance of the

Palais Cardinal on December 4, 1642, about noon; he was then fifty-eight years old.

Emperor Julius Caesar[88] once honored the city of Rome by planning a very fine library for public use; today we have that great Roman cardinal, Jules Mazarin, minister of state to their majesties, who in no less a way honors the city of Paris by the sumptuous and exquisite library which he founded a year ago[89] upon the book collection of the late Jean Descordes, canon of Limoges.[90] Descordes had been

<u>Card. Mazarin's library</u>

---

bookseller Blaise; a copy of this manuscript catalog is preserved today in the Bibliothèque Mazarine. Later, in 1648, Geoffroy, together with François Desclos, advocate in Parlement, prepared another inventory of the cardinal's library (<u>ibid</u>., pp. 273-74).

[88] Julius Caesar was proclaimed perpetual dictator, and he wore the garb of an <u>imperator</u> ("victorious commander-in-chief") at all public festivals, but the latter term did not yet mean "emperor" in the wider sense; Augustus Caesar is rightly regarded as the first of the Roman emperors.

[89] On the Mazarin library, see Gabriel Naudé, <u>News from France, or a Description of the Library of Cardinal Mazarin</u> ("Literature of Libraries in the Seventeenth and Eighteenth Centuries"; Chicago: A. C. McClurg, 1907); Gabriel Naudé, <u>Iugement de tout ce qui a esté imprimé contre le cardinal Mazarin</u> [hereafter cited as <u>Mascurat</u>] ([2d. ed.; Paris, 1650]), pp. 242-56; Franklin, III, 37 ff.; Delisle, I, 279-83; Alfred Franklin, <u>Histoire de la Bibliothèque Mazarine et du Palais de l'Institut</u> (2d ed.; Paris: H. Welter, 1901); Louis-Charles-François Petit-Radel, <u>Recherches sur les bibliothèques anciennes et modernes, jusqu'à la fondation de la Bibliothèque Mazarine</u> (Paris: Rey et Gravier, 1819), pp. 249 ff.; and publications dealing with Gabriel Naudé, Mazarin's librarian (n. 96 below). In the opinion of Perkins, II, 442, "The work [on Mazarin's part] which, perhaps, most deserves commendation was the collection of a great library."

[90] As the seventeenth-century librarian and bibliophile Paul Colomiès noted, Descordes had possessed "one of the finest libraries of Paris" (Colomiès, p. 132). Descordes (d. 1643) had lived almost solely for this library of some 6000 volumes and had insisted in his will that it be sold to a single buyer. Gabriel Naudé, who was his close friend, drew up a catalog of the collection in order to show Mazarin the wisdom of purchasing it.

another Varro of his time in his search for worthwhile books, and had purchased the library of the scholarly writer Siméon Dubois.[91]

But the truth is that Julius' plan to open his library to the public never became more than an intention. Our cardinal, however, has really given his library to the public, for every Thursday from morning till evening, to the great satisfaction of the learned, his library is open to all those who wish to go there for study.[92]

This catalog, with its subject arrangement, gives an excellent picture of the original state of the Mazarin library (Descordes limited his collection almost entirely to two fields--theology and history), and, through the biographical eulogy which Naudé wrote as a preface, it also provides valuable information on Descordes himself (see **Naudé**, **Bibliothecae Cordesianae catalogus, cum indice titulorum** [Paris: Vitray, 1643]). Archer Taylor says of this inventory that it was "the first catalogue of a private library to find general use as a reference book and therefore a landmark in the history of libraries" (Gabriel Naudé, Advice on Establishing a Library, ed. Archer Taylor [Berkeley: University of California Press, 1950], p. ix; cf. Archer Taylor, Book Catalogues: Their Varieties and Uses [Chicago: Newberry Library, 1957], pp. 109-10).

[91]Dubois (Latin, Bosius), ca. 1535-ca. 1580, was lieutonant general of the seneschalsy of Limoges and a philologist of note in his own time (a eulogy appears in Scévole [I] de Sainte-Marthe, p. 135). However, it is now known that he engaged in the indefensible practice of inventing manuscript codices to support his textual emendations.

[92]Because of Mazarin's influential position, the public opening of his library constituted a valuable precedent in French librarianship. At this time in Europe there were only four other libraries to which all scholars had free access: the Ambrosian library at Milan, which Cardinal Borromeo had founded ca. 1608; the Bodleian library, opened in 1612; Angelo Rocca's Bibliotheca Angelica, founded in 1620 at Rome, and the Rouen Cathedral library, opened to the public in 1634 (see below, n. 463). Richelieu had intended his library to serve a similar public function, as we note from his testament, but death prevented the full realization of his objectives. Thus when Mazarin opened his library from eight to eleven and from two to five each Thursday, he provided French scholars with a wonderful opportunity, and they were quick

Though I have previously noted (on p. 94 [Pt. I]) that his eminence possesses a very considerably library in his Quirinal palace at Rome,[93] the library here at Paris is in an entirely different class. It is one of the most complete libraries of Europe with respect to abundance of printed books and best available editions. Besides this, the library has been continually augmented with all the rarest works printed both within and without the kingdom of France. As for manuscripts, the library contains nearly 400 folio volumes, bound in rose-colored morocco with gold threads.[94]

Thus although his eminence labors constantly for the welfare and peace of this realm, with the universal commendation of all France and of foreign countries, he loses no opportunity to promote the expansion of knowledge--whether by recognizing

---

to take advantage of it; eighty to one hundred persons came there to study each week. The contemporary poet Auberoche gives in his Juliade the names of those who most frequented the library--and here one encounters the great scholars and literary figures of the time, such as Gassendi, Grotius, Colletet, Sirmond, Vulson, and Moreau (the passage from Auberoche is quoted by Naudé, Mascurat, pp. 245-46). When one considers that by the end of 1643 the Mazarin library already contained 12,000 printed works (as compared, for example, with the royal library, which had half that number), the significance of the cardinal's decision can be seen even more clearly (Franklin, Les anciennes bibliothèques ..., III, 42-47). By 1650, the cardinal's library had grown to over 40,000 volumes (Naudé, Mascurat, p. 224).

[93]It thus seems probable that Cardinal Mazarin was engaged in book collecting even before he became Richelieu's favorite. Franklin notes that a 34-page, quarto manuscript inventory of the contents of Mazarin's Quirinal library has been preserved (Franklin, Les anciennes bibliothèques ..., III, 37-38). On Mazarin's Quirinal palace at Rome, see Mazarin, homme d'état et collectionneur, 1602-1661. Exposition organisée pour le troisième centenaire de sa mort (Paris: Bibliothèque Nationale, 1961), pp. 132-33.

[94]Delisle, I, 282, cites specific extant volumes from Mazarin's library which illustrate the bindings executed for him.

the abilities of men of letters, or by directing the growth of his Parnassus of the Muses. In praise of that library Pierre d'Auberoche, doctor of theology, has composed numerous Latin epigrams; I shall here quote only the following:

> Jules, with lofty endowments of wondrous genius,
>   brings his far-flung virtues together in so many
>   volumes.
> And since the state requires all of his genius,
>   it is his wish, O guest, that you become the
>   master of these books.
> This is indeed the act--the innovation--of a
>   beneficent hero
>   who desires thus to make his own gifts available
>   to all.95[L]

Now although his eminence deserves undying glory for creating this library, it is quite certain that he must receive no less praise for the choice of his vigilant and indefatigable librarian, M. Gabriel Naudé.[96] Naudé, canon of Verdun in Lorraine and prior of Artige, is completely knowledgeable where books are concerned, and for this reason all who are privileged to be acquainted with him consider him another Demetrius of Phalerum.[97] My fear of offending his modesty causes me to borrow

---

[95]Pierre d'Auberoche, _Eminentissimo principi Julio cardinali Mazarino_ (Parisiis: A. Coulon, 1644), p. 9. Note that this work was published in the same year as Jacob's _Traicté_, and thus has similar primary-source value for the history of the Mazarin library. On the basis of Auberoche's text, "attis" in the first line of Jacob's quotation has been corrected to "altis."

[96]On Naudé, whom Alfred Hessel terms "the _beau ideal_ of library directors" (_A History of Libraries_, tr. Reuben Peiss [Washington, D.C.: Scarecrow Press, 1950], p. 56), see James V. Rice, _Gabriel Naudé, 1600-1653_ ("Johns Hopkins Studies in Romance Literatures and Languages," No. 35; Baltimore: Johns Hopkins Press, 1939); and Bob L. Mowery "Gabriel Naudé, Librarian" (unpublished M.A. dissertation, University of Chicago, 1951). Jacob discusses Naudé's personal library below (see the text at n. 229).

[97]Demetrius of Phalerum inspired Ptolemy Soter to found the Alexandrian Museum-Library (see Edward Alexander Parsons, _The Alexandrian Library_ [Amsterdam and New York: Elsevier Press, 1952], Chapter VI, pp. 83-105).

from elsewhere testimonies to his merits, rather than to present my own. One of the eloquent voices of our time will serve as my oracle--M. François de La Mothe le Vayer, a Parisian, formerly royal councillor and deputy attorney general in the Paris Parlement, who dedicates the second volume of his Opuscules to Naudé. Here then is how he addresses Naudé in the portion of his dedicatory epistle pertaining to our subject:[98]

> I prefer to treat you as a friend, and, as Pliny the younger says, avoid all encomiums which you could call burdensome. And I shall follow this course the

---

[98] François de la Mothe le Vayer, Oeuvres (3d ed.; Paris: A. Courbé, 1662), II, 62-63. La Mothe le Vayer (1588-1672), scholar, prolific writer, tutor to Louis XIV, and in many ways precursor of the skeptical, libertarian Weltanschauung of the eighteenth-century French Enlightenment, was one of the four members of Naudé's avant-garde "Tétrade" and a close personal friend of the "father of modern librarianship." The connection between the two men is well illustrated by the fact that the Englishman John Evelyn, who travelled in France and Switzerland from 1641 to 1647, translated La Mothe le Vayer's La liberté et servitude, and a few years later provided the first English translation of Naudé's Avis pour dresser une bibliothèque. La Mothe le Vayer's relationship with Naudé and his scholarly circle is well described in the section on "His Friends" in the excellent biography by Florence L. Wickelgren, La Mothe le Vayer, sa vie et son oeuvre (Paris: E. Droz, 1934), pp. 23 ff.; see especially pp. 32-33. La Mothe le Vayer had a literary circle of his own which gathered at his country home during the years 1636-1660; Naudé was a member of the group (de Boer, PMLA, LIII, 760-62). The general position of La Mothe in the scholarly society of the time is best seen in René Pintard, Le libertinage érudit dans la première moitié du XVIIe siècle (Paris: Boivin, 1943), passim; cf. Richard H. Popkin, "Skepticism and the Counter-Reformation in France," Archiv für Reformationsgeschichte, LI, No. 1 (1960), 77-78. We know that La Mothe possessed a valuable personal library, for Colletet relied heavily upon it in his researches (de Boer, PMLA, LIII, 754). Jacob's contact with La Mothe came through two literary groups of which they were both members, along with Naudé and many other leading scholars of the time--Colletet's circle (see n. 136 below), and "le cabinet Dupuy" (n. 244 below).

more willingly because, as everyone knows, you were chosen by that great cardinal who has put his trust in you no less for the common good than for his personal satisfaction (which he places second to the public welfare); this is the pinnacle of all the eulogies which I know how to present to you. You must, however, allow us to reflect a bit on that wise choice by his eminence when he committed his famous library to one whom he regarded, in the words Eunapius used in trying to convey the merits of the sophist Longinus, as a living library or an animated, walking museum. However, your vast knowledge of all kinds of literary material was not alone sufficient to place you ahead of all others. Had you been like those whom the Apostle describes as inflated and full of vanity, your erudition would not have been suitable for your present position. It is your characteristic gentleness and affability which give you the advantage over the majority of learned men. And what Emperor Antoninus[101] admired so greatly in the philosopher Sextus—a deep learning free from all ostentation—"τὸ πολυμαθὲς ἀνεπιφάντως"—is the heavenly quality which you possess. This gift of yours has been judiciously regarded by those who sorted you out, as it were, from among so many men of letters; and in their choice of you, they have shown the same acumen which renders all their decisions brilliant.

"Love by its very nature does not permit an overloading with encomiums" (Bk. I, epistle 14) [L].[99]

"βιβλιοθήκη ἔμψυχος, καὶ περιπατοῦν μουσεῖον [a living library and a walking museum]" (Life of Porphyry).[100]

Meditations, Bk. I.

---

[99] Pliny concludes this letter by saying of Minicius: "For the very reason that I love him so much, I would not overload him with encomiums."

[100] Eunapius, Lives of the Philosophers and Sophists, par. 456; see Philostratus and Eunapius, The Lives of the Sophists, ed. and tr. W. C. Wright ("Loeb Classical Library"; London: W. Heinemann, 1922), pp. 352-53.

[101] I.e., Marcus Aurelius Antoninus. The Greek phrase from his Meditations (To Himself) i. 9, which Jacob quotes, has been well rendered as "to possess great learning but make no parade of it": The Communings with Himself of Marcus Aurelius Antoninus, ed. and tr. C. R. Haines ("Loeb Classical Library"; London: W. Heinemann, 1930), pp. 8-9. This humble willingness to place one's learning at the disposal of others—a characteristic which Naudé apparently possessed to

Besides this eulogy, I shall give the epigram which M. d'Auberoche wrote for Naudé as librarian to his eminence:

> Every one of you who enters the museum of this prince
> of the church,
>   harken to him who shows its Palladian wealth to you.
> As so many choice volumes capture your vision,
>   it is Naudé,
>   the talking library, who delights your ears.[102]

I shall note further that Father Marin Mersenne, a Minim friar and man of great learning, speaks of this library in his Latin treatise, <u>De magnete</u>, which he dedicated to M. Naudé.[103]

---

a high degree--has been considered one of the most important qualities of the librarian. In 1780, Jean-Baptiste Cotton des Houssayes said of the ideal librarian: "Neither cold nor heat, nor his multiplied occupations, will ever be to him a pretext for evading the obligation he has contracted to be a friendly and intelligent guide to all the scholars who may visit him. Forgetting himself, on the contrary, and laying aside all occupations, he will lead them forward with a cheerful interest, taking pleasure in introducing them to his library; he will examine with them all its parts and divisions; every thing precious or rare that it may contain he will himself put before them" (<u>The Duties & Qualifications of a Librarian</u> ["Literature of Libraries in the Seventeenth and Eighteenth Centuries"; Chicago: A. C. McClurg, 1906], pp. 39-40). Recently Franz Grasberger has warned against misuse of the "service" theme by librarians: "We ourselves, by always insisting that ours is a 'service to others,' may have contributed to a misinterpretation of our calling. In actual fact, the library profession is as independent as any other. . . . If we must speak of 'service,' then, at least, both scholar and librarian can be said to serve a common cause" ("On the Psychology of Librarianship," <u>Library Quarterly</u>, XXIV [January, 1954], 35-46).

[102] Auberoche, <u>Eminentissimo ...</u>, p. 11; see above, n. 95. Auberoche's text permits the correction of the impossible "Palladios" to "Palladias" (modifying "opes").

[103] Marin Mersenne, <u>Cogitata physico-mathematica</u> (Parisiis: A. Bertier, 1644), [Pt. I], p. 245; the "Tractatus de magnetis proprietatibus," which Mersenne dedicates "ad eruditissimum virum Gabrielem Naudeum, Eminentissimi Cardinalis Mazarini bibliothecarium," is part of the subsection "Ars navigandi" in the first major portion (entitled, "Hydraulica pneumatica; arsque navigandi") of the book. In a brief dedicatory paragraph to the "Tractatus," Mersenne suggests that Naudé's patron Mazarin sponsor scientific expeditions which would have as a by-product the

M. Charles de Valois, natural son of King Charles IX of France, duke of Angoulême, and a brave and learned prince who has always held aloft the glory of arms and the splendor of letters (as Father Hilarion de Coste remarks in his Traicté des gouverneurs du Dauphiné),[104] has in his palace a fine library containing very worthwhile books. I have learned this from Father Hilarion, to whom I am under great obligation for having supplied me with many notes for the present work. Lord Charles de Valois is now, in 1644, seventy-two years old, and lives in Paris.

The duke of Angoulême

Monseigneur de Bassompierre, marshal of France, is reputed to be very accomplished in the sciences, for he engages in continual study, and, moreover, takes care to search out the best books to enrich his famous library of more than 4000 volumes.[105]

Marshal de Bassompierre

---

collecting of manuscripts from all parts of the world for the library under Naudé's care. Mersenne (1588-1648), a friend of La Mothe le Vayer (Wickelgren, p. 26) as well as of Naudé, was a strange combination of opposites. On the one hand, he maintained a strict theological orthodoxy; on the other, he devoted himself, especially in his later years, to advanced scientific researches, and he defended Descartes with great vigor. The relationship between Mersenne and Naudé is well described in the detailed work by Robert Lenoble, <u>Mersenne, ou la naissance du mécanisme</u> (Paris, J. Vrin, 1943), especially pp. 179, 488, 594-95; see also Mersenne's <u>Correspondance</u>, ed. Mme. Paul Tannery and Cornelis de Waard (3 vols.; Paris: G. Beauchesne [Vols. I and II] Presses Universitaires de France [Vol. III], 1932-1946), <u>passim</u>. For Mersenne's influence on the scholarly and scientific activity of his time, see Yates, pp. 284-90, and Pintard, <u>passim</u> (especially pp. 348-49). Mersenne, Naudé, and Jacob were members of "le cabinet Dupuy" (see below, n. 244), and Mersenne and Naudé also participated in Gui Patin's circle (n. 233 below).

[104]I.e., <u>Les éloges de nos rois, et des enfans de France qui ont esté daufins de Viennois</u>, p. 334. See above, n. 5.

[105]For the contents of the library of the famed courtier

Among the libraries which are held in high esteem in the city of Paris is that of Monseigneur Pierre Séguier, knight, count of Guienne, and chancellor of France.[106]

M. Séguier, knight of France

This library's reputation stems not only from its physical beauty but more from the good books in all languages and branches of learning which its lord constantly adds to it. Today this personage enlightens Europe by his uncommon merits and great erudition--a

---

Marshal de Bassompierre (1579-1646), whose Mémoires are an important source for history of the period, see the Inventaire et prisée des Livres trouvés en la Bibliothèque de hault et puissant Seigneur Messire François de Bassompière ... faite a la requeste de Monsieur le Procureur du Roy au Chastelet, et ensuivant l'ordonnance de Monsieur le Lieutenant civil (Paris: S. Cramoisy, 1646). Peiresc, in a letter of 1634, says that he has heard that Bassompierre, imprisoned in the Bastille by Richelieu, managed to have part of his library incarcerated with him; Peiresc calls this prison collection "une bibliothèque toute entière de trez bons livres" (Nicolas Claude Fabri de Peiresc, Lettres, ed. Philippe Tamizey de Larroque [7 vols.; Paris: Imprimerie Nationale, 1888-1898], III, 51).

[106]"Throughout the middle of the century there are brief but constant references to a private group of writers that met in Séguier's beautiful new home in the rue de Grenelle-Saint-Honore. From the close of 1633 until 1643, when Séguier became official patron of the French Academy, this smaller circle was especially important. It met in Séguier's handsome library rich in Latin, Greek, Turkish, and Arabic manuscripts" (de Boer, PMLA, LIII, 755). By the time of Séguier's death in 1672, his magnificent library had become one of the foremost of the day, its manuscripts alone numbering 4000 and representing a great variety of languages. Bernard de Montfaucon's Bibliotheca Coisliniana, olim Segueriana of 1715 provides a catalog of the Greek manuscripts in the collection. In the Saint-Germain-des-Prés fire in 1794 a majority of the printed books and part of the manuscripts which had belonged to this library were destroyed; what remains is now for the most part in the Bibliothèque Nationale. For details on the history and contents of this library, see Delisle, II, 78-99; Franklin, Les anciennes bibliothèques ..., I, 117-20; Le Roux de Lincy, Researches concerning Jean Grolier, pp. 91-94; René Kerviler, Le chancelier Pierre Seguier (2d ed.; Paris: Didier, 1875), pp. 166-75, 441-688; and Robert Devresse, Le fonds Coislin (Paris: Bibliothèque Nationale, 1945).

quality truly intrinsic in the very illustrious Séguier family, as will be seen in our Bibliothèque universelle des autheurs de France,[107] where I shall list individually the works of those members of the family who have written. Finally, this library also contains various old and valuable manuscripts which give it great splendor. Pierre Blaise has charge of the library, and he works with great zeal for its expansion.[108]

The integrity, honesty, and erudition of Monseigneur Mathieu Molé, knight, caused his elevation to the dignity of

M. Molé, 1st president

first president of the august Parlement of Paris by our victorious monarch of blessed memory, Louis XIII. Lord Molé's affection for books is so great that his library can be put on an equal plane with the finest collections in France in regard to rare and interesting volumes. Such works--and he is fully conversant with them--are added at great expense through his efforts.[109]

---

[107] See above, editor's Introduction at n. 89.

[108] Several examples of correspondence from Séguier to his librarian Blaise (or Blaize) are given in Delisle, II, 79, 83, 85-86. Blaise was active in Séguier's literary circle (de Boer, PMLA LIII, 755).

[109] Molé (1584-1656), like Bassompierre a writer of historically-important Mémoires, is remembered chiefly for his conciliatory role in French politics during the Mazarin period (see Amable-Guillaume-Prosper de Barante, Le Parlement et la Fronde [Paris: Didier, 1859]). His book collecting interests are mentioned by V. Cousin, "Des carnets autographes du cardinal Mazarin, conservés à la Bibliothèque impériale. Cinquième article," Journal des savants, December, 1854, p. 761; cf. also Delisle, I, 443-44.

Dear Reader: I candidly admit to you that I have been very uneasy as to how I could arrange all the libraries of Paris according to their owners' ranks. So, since I am not acquainted with all these lords and others, I have resolved (with the advice of the most learned and intelligent) to present them below in alphabetical order. And I entreat those worthy library owners not to take offence, for I do this that I may not incur the blame of having arranged them inconsistent with their merits. I trust that their indulgence will make good what is lacking, and that they will approve my procedure-- since it is honestly conceived. I shall, therefore, begin with the proposed arrangement as the most suitable one.

M. Jacques Amelot of Beaulieu, first president of the Court of Aids,[110] collected a famous library which is stocked not only with Greek, Latin, and French books of the best editions, but also with a variety of ancient and modern manuscripts, and many political and historical collections, treatises, and memoirs, in manuscript, from recent times.[111]

M. Amelot's library

---

[110] "In relation to the finances extraordinaires [the more modern, non-demesne revenues, such as the taille, on which the monarchy now chiefly relied for income] . . . the Cour des Aides was set up as a supreme appellate tribunal with authority to determine all cases, civil and criminal, and with power to inflict the death penalty upon delinquents. . . . Though the court had been confirmed in a supreme appellate jurisdiction, its proceedings might at any moment be arbitrarily quashed either by the evocation of a cause to the Grand Conseil or by the setting up of an extraordinary commission" (Bridge, V, 124).

[111] In the DBF II, 624-27, M. Prevost provides a detailed biographical article on Jacques Amelot de Mauregard (1602-1668), who was an important figure in the French political life of his day, and is mentioned in such standard memoirs of the time as those by Molé and Retz.

One notes also in this library numerous printed proclamations and other addresses of the last eighty years. The library was first of all augmented by the collection of M. Chenard, advocate in Parlement, and then by that of the late M. Gilles de Souvré, bishop of Auxerre.[112] The bishop was deeply versed in sacred literature, as you will be able to see from our Bibliothèque universelle des autheurs de France,[113] where I shall cite the books which that learned prelate has left to posterity--but which his heirs have kept in manuscript to the present day.

M. Chenard's library

M. de Souvré

Queen Marguerite, first wife of King Henry the Great, was endowed with a positive attitude toward learning. It is for this reason that she was a patron of men of letters, and held them in great esteem. Among these the Augustinian fathers were her favorites, as can be seen from that noble monastery which she built for them in the Saint-Germain quarter. There one finds quite a considerable library, for it contains about 4000 volumes.[114]

The library of the Petits-Augustins

---

[112] On Souvré, see Jean Lebeuf, Mémoires concernant l'histoire ecclésiastique et civile d'Auxerre (2 vols.; Paris: Durand, 1743), I, 670-81.

[113] See above, editor's Introduction at n. 89.

[114] Henry IV's first wife Marguerite summoned the Petits-Augustins to Paris in 1612 to replace the discalced Augustinians with whom she had become displeased; the Petits-Augustins thus moved into quarters which had formerly been occupied by the discalced Augustinians. Leprince informs us that the Petit-Augustins bought part of their 4000-volume library with their own savings (Nicolas-Thomas Leprince, Essai historique sur la bibliothèque du

111

M. de Barillon's library President de Barillon is impelled by a praiseworthy love of learning to search out good books for the enrichment of his fine library; and he is at great pains to accomplish this.[115]

M. Bignon's library Although on page 88 I have spoken of M. Jérôme Bignon (previously advocate general, and now councillor of state) as master of the library of our most Christian king, it is here to be noted that he has a distinguished library of his own. In it are kept the best currently available books on all subjects, and from them he has derived the vast learning that appears in the works with which he has honored the public.[116]

Roi [Paris: Belin, 1782], p. 360). For the later history of this library, see Franklin, Les anciennes bibliothèques ..., II, 345-49.

[115] Jacob refers here to Jean-Jacques Barillon, president of the Chamber of Inquests of the Paris Parlement (1601-1645). The Bibliothèque Nationale preserves many of his letters, as well as contemporary documents concerning him (mss. fr. 15610-11 and 20632-35); for primary-source published material, see Agathius Matthaei, Aeternae memoriae Joan. Jac. Barrillon (n.p., [1645]), and Antoine Rivière, Les dernières actions et paroles de M. le président de Barillon (Paris: S. Martin, 1649). As president of the Chamber of Inquests, Barillon was the leading figure in that Parlement court which, subject to judicial revision by the Grand Chamber "exercised jurisdiction in nearly all cases which did not depend upon oral evidence; there thus came within its purview numerous appeals by way of special case from the provincial courts of the kingdom. It is worthy of remark that the Chambre des Enquêtes was a court of investigation only: it is a somewhat curious feature of its procedure that no pleaders ever appeared at its bar, and that it never came directly into contact with the litigants whose disputes it determined" (Bridge, V, 87).

[116] On Bignon, cf. n. 66 above. From about 1642 to his death in 1656, Bignon's library in the rue des Bernardins served as the meeting place for his literary circle; this circle is frequently mentioned at the time, but of it "we know very little" (de Boer, PMLA, LIII, 768). His magnificent personal library was increased by his son and grandson, and the latter (Jean-Paul Bignon)

112

M. Bluet

M. Bluet, advocate in Parlement, has established a library which is important for the quality of its books on law, history, and other disciplines.¹¹⁷

M. Bordier

I can say the same about the library of M. Bordier, secretary of the Council, who very assiduously hunts for good books to embellish it.¹¹⁸

<M. Bossu's library>

<M. Bossu, advocate general of the Court of Aids, has collected a library which is held in esteem for its good books.¹¹⁹>

M. de Bournonville

The literary knowledge possessed by M. Henri du Bouchet, lord of Bournonville and councillor in Parlement, is sufficient evidence of the exacting pursuit which he carries on to augment his excellent library. The library contains approximately 6000 volumes chosen from the best in all subjects and

---

when appointed master of the royal library in 1718, gave the Chinese, Tartar, and Hindu books to the royal library, and sold the rest of the 60,000 volume collection, in order to avoid conflict of interest in his new position (see Franklin, Les anciennes bibliothèques ..., II, 191-92).

¹¹⁷Bluet's library is mentioned in Delisle, II, 86.

¹¹⁸Jacques Bordier (d. 1660), who came to hold the offices of secretary to the king and intendant of finances, had made a fortune in business and spent absurdly large sums on his château at Raincy; a pamphleteer of the time said that he was a man characterized by great personal insolence. (Cf. Gédéon Tallemant des Réaux, Les historiettes [6 vols., 3d ed.; Paris: Techener, 1862], III, 441-49.)

¹¹⁹On the Court of Aids, see above, n. 110. Jacob refers here to Jean Le Bossu, lord of Courbevoie and father of the more famous René Le Bossu (1631-1680), a member of the Canons Regular who served as a librarian at Sainte-Geneviève (Louis Moréri, Le grand dictionnaire historique [10 vols.; Paris: Libraires Associes, 1759], II, Pt. 2, 101).

languages.[120]

<Gilles Bourdin's library> The memory of the erudite Gilles Bourdin, king's attorney general in the Parlement of Paris, is noteworthy not only because of the great mental powers he possessed, or even because of his learned observations on the ordinance of Moulins which he left to the public, but still more on account of the very exquisite library which he established at great expense and with great labor.[121] This library merited

---

[120] Du Bouchet bequeathed his outstanding library to the abbey of Saint-Victor in 1652. His testament carefully set out various conditions for the monks to fulfil if they wished to receive the collection. The most important stipulation was that the library would have to be opened to the public seven hours each Monday, Wednesday, and Saturday (at that time the only library in Paris which gave scholars general public access to its collection was the Mazarin library). Also, du Bouchet made provision for a yearly inspection of the library by members of Parlement, and specified that on those occasions they inform the monks of any complaints they had received from scholars using the library. On his death in 1654, the monks faithfully carried out the terms of the will, and in fact placed a marble bust of the donor in the library with the appropriate clauses of his testament inscribed upon it. Parlement likewise respected the wishes of the deceased; each year a solemn visit was made to Saint-Victor, and on that occasion the librarian delivered before those assembled a Latin oration on the value of public libraries. See Franklin, Les anciennes bibliothèques ..., I, 154-59, 180-82, for details concerning this collection, including a transcription of du Bouchet's epitaph and a lengthy extract from his will; and cf. Delisle, II, 228, 233-34.

[121] Gilles Bourdin (1517-1570), an ardent Catholic and a powerful legal figure who opposed such notables of his time as the prince de Condé and Coligny, was highly regarded for his learning even by his adversaries. His principal work is the Paraphrasis in constitutiones regias of 1549, which went through many editions (see François d'Amboise, Tumulus amplissimi viri D. Aegidii Burdini [Paris: D. Du Pré, 1570]; and François de La Croix du Maine, Les bibliothèques françoises de La Croix du Maine et de Du Verdier, ed. Rigoley de Juvigny [6 vols., new ed.; Paris: Saillant & Nyon, 1772-1773], I, 285-86). Laumonier (in Ronsard, X, 269), following Richelet, mentions Bourdin's book on the ordinance of Moulins (a 1566 ordinance which introduced

considerable praise from two excellent poets of his time. One of these is Pierre Ronsard; in Bk. V, Ode 23 (written to Pierre Belon) he says:

> He has landed in the haven
> Of the learned Bourdin, his patron.
> Bourdin, as an erudite Ptolemy,
> has amassed without regard to cost
> Those books of past ages
> To which fame has given the laurel.
>
> In his breast Bourdin holds
> Equity, innocence, and truth;
> He is a prime foe of evil.
> Beloved by the nations and by God,
> He appears as the image of justice
> From the Palace to the market place.
>
> Beyond all others he deserves the prize,
> For he is well versed in the three languages,
> And to a unique degree he honors men of learning;
> By his own erudition, which is so highly esteemed,
> He has, almost singlehandedly, restored to gold
> This age of iron in which we live.[122]

---

sweeping reforms in the French judicial machinery; Chancellor Michel de L'Hospital was chiefly responsible for it, and it was one of his great accomplishments, for had it been observed, it would have remedied many of the abuses of the Old Régime).

[122] Jacob here transcribes ll. 79-96 of Ronsard's ode to André Thevet (ibid., pp. 269-70), which, perhaps because Thevet did not include Ronsard in his Vrais portraits et vies des hommes illustres of 1584, was dedicated instead to Pierre Belon by the poet or his executors in the posthumous editions of his works. Both Thevet (a traveller, collector, and eventually royal garde des curiosités) and Belon (likewise a traveller, but remembered today as a naturalist and early comparative anatomist) were close friends of Ronsard and Bourdin. In the 1587 edition of Ronsard's Oeuvres (Odes, Bk. V), this ode carries the number 23, but in the earlier editions (and in Laumonier's critical edition) it is designated 21. It is of interest that in the 1580 edition of the Oeuvres, and in Thevet's Cosmographie universelle of 1575 (where the ode is reproduced in the preliminary pages) the name of Bourdin is removed from l. 80 (l. 2 of Jacob's quotation), and "Of the great cardinal" is substituted. Laumonier identifies him either as Charles, cardinal of Lorraine, or Jean Bertrand, cardinal archbishop of Sens; the latter was keeper of the seals from 1557 to 1560 and Thevet dedicated to him his Singularitez de la France antarctique of 1558. The reference to "three languages" in l. 92 (l. 14 in Jacob's quotation of course means Greek, Latin,

The second author who bestowed honors on this library is Jean Dorat, who, in writing an epigram for Bourdin, leaves a fine testimony to his library.

> When a youth he was versed in the Greek and
> Latin tongues; then,
> in his later years, he knew the Hebrew and
> Aramaic as well.
> But he also acquired various arts, and made use of
> all men
> through whom one could hope to learn anything new.
> He spared no outlay for suitable books or scholars
> if he himself might make a contribution through them.
> His library will be a lasting testimony to this,
> for no more illustrious exists in Paris[123][L].

One must include among the men of this century who are learned and have a thirst for knowledge the late M. Jean Bourdelot. He was well acquainted with the Eastern languages and with good books, and for the sake of building up his library he expended great effort to collect worthwhile publications. This library consists of printed works and a variety of Arabic, Hebrew, Greek, and Latin manuscripts; today it is owned by M. Pierre Bourdelot, his nephew, who is physician to his Royal Highness the Prince of Condé and who augments it with the best current literature.[124]

M. Bourdelot

---

and Hebrew. In 1530 the Collège royal (the future Collège de France) was founded (see above, n. 31); Clément Marot specifically called it the "trilingual academy," and its instruction in the Biblical languages was offered outside of, and in opposition to, the Sorbonne (Ronsard, X, 270).

[123]Dorat, III, 165; the Latin lines are elegiac stanzas. On Dorat, see above, n. 46.

[124]Much information on the relation of the Bourdelots to the scholarly activities of their time is given in Pintard, passim. Of Jean Bourdelot, a fellow member with Jacob of "le cabinet Dupuy" (see below, n. 244), M. Prevost writes: "He was born at Sens, was an advocate in the Parlement of Paris, and in 1627 became Marie de Médicis' master of requests. He is less

Although M. Julien Brodeau, advocate in Parlement, is well thought of for the contribution made by his excellent court judgments (they are in the hands of all members of his profession), yet his fascinating library should provide him with no less future glory.[125]

M. Brodeau

---

known as a jurist than he is for his editions of Greek, Latin, and Eastern texts—of the frequently-edited Heliodorus, Lucien, and Petronius, and of the psalms of David Kimhi. He died in 1638, transmitting his name and fortune to his sister's son, Pierre Michon, who then took the name Abbé Bourdelot. Jean's brother, Edme, was Louis XIII's personal physician" (DBF, VI, 1439). Pierre Bourdelot (1610-1684) studied medicine at Paris and there became acquainted with Gassendi, Peiresc, and other celebrated scholars. He served as physician to various notables, and was immersed in the political and court life of the time. While serving as first physician to Queen Christina of Sweden, his rather questionable sense of humor was a cause of a general exodus of French scholars from the Swedish court in 1653; Naudé was the last to leave, and died on the return journey to France (Rice, pp. 42-43). Bourdelot wrote two works on music which were published posthumously (Histoire de la musique et de ses effets, 1715; Histoire générale de la danse sacrée et profane, 1732). Cf. Henri Malo, Le Grand Conde (Paris: Albin Michel, 1937), pp. 459-62; Jean Lemoine and André Lichtenberger, Trois familiers du Grand Conde: l'Abbé Bourdelot, le Père Talon, le Père Tixier (Paris: H. Champion, 1909), pp. 1-138; and Harcourt Brown, Scientific Organizations in Seventeenth Century France, 1620-1680 (Baltimore: Williams & Wilkins, 1934), Chapter XI ("The Academy of the Abbé Bourdelot"), pp. 231-53. The ultimate disposition of the excellent Bourdelot library is not known. Abbé Bourdelot bequeathed the collection to his nephew Pierre Bonnet-Bourdelot with the request that the latter eventually pass it on to the École de Médecine; however, the Medical Faculty was in such poor financial condition as a result of war and taxation when the library was offerred to them in 1691-1693 that they were hesitant to accept responsibility for it. The library may therefore have never been transferred to the École, or it may have actually been accepted but then lost as a result of what has been termed the "incredible disorder" in the Faculty at that time (Franklin, Les anciennes bibliothèques ..., II, 29-30). Delisle regrets that he "cannot say what became of that collection," but he notes that a manuscript catalog of its Hebrew books has been preserved (Delisle, I, 321; cf. II, 343).

[125]Julien Brodeau (ca. 1585-1653) wrote extensively in the legal field, but most of his works were not published until after his death (for a partial list of them, see M. Prevost's article in DBF, VII, 393-94). Jacob undoubtedly refers here to Brodeau's

The library of the Capucins of Saint-Honoré

The library of the Capucin fathers whose residence is in the Saint-Honoré quarter is worth considering for the quantity and quality of its books.[126]

The library of the Capucins of Saint-Jacques

As for the library of the Capucin fathers who reside in the Saint-Jacques quarter, it is not inferior to the preceding.[127]

The library of the discalced Carmelites

The monastery of the discalced Carmelites located in the Saint-Germain quarter was founded in the year 1611 by permission of Queen Marie de Médicis. In this monastery there is a distinguished library containing worthwhile books.[128]

---

expanded editions of Georges Loüet's *Recueil d'aucuns notables arrests donnez en la cour de Parlement de Paris* (9th ed., Paris: C. Cramoisy, 1633; 11th ed., Paris: M. Guillemot, 1633; etc.), whose popularity is evidenced by its frequent issue. Books from Brodeau's fine library eventually entered such collections as that of Étienne Baluze and the Bibliothèque du roi; among Brodeau's books were many manuscripts whose bindings had been executed for Jean Grolier and which had been in his library (Delisle, I, 300-301, 365; cf. Franklin, *Les anciennes bibliothèques ...*, II, 187).

[126]This library is discussed in detail *ibid.*, pp. 235-44. At the time of the Revolution its library of 18,000-24,000 volumes was, according to the official Déclaration, "the largest and finest of all those of the same order in France."

[127]See *ibid.*, pp. 357-58. In later years it did not progress as rapidly as the preceding collection; at the time of the Revolution it contained scarcely 3000 volumes.

[128]The later history of this library is discussed *ibid.*, pp. 311-14. Books to the number of 18,181 entered the dépôts littéraires from this collection. It is of more than routine interest that a chapter in the *Rule* of the discalced Carmelites was devoted to the specific duties of the librarian; these duties were set forth in the fullest detail by way of eighteen articles.

The Celestin fathers possess a considerable library, in which is carefully preserved a great manuscript Bible on

The library of the Celestins

vellum. This Bible was given to them by Louis d'Orléans, count of Valois, Blois, and Beaumont, and second son of Charles V of France, and it contains the signatures of these princes. The duke of Orléans also donated a great four-volume folio Bible on vellum; it has always served--and is used today--for reading when the monks take their meals.[129]

Our most Christian king Saint Louis founded the monastery of the Carthusian fathers, where piety and erudition have always

The library of the Carthusians

been held in esteem. Their solitary lives are an indubitable mark of this, and so is their famous library, which provides them with diversion after serious application to devotional exercises.[130]

---

[129]See *ibid.*, pp. 89-100. Franklin discusses the two donations mentioned by Jacob, and reproduces the signatures of Charles V and Louis d'Orléans on the first of these Bibles. The king had had this Bible executed for his personal use, and it was said that he read it in its entirety each year on his knees with head bared. Louis collected a fine library himself, and passed it on to his son Charles d'Orléans, who in turn enlarged it and transmitted it to his son, Louis XII; this was the famous library of Blois. The interest of the Celestins in libraries is shown by the fact that their *Constitutiones* devotes one of its chapters to the librarian's responsibility.

[130]The Carthusians placed great emphasis upon learning, study, and the copying of manuscripts; their first *Rule* (dated 1110) enumerates the equipment to be included in a copyist's cell. By the seventeenth century, their austerity had become more apparent than real, and their solitary cells had become three-room apartments, including individual book collections. The latter were of minor importance, and Jacob's remarks on the Carthusian library refer to the common library, which contained some 4400 volumes at the time of the Revolution. The books were

If death has repeatedly cut off the men of letters of our time, one must admit that such has indeed been the case with that very famous royal historian M. André Duchesne of Touraine.

<u>The library of M. Duchesne</u>

He will be remembered forever among the Muses for producing so many fine works and for intending to publish so many more on the basis of the extensive research which he continually carried on.[131] Moreover, his library is very precious for its histories of all nations; it is now enjoyed by his son M. François Duchesne, royal historian and advocate on the Privy Council, who has already shown that his father's qualities live

---

not noteworthy for age or rarity, but among them were a surprising number of works on architecture (<u>ibid</u>., I, 323-28).

[131] André Duchesne, or Quercetanus, or Querneus (1584-1640) is generally viewed as the father of French history. He enjoyed Richelieu's patronage, and through him was appointed historiographer and geographer to the king. Duchesne and Jacob were both members of "le cabinet Dupuy" (see below, n. 244). His death, to which Jacob here alludes, occurred under tragic circumstances: he was run down by a carriage when on his way from Paris to Verrière, where his country house was situated. Among his extensive and still important published historical writings are a work on the antiquities of the French kings, a work on the antiquities of all the towns and châteaux of France, a collection of early writings on Norman history (today the only source for some of the texts), a partially completed source collection for medieval French history, and numerous genealogies of noble families. Jacob refers to Duchesne's frustrated intention to publish many more works; after his death, his son François edited several of his father's works for publication, but these comprised but a small proportion of the total number--more than one hundred folio volumes of his manuscript extracts still exist in the Bibliothèque Nationale (Delisle, I, 333-34; II, 333). On Duchesne as an historian, see Molinier, V, pars. 230-31, where it is noted that Duchesne "had been able to explore over a long period the rich libraries of Pithou, Pétau, and de Thou"; and Bourgeois, entries 251-52, 1412, 1418, 1430, 1441, 1449. It is known that manuscripts from Duchesne's library eventually entered the Bibliothèque du roi (via Colbert's magnificent private library) and the library of the queen of Sweden (Delisle, I, 452; Franklin, <u>Les anciennes bibliothèques ...</u>, II, 198).

again in him, and that he will manifest an equal love for the public welfare.¹³²

  Our invincible monarch Henry IV had as his tutor the learned Q. Septime Florent Chrestien, a native of Orléans.¹³³ He was survived by his son M. Claude Chrestien, advocate in Parlement and later councillor to the King and lieutenant in the Constabulary and Marshalsea of France.¹³⁴ He has built up a considerable

M. Chrestien

---

 ¹³²François Duchesne (1616-1693), André Duchesne's only son, succeeded his father as royal historiographer, but fell short of him in scholarly attainment; most of his works consisted of posthumous editions of his father's writings. Of his own publications, the most significant appears to be Le nouveau style du Conseil d'Estat et privé du Roy (Paris: Rocolet et Foucault, 1662), a comprehensive manual of procedure and personnel, with lists of councillors, masters of requests, royal advocates, etc.; the work was based on François Duchesne's own experience in the Privy Council, and the book is termed "very important" by Bourgeois (entry 6136; cf. entries 6126 and 6837).

 ¹³³Florent Chrestien (1541-1596) was the son of Guillaume Chrestien, who distinguished himself as physician to the duke of Bouillon, Francis I, and Henry II, and as a medical writer and a translator of Galen and Hippocrates. Florent learned Greek under Henri Estienne, and entered the service of the future Henry IV, first as his tutor, and later as librarian of cardinal de Bourbon's library, which Henry maintained at Vendôme. He wrote prolifically (French poems, Latin commentaries on Aristophanes, biting satires against Ronsard), and translated works not only from Greek into Latin, but also from Latin into Greek (e.g., Catullus' Epithalamium On Chrestien, see La Croix du Maine, I, 197-98; and cf. Robert Vergès, "Ronsard et Florent Chrestien à propos d'un sonnet anonyme, Mélanges de littérature, d'histoire et de philologie offerts à Paul Laumonier (Paris: E. Droz, 1935), pp. 257-67. It is noteworthy that Chrestien also served as librarian of the de Mesme library, a position which Gabriel Naudé later filled with great distinction (Franklin, Les anciennes bibliothèques ..., II, 196).

 ¹³⁴Claude Chrestien was born in 1567; "he was very learned, as was his father, but he published nothing, and we have from him only those letters which are included among the correspondence addressed to Scaliger" (M. Prevost, in DBF, VIII, 1277). The Joseph Scaliger correspondence here referred to was published at Harderwick in 1624.

library containing books in the best available editions and a number in such Eastern languages as Arabic, Syriac, Aramaic, and Hebrew. This library also has some manuscripts in it, including a translation of Julius Caesar's *Commentaries* made by King Henry IV.

<u>M. Clément</u>

M. Clément, councillor in the Inquests, has a great interest in searching out books to furnish his library. The collection is admired for its books of emblems, devices, and escutcheons.[135]

<M. Colletet>

<Among the famous poets and orators of our time we have M. Guillaume Colletet, advocate on the Privy Council. His charming poems and his eloquent translations provide conspicuous testimony to his importance. And since he is entirely devoted to honoring the Muses, he also uses all his energies to make his library outstanding for its poetical and oratorical works. He possesses a great number of these, especially Latin and French poets; indeed, I think that no one in France has more than he.[136]>

---

[135] On the Chamber of Inquests, see above, n. 115. No corroborating data have been found on Clément.

[136] In the original text the preceding paragraph appears as an "Addition" between the Corrigenda and the Privilege at the end of the volume; it has been transferred to the present position in accord with our author's specific instruction accompanying it. Colletet (1596-1659) was highly regarded by his contemporaries for his poetry and his translations; he was educated at the Collège royal, enjoyed Mazarin's patronage, and was one of the first members of the linguistic Académie Française (M. Prevost, in DBF, IX, 272-74; Yates, pp. 28-30). Colletet's connection with Naudé's circle is evident from his epigram addressed "aux doctes amis MM. Gassendi, de La Mothe le Vayer, Deodati et Naudé, estant au village d'Arcueil 1644" (quoted in Wickelgren, p. 32). Moreover, "when Heinsius visited France in 1645, he was entertained at Gentilly and Colletet composed in honor of the occasion a 'Sonnet

M. Corbin

The writings of M. Jacques Corbin, advocate in Parlement, are evidence of his love for good books; he is at pains to fill his library with worthwhile literature.[137]

à Monsieur Nicolas Heinsius sur la maison de Monsieur Naudé à Gentilly'" (Rice, p. 31; see also Josephine de Boer, "Life and Works of Guillaume Colletet" [unpublished Ph.D. dissertation, Johns Hopkins University, 1925], p. 78; and de Boer, PMLA, LIII, 759). Colletet had a literary circle of his own, which, from 1632 to 1652, met in the house once occupied by Ronsard on the rue des Morfondus, just beyond the Porte Saint-Marcel. "On mild days the company gathered in the garden under a large mulberry tree at the square stone table, where Ronsard and his friends loved to dine and where Baïf's Academy occasionally met on warm summer afternoons. In winter the meetings took place in Colletet's famous library, assembled with the help of his friend Gabriel Naudé and unique in its collection of sixteenth-century poetry, source of the monumental Histoire des Vies des poètes françois" (ibid., pp. 751-52). Naudé's brother Gilles, on his marriage in 1635, became Colletet's neighbor; besides the Naudé's, members of this circle included La Mothe le Vayer, Ménage, Gui Patin, Gassendi, Deodati, Michel Le Masle, Hilarion de Coste, and our author Louis Jacob (ibid., pp. 752, 754). Jacob dedicated to Colletet the 1647 volume of his Bibliographia Gallica universalis (for 1646), and both Colletet and his son François wrote laudatory epigrams on an earlier volume of this work (these poems are quoted in Louise-Noëlle Malclès "Le fondateur de la bibliographie nationale en France, le R. P. Louis Jacob de Saint-Charles (1608-1670)," Mélanges d'histoire du livre et des bibliothèques offerts à Monsieur Frantz Calot [Paris: Librairie d'Argences, 1960], p. 255). Richelieu encouraged Colletet to produce a Vies des hommes illustres, and Colletet did prodigious research for it, though only the Vies des poètes was completed (and it survives only in those few portions separately copied or printed before the Louvre fire of 1871 destroyed Colletet's manuscript). "The collection of all this material and his intensive research in the Bibliothèques du Roi, de l'Abbaye de Saint-Victor, des Jesuites de l'Hôtel de Clermont, as well as those of his patrons, Richelieu, Mazarin, and Séguier, brought him into constant relations with bibliophiles and scholars. Throughout the '40's, these men were attracted to his own 'belle et curieuse Bibliothèque du Faubourg Sainct-Marcel,' which contained all the general reference books and many Latin as well as French poets from Villon to their own day. Colletet was generous in sharing his books and in offering to lend foreign works, sent him by Naudé and others, to anyone who cared to translate them. Besides several manuscripts and a full collection of the works of Ronsard, he had accumulated much unusual first-hand information about sixteenth-century writers, which especially figures in his Vies of the Pléiade poets" (de Boer, PMLA, LIII, 754

[137]Two of the works of Corbin (ca. 1580-1653) are cited by Bourgeois (entries 6260, 6586): his Code Louis XIII contenant ses

M. Cordeau   M. Jacques Cordeau, advocate in Parlement, is engaged in hunting for books to perfect his library.[138]

M. Deodati   The library of M. Élie Deodati, likewise an advocate in Parlement, is full of interesting books in various languages and branches of learning.[139]

M. L'Escuyer   The great collection of books made by M. Sebastien L'Escuyer, councillor-clerc in Parlement, is worthy of praise, for his fine library is as well stocked with good books as are a number of the other excellent libraries of this city, and he spares no expense to bring together those books which can serve to improve it.[140]

The illustrious family of the Fayes, sieurs d'Espeisses,

ordonnances et arrêts de ses cours souveraines of 1628, and his Nouveau recueil des edits, ordonnances et arrêts de l'autorité, juridiction et connaissance des Cours des aides de Paris, Rouen, Montferrand et Montpellier of 1612 (another ed., 1623).

[138] No corroborating data have been found on Cordeau.

[139] Deodati (or Diodati) was a member of Naudé's "Tétrade" as well as of several other Parisian literary groups of the time; contact with Jacob came through Colletet's circle and "le cabinet Dupuy" (de Boer, PMLA, LIII, 731, 754, 759-60, 762, 773). In discussing the friends of La Mothe le Vayer, Wickelgren has the following to say about Deodati: "Élie Deodati, whom La Mothe le Vayer mentions in his letter De la mort des amis, was as learned as our author. A friend of Galileo, he published in 1636 a Latin translation of one of his works. He acted as intermediary when Galileo offered to the Estates-General his plan for determining longitude, so that this could be done without the Inquisition's knowledge. Gassendi and Deodati visited Galileo between 1636 and 1641. Like Gassendi, Deodati was en rapport with Naudé, Luillier, Peiresc, and the brothers Dupuy. There are frequent references to Deodati in the correspondence of these friends" (Wickelgren, pp. 33-34); see also Pintard, passim.

[140] Sebastien L'Escuyer was received as a councillor on May 6, 1632 (François Blanchard, Les presidens au mortier du Parlement de Paris ... ensemble un catalogue de tous les conseillers selon l'ordre des temps & de leurs receptions [Paris: Cardin Besongne, 1647], Pt. II, p. 124).

can boast of erudite persons among their members--for example,

M. d'Espeisses Barthélemy, councillor of the Court, who had a son Jacques, member of the Royal Council of State and Privy Council, king's advocate, and later president of Parlement; and Jacques in turn had a son Charles, who was royal councillor and ambassador to Holland. All of these members of the family have written, and they have worked to build a good library which is still kept in the family today.[141]

The Feuillant fathers of the rue Saint-Honoré have established a choice library for their use.[142] Fathers Jean de Saint-François, Eustache de Saint-Paul, Pierre de Saint-Joseph,[143] and other learned personages have used this library to produce the fine works which they have offered to the public.

The library of the Feuillants

---

[141] On these distinguished statesmen, see Eugène Halphen (ed.), <u>Lettres inédites de Jacques Faye et de Charles Faye</u> (Paris: Champion, 1880), and Édouard Faye de Brys, <u>Trois magistrats français du seizième siècle, études historiques</u> (2d ed.; Paris: Au Comptoir des imprimeurs-unis, 1845), pp. 161-211, 321-33. Representative writings of Barthélemy, Jacques (1543-1590), and Charles (1577-1638) may be found in the <u>Catalogue général des livres imprimés de la Bibliothèque Nationale</u>.

[142] The chief benefactor of this library before 1644 was Jacques Le Bossu, a Benedictine and sometime tutor to Cardinal Henri de Guise, who bequeathed his library to a Feuillant friend in 1626; included in the collection were many interesting manuscripts. The next major donation came in 1652, when a converted Protestant minister, Jean de Vassan (in religion: Jean de Saint-Paul) donated his library, consisting almost exclusively of heterodox works. These were isolated from the general collection and placed in a garret called--appropriately--"The Hell" (<u>l'Enfer</u>). At the time of the Revolution, the total Feuillant library numbered 16,000-24,000 volumes (Franklin, <u>Les anciennes bibliothèques ...</u>, II, 281-86).

[143] Jean Goulu (1576-1629; in religion: Jean de Saint-François) and Eustache Asseline (1573-1660; in religion: Eustache de Saint-Paul) are cited in Bourgeois (entries 1510, 1666, 2697). Goulu was superior general of the Feuillants, and the biographer

M. Pierre Frizon, doctor of Navarre, has built up a library quite worthy of consideration for the good books in all

M. Frizon   branches of knowledge which, after great searching, he includes in it. To Frizon the public owes the enjoyment received from the Gallia purpurata.[144]

The wide acquaintance with languages and learning possessed by M. Gilbert Gaulmin of Moulins in Bourbonnais earned

M. Gaulmin   him the honor of becoming master of requests at the Hôtel of the king and the reputation there of being

a great authority. His ability is evidenced by the Greek and Latin works which he has written; and he can compliment himself for having an excellent library of good books, especially works in the Greek, Hebrew, and Arabic languages.[145]

---

of François de Sales. Asseline is remembered especially as counsellor to Cardinals de La Rochefoucauld and de Retz; in 1604 he served as librarian of the Sorbonne (Franklin, Les anciennes bibliothèques ..., I, 296). Pierre Cornagère (in religion: Pierre de Saint-Joseph) is represented in the Catalogue général des livres imprimés de la Bibliothèque Nationale by over eight columns of works published between 1627 and 1664. It is of interest that Jean Goulu gave to this library a twelfth-century French translation of forty-four sermons of St. Bernard, which volume Goulu had received from Nicolas Lefèvre, tutor to Louis XIII; this manuscript is still valuable for studying the evolution of the French language (Delisle, II, 252; III, 292-93).

[144]Frizon (d. 1651), a theologian and historian is especially remembered as an intimate friend and scrupulous biographer of Henri de Sponde (Bourgeois, entry 1897). Jacob refers to Frizon's Gallia purpurata (Lutetiae Parisiorum: S. Le Moine, 1638), a huge compendium of historical data on the popes, French cardinals, French church councils, etc.

[145]On Gaulmin or Gaumin (1585-1665) see Pintard, pp. 184, 272. He is perhaps best known as the source of the French expression mariage à la gaulmine (or gaumine, or gomine), referring to the situation in which a couple, while in the presence of a priest who refuses to marry them, declare themselves married; Gaulmin is supposed to have entered into such a quasi-clandestine marriage and thus given rise to the term (cf. Alessandro Manzoni, The Betrothed, tr. Archibald Colquhoun ["Everyman's Library,"

The library of the Benedictine abbey of Saint-Germain-des-Prés is very rich,[146] for it contains a great number of printed and manuscript books which were placed there in part by Guillaume Briçonnet, bishop of Meaux and abbot of this monastery,[147] and partly by many of the monks themselves.

Saint-Germain-des-Prés

No. 999; London: Dent, 1956], pp. 72-74, 98). Costar said that Gaulmin knew all languages--but excelled particularly in Greek, Hebrew, Arabic, Turkish, and Persian. He was a member of "le cabinet Dupuy," as was Jacob (see below, n. 244), and he was highly regarded by Patin, Colomiès, Nicolas Bourbon, and Baillet. Gilles Ménage said that a collected edition of his poetry deserved to be published, and one of his poems is included in the 1729 edition of the Ménagiana (4 vols., new ed.; Paris: Delaulne, 1729), I, 296-98; cf. Menagiana (Amsterdam: A. Braakman, 1693), pp. 100, 398, where Abbé Chastelain and M. Baudelot are listed as contributing Ménage's comments on Gaulmin. He was also known for his translations (e.g., Latin renderings of Greek romances) and editions of Greek and Hebrew works; a number of his publications are listed in the Catalogue général des livres imprimés de la Bibliothèque Nationale. Gaulmin, who had opposed Parlement's sale of the Mazarin library, left at his death a collection consisting of 127 Hebrew manuscripts, 461 Arabic, Persian, and Turkish manuscripts, 2 Greek manuscripts, and 615 printed works. Queen Christina of Sweden, who had obtained some manuscripts from this collection about 1650, badly wanted the whole library, but recoiled at the "monstrous price" asked by Gaulmin's heirs; whereupon Colbert without hesitation paid them 2,685 pounds and in 1667 obtained the collection for the Bibliothèque du roi (Franklin, Les anciennes bibliothèques ..., II, 175-76; III, 81; Delisle, I, 270).

[146]On the Saint-Germain-des-Prés library, its benefactors (such as Briçonnet), its incorporations (such as the Corbie abbey library), and its treasures (such as the Psalter, wax tablets, and Poissy Bible about to be mentioned by Jacob), see Franklin, Les anciennes bibliothèques ..., 1, 108-34; and cf. Lomeier, sec. "France," nn. 8-9.

[147]Briçonnet (1470-1534) was much involved in French church reform activities at the time of the Protestant revolt. He became abbot of Saint-Germain-des-Prés in 1507 (thus succeeding his father, Cardinal Guillaume Briçonnet), and later received the bishopric of Meaux. In order to improve diocesan morals, he invited there such men as Lefèvre d'Etaples and Guillaume Farel, who preached evangelical doctrine and introduced vernacular translations of Biblical portions. Although he restrained Farel when the latter attacked Rome, he was charged with Lutheran sympathies

It is also to be noted that the manuscripts of the library of Saint-Pierre de Corbie were brought there some time ago for purposes of preservation, and this acquisition makes the Saint-Germain library one of the most substantial in Paris. Its importance is maintained through the extensive and constant efforts of the monks to find the best available books. Laurent Bouchel, advocate in Parlement, provides a full description of this library in the first volume of his Bibliothèque du droict françois (see "Bibliothèque").[148] Here he notes, among other things, that about the year 542 King Childebert I brought from the spoils of the city of Toledo in Spain the Psalter of the glorious bishop Saint Germain; it is written in silver letters on purple or violet parchment, and where the divine names, Deus or Dominus, occur in the text, they are lettered in gold, and are as resplendent as they ever were.

The library of Saint-Pierre de Corbie

---

by the Cordeliers. Finally, Briçonnet, whose own position was media via, wrote a formal submission to Parlement, and Francis I stopped proceedings against him (Amy Gaston Bonet-Maury, in The New Schaff-Herzog Encyclopedia of Religious Knowledge [hereafter cited as New Schaff-Herzog], ed. Samuel Macauley Jackson [13 vols. plus 2 supplementary vols., reprint ed.; Grand Rapids, Michigan: Baker Book House, 1958], II, 264-65). Cf. also Guy Bretonneau, Histoire généalogique de la maison des Briçonnets (Paris: J. Daumalle, 1620); and Florence Whitfield Barton, The Sage and the Olive (Philadelphia: Muhlenberg Press, 1953), an historical novel which well captures Briçonnet's personality and the bibliophilistic interests of the time.

[148]Laurent Bouchel, La bibliothèque ou thresor du droict françois (2 vols.; Paris: J. Gesselin, 1615), I, 364; Bouchel here reproduces verbatim the account given by Du Breul (see the following note). Bouchel (1559-1629), a historian and canonist, served for forty years as an advocate in the Paris Parlement, and produced a number of juridical compilations (M. Prevost, in DBF, VI, 1195); from the bibliothecal standpoint, one of his most interesting works is the Recueil des statuts et règlements des marchands libraires et imprimeurs de Paris of 1620 (discussed in Bourgeois, entry 5662).

128

Numerous other ancient books are also preserved there--even including wax tablets (which people long ago used as writing surfaces). In this same library one sees the Bible used at the colloquy of Poissy. Father Jacques Du Breul, who is a monk in this monastery, has given the same account of this library in the second book of his Antiquitez de Paris.[149]

⟨M. Isaac Habert, canon and theologal of the Church of Paris, abbot of Sainte-Marie des Alletles, doctor of the Sorbonne, and councillor and preacher in ordinary to the ⟨M. I. Habert⟩ king, is known to all for his wide acquaintance with literature and the Greek language. This academic background made it possible for him to produce that fine version of the Greek Pontifical which the public now enjoys. The library he has formed is worthy of consideration because of its holdings in theology and church history.[150]⟩

---

[149]Du Breul, Le théâtre des antiquitez de Paris, pp. 375-78. Du Breul himself acquired for the Saint-Germain library a great number of old editions and rare books, and wrote a valuable manuscript history of the abbey (Franklin, Les anciennes bibliothèques. I, 108-109); see above, n. 13.

[150]This paragraph has been moved from the end of the present chapter to its proper alphabetical location. After discussing this library (and that of Jean de la Haye), Jacob says: "These last two libraries came to my attention only when this sheet was being printed, and thus could not be entered in their correct order at the letter H." Habert, who became bishop of Vâbres in 1645, died in 1668. His bibliothecal interests are indicated by the fact that he praises in Latin verses the paintings in Chancellor Séguier's library (ibid., p. 118). He had been a member of "L'Académie des Puristes" which gathered in Marolles' rooms during 1619-1624 to engage in the serious study of language (de Boer, PMLA, LIII, 742). Most of his writings were polemic in character, directed chiefly against the Jansenists. Jacob refers to his Liber pontificalis graecè et latinè cum notis of 1643, whose annotations demonstrate great erudition. By "Church of Paris" Jacob means the Cathedral of Notre-Dame (see the following chapter).

M. Hallé

M. Hallé, councillor to the king and master of accounts,[151] has a fine and interesting library which is mentioned by Gabriel Naudé in his *Avis pour dresser une bibliothèque*,[152] by Pierre Blanchot the Minimite in his *Idea of a Universal Library*,[153] and by Raoul Boutrays,

---

[151] Not Pierre Hallé (1611-1689), a poet and a doctor of law, but Jean Hallé (as the index to Jacob's *Traicté* specifies). Jean Hallé is mentioned by Peiresc in a letter of 1627; Peiresc says that Hallé did not want to return one of Peiresc's books to him (Peiresc, I, 150).

[152] Naudé refers to Hallé's library in the following passage: "The first [means of learning how to establish a library] is to take the counsel and advice of those who are capable of giving it, of planning, and of animating us *viva voce*, whether they are able to do so because they are men of letters . . . , or because they also are pursuing the same enterprise with a reputation for better success, and for acting with greater diligence, caution, and judgment than others are doing, such as are at present MM. de Fontenay, Hallé, Du Puy, Ribier, Descordes, and Moreau, in following whose examples one cannot err, since, as Pliny the younger says, 'It would be exceedingly stupid not to set oneself the best models'; and, for what concerns you in particular, the variety of their procedures may continually provide you with some new skill and enlightenment which will, perhaps, be serviceable to the progress and advancement of your own library, in the choice of good books and of whatever else is most interesting in each of theirs" (*Advice on Establishing a Library*, pp. 10-11; the editor, Archer Taylor, wrongly attributes the Hallé reference to Pierre Hallé in the index to the volume). On Naudé, see nn. 96 and 229. With his *Avis* should be consulted E. Dacier, "En lisant Gabriel Naudé," *A & B*, 1935, pp. 5-9; and E. Albrich, "Der Avis pour dresser une bibliothèque von Gabriel Naudé" (unpublished dissertation, Erlangen University, 1949).

[153] The passage reads: "And indeed we have in this city famous and magnificent libraries to which we are quite certain to be given access by their curators--the royal library, Richelieu's library, the Sorbonne library, the library of Saint-Victor's, the libraries of the Collège de Navarre and of the Jesuit College de Clermont, and the libraries of de Thou, de Mesme, Hallé, de Lauzon, Ribier, Descordes, and Moreau" (*Idea bibliothecae universalis* [Parisiis: S. Cramoisy, 1635], leaf Aiiij); the preface to the work is dated 1631. This publication consists of only five leaves (two title-pages, the proposal itself, covering four pages, and a four-page example), but its importance cannot be measured by its size (see Tamisey de Larroque, in *Bulletin du bouquiniste*, October 15, 1867, p. 518). It is one of the earliest expressions of a hope which has reappeared throughout bibliothecal history, and it

advocate on the Grand Council, in his description of Paris.

> . . . he is inflamed with a like passion.
> Neustria is honored and Hallé brings glory to himself
> By his amazing quantity of books whose very age makes them valuable.[154][L]

With regard to the library of M. Hardy, councillor at the Châtelet, it indicates clearly his knowledge of good books,

M. Hardy
particularly mathematical works and publications in the Hebrew and Arabic tongues.[155]

---

reflects the universal interests of Naudé's circle. "Mersenne of course knew of Blanchot's project, and he spoke of it to Descartes, who approved of it" (Lenoble, p. 592). Lenoble calls Blanchot one of Mersenne's "confrères."

[154]Boutrays (1564-ca. 1630) produced a great quantity of Latin poetry, much of it biographical and laudatory (P. Vaucelles, in DBF, VII, 65), and also some historical works of primary-source value for seventeenth-century French history (Bourgeois, especially entries 3476, 6366). Jacob refers to his 4000-line dactylic hexameter poem, Lutetia (Lutetiae Parisiorum: R. Thierry, 1611), p. 28, where he devotes eleven lines to "Distinguished libraries." First he asserts that the royal library is superior to the Alexandrian library, to the Vatican, and to Cosmo de' Medici's library, and then he praises the library of "Portaeus" (i.e., the poet Philippe Desportes, whose book collection is discussed later on by Jacob) and the library of Hallé. (In the first quoted line of the poem, the "like" refers to Desportes.) The Grand Council on which Boutrays was an advocate was "created and preserved by the Crown as a counterpoise to the Parlement" (Bridge, V, 38); in theory it "decided questions of jurisdiction between the other Sovereign Courts," i.e., between the Paris Parlement, the Chamber of Accounts, and the Court of Aids (Arthur Hassall, Mazarin [London: Macmillan, 1903], p. 186).

[155]Jacob refers here to Claude Hardy (d. 1678), the "intimate friend" of Descartes (Adrien Baillet, Vie de Monsieur Descartes [n.p.: La Table Ronde, 1946], p. 112). He was supposed to have had a knowledge of thirty-six Eastern languages or dialects, and in 1625 he brought out the first Greek edition, with Latin translation and commentary, of Euclid's Data (Moritz Cantor, Vorlesungen über Geschichte der Mathematik [4 vols., 2d ed.; Leipzig: Teubner, 1894-1908], II, 655). Hardy's book collecting interests, as well as his relations with Descartes, are well illustrated by the following passage from Haldane's biography of Descartes: "As regards his correspondence, a very natural little touch is given in what he writes in reference to a copy of Cicero, which he had been commissioned to obtain for Hardy. The book was sent, and the recipient wished to pay the cost, twelve and a half

M. Achille de Harlay, master of requests at the Hôtel of the king, possesses an excellent library which incorporates

M. de Harlay   that of the late M. Achille de Harlay, his grandfather, who was a first president in the Parlement of Paris.156

The library of M. Jean-Baptiste Hautin, councillor at the Châtelet (d. 1640), is now maintained by his sons and by

M. Hautin   Chandelier, his son-in-law, and they have the responsibility of adding new books to it. The library formerly consisted of more than 10,000 volumes, but at present it is divided three ways, namely, among his two sons (an ecclesiastic and a councillor at the Châtelet) and M. Chandelier, who is an advocate in Parlement.157 Each of these individual collections contains more than 4000 items,

---

francs. This sum, Descartes declared, was beneath his notice; but if it would enable Hardy to employ him once more in carrying out his wishes, he said he would be glad if the money were given to Mersenne's porter to meet the postage of his letters, which could not have been small" (Elizabeth S. Haldane, <u>Descartes: His Life and Times</u> [London: John Murray, 1905], pp. 248-49); this event occurred in 1643, one year before Jacob's <u>Traicté</u> was published. At the time of Hardy's death, Colbert acquired four hundred and forty-three manuscripts from his library, at a cost of five hundred pounds (Delisle, I, 469). On Hardy's library, see Paul Colomiès, <u>Opera</u>, ed. J. A. Fabricius (Hamburgi: C. Liebezeit, 1709), p. 319.

156This library, of which Jacob himself later became librarian, is described in the editor's Introduction above, <u>q.v.</u>

157The majority of Jean-Baptiste Hautin's manuscripts were acquired by Étienne Baluze, but about fifty of his valuable manuscripts were obtained by John Moore, bishop of Ely, and after his death in 1714 they were given to Cambridge University by King George I (Delisle, I, 365; III, 370, 384). In 1674 Colbert acquired at a cost of four hundred and forty pounds, one hundred and thirty-four manuscripts which had belonged to Chandelier; they were "precious volumes for the most part" (<u>ibid</u>., I, 451). On Hautin's connection with the Bibliothèque du roi, see above, the text at n. 72.

excluding the cabinet of medals which Hautin had had a great interest in collecting. He was versed in French and foreign historical writings and even in family histories, and for this reason was highly regarded by the writers of the time--among others, André Duchesne (see various of his works), Saint-Amand (see his <u>Memoires historiques</u>), and Pierre Gassendi (see his <u>Life of Nicolas de Peiresc, Councillor in the Parlement of Aix</u>).[158]

<The Rev. Father Jean de la Haye of Paris, a Franciscan monk, royal preacher, and bursar general of his order in France,

<The library of Father de la Haye> continually shows the public his great love of literature, both by his writings and by his library. He has published learned commentaries on Genesis and Exodus; he has recently edited a great Bible in five volumes folio with textual

---

[158] On Duchesne, see above, n. 131. By "Saint-Amand" Jacob undoubtedly refers to the noted poet Marc-Antoine de Gérard, sieur de Saint-Amant (1594-1661), with whom Jacob had contact in Retz's literary circle from about 1640 to 1652 (de Boer, <u>PMLA</u>, LIII, 756); no known work by Saint-Amant has the title "Mémoires historiques," but Jacob may well be indicating by this common expression a diary-like record which has not come down to us. On Gassendi and Peiresc, see Pintard, <u>passim</u>, and Lomeier, sec. "Italy," n. 7 and sec. "France," n. 23; Jacob was associated with both Peiresc and Gassendi in "le cabinet Dupuy" (see below, n. 244). Gassendi writes of Hautin's literary and book-collecting interests: "Moreover he [Peiresc] procured for Learned men the Copies of very many Manuscripts, as namely out of the Escuriall and Vatican libraries: out of which, besides others, he got a Coppy of Syncellus, with which he helped the Learned Johannes Baptista Altinus [i.e., Hautin], who was then setting forth the said author with Expositions. And whereas upon that occasion, he had sent to Alemannus an exquisite Ichnographiall description of the Porch of Sancta Genovesa, and of divers other places, he received of him for the foresaid Altinus, a Copy of the Anecdota of Procopius, to the end they might be printed" (<u>The Mirrour of True Nobility & Gentility. Being the Life of the Renowned Nicolaus Claudius Fabricius Lord of Peiresk</u>, tr. W. Rand [London: H. Moseley, 1657], [Pt. I], p. 208 [for the year 1622]; for the Latin text see <u>Viri illustris Nicolai Claudii Fabricii de Peiresc ... vita</u> [Parisiis: S. Cramoisy, 1641], p. 188).

annotations; he has produced the works of St. Francis, and of Sts. Anthony of Padua and Bernard of Siena, corrected and augmented from the manuscripts, in three volumes; also, he now has in press three volumes on the Apocalypse. He established his celebrated library for his own use by permission of the superiors of the royal monastery of Sainte-Claire in the Saint-Marcel quarter, where he customarily resides. It contains close to 4000 volumes, the majority devoted to positive and scholastic theology; moreover, it should be noted that there are also some very fine old manuscripts there which have not been printed--but Father de la Haye feels such concern for the public that he will make these treasures available to posterity.[159]

The pious and learned M. Jacques Hennequin, doctor and professor royal of the Collège de Sorbonne, has spent--and is still spending--the greatest proportion of his in-

M. Hennequin come on good books, in order to augment his library which is very strong in theological materials.[160]

---

[159]This paragraph has been moved from the end of the present chapter to its proper alphabetic location. After discussing this library (and that of Isaac Habert), Jacob says: "These last two libraries came to my attention only when this sheet was being printed, and thus could not be entered in their correct order at the letter H." La Haye continued to augment his library for many years after Jacob's Traicté was published; fifteen years later the library had increased to over 6000 volumes (Henri Sauval, Histoire et recherches des antiquités de la ville de Paris [3 vols.; Paris: C. Moette, 1724], III, 52). Franklin cites an extant manuscript catalog of the collection (Les anciennes bibliothèques ..., I, 205). La Haye died in 1661, and bequeathed his library to the Cordeliers; cf. n. 286 below. For an excellent biographical sketch of him, including references to his theological publications, see Thomas Plassmann's article in the Catholic Encyclopedia (16 vols.; New York: Appleton, et al., 1907-1914), VIII, 742.

[160]Hennequin receives mention as a "venerable et scientiffique [sic] personne" in the two contracts of donation (March 16 and 17, 1646) by which Michel Le Masle gave his library to the

134

As vital a concern for books, antiquities, and rarities is demonstrated by M. Hesselin as by any man in France, according to Father Jean-François Nicéron, the Minimite. In his *Perspective curieuse*, Bk. III, p. 77, Nicéron gives an extensive description of Hesselin's library and museum, and I shall quote his testimony here.

M. Hesselin

> Those who have seen a similar device at Rome in the Borghese vineyard (Nicéron is speaking at this point of certain machines) will not have difficulty believing this. And at Paris, which can be called the museum of Europe because of the wonders of nature and art to be seen there--wonders which even today are brought there from far and wide--people have not been deprived of this curious object since a noteworthy contrivance of this kind was set up by M. Hesselin, royal councillor and master of the king's treasury. Hesselin's interest in it stemmed from his determination to include in his museum every item of interest that could be obtained at any price whatever. I call his entire mansion his museum, for truly it is filled with so many decorative rarities! There one sees numerous fine articles of crystal, handsome mirrors, rare paintings, pieces of furniture which entrance one by their round bosses and reliefs, and a great quantity of good books in all areas of learning. Thus one can view his mansion as the epitome of the museums in Paris; the diverse rarities which appear here and there in all the others are found carefully assembled in this museum, and they are a sufficient evidence that the master's intellect is absolutely catholic in these realms of knowledge.[161]

Sorbonne; the texts of these documents are given in Franklin, *Les anciennes bibliothèques ...*, I, 314-16. Hennequin was one of those who represented the Sorbonne in this transaction. Jacob discusses the Le Masle library further on; see n. 205.

[161] In the 1663 edition of Nicéron's *Perspective curieuse* (Paris: Jean Du Puis, 1663), the quoted passage appears on p. 150. Nicéron's *Perspective* is cited in Cantor, IV, 592. Nicéron (1613-1646) was a student of Mersenne and his close friend (Lenoble, pp. 393, 430). Lenoble, Mersenne's biographer, implies that the *Perspective* was left unpublished at its author's early death; that Mersenne intended to publish it but died without doing so; and that Roberval eventually issued it in 1652 along with Mersenne's posthumous *L'Optique et la Catoptrique* (Lenoble, pp. xxx, 20, 56); however, an edition of the *Perspective* had already been published during Nicéron's lifetime (Paris, 1638), and it is to this edition that Jacob refers. The "machines" or "devices" of which Nicéron speaks consisted of a combination of mirrors of various shapes to

All who are knowledgeable in things literary admire the
great mind of M. Michel de L'Hospital, chancellor of France
during the reign of Francis II.[162] His library
Chancellor was so highly valued that he devoted space to it
de L'Hospital in his will, the text of which appears in the
third volume of Laurent Bouchel's Bibliothèque
du droict françois. Here are the pertinent clauses:[163]

> By this testament I leave and bequeath my library and
> book collection to Michel Hurault de L'Hospital, who
> seems to me to have more ability in and love for lit-
> erary study than my other grandsons. However, I want
> my wife and daughter to maintain supervision over my
> library so that no one can make away with anything,
> and I wish them to place it in the said Michel's hands
> when he comes of age--on condition that it be open for
> the convenience of members of the family, our family

---

give the impression of multiple objects when only few were actually present--a kind of "hall of mirrors" effect.

[162] L'Hospital or L'Hôpital (ca. 1505-1573) is remembered for his enlightened chancellorship during a particularly difficult decade of French history; he was "a liberal who was regarded as neither a good Catholic nor a true Protestant, because he believed in a policy of compromise and advocated tolerance" (W. J. Stankiewic Politics & Religion in Seventeenth-Century France [Berkeley: University of California Press, 1960], p. 18). Since he became chancellor in the year of Francis II's death (1560), his chancellorship was actually under Charles IX. When he was dismissed in 1567, "the road lay open to intolerance" against the Reformed and to the civil wars (ibid., p. 22). On L'Hospital, see Théodore Seitte, Un apôtre de la tolérance au XVIe siècle: Michel de l'Hospital (Montauban: J. Granié, 1891), and Christopher Thomas Atkinson, Michel de l'Hospital (London: Longmans, 1900).

[163] L'Hospital's will is printed in Colomiès, Bibliothèque choisie, pp. 52-70 (French text), and in L'Hospital's Oeuvres complètes, II, 501 ff. (Latin and French texts). On Bouchel, see above, n. 148. Michel Hurault de L'Hospital, the recipient of Michel de L'Hospital's library, became councillor in Parlement in 1581, and a master of requests in 1585; he also served as chancellor of Navarre and as a member of the Council of State and Privy Council (Maugis, III, 262-63). He was a nephew of Jean (II) Hurault, lord of Boistaille (see above, n. 52).

domestics,[164] and those who are frequent visitors in this house.

And farther on:

> My son-in-law will take care and see to it that the books on civil law which as a youth I wrote out in a systematic fashion as a learning device not be torn up or burned, but that they be given to one of the most capable of my grandsons who will perchance be able to complete them by imitating his grandfather.

The chancellor died in the year 1573 at the age of seventy-five.

The Reformed Jacobin fathers of the rue Saint-Honoré have established a library whose physical characteristics are very sumptuous, but whose book collection is not of comparable quality, since at present it contains only 3000 or 4000 volumes.

The library of the Jacobins of Saint-Honoré Among the books are medical works definitely worth noting; they come from the library of a German physician whose son is a member of that order.[165]

There is a library at that same order's community on

---

[164] The noun "domestic" (domestique), which in modern French means simply "servant," had a more specialized denotation in the seventeenth century. It referred to a "person attached to the household of a king, of a great lord, of a bourgeois, etc., who exercised functions of particular importance there. . . . It is applied to members of the bourgeoisie, even to gentlemen: . . . La Bruyère, Parisian bourgeois and tutor to the duc de Bourbon, Saint-Évremond, descendant of one of the best families of Normandy, Daniel de Cosnac, future archbishop of Aix, have no other title in the household of the Condé" (Cayrou, p. 290).

[165] This library, with its "very sumptuous" gallery, is described in detail by Franklin, Les anciennes bibliothèques ..., II, 315-21. By 1727, the library had grown to 20,000 volumes, and by 1787, it contained 32,000 printed books and 232 manuscripts. Thus, although at the time Jacob wrote his Traicté its collection was not impressive, this Jacobin house "soon had a more precious library than that of the Jacobins of the rue Saint-Jacques" (Delisle, II, 245). The "German physician" mentioned here by Jacob has not been identified (Franklin, Les anciennes bibliothèques ..., II, 316).

the rue Saint-Jacques. This library is much finer than the one just described in respect to its printed works and manuscripts; but this cannot be said of its physical facilities.¹⁶⁶

The library of the Jacobins of Saint-Jacques

The Jesuit monastery of Saint-Louis on the rue Saint-Antoine was formerly the Hôtel d'Anville, which Cardinal Charles de Bourbon bought and gave to the Jesuit fathers around the year 1580. The books in this monastic library were excellently bound in morocco; but because the Jesuits were driven out of France this entire library was dispersed. When Henry IV restored their position throughout the kingdom, they established another very rich library which they now augment daily.¹⁶⁷

The Jesuit monastery

Cardinal de Bourbon

---

¹⁶⁶The early history of this monastic collection was very distinguished. As early as 1260 it received the entire library of a learned doctor of the Sorbonne, one Laurentius Anglus, and the monks built up the collection on this foundation. Saint Louis bequeathed books to the library (1270). It was here that Thomas Aquinas and Albertus Magnus wrote their commentaries on Peter Abelard's Sentences, and Aquinas returned there towards the end of his life to write his Summa contra gentiles. In 1345, Richard de Bury praised this monastic community in these words: "Though by our manifold intercourse with all the religious we have obtained an abundant store of works, both new and old, yet in this respect we extol the Preachers deservedly with special notice, since we found them free from jealousy in sharing generously their possessions, imbued with divine liberality, and not avaricious but rightful possessors of luminous wisdom" (The Philobiblon, ed. Archer Taylor [Berkeley, University of California Press, 1948], pp. 53-54). By the end of the sixteenth century, however, the library had fallen into almost complete ruin. In 1721, it contained only 8000 volumes; at the time of the Revolution, the collection amounted to 14,000 printed works and about 250 manuscripts. During the revolutionary period, books from this library entered the library of the Collège Mazarin (Franklin, Les anciennes bibliothèques ..., I, 191-96; III, 129).

¹⁶⁷On this library, see ibid., II, 269-79. The Cardinal

The founder of the Jesuit Collège de Clermont on the rue Saint-Jacques was Guillaume Duprat, bishop of Clermont in Auvergne. He had a great affection for men of letters, and consequently, when he saw the love of learning possessed by the Jesuit fathers, he took them under his patronage and secured their advancement by the founding of the Collège.[168] There they established a library, which was notably enlarged by Jérôme de Varade's bequest of his private library. Varade was a distinguished member of the Paris Medical Faculty and later a municipal magistrate; his bequest was made out of regard for one of his sons, who was in the order and held the position

<u>The library of the Collège de Clermont</u>

<u>J. de Varade</u>

Charles de Bourbon here mentioned is the famous Charles X of the League; he was born in 1523 and died in 1590. Du Breul, the cardinal's biographer, tells us that Bourbon provided him with a good library which was well-known to the savants of the period, and that the learned discussions carried on there between Breul, the cardinal, and Marien de Martimbos, one of his canons, often lasted far into the night (Jacques Du Breul [ed.], <u>Sancti Isidori, Hispalensis episcopi, opera omnia quae extant</u> [Parisiis: L. Sonnius, 1601], Dedicatory Epistle). The Jesuits were expelled in 1594, and restored in 1603. The most important later acquisition which the Jesuit library received was the book collection of Pierre Daniel Huet (1630-1721), the polymath, who became a friend of Gabriel Naudé in 1651 (Rice, p. 39); Huet's library was eventually incorporated into the Bibliothèque royale. By 1754, the monastic library totaled 30,000 volumes. In 1762, the Jesuits were again expelled from France, and their book collection was sold at auction.

[168]Guillaume Duprat (1507-1560), son of Cardinal and Chancellor Antoine Duprat, was a prime leader at the last sessions of the Council of Trent, as well as an ardent patron of the Jesuits; on him see Ferdinand Tournier, "Monseigneur Guillaume du Prat au Concile de Trente," <u>Études: revue fondée en 1856 par des pères de la Compagnie de Jésus</u>, XCVIII (January-March, 1904), 289-307, 465-84, 622-44. The library of the Collège de Clermont (later, the Collège Louis-le-Grand) is discussed in detail by Franklin, <u>Les anciennes bibliothèques ...</u>, II, 245-65.

of rector of the College.[169] I realize that Pierre Bonfons, in his Antiquitez de Paris, mentions Varade's library directly after speaking of the library which Cardinal de Bourbon gave to the monastery of Saint-Louis;[170] however, Varade's book collection must be associated with the College library, according to what I am told by the Rev. Father Jacques Sirmond, confessor to the late King Louis XIII.[171] From Sirmond I have also learned that this Collège once possessed a good library which came from

F. de Saint-André M. François de Saint-André, president of Parlement, who died on January 6, 1571.

He had purchased Guillaume Budé's book

---

[169] Jérôme de Varade became municipal magistrate on August 16, 1568 ([Gilles Corrozet], Les antiquitez et choses plus remarquables de Paris, recueillies par M. Pierre Bonfons, ... augmentees, par frère Jacques du Breul [Paris: N. Bonfons, 1608], folio 431, recto and verso). Jerôme's son here referred to was Claude de Varade, who was burned in effigy in 1595 as a result of being compromised in the proceedings against Jean Chastel, a pupil of the Jesuits, who made an attempt on the life of King Henry IV in 1594 (Pierre de L'Estoile, Registre-Journal de Henri III, Henri IV et Louis XIII ["Nouvelle collection des memoires," ed. J.-F. Michaud and J.-J.-F. Poujoulat, Vol. XIII; Lyon: Guyot, 1851], entry for January 25, 1595).

[170] The Antiquitez containing this error is not by Bonfons, but by Jacques Du Breul and Claude Malingre: Les antiquitez de la ville de Paris [Paris: P. Rocolet, et al., 1640], p. 661. For the authorship identification of this anonymous work, see below, n. 323.

[171] Sirmond (1559-1651) was associated with Jacob in "le cabinet Dupuy" (see below, n. 244), and was a frequent user of the Mazarin library (see above, n. 92). This industrious Jesuit contributed much to the fields of history and textual scholarship. Sandys, II, 283, cites his 1614 edition of Apollinaris Sidonius. Perhaps his greatest historical productions were his editions of the capitularies of Charles the Bald, and of the councils of ancient France. In 1617 he became rector of the Collège de Clermont. See Augustin de Backer, Bibliothèque de la Compagnie de Jesus, ed. Carlos Sommervogel (10 vols.; Bruxelles: O. Schepens, 1890-1909), VII, 1237-61.

collection, including his manuscripts.[172] These libraries were preserved until the Jesuits were driven from France, and were then dispersed, with great loss to the realm of letters. But after the Society of Jesus was restored, the fathers again created a very precious library by combining numerous other book collections donated to them. In particular, Cardinal François de Joyeuse, archbishop of Rouen,

G. Budé

---

[172]François de Saint-André became a councillor in Parlement in 1515, president of the Chamber of Inquests in 1533, fourth president of Parlement in 1535, and served as second president from 1548 to 1563. His correct death date is June 10, 1571; he died at age eighty-one (Maugis, III, 150, 159, 189, 216; Blanchard, Pt. I, pp. 183-84). Franklin, though relying upon Jacob, incorrectly has "Pierre" (François' father) for "François" de Saint-André (Les anciennes bibliothèques ..., II, 246). François de Saint-André's purchase of Budé's library is confirmed by Leprince, p. 23. Budé's library had had a central place in his brilliant academic career (see n. 56 above). As a young man he wrote: "At last intercourse with Italy having aroused a feeling for literature in France, and Greek and Latin books gradually finding their way here, I spared neither money in buying books, nor labour in studying them" (quoted in Tilley, p. 270). The following anecdote is characteristic: "Once, when he was busy reading in his library, one of the servants suddenly rushed in to inform him that the house was on fire. The scholar, without lifting up his eyes from his book, simply said to his informant:--'allez avertir ma femme; vous savez bien que je ne m'occupe pas des affaires du menage!'" (Sandys, II, 172). The basis of Budé's library was the book collection of his father, Jean Budé (d. 1502), whom his son called a librorum emacissimus; on the contents of the libraries of both father and son, and the location of surviving manuscripts from these collections, see Henri Omont, "Notice sur les collections de manuscrits de Jean et Guillaume Budé," Bulletin de la Société de l'histoire de Paris et de l'Ile-de-France, XII (1885), 100-113, and cf. Delisle, I, 181, III, 353, and Louis Delaruelle, Guillaume Budé ("Bibliothèque de l'École des Hautes Études. Sciences historiques et philologiques," No. 162; Paris: H. Champion, 1907), pp. 223-27. The Budé volumes suffered in the general pillage of the Collège de Clermont library at the time Henry IV expelled the Jesuits from France (Lestoile, entry for January 5, 1595); the total Collège collection had by then reached a size of 20,000 volumes ([Jean Garnier], Systema bibliothecae collegii Parisiensis Societatis Jesu [Parisiis: S. Marbre-Cramoisy, 1678], p. 4). Jacob has indicated previously that upon the expulsion of the Jesuits Henry moved the royal library into the Collège de Clermont, where it remained until after the Jesuits were restored (see above, the text at n. 48).

directed that his celebrated library, which had been formed of three others, among which was that of the learned Pierre Pithou of Troyes in Champagne, should be divided among the Jesuits of Pontoise and those of this College.[173] Father Antonio Possevino praises the Cardinal's library in his Sacred Apparatus: "François de Joyeuse could not but have a most abundant library--one worthy of first rank--for he built it out of three others, and among them that of Pithou"[174][L]. The second addition which

[marginalia: Cardinal de Joyeuse; P. Pithou]

---

[173] François de Joyeuse (1562-1615), brother of the more famous Henri, duc de Joyeuse, and a relative of Ronsard (Yates, p. 179), is remembered chiefly for having negotiated peace in the name of Henry IV between Pope Paul V and the Republic of Venice; he receives mention in Bourgeois, entries 1350, 1711. The two unnamed collections which were incorporated into his personal library have not been identified. His donation to the Collège de Clermont is confirmed in Garnier, p. 5. Pierre Pithou (1539-1596), in later life a promoter of Gallicanism (Stankiewicz, p. 67), "had a fine library including an important collection of MSS. He produced the first important text of Juvenal and Persius (1585) founded on the 'codex Pithoeanus' formerly in the Benedictine abbey of Lorsch, and now at Montpellier, and the editio princeps of Phaedrus (Autun, 1596), the Pervigilium Veneris (1577), Salvianus (1580), and the Edict of Theodoric (1579). He also produced an improved edition of Petronius. He narrowly escaped death in the massacre of St Bartholomew (1572), and became a Catholic in the following year. When Scaliger left for Leyden in 1593, Pithou was perhaps the ablest scholar in France; but a decline in Greek scholarship is indicated by the fact that Scaliger describes Pithou as 'nothing of a Greek scholar'" (Sandys, II, 192) cf. Molinier, V, entry 229. Joyeuse acquired only printed books from Pithou's library; President de Thou obtained the ancient manuscripts. François Pithou, Pierre's younger brother, was also a recipient of printed and manuscript books from Pierre's library. A very full discussion of the Pithou library, with extensive bibliography, is provided by Franklin, Les anciennes bibliothèques ... II, 249-51.

[174] Antonio Possevino, Apparatus sacer (2 vols.; Coloniae Agrippinae: J. Gymnicus, 1608), I, 229 (art. "Bibliotheca"). The Apparatus sacer was in the seventeenth century "a widely used handbook of theological bibliography" (Archer Taylor, in de Bury, The Philobiblon, p. xii). On Possevino (ca. 1534-1611), see Backer,

that library received was a portion of the private book collection of Philippe Desportes of Chartres, abbot of Tiron, who

Ph. Desportes had a very considerable library according to Scévole de Sainte-Marthe. Sainte-Marthe writes in his eulogy of Desportes: "No one surpassed him either in liberal feasts for his guests, or in the zeal and expense of establishing a library, or (briefly) in total splendor of private life"[175][L].

VI, 1061-93; and the Enciclopedia biografica e bibliografica "Italiana" (Milano: Istituto ed. Ital., Bernardo Carlo Tosi, 1936--), series 38, p. 347.

[175] Scévole (I) de Sainte-Marthe, p. 260. Desportes (1546-1606) was one of the most important poets of his time; though chiefly an imitator of Italian models, his graceful and dainty verse had considerable influence on English poets. He "was once described by Du Perron as the most learned man in all Christendom, and as Du Perron himself was universally held to be an encyclopaedic mind of positively prodigious capacity, the testimony is impressive" (Yates, pp. 128-29); cf. Robert M. Burgess, Platonism in Desportes ("University of North Carolina Studies in the Romance Languages and Literatures," No. 22; Chapel Hill: University of North Carolina Press, 1954). An attempt to reconstruct Desportes' magnificent library has been made by Jacques Lavaud, Philippe Desportes (Paris: E. Droz, 1936), pp. 409-25. The library contained a very large number of theological works, both Catholic and Reformed, and was strong in philosophy and medieval belles-lettres; mysticism and science were also represented. This library had a very high reputation at the beginning of the seventeenth century (see above, n. 154). Desportes was so generous in giving others access to his collection that de Thou said the library could almost be considered public. Jacob informs us that only a portion of Desportes' collection became part of the Collège de Clermont library. It is ordinarily argued that the rest of Desportes' books were dissipated by his illegitimate son (a lawyer whose name was also Philippe Desportes). There is undoubtedly some truth in this, for in a surviving portion of Colletet's Vies des poètes françois we read: "I once saw some pages of the manuscript book of the institution of this noble and famous Academy [i.e., Baïf's Academy] in the hands of Guillaume de Baïf, son of Antoine de Baïf, who had rescued them from the shop of a pastrycook to whom the natural son of Philippe Desportes, who did not follow in the glorious footsteps of his father, had sold them together with other learned and curious manuscripts. An irreparable loss which I felt very deeply indeed" (Yates, p. 28). However, Lavaud,

143

At present this library contains a variety of fine old Greek and Latin manuscripts which derive in part from the book collection of an abbot of Lorraine who was much interested in manuscripts. After his death his heirs treated them with neglect, for they sold them to a bookbinder to use for binding material; but God had another purpose for these books. The erudite Father Jacques Sirmond was then travelling through Lorraine and received warning of this peril to the Muses. Thereupon he averted the tragedy by going without delay to that binder and buying the books from him for fifty crowns. Then he had them transported to Paris in a cart and placed in the Collège, where they are now preserved in a room at the far end of the library.[176]

<u>Father Jacques Sirmond</u>

The library of the Jesuit fathers of the Noviciate, whose residence is in the Saint-Germain quarter, is also well worth consideration. Indeed, it contains good books to the number of 4000 or 5000 volumes.[177]

<u>The library of the Noviciate</u>

---

pp. 422-24, argues that as a bastard Desportes' son could not have inherited the library, and, in the absence of a specific clause in the poet's will, the library must have passed to his general heir, namely, his brother Thibault Desportes; to Lavaud it seems most reasonable, on the basis of circumstantial evidence, that Desportes heirs were responsible for the dispersal (<u>ca</u>. 1627) of a large portion of the poet's book collection. Lavaud also notes that some private libraries of the time acquired manuscripts from Desportes' collection, and he specifies certain volumes which may be seen today in the Bibliothèque Nationale.

[176]The "abbot of Lorraine" here mentioned has not been identified (Franklin, <u>Les anciennes bibliothèques ...</u>, II, 252).

[177]This library underwent considerable deterioration after Jacob's time. When the Jesuits were expelled from France in 1763, the books at the Noviciate were sold at auction, as was the case with the other Jesuit libraries of Paris (<u>ibid</u>., III, 366-67).

M. Joubert

    M. Joubert, advocate in Parlement, has built up his library through his great efforts to acquire fine books.[178]

M. Jouvin

    A like passion has driven M. Nacques Jouvin, doctor of the Faculty of Medicine at Paris, and a Parisian by birth, to collect a library.[179]

M. Justel

    Although M. Christophe Justel, secretary to the king, is known by the fine works he has written and continues to produce (e.g., the History of the Dauphins of Auvergne and the Histoire de la maison de La Tour), his interesting library will commend him even more to posterity.[180]

---

[178] J. Joubert is known to have restored fifteen books to Mazarin's library after the dispersal of the Fronde; among these books returned in 1654 was Mazarin's copy of the 42-line Gutenberg Bible, and Joubert's ex-libris may still be seen in it (Mazarin, homme d'état et collectionneur ..., pp. 179, 189).

[179] Jacques Jouvin was a close friend of Gabriel Naudé (see Pintard, p. 157). It is apparently this Jouvin who is mentioned in a letter written by Gui Patin on October 22, 1660: "One of our physicians, a man by the name of Jouvin, died this morning at the age of sixty-five. He was not one of those great arbalesters who kill so many, for he hardly ever saw patients. He was rich, the son of a merchant and provincial collector of tithe rents in the tax-area of Lyon" (Gui Patin, Lettres, ed. J.-H. Reveillé-Parise [3 vols.; Paris: J.-B. Baillière, 1846], III, 283).

[180] Christophe Justel (1580-1649), an ecclesiastical antiquarian and canonist, and a friend of the Dupuys, became secretary in 1610 to Henri de La Tour, duc de Bouillon. The latter commissioned him to collect the library for the University of Sedan which he founded. This library became one of the richest collections of the seventeenth century. Justel was a Protestant; under Henry IV he served as royal councillor and secretary. The two works of Justel mentioned by Jacob are, respectively, his Stemma arvernicum of 1644 and his Discours du duché de Bouillon of 1633. Cf. Bourgeois, entry 1408; and Delisle, III, 213. It is of interest that Christophe Justel's son Henri (1620-1693), who inherited his father's rich library, went to England in 1681 and became keeper of the library of St. James; a valuable chapter on him appears in Harcourt Brown, pp. 161-84.

It is true that there are many libraries in the city larger than that of M. Jacques Kerver, councillor-secretary to the crown and royal household, and tax collector general for the state in Paris; however, I find no library here with a better selection of titles, good editions, and important papers. With great effort and expense Kerver continually enlarges his library. Moreover, he possesses a fine collection of medals and antiquities, for he is well versed both in literature and in such rarities.[181]

M. Charles Labbé, advocate of the Court, began his library a long time ago, and thus today it is of definite significance.[182]

<M. Jacques Lambin, advocate in Parlement, truly reflects the fine qualities of his great-uncle Denis Lambin, who left such excellent and learned works to posterity. This eloquent advocate has spared no effort in his quest

Marginalia: M. Kerver; M. Labbé; <The library of M. Lambin>

---

[181] Additional data on Kerver have not been found.

[182] Charles Labbé (1582-1657), who manifested great scholarly precocity, wrote both in the juridical and in the philological field. He was unable to complete the edition of the Glossaries of Cyril and Philoxenus which he had begun on the insistence of Joseph Scaliger and Isaac Casaubon; he left the manuscript to Ménage, and Ducange finally published the work in 1679 (Johann Albert Fabricius, Bibliotheca graeca [14 vols.; Hamburgi: C. Liebezeit, 1705-1728], X, 61). It was Labbé who issued the collected works of Pierre Pithou. On Labbé, see Johann Klefeker, Bibliotheca eruditorum praecocium (Hamburgi: C. Liebezeit, 1717), pp. 189-90. One Latin manuscript from Labbé's library has been identified in the Bibliothèque Nationale collection (Delisle, II, 374), and a testimony to his bibliothecal interests (and, incidentally, to his questionable ethics) is provided by the following manuscript note by Peiresc in one of the latter's books: "Here are lacking certain leaves . . . which Charles Labbé of Paris pilfered from me in 1612 in order to complete his copy of the same book which was mutilated at this section" (quoted ibid., I, 284).

for books in all fields of knowledge for his library.[183]

M. Laisné M. Laisné, lord of La Marguerie and master of requests of the king's hôtel, has a library which is considered of high quality.[184]

M. de Longueil M. René de Longueil, knight, lord of Maisons, previously first president of the Court of Aids at Paris and now president à mortier of Parlement, is descended from the illustrious Longueil family which gave to the Roman church a cardinal named Richard-Olivier de Longueil. The latter was bishop of Oporto, legate of Umbria, and minister of state under King Louis XI; he died at Perugia and his remains were interred at St. Peter's in Rome, where he had been an archpriest.[185] This indicates how high a reputation

---

[183] The accomplishments of Denis Lambin (1520-1572), the great classical scholar, are set forth by Sandys, II, 188-91. Apparently Jacques Lambin had to build up a book collection largely on his own, for Joseph Scaliger stated that Denis Lambin "owned very few books" (Scaligerana [Cologne (i.e., Amsterdam?), 1695], p. 228).

[184] Laisné's first initial is given as "J" in Jacob's general index. Blanchard, Pt. II, p. 117, mentions a Jean Laisné who was received as councillor in the Paris Parlement on August 20, 1613. This is undoubtedly the Laisné or Lesné to whom Jacob is referring, for in an anonymous account of the members of the Paris Parlement transcribed ca. 1662 by Robert Hubert (1620-1694), chaplain to the king, and almost certainly composed in 1661-1662, Laisné is described as a "diligent student of literature, and especially of the Greek language, which he prefers above all other disciplines, and he is much involved in building a collection of Greek books" (A. Duleau [ed.], "Portraits des membres du Parlement de Paris et des maîtres des requêtes vers le milieu du XVIIe siècle, Revue nobiliaire héraldique et biographique, I [1862], 115).

[185] Detailed biographical sketches of René de Longueil (d. 1677) and of Richard-Olivier de Longueil (ca. 1410-1470) are given in Blanchard, Pt. I, pp. 461, 470-71. Of Richard-Olivier's death, Blanchard says: "He died in 1470 at Sutri, a town in Italy, and not at Perugia as some have thought, and he was buried in the chapel of Saints Processus and Martinian." On the Court of Aids, see above, n. 110. René de Longueil, who is mentioned in the

the family has had and continues to have—not only because of its nobility, but also on account of the distinguished library in Lord René's mansion. He inherited this library from M. Nicolas Chevalier, a first president of the Court of Aids,

M. Chevalier   and he adds to it constantly.[186] I can state that this library is one of the most excellent in Paris with respect to its bindings. The books are all bound in calf dotted with fleurs-de-lis, and are gilt-edged. The collection also contains some very rare manuscripts, bound in velvet, which should be of much value to the public,

---

Mémoires of Cardinal de Retz, had Mansard construct for him at Maisons-sur-Seine a splendid château, which later became the property of the financier Laffitte; it was undoubtedly here that he kept his library. Richard-Olivier de Longueil likewise had had bibliothecal interests; he was one of those most responsible for the founding of a library at Saint-Lô around 1470 (Delisle, I, 544-45). He is remembered chiefly for his spirited defense of Jeanne d'Arc while he was serving on the papal commission that reconsidered her condemnation and rehabilitated her; he obtained his cardinal's hat as a consequence of this (see Jeanne d'Arc, defendant, Procès de condamnation et de réhabilitation, ed. Jules Quicherat [5 vols., "Societe de l'histoire de France. Publications in octavo," Nos. 24, 37, 42, 46, 60; Paris: J. Renouard, 1841-1849], II, 73).

[186]Chevalier is mentioned in the correspondence of Peiresc and of Jacques Dupuy during 1627-1628 (Peiresc, I, 200, 537, 832-33). He became first president of the Court of Aids in 1610, and preserved the magnificent library of Étienne Chevalier, treasurer of France (d. 1474). "Étienne Chevalier was one of the most enthusiastic of bibliophiles. The few manuscripts belonging to his library, preserved until the present day, are masterpieces of calligraphy and painting. He protected and gave work to Jean Fouquet, long obscure, now celebrated, who painted the portrait of his benefactor with that of Agnès [Sorel]. The fragments of the Livre d'Heures which this artist executed for Étienne Chevalier, to the number of forty-two leaves, are certainly the most beautiful miniatures of the French school in the XV century. During the last years of his life, he built in Paris, in the rue de la Verrerie, a large house filled with devices and allegorical paintings in praise of the beautiful Agnès. It was there that the exquisite, 'rare, velvet-covered' manuscripts of Étienne Chevalier were preserved by one of his descendants, Nicolas Chevalier" (Le Roux de Lincy, Researches concerning Jean Grolier, pp. xxxviii-xxxix).

and especially to old families of noble rank.

President de Lauzon formed a library which is classed
among the notable book collections of Paris,
M. de Lauzon according to the testimonies I find in Gabriel
Naudé's <u>Avis pour dresser une bibliotheque</u> and
Pierre Blanchot's <u>Idea of a Universal Library</u>.[187]

M. de Mangot, abbot of Sainte-Colombe and son of Claude
de Mangot, keeper of the seals of France, is well acquainted
with good books, and has searched and still searches
M. Mangot continually for them to embellish his famous library.
At present this library contains about 6000 well
selected volumes representing the best editions.[188]

I feel compelled here to remark that the art of printing,
that wonderous secret and rich scientific treasure,
M. Mentel was discovered at Strassburg, a city in Alsace,
Germany, around the year 1442 (I say this notwithstanding the fables which people would relate from Chinese sources).[189] One of our poets calls printing "the image and

---

[187]President de Lauzon (Lauson, Lozon) is not mentioned by Naudé, but is referred to by Blanchot (see above, n. 153). His name appears frequently in the Peiresc correspondence; on his collecting interests, see especially Peiresc, I, 895-96; VI, 87-88.

[188]Claude de Mangot, lord of Villarceaux, became councillor in the Paris Parlement in 1592, master of requests in 1600, and secretary of state in 1612. He receives mention in the <u>Mémoires</u> of Richelieu and of Molé; Bourgeois cites several tracts attacking him (entries 2300, 2308, 3401).

[189]Naudé, <u>Addition ...</u>, pp. 239-42, likewise dismisses the claim that printing originated in China and was imported into Europe; however, he lists some ten authors (prior to 1630) who argued for Chinese priority of invention. Today, for lack of evidence, the presumption is against a direct connection of European typography with China; but at the same time it is thoroughly established that the Chinese and Koreans engaged in printing from

the mirror of all adornments."[190] It would indeed be hard to say who has gone to the most trouble to identify the inventor of this art—or who has shown the greatest temerity in writing on the subject while impelled by vain glory for his family or country—or who has shown most negligence through following such writers without a concern to seek out the origin of printing for himself. Now it is unreasonable that truth should forever remain hidden, and that Gutenberg, Fust and Schoeffer—or the more recently suggested Coster[191]—should carry off the laurels for that divine invention. These men deserve only the praise due to the first practitioners of that art. On the same ground, Mainz might be able to edge out other places, for there Gutenberg, an expert goldsmith, withdrew with Fust, and by enticing[192] away one of the servants of Johann Mentel of Strassburg, the true

Blanchon, "Mélanges", Bk. III

---

movable type long before Gutenberg. See on this subject Thomas Francis Carter, The Invention of Printing in China and Its Spread Westward, ed. L. Carrington Goodrich (2d ed.; New York: Ronald Press, 1955), especially pp. 238-44.

[190]Joachim Blanchon, Les premières oeuvres poétiques (Paris: Thomas Perier, 1583), p. 286. On Blanchon (ca. 1540-ca. 1597) a minor poet who devoted much of his verse to the glories of his province of Limoges, see Paul Ducourtieux, Le poète Joachim Blanchon (Limoges: Ducourtieux, 1923).

[191]The argument in behalf of Lourens Janszoon Coster of Haarlem as the inventor of printing is well summarized and its weaknesses are effectively pointed out by Douglas C. McMurtrie, The Book (New York: Oxford University Press, 1943), Chapter XI ("The Case of Rival Claimants"), pp. 165-80.

[192]The text has the impossible besbauché for desbauché (modern French, débauché).

and legitimate inventor of that noble art,[193] commenced to print Durand's De ritibus ecclesiae[194] in 1461 and a two-volume, folio edition of the Bible in 1462.[195] The latter may still be seen today in the library of the Carmelites of the Place Maubert,

The library of the Carmelites   and in the library of Sainte-Croix-de-la-Bretonnerie at Paris, where Fust and Schoeffer are simply called "ministres."[196] And yet they and their successors tried to insinuate that they were the actual inventors of printing--with the result that Mentelin (as his name is pronounced in his own country) had to

---

[193] Johann Mentelin was the first printer of Strassburg (HB, I, 433-35; Karl Schorbach, Der Strassburger Frühdrucker Johann Mentelin (1458-1478) ["Veröffentlichungen der Gutenberg-Gesellschaft," No. 22; Mainz: Gutenberg-Gesellschaft, 1932]). However, the claim that he invented printing from movable type cannot be sustained. Here Jacob took a position in opposition to Naudé, who in his Addition ..., pp. 277 ff., argued that Gutenberg discovered the art in Strassburg, and perfected it with the aid of Fust and Schoeffer in Mainz. Later, in the Mascurat, pp. 172-79, Naudé altered his position and defended Fust as the inventor and Mainz as the city where the invention occurred. Naudé's original position is the one most widely accepted by present-day scholarship.

[194] Jacob here undoubtedly refers to the first printed edition of the Rationale divinorum officiorum, published by Fust and Schoeffer at Mainz in 1459 (Gesamtkatalog der Wiegendrucke [Leipzig: Hiersemann, 1925--], VII, 727). Cf. n. 7 above.

[195] This Mainz, 1462 edition of the Latin Bible is described ibid., IV, 75-77. Naudé transcribes the colophon of the Bible in his Addition ..., pp. 289-90; and in the Mascurat, p. 175, he asserts that a copy is to be seen not only at Sainte-Croix-de-la-Bretonnerie and at the Carmelite monastery of the Place Maubert, but also in Harlay's library.

[196] I.e., "servants" or "agents". The connection between early printing and the priory of Sainte-Croix-de-la-Bretonnerie was a strong one. "It is known that from 1475 Peter Schoeffer and his associate Conrad Heinlif maintained at Paris a stock of books which they had printed at Mainz; it is now recognized that that stock was kept with the monks of Sainte-Croix" (Franklin, Les anciennes bibliothèques ..., I, 330). On the library of the Carmelites of the Place Maubert, see ibid., II, 1-11.

prove to them that this was not so. Indeed, he had the authority of Emperor Frederick III on his side, for Frederick in 1466 acknowledged and recognized him as the inventor-discoverer of "typography," and honored him and his posterity with prerogatives and titles of nobility; we are informed of this by M. de la Colombière in his Traicté de la science héroîque.[197] Wimpheling, Jacob Spiegel, H. Gebwiler, Andreas Althamer,[198] and other renowned authors who flourished only a very short time after the invention of the art provide the same testimonies to him in their writings.

Since the excellence and richness of libraries is due to the art of printing, I have taken this opportunity to give the historically-sound account of its invention, in order to show how heavy our obligation is to that great Mentel. His memory must forever remain dear to men of letters, and his posterity

---

[197] Marc Vulson de la Colombière, La science héroïque (Paris: Cramoisy, 1644), p. 248. Vulson (d. 1658), an heraldic writer, is cited in Bourgeois, entry 1302, for his Portraits des hommes illustres français of 1650, etc. (1673 and later editions under the title, Histoire des illustres et grands hommes de notre temps). He was a frequent user of the Mazarin library (see above, n. 92).

[198] The testimonies of Jacob Wimpheling (1450-1528), an Alsatian Latin poet and humanist, of Jacob Spiegel (1483-1547), Austrian humanist and imperial secretary, of Hieronymus Gebwiler (ca. 1480-1545), German philologist, and of Andreas Althamer (1498-1564), German humanist and reformer, are employed passim by Jacques Mentel in his De vera typographiae origine paraenesis (Parisiis: R. Ballard, 1650); see especially pp. 8-10, 42-43, 46, 99. In this work Mentel argues that his ancestor, Johann Mentelin, was the true inventor of printing. Later in the present chapter Jacob discusses the libraries of Spiegel and his uncle Wimpheling. In actuality, Wimpheling is much better used as a testimony in behalf of Gutenberg, for it is he who made the famous statement that "Johann Gutenberg of Strassburg first invented the printing art in the city of Strassburg, and then, moving to Mainz, felicitously perfected it there" (quoted in Naude, Addition ..., p. 283; cf. McMurtrie, p. 162).

must always be given recognition and honor. Indeed, descendants of Mentel are still living today in some parts of Germany and elsewhere--as for example in France near Champagne. From there comes M. Jacques Mentel, doctor of medicine on the Paris Faculty, a man possessed with as great integrity and erudition as profound interest in good books. He owns four to five thousand such volumes, and they are finely bound and in excellent condition.[199] Many of them come from the libraries of the late M. Jean Passerat[200] and M. Jean

<u>Jean Passerat</u>

---

[199] Jacob's high opinion of Jacques Mentel is evidenced by the fact that he dedicated the first volume of his <u>Bibliographia Gallica universalis</u> (for 1643-1645) to him. Mentel was a close friend of Naudé; Naudé praised his library thus: "Riolan, Moreau, Patin, and Mentel--all four have the finest and best-stocked libraries of medicine in this city--or in any other, in my opinion" (<u>Mascurat</u>, p. 167). A few pages later in this work, the question is asked: "A little while ago when you spoke of Mentel's library I believed you were one of his friends, but now that you hold a view contrary to his with regard to the invention of printing, I do not know what to say, for without qualification he wishes us to be indebted to one of his ancestors with the same name as his, Mentel or Mentelin." To which the reply is given: "That difference of opinion does not keep us from being good friends, for, as the maxim says, 'Diversum sentire duos de rebus iisdem/ incolumi licuit semper amicitia'" (<u>ibid</u>., pp. 172-73). Naudé bequeathed many books to Mentel when he died (Leprince, p. 57). Michel de Marolles said of Mentel: "He was admirably versed in the knowledge of all the finest books, as well as in the most important skills of his profession" (<u>Mémoires</u>, II [Amsterdam, 1755], 217). At the time of Mentel's death, his library had grown to 10,000 printed works, and about 136 excellent manuscripts (Jean-Baptiste-Louis Chomel, <u>Essai historique sur la médecine en France</u> [Paris: Lottin aîné, 1762], pp. 70-71). Virtually the entire collection was purchased in 1670 for the Bibliothèque du roi at a cost of 25,000 pounds; a manuscript catalog of Mentel's printed books still exists (Delisle, I, 286; III, 367).

[200] Jean Passerat (1534-1602) "succeeded Ramus as Royal Professor of Eloquence in 1572. He is said to have published nothing before the age of sixty, when he wrote the french verses at the close of the <u>Satire Ménippée</u> (1594). In Latin, his favourite author was Plautus, whom he is said to have read through forty times. He lost his sight five years before his death. He is best known for two of his posthumous works:--a treatise <u>De literarum</u>

Jean Grangier

Grangier,[201] formerly royal professors of Latin eloquence at Paris.

M. Marescot

The late M. Guillaume Marescot, royal councillor and master in ordinary of request of the king's Hôtel,[202] labored with great effort for fifty years to build his rich, handsome library. The collection numbers

---

inter se cognatione ac permutatione (1606), and an annotated edition of Catullus, Tibullus and Propertius (1608)" (Sandys, II, 191). He was an "elegant Latin versifier," and a member of the scholarly circle which met at the home of President de Thou, and of which Pierre Pithou had been a presiding genius (ibid., pp. 205-206). Henri de Mesme was Passerat's friend and patron (see below, the text at n. 213). On Passerat, see Prosper Blanchemain (ed.), Les poésies françaises de Jean Passerat (2 vols.; Paris: Lemerre, 1880), I, i-xxiii.

[201] Jean Grangier (1576-1643) received the chair of Latin eloquence at the Collège de France in 1617, succeeding the Flemish humanist Théodore Marcile. His high reputation in his field is indicated by the following distich, in which his contemporaries compared his talents with those of Marcile and of Nicolas Bourbon: "Grangerius dicit: scribit Borbonius: unus/ Marcilius doceat: cetera turba, tace." For a detailed biographical sketch of Grangier, and a bibliography of his works, see Jean-Pierre Nicéron, XXXVII, 260-68.

[202] "When he had abandoned the primitive practice of sitting personally 'in the gate,' the King had appointed certain professional members of the curia regis to receive petitions addressed to him; and when the curia regis was split into sections, some of these had been attached to the Council as Maîtres des Requêtes of the Hôtel and some to the Parlement as Maîtres des Requêtes of the Palais de Justice" (Bridge, V, 87-88); see n. 55 above. "The special jurisdiction of the masters of requests, called requests of the Hôtel, was 'ordinary' and 'extraordinary.' Their ordinary jurisdiction gave them the right to be the court of first instance for the cases of princes, officers of the crown, guests of king's household, and other persons having the right of committimus . . . . Appeals from the sentences they rendered were made to the Parlement. The extraordinary jurisdiction of the masters of requests was that of a final court of appeal: they dealt with disputes which occurred with reference to the titles of royal offices, with the cases which the Council of State referred back to them, and with the counterfeiting of seals--and in general with all proceedings relating to the seal, for example, the privileges accorded to authors and to booksellers for the printing of books" (A. Chéruel, Dictionnaire historique des institutions, moeurs et coutumes de la France [2 vols., 5th ed.; Paris: Hachette, 1880], II, 718).

more than 6000 volumes, and consists principally of outstanding histories of France and of all the foreign countries of Europe. Marescot had in his youth travelled through the provinces of Spain, Italy, and Germany, and learned the languages of these regions; this brought about his decision to collect all the best books of these countries. Moreover, when he was sent on numerous missions to these areas in the service of the king, he spared neither concern nor diligence in carrying out his noble plan to make his library of great significance. And it was easy for him to do this, because he had a wide acquaintance with books--having loved them deeply right up to the time of his death at age eighty.[203] He left this precious monument of the Muses to his son who is also a master of requests. This son is the true heir of his virtues and learning, for he desires the library to remain solely in his possession, and he intends that after his death it shall not be split up but shall go to his heirs of the same name. He believes that this great work should not be dispersed--that it ought to be kept in its entirety in his family as long as it pleases God to maintain that house in the honors and dignities which its members possess today.

M. Martin

M. Claude Martin, bachelor of the Faculty of Medicine at Paris, has a library noteworthy for its books on medicine and mathematics.[204]

---

[203] Strictly speaking, Guillaume Marescot (1567-1643) died at age seventy-six. He took a doctor of law degree under Cujas at Bourges in 1586, and became an advocate that same year--when still eighteen years old. In the course of his career he taught for five years at Heidelberg University. On him, see Peiresc, I, 804, and Antoine Loisel, Divers opuscules, ed. Claude Jolly (Paris: J. Guignard, 1656), pp. 601 ff.

[204] Additional data on Martin have not been found.

The library of M. Michel Le Masle, abbé Desroches, canon
and cantor of Notre Dame, is highly esteemed for the quality and
quantity of books which its owner has collected
M. Desroches   over a long period of time. After his death he
wants his library preserved in the Collège de Sorbonne, but separated from the Collège library for the benefit of
those who wish to study the books in it. To this end he is be-
queathing money for a librarian to administer it as a special
collection.[205]

The Roman senator Severinus Boethius,[206] a great mind
and a great statesman, was descended from a very distinguished
old Roman family. The same can be said of M. Henri de Mesme,

---

[205] Le Masle was associated with Jacob in Colletet's
literary circle during the 1640's (de Boer, PMLA, LIII, 754);
see above, n. 136. Le Masle served as secretary to Richelieu,
and quite naturally wished to donate his fine library to the
institution which had had Richelieu as its patron. The Le Masle
collection was highly regarded in its day, especially for its
fine bindings; testimonies are collected in Franklin, Les anciennes
bibliothèques ..., I, 266-68. Michel Le Masle gave the Sorbonne a
yearly income of 4000 pounds to maintain and expand the collection,
and specified that 800 pounds be used each year as the salary for
a member who would serve as its librarian--Michel's cousin Hubert
Le Masle being given first preference for the office (ibid., p. 269,
and pp. 314-16 where the contracts of donation are transcribed in
full). There seems to be no evidence in the documents that Le
Masle actually requested that his library be kept separate from
the general Sorbonne collection; moreover, "even if the Sorbonne
had accepted such a condition, it is very improbable that it would
have been carried out" (ibid., p. 269). As a result of Le Masle's
donation, he was honored with the title of socius of the institution
and the privilege of residing at the Collège (André Chevillier,
L'origine de l'imprimerie de Paris [Paris: J. de Laulne, 1694],
p. 89). The Sorbonne clearly viewed Richelieu and Le Masle as its
two chief bibliothecal benefactors, for full-length portraits of
the two men once graced the two monumental fireplaces at each end
of the library (Franklin, Les anciennes bibliothèques ..., I, 298).
A manuscript catalog of the Le Masle collection still survives
(ibid., p. 317). On the Le Masle donations, cf. n. 160 above.

[206] The author of The Consolation of Philosophy.

knight and president à mortier of the august Parlement of Paris.²⁰⁷ He has an exceptional intellect

M. de Mesme himself, but beyond this his family background includes the illustrious Amané de Mesme of Scotland, the father of Jean-Jacques²⁰⁸ who was a great lover of literature according to Scévole de Sainte-Marthe's eulogy of him.²⁰⁹ And Jean-Jacques' son Henri followed him in his literary interests; this Henri was lord of Roissy and Malassise, master of requests, ambassador to Siena for King Henry II, and later chancellor of Navarre.²¹⁰ He began the opulent family library and put in it, besides printed books, a great number of manuscripts in Greek, Latin, French, and other languages. We are informed of this by François de La Croix in his Bibliothèque des autheurs françois (see the letter H),²¹¹ and the fact is

---

²⁰⁷Henri de Mesme (d. 1650), to whom Gabriel Naudé, his librarian, dedicated the Avis pour dresser une bibliothèque.

²⁰⁸A de Mesme genealogy appears in Blanchard, Pt. I, pp. 387-97. No Amané de Mesme is mentioned, and the name of Jean-Jacques' father is given as Georges de Mesme (ibid., pp. 391-92). However, the following statement is made concerning the family: "The common tradition holds that it derived from a noble family of Scotland, of which a younger brother came and settled in Guienne when the wars between King Philip Augustus of France and King Henry of England gave many foreign noblemen reason to enter France" (ibid., p. 389). The distinguished political career of Jean-Jacques de Mesme (1490-1569) is described in detail ibid., pp. 392-93.

²⁰⁹Scévole (I) de Sainte-Marthe, pp. 212 ff. Cf. La Croix du Maine, I, 521.

²¹⁰For a sketch of the public life of Henri de Mesme (1531-1596), see Blanchard, Pt. I, pp. 394-95.

²¹¹La Croix du Maine, I, 369. Henri was chiefly responsible for creating the renowned de Mesme library. His generosity in allowing the scholars of his day to use it was unbounded; in a letter of October 27, 1601, Joseph Scaliger wrote: "He opened his

157

confirmed by Denis Lambin in a prefatory letter addressed to Henri, where he speaks of the library in the following terms:

> How can I justly avoid speaking here of all your acts in behalf of the state? But I shall cite only your library, built up at great expense and filled to overflowing with every kind of manuscript and printed book--the library which you throw open to all men of our class so freely that you seem to have provided it not for yourself but for everyone. For you willingly and gladly share with them the oldest and most faithful copies in the library, and there is no question of your ability and desire to impart to the community the delights you enjoy there212[L].

The royal professor of eloquence Jean Passerat gives a similar testimony to this library in a poem written on the subject in the year 1571; I shall quote it here.[213]

> This ample library takes pride in its numerous Greek books
> And Latin volumes--so many as to cause wonder in Athens
> At her height or in lofty Rome before she was subdued
> By the barbarian heel. Here flourish the deeds of kings and nations:
> Here one finds Socrates' secret home, and the illustrious domicile

---

library to me in such a way that his own things were offered to me unasked and he often sent me books to be used without my even requesting them" (Epistolae, p. 194). De Mesme's library served as a frequent meeting place for the learned men of his time; his circle included, among others, Henri Estienne, Jean Dorat, Jean Passerat, Pierre de Montdoré, Denis Lambin, Adrien Turnèbe, and Claude Fauchet (Janet Girvan Espiner-Scott, "Note sur le cercle de Henri de Mesmes et sur son influence," Mélanges offerts à M. Abel Lefranc [Paris: E. Droz, 1936], pp. 354-61). On this library, see also Édouard Frémy (ed.), Mémoires inédits de Henri de Mesmes (Paris, n.d.), p. 109, and Pierre de Nolhac, Ronsard et l'humanisme (Paris: H. Champion, 1921), p. 76.

[212]Denis Lambin (ed.), Titi Lucretii Cari De rerum natura libri sex (Parisiis: Rouillius, 1563), Bk. I, dedication. On Lambin, see above, n. 183.

[213]Jean Passerat, Kalendae Ianuariae, & varia quaedam poëmatia (Parisiis: A. l'Angelier, 1606), p. 4. The meter of the quoted lines is dactylic hexameter (heroic verse). This volume of poetry is dedicated to Jean-Jacques de Mesme, Henri de Mesme's son. On Passerat, see n. 200 above.

Of the ancient Coan,[214] fickle fame and eloquent
 tongues are here;
Also Parnassus and Helicon, and a glory equal to
 Mt. Pindus.
Here is sand and the geometer's drawing rod, and a
 sphere rivalling the globe of the world.
All the monuments of every age are present, and the
 largest share
Are recorded in plain characters. . . .[L]

See how high a reputation this library attained in that lord's lifetime; indeed, besides the authors here cited, numerous other learned men have spoken with great approbation concerning it-- such men as President Claude Fauchet, André Turnèbe, and Marsil.[215] M. Jean-Jacques de Mesme, Henri's son and a president of the same Parlement, has not been any less an ornament to that family, for because of his fine personal qualities he merited important appointments from our sovereigns.[216] He possessed an admirable

---

[214] I.e., inhabitant of Cos, referring probably to the physician Hippocrates, or to the poet-grammarian Philetas, or to the artist Apelles. Philetas was the only poet we know of at the court of Ptolemy I, who made him preceptor to his son and successor Ptolemy Philadelphus; an allusion to the Alexandrian library may thus be intended. We are told by Aelian that Philetas studied so hard that in his emaciated condition he had to wear lead soles to prevent his being blown away by the wind.

[215] Claude Fauchet (1530-1601), an antiquarian and historian whose accurate writings on French history have continuing value, has received detailed biographical treatment in Janet Girvan Espiner-Scott's *Claude Fauchet, sa vie, son oeuvre* (Paris: E. Droz, 1938); his laudatory opinion of de Mesme's library (to which he received access in 1564) is given on p. 30. On Fauchet's own library, see below, n. 235. Adrien (not André) Turnèbe (1512-1565), a specialist in Greek textual criticism and, from 1552 to 1556, director of the Imprimerie royale, is discussed in Sandys, II, 185-86; he praises de Mesme's library in his most important work, the *Adversaria* (2 vols.; Parisiis, 1564-1565), II, preface. By "Marsil" Jacob undoubtedly means the Dutch scholar Théodore Marcile (1548-1617); see the *Allgemeine deutsche Biographie* [hereafter cited as *ADB*] (56 vols.; Leipzig: Duncker, 1875-1912), XX, 303; Jean-Pierre Nicéron, XXII, 51-56; and n. 201 above.

[216] The career of Jean-Jacques de Mesme, often referred to as M. de Roissy (d. 1642) is outlined in Blanchard, Pt. I, pp. 395-96; although he held many important state positions, he does not

interest in literature, as we see from the fact that he spared neither effort nor expense in enlarging his father's library. We learn from King Solomon that "a wise son is his father's glory" [L],[217] and this sacred axiom is truly manifest in Jean-Jacques' son, M. Henri de Mesme, who is likewise a president à mortier. If you cast your eyes upon his intellectual ability, it dazzles the most erudite; if you contemplate his integrity, his life is a flawless pearl; if you ponder his dignity, it is that of the foremost men in the noblest Parlement on earth. In short, his acquaintance with the realms of knowledge makes him one of the most highly regarded men in the kingdom. All these qualities, together with his love of books, inspire him to patronize literature and the sciences, and thus he has made his library one of the most complete in Paris.[218] That genius of libraries, M. Naudé, was formerly librarian of the collection, and on

---

seem to have been a president of Parlement. The treasures of the de Mesme library in Jean-Jacques' time were listed by Peiresc on the occasion of his visit to the library on March 9, 1606; Peiresc's manuscript note is transcribed in Delisle, I, 398-99

[217]Cf. Prov. 10:1; 15:20; 23:24.

[218]In actuality, Henri de Mesme (d. 1650), whose political biography is given in Blanchard, Pt. I, pp. 387-88, 397, (cf. Maugis, III, 324), did not have his predecessors' stature as a library patron. He made it extremely difficult for scholars to consult the collection, and he did not like to have his manuscripts collated; his jealous attitude toward his books is seen from the letters of Nicolas Heinsius and Isaac Vossius in 1645 (Delisle, I, 399). However, it should be noted that these negative testimonies come long after Gabriel Naudé gave up his post as Henri de Mesme's librarian (1626). "With Naudé as librarian, the Bibliotheca Memmiana grew to be one of the best in seventeenth-century Paris, and its fame spread over all Europe. . . . . It is certain that whatever glory de Mesme may have derived from his collection was in great measure due to the devotion of his librarian" (Rice, p. 11). A history of the de Mesme library after the time of Henri is given in Delisle, I, 400 ff.

the subject of librarianship we profit from his scholarly and absorbing book entitled, Avis pour dresser une bibliothèque, which he dedicated to Henri de Mesme.[219] Another rare intellect of our time—a man no less pious than learned—the Rev. Father Léon de Saint-Jean, royal preacher and provincial of the Reformed Carmelites of Touraine province, has by order of Henri de Mesme written a Latin work on librarianship; he will soon publish it in his Opuscules under the title, Idea bibliothecae viventis & mortuae, ad Henricum Memmium, etc.[220] <Today it is M. Florent, doctor of the University of Orléans, who has charge

<M. Florent's library> of this library; and he has quite an interesting library of his own.[221]>

M. de Metz, commissioner of war, uses all his energy in building an outstanding library; it excells in books on mathematics.[222]

M. de Metz

---

[219]See above, n. 152.

[220]Jean Macé (1600-1671; in religion: Léon de Saint-Jean) assisted Richelieu in his last hours and wrote a hagiographical description of his death. He also produced funeral orations for Father Joseph (the "Grey Eminence") and for Mazarin. (See Bourgeois, entries 1750, 1863.) The projected work to which Jacob refers "never appeared" (Joannis [sic] Guigard, "Bibliothèque de la famille de Mesmes," Bibliophile français, VI [August, 1872], 251). Macé's broad intellectual interests are evident from his book, Le portrait de la sagesse universelle, avec l'idée générale des sçiances [sic] et leur plan representé en cent tables, which was issued in a number of editions in the seventeenth century.

[221]François Florent (ca. 1590-1650), a celebrated legal scholar of his time, became professor of law at Orléans in 1630. He spent his vacations each year with his friends at Paris, and by their solicitation he received a chair of canon law on the Paris Faculty in 1644. His Dissertationum selectarum juris canonici libri duo (Parisiis: J. Camusat, 1632) is dedicated to Henri de Mesme. See the biography of Florent by his successor J. Doujat in his edition of Florent's Opera juridica (2 vols.; Parisiis: J. de la Caille, 1679).

[222]M. de Metz (or Mets) is included in Hilarion de Coste's

The library of the Minimites of the Place Royale is indeed a rich Parisian chamber of the Muses, for it contains 8000 volumes in all fields of knowledge. These were provided in part through the solicitude of Father Robert Renaud, who had a profound knowledge of good books, and also through the efforts of many other learned monks of that monastery who have honored and continue to honor the public in this way; here I refer to such men as Father Marin Mersenne, François de La Noue, Hilarion de Coste, and Jean-François Nicéron.[223]

<u>The library of the Minimites</u>

M. de Montchal, master in ordinary of requests of the king's hôtel, and brother of Archbishop Montchal of Toulouse, testifies publicly to his love of knowledge by the collection of good books which he has built up in an effort to create a distinguished

<u>M. de Montchal</u>

---

list of the friends of Marin Mersenne (Mersenne, <u>Correspondance</u>, I, xl.

[223] On de Coste, Mersenne, and J.-F. Nicéron, see above, nn. 5, 103, and 161 respectively. François de La Noue (1595-1670), whose baptismal name was Claude, has been considered one of the most learned men his order produced. Although elevated to various high dignities in the Minimites, he asked and received permission to return to the status of a simple monk so that he could concentrate on his studies. He had a thorough knowledge of Hebrew, Greek, Latin, Italian, and Spanish, and his academic interests and numerous writings embraced almost all fields of knowledge. Most of his productions were left in manuscript in the Minimite library; he published only two essays. A biographical eulogy, together with a six-page catalog of his completed and projected works, is given in Renatus Thuillier, <u>Diarium patrum, fratrum, et sororum ordinis Minimorum provinciae Franciae sive Parisiensis qui religiose obierunt ab anno 1506 ad annum 1700</u> (Parisiis, 1709), Pt. II, pp. 7 ff. The Minimite library, which was frequented by the scholars of Jacob's time, grew to be one of the most valuable in Paris; its later history, treasures, and catalogs receive detailed treatment in Franklin, <u>Les anciennes bibliothèques ...</u>, II, 324-35.

library.[224]

The variety of libraries in Paris is a source of great satisfaction to men of letters, and it testifies to what extent learning is cultivated here. The scholarship and intellectual curiosity of M. Morand, councillor on the Grand Council, motivate him to build a notable library.[225]

M. Morand

Although M. René Moreau, doctor of the Paris Faculty and royal professor of medicine, has acquired a great reputation from his learning, I find that his excellent library provides no less a ground for prestige.[226] It is very

M. Moreau

---

[224] We learn from a letter which Jacques Dupuy wrote to Rigault from Paris on October 5, 1652, that M. de Montchal was one of Archbishop Montchal's heirs, and that he had little interest in his brother's manuscripts: "M. de Montchal, master of requests and brother of the late M. de Toulouse, has died at his home in Annonay. I don't know what will become of the books that belonged to his late brother. He had a wealth of manuscripts, but M. de Montchal didn't plan to keep them--he was just waiting for a more opportune time to sell them here" (manuscript extract quoted in Delisle, I, 271). Archbishop Charles de Montchal (1589-1651) had collected a library which was held in great esteem by the learned in the seventeenth century; its catalog has been published by Bernard de Montfaucon, Bibliotheca bibliothecarum manuscriptorum nova (2 vols.; Parisiis: Briasson, 1739), II, 896. Foucquet acquired the Archbishop's manuscripts, and later Charles-Maurice Le Tellier, archbishop of Reims, obtained possession of almost all of them; it was Le Tellier who presented them to the Bibliothèque du roi (Delisle, I, 271-73, 302-305). Jacob had contact with Charles de Montchal through "le cabinet Dupuy" (see below, n. 244).

[225] Thomas Morand (1616-1692), marquis of Mesnil-Garnier and count of Penzès, became councillor in the Grand Council on September 18, 1636, master of requests on August 1-6, 1643, and honorary master of requests in 1663 (Duleau, Revue nobiliaire héraldique et biographique, I, 179). On the Grand Council, see above, n. 154.

[226] Moreau (1587-1656), who is included in August Hirsch (ed.), Biographisches Lexikon der hervorragenden Ärzte aller Zeiten und Völker (5 vols., 2d ed.; Berlin: Urban & Schwarzenberg, 1929-1935), IV, 258-59, was associated with Jacob and Naudé in "le cabinet Dupuy" (see below, n. 244), and, with Naudé, was also a member of the avant-garde group that met informally in Gui Patin's

well stocked with books on medicine and philosophy. Moreover, several writers speak highly of it; for example, Gabriel Naudé, on page 91 of his Addition à l'histoire de Louys XI, calls it "a fine, rich collection", and in his Bibliographie politique Naudé classes it with the substantial libraries of Paris; and Father Pierre Blanchot, the Minimite, in his Idea of a Universal Library, also places it among the splendid and celebrated libraries of the city.[227] This erudite physician takes special care that searches are made in Germany, Flanders, Holland, England, and Italy for all the best books relevant to his praiseworthy objectives.

---

library (see below, n. 233). Patin said of the relationship among Moreau, Naudé, and himself: "M. Naudé was a very wise, very prudent, and very methodical man, and a good friend; he put his confidence only in M. Moreau and in me. . . . We became close friends in 1620, and in 1622 we studied medicine together under M. Moreau" (Gabriel Naudé and Gui Patin, Naudaeana et Patiniana [2d ed.; Amsterdam: F. vander Plaats, 1703], sec. "Patiniana," pp. 39-40). From Patin's correspondence, we know that after Naudé's death Moreau began a biography of him which was never finished (Patin, Lettres, ed. Reveillé-Parise, I, 216). As we have seen, Moreau was a frequent user of the Mazarin library (see above, n. 92).

[227]A chapter is devoted to Naudé's Addition in Rice, pp. 73-85. Naudé refers to Moreau's library in the following terms in his Bibliographie politique (Paris: G. Pelé, 1642), pp. 5-6: "It is true that the ardent love of books which has possessed me from my earliest years and brought about a strong inclination to search out volumes, together with the position of librarian which was given me a long time ago by President de Mesme, and later by his eminence Cardinal de Bagny, my very liberal Maecenas and benefactor, have provided me with some slight acquaintance with authors; however, for two years I have been separated from my collection of books at Paris and from the substantial libraries of MM. Dupuy, Moreau, Descordes, and my other friends." Naudé addresses his work to Jacques Gaffarel (see above, n. 83, and Pintard, passim), and in fact wrote the book at the request of this friend (cf. Rice, p. 106). The French edition of 1642 is a translation from the Latin original (Bibliographia politica [Venetiis: F. Baba, 1633]); in the Latin edition the above passage appears on p. 7, with slight verbal alterations. It is clear that Jacob refers to the French edition. Naudé also praises Moreau's library in his Avis (see above, n. 152) and in his Mascurat (see above, n. 199). For Blanchot's reference to Moreau's library, see n. 153 above.

The royal Collège de Navarre has always been a seminary where the most famous theologians receive their training--doctors who have shed lustre upon the church of God through *Navarre* their good lives, and upon the public through their learning. One thinks of Cardinal Pierre d'Ailly, the venerable Jean Gerson, and many others. These men left their works to the College in order to honor its magnificent library, which was built through the liberality of King Charles VIII, and which houses divers ancient manuscripts.[228]

It will not seem unreasonable that M. Gabriel Naudé is called a living library on account of his extensive knowledge of books and their subject matter, if we realize that for *M. Naudé* this very reason he has been honored with the librarianship of the most famous libraries of Europe. First, he was in charge of President de Mesme's library, then of Cardinal

---

[228] The library of the Collège de Navarre was one of the outstanding libraries of Paris in Jacob's day (see above n. 153), owing chiefly to the fact that in 1637 it bought almost the entire book collection of Peiresc (Franklin, Les anciennes bibliothèques ..., I, 401; a detailed history of the Navarre library is provided on pp. 393-404). Charles VIII's liberality in relation to the monastery consisted of a donation of 2400 pounds to expedite the work of restoration which had been ordered by Charles VII and begun in the reign of Louis XI. The gallery to house the library was finally completed in 1506 (ibid., pp. 398-99). Pierre d'Ailly (ca. 1350-1420), "the eagle of the doctors of France," and Jean Gerson (1363-1429), "doctor Christianissimus," were two of the first students of the College. D'Ailly left his whole library to the College, and one who saw it praised it highly (Aubert Le Mire, Bibliotheca ecclesiastica [Hamburgi: Liebezeit & Felginer, 1718], Pt. I, Chapter CCCCLIV). Gerson, however, bequeathed his books to the Celestins of Avignon, and forbade any change in their ownership (Jean de Launoy, Regii Navarrae gymnasii Parisiensis historia [Parisiis: E. Martinus, 1677], pp. 492-93); see n. 339 and corresponding text. A number of early manuscript donations to the College by its students and faculty are discussed in Franklin, Les anciennes bibliothèques ..., I, 395-97.

Bagny's at Rome. After the latter's death, Cardinal Antonio Barberino gave him supervision over his book collection. He served in this capacity for some months, until Cardinal Mazarin appointed him to be his domestic[229] and librarian. In that post he occupies himself in so worthy a manner that he no longer thinks in terms of augmenting his own rare and interesting library of over 8000 volumes--with as many still in Rome as are here in Paris. Now he is concerned only to enrich his eminence's library with all the better and rarer books available in Europe; he has freely renounced his own interests in order better and more readily to

---

[229] On the seventeenth-century meaning of this word, see above, n. 164. This passage gives further validation to the assertion of Pintard, p. 615: "Naudé returned to France, called not by Richelieu, but by Mazarin, and to serve Mazarin." Taylor is thus in error when he writes: "In 1642, Cardinal Richelieu recalled him [Naudé] to Paris to be the librarian of his personal collection. Soon after Naudé arrived, Richelieu died, and he was employed by Cardinal Mazarin instead" (Naudé, Advice on Establishing a Library, p. viii). Literature dealing with Naude has been cited previously (nn. 96, 152). Naudé's personal library was acquired en bloc by Mazarin at the time of Naudé's death. Manuscript catalogs of the library still exist; one is entitled, "Inventory of my books which are at Rome," the second is titled, "Catalog of the books which are in the study of G. Naudé at Paris," and the third lists Naudé's manuscripts (Delisle, I, 285). Naudé's influence on his scholarly contemporaries is evident from his own avant-garde literary circle which met from 1644 to 1652 and included Le Mothe le Vayer, Gassendi, and Deodati (comprising, with Naudé, "la Tétrade"), as well as Patin and Colletet (de Boer, PMLA, LIII, 759-60); and from his association with other scholarly circles of his time such as "le cabinet Dupuy" (see below, n. 244) and Colletet's group (see above, n. 136), to both of which Jacob also belonged. (On these circles, and Naudé's place in them, see the definitive study by Pintard, passim.) The relations between Naudé and our author were always very close. Jacob's name appears frequently in Naudé's account-book, and it is evident that on more than one occasion they put themselves under obligation to each other (Franklin, Histoire de la Bibliothèque Mazarine ..., p. 25). Jacob dedicated the first volume of his Bibliographia Parisina to Naudé, and it was Jacob who, of all Naudé's friends, produced the memorial volume for him after his death (V. cl. Gabrielis Naudaei tumulus); see Rice, p. 44.

fulfil his duties in the service of so good a master. It has been over seventeen years since he gave us his approach to this task in his Avis pour dresser une bibliothèque.[230]

Cardinal Pierre de Bérulle will always be held in blessed memory for having founded the devout congregation of the Oratorians at Paris. This congregation has, to its own glory and that of the order, produced a number of learned persons who have all contributed to the establishment of a distinguished library.[231] This library contains more than 6000 volumes, among which are all the Hebrew manuscripts dealing with theology and philosophy which M. de Sancy brought from Constantinople when he was our royal ambassador to its great sovereign. Later Sancy turned his back on the grandeurs of this world in order more perfectly to acquire eternal rewards, and donned the habit and accepted the way of life of this Oratorian congregation; and there he remained until the

The library of the Oratorian fathers

M. de Sancy

---

[230]First published in 1627. The second edition was brought out by Rolet Le Duc in conjunction with Jacob's Traicté in 1644 (cf. Naudé and Patin, Naudaeana et Patiniana, sec. "Naudaeana," pp. 237-38).

[231]The bibliothecal history of the Oratory is described in Franklin, Les anciennes bibliothèques ..., II, 337-43. At the time of the Revolution the library contained at least 37,750 volumes, including 1580 manuscripts. Pierre de Bérulle (1575-1629), the cardinal and statesman who encouraged Descartes' philosophical studies and founded the Oratory in 1611, contributed the first books to the Oratory library; these consisted of controversial works and volumes which he had obtained in Spain. (On Bérulle, see the several biographical studies by Michel Houssaye, especially Le père de Bérulle et l'Oratoire de Jésus [Paris: E. Plon, 1874]; and [Henrietta L. F. Lear], The Revival of Priestly Life in the Seventeenth Century in France [London: Rivingtons, 1873], pp. 31-50).

late King Louis XIII provided him with the bishopric of Saint-Malo in Bretagne, where he lives in an exemplary manner today.[232]

M. Gui Patin of Beauvais, doctor of the Faculty of Medicine at Paris and dean of their schools, should be praised not only for his fine intellect and mental acumen but also

M. Patin for his remarkable efforts to find good books with which to enlarge his excellent library. At the present time this library exceeds 6000 volumes in all fields of knowledge.[233]

---

[232]Blanchard, Pt. I, p. 242, provides an overview of the career of Achille Harlay de Sancy (1581-1646), and asserts that while he was in the East, "he learned the Eastern languages with such perfection that he spoke them as he did French." During his ten years in the Levant, Sancy brought together a magnificent collection of oriental manuscripts, which he gave to the Oratory; of the 1580 manuscripts in the Oratory library at the time of the Revolution, 300 were written in Eastern languages and had belonged to Sancy. Sancy's portrait was one of the two hanging in the library of the Oratorians (Franklin, Les anciennes bibliothèques ..., I, 122; II, 338, 341). The entire oriental portion of the Oratory library is now in the Bibliothèque Nationale (Delisle, II, 257).

[233]Patin's library, which his close friend Naudé considered one of the four best medical libraries in Paris (see above, n. 199), was the meeting place of his "l'académie libre," an informal discussion group whose atmosphere of free inquiry paralleled that in Naudé's own circle and in the meetings at La Mothe le Vayer's. Among Patin's favorite friends were, besides the two savants just mentioned, Moreau (cf. n. 226 above), Gassendi, Deodati, Mersenne, Marolles, Riolan, and Charles Sorel. "Having begun during the preceding decade in Patin's humbler quarters of the rue des Lavandières-Sainte-Opportune, these meetings were transferred early in 1651 to the large, bright library of his new home in the place du Chevalier-du-Guet, where they continued till his death on March 30, 1672. . . . These congenial spirits conversed very freely on religion, politics, history, the sciences, coins, manuscripts, etc. But in literature, according to Sorel, their tastes were distinctly of their own generation and rarely did they enjoy a new book of the '50's. Indeed, having learned the classics well, they were inclined to favor both ancient and modern Latin literature, to thoroughly disapprove of translation, and to scoff at Sorel's proposal of a non-classical education in France" (de Boer, PMLA, LIII, 763). From Patin's correspondence we receive a detailed picture of his new library. Above the mantle of the fireplace a painting of the crucifix was flanked by portraits of himself and his wife, and below the crucifix, those of his mother

168

M. Pétau, councillor in the Parlement of Paris, began the Pétau family library. This collection is very rich and noteworthy with respect to its manuscripts;

M. Pétau   these are present in great numbers, and were sought out by Paul Pétau with much care and at considerable expense.[234] The manuscripts come in part from the libraries of

---

and father. A large portrait of Erasmus hung to one side of the fireplace, and a portrait of Joseph Scaliger balanced it on the other. A beam traversed the middle of the study, and portraits of illustrious men were placed on either side of it. Included were Naudé, Saumise, Heinsius, Julius Caesar Scaliger, Lipsius, Casaubon, Muret, Grotius, Rabelais, Montaigne, François de Sales, F.-A. de Thou, and others (Patin, Correspondance, ed. Armand Brette [Paris, A. Colin, 1901], pp. 102, 112). Twenty portraits, representing Patin's gallery, are reproduced at the back of Pierre Pic, Guy Patin (Paris: G. Steinheil, 1911). By January 14, 1651 Patin's library had grown to 10,000 volumes, as we learn from his letter of that date (Patin, Correspondance, p. 109). His bibliophilistic interests and his intimate friendship with Naudé are well set forth from the documents by Francis R. Packard, Guy Patin and the Medical Profession in Paris in the XVIIth Century (New York: Hoeber, 1925), pp. 70-79, 91-99, 139-145. Patin's influence on Paris society in his capacity as two-time elected dean of the Medical Faculty will be better understood in the light of Packard's statement that "the term Faculté de Médicine, did not imply a few professors or teachers of medicine, but a corporate body of physicians under the control of which was placed the medical teaching of the University, and the control of the practice of medicine in the city of Paris" (ibid., pp. 44-45). Jacob's respect for Patin is evident by the fact that he dedicated the second (1646) volume of his Bibliographia Parisina (for 1645) to him; they were associated in "le cabinet Dupuy" (see below, n. 244) and in Colletet's circle (see above, n. 136). For further information on Patin, see Félix Larrieu, Gui Patin (Paris: A. Picard, 1889); and René Pintard, La Mothe le Vayer--Gassendi--Guy Patin; études de bibliographie et de critique suivies de textes inédits de Guy Patin ("Publications de l'Université de Poitiers. Série des sciences de l'homme," No. 5; Paris: Boivin, n.d.), especially pp. 47-61 (dealing with the origin of the "Naudaeana" and "Patiniana").

[234]Paul Pétau was received as a councillor in the Paris Parlement in 1588 (Blanchard, Pt. II, p. 106). On April 6, 1593, this "learned bibliophile and jurist" was received as councillor in the Parlement of Tours, and during the reign of Henry IV he was confirmed as councillor in the Parlement of Paris (Maugis, III, 293, 308). "He established a fine library, rich in rare books and excellent manuscripts. It was there that he entertained a

the late M. Claude Fauchet, president of the Court of Monies,[235]

M. de Fauchet and of Pierre Daniel, bailiff of Saint-Benoist-sur-Loire.[236] One can judge the rarity of these
P. Daniel manuscripts from the fact that several have been employed by Father Jacques Sirmond in preparing

his published editions of great works, and particularly by the fact that the late M. Duchesne used them in producing his corpus

---

number of illustrious and erudite friends, to whom he freely loaned his manuscripts and books; and there he wrote the admirable works which we have from his own pen. The most notable are: Veterum numismatum γνώρισμα; Antiquariae supellectilis portiuncula; Syntagma de Nithardo comite, Caroli M. ex filia nepote; Dissertatio de epocha annorum incarnationis Christi" (Moreri, VIII, Pt. 2, 226). Petau's library was especially strong in classical authors, the church fathers, the older French historians, and ancient French poets (Delisle, I, 287). On the Pétau family library in general, see Paulin Paris, Les manuscrits françois de la Bibliothèque du roi (7 vols.; Paris: Techener, 1836-1848), IV, 51 ff.; and cf. Le Roux de Lincy, Researches concerning Jean Grolier, pp. 89-90.

[235] On Fauchet, see above n. 215. The Cour des monnais was "a court of last resort for all cases dealing with monies" (Chéruel, I, 249); its jurisdiction related to mint and coinage matters (cf. Bridge, V, 122-23). Fauchet himself said that his library consisted of 2000 volumes, and a thorough attempt to reconstruct it has been made by Janet Girvan Espiner-Scott, in her Documents concernant la vie et les oeuvres de Claude Fauchet (Paris: E. Droz, 1938), pp. 203-30. Manuscripts from Fauchet's library were obtained not only by Pétau, but also by M. de la Brulonnière (see the text at n. 458) and by Denis Godefroy, Fauchet's nephew (Peiresc, I, 267). Today, the greatest number of Fauchet manuscripts are in the Bibliothèque Nationale and in the Vatican library (the latter having received them in the bequest of Queen Christina of Sweden); other libraries with manuscripts from the Fauchet library are the British Museum, Berlin, Berne, Leiden University, Aix, and Dijon.

[236] Saint-Benoist-sur-Loire is the abbey of Fleury. Pétau and Jacques Bongars divided between them the abbey books which Pierre Daniel, an Orléans advocate, had saved from Protestant depredation (Delisle, II, 364-65). On Daniel, see M. Dupré's notes in the Bulletin de la Société archéologique de l'Orléanais, LII (1866), 333; and Hermann Hagen, Zur Geschichte der Philologie (Berlin: S. Calvary, 1879), pp. 1-52 (on pp. 55-216 much information is to be found on Bongars).

of French historians.[237] Death, which so frequently carries off men of letters before their time, deprived the public of the learned senator Pétau in 1614, but not before he left to posterity various interesting and valuable works which are now in the hands of the studious. In the poetry of Nicolas Bourbon there is an epitaph for Pétau which renders particular testimony to his books and curiosities; since it contributes to our subject, I shall quote it here.

> DEDICATED TO THE PIOUS SHADE AND TO THE MEMORY
>
> of Paul Pétau, Parisian senator; especially to be esteemed for the integrity of his life; celebrated throughout Europe for his knowledge of things divine and human, as evidenced by the published offspring of his genius; not only an authority on ancient law, but also a thorough student of all antiquity--of age-old rites and of primitive seals and coins which contribute to classical learning. For him, struck down by a premature death, Pallas and Astraea feel equal loss and sorrow, and both join his funeral procession; and his wife, his son-in-law and successor in public office, and his surviving children have erected to their beloved husband, father-in-law, and parent this little monument of their enduring grief.
>
> Only Pétau's bones are left on earth; his soul is engrafted
> On the stars. For the deserved praise of a better time
> And because he was weary of our corrupt age, he hastened
> his journey to heaven. Though subject to that fate,
> Like a restored Astraea he seemed to show to a condemned
>   world
> A strength of an extraordinary kind, and virtues rivaling
> Cato's. Yet even when he turned to the Palladian arts, as
>   he frequently did,
> He succeeded in penetrating into the hidden recesses of
>   ancient times;
> Whatever the long years concealed in alien gloom,
> He learned. Behold, this man's knowledge was so venerable
>   that
> It deceived the unreliable Lachesis; for however wide his
>   knowledge,
> At his death he had hardly knocked at the door of his
> Tenth lustrum: it is false that length of life is predictable.

---

[237] Duchesne and Sirmond have already been mentioned above (nn. 131 and 171 respectively).

He died on the 17th of September in the year of our Lord 1614, at the age of 46 years, 4 months, and 2 days[238][L].

Paul Pétau's son, M. Alexandre Pétau, is also a councillor in the Paris Parlement, and mirrors his father's virtues and goals. Every day he enlarges this library of the best printed books and manuscripts.[239] For example, he bought many

---

[238] Nicolas (II) Bourbon (1574-1644) studied under Jean Passerat at Paris, held a professorship of Greek in the Collège royal, and was admitted to the Academy in 1637. He received a pension of two hundred crowns from Richelieu. His contemporaries considered him to be a foremost--if not the foremost--Latin poet of the time (see René Kerviler, "Nicolas Bourbon," La Champagne à l'Académie française [Paris: H. Menu, 1877]). From about 1620 to his death in 1644, Bourbon was the center of an erudite group which met in his rooms at the Oratory. Among his intimate friends were Patin (Packard, pp. xvii-xviii), Naudé, Gassendi, Colletet, Ménage, and Balzac (Bourbon and Balzac were eventually reconciled after their quarrel in 1628). "Although primarily attracted by Bourbon's profound knowledge of Latin and Greek literature and the pleasant and instructive conversation drawn from his wide learning and long experience in the literary world of Paris, the discussions of these independent spirits covered an unusually wide field" (de Boer, PMLA, LIII, 737). Jacob had contact with Bourbon in "le cabinet Dupuy" (see below, n. 244). The Pétau epitaph appears in Bourbon's Poematia exposita (2 vols.; Parisiis: R. Sara, 1630-1633), I, 157-58; it consists of dactylic hexameters. Some minor difficulties in Jacob's text of the epitaph have been resolved by comparison with this edition.

[239] Alexandre Pétau was received as councillor on February 11, 1628 (Blanchard, Pt. II, p. 123). At the time Jacob wrote, he certainly did "mirror his father's virtues and goals," as can be seen from his 1645 catalog of his library, published at least in part by Montfaucon, I, 61-96. However, subsequent events were to paint a much different picture of him. In 1650, having lost interest in his library, he sold almost all the manuscripts in it to Queen Christina of Sweden, and the rest of the family collection was dispersed far and wide. Some manuscripts entered the libraries of Mazarin, Claude Joly, Bigot, Séguier, and Harlay; Baluze later obtained a number of printed books from the collection. The general result was tragic: "thus vanished one of the finest manuscript collections which had existed in France" (Delisle, I, 289; cf. III, 367). Moreover, as one of those commissioned by Parlement to witness the sale of the Mazarin library during the Fronde, Alexandre Pétau apparently obtained manuscripts for himself by underhanded methods--if we can believe Naudé, who of course was profoundly disturbed by the sale (see Naudé's letter of January 9, 1652 to Mazarin, quoted in Franklin, Histoire de la Bibliothèque Mazarine, p. 83; cf. pp. 87-88).

manuscripts from the library of the late M. Jean de Saint-André, canon of Notre Dame and councillor in the Grand Chamber; these are very rare, for they include some Greek manuscripts from Calabria which Cardinal Sirleto sent to Saint-André for his library.[240]

M. Louis Phélypeaux, knight, lord of La Vrillière, royal councillor, king's secretary, and grand master of ceremonies of the order of the Knights of the Holy Spirit, performs important duties in the affairs of state, but does not neglect to have good books ferreted out to embellish the sumptuous library which he has established in his palace.[241]

M. Phélypeaux

The library of M. Duplessis, baron of Montbart in Burgundy and councillor of state, is composed of the best available books in all fields of knowledge. This collection shows how great his literary knowledge is; and I can affirm that his fine reputation and intellectual acumen place him among the most accomplished men of our time.[242]

M. Duplessis

---

[240] On the library of Jean de Saint-André, see below, the text at n. 282.

[241] Louis Phélypeaux was made councillor of state on December 20, 1620, secretary of state on June 26, 1629, and commander, provost, and master of ceremonies of the orders of the king on April 1, 1643; he died in 1681 at the age of eighty-three (Moréri, VIII, Pt. 2, 259). Some additional data on the Phélypeaux family library are given by Delisle, II, 20, 286.

[242] Christophe Duplessis (d. 1672) eventually retired to the Séminaire des Missions Étrangères, and willed his book collection to this institution, which had been founded at Paris in 1663. A manuscript catalog of the bequest, which tripled the size of the Séminaire library, still exists (Franklin, Les anciennes bibliothèques ..., III, 164-66; Delisle, II, 258).

M. du Plessis de Guénégaud, secretary of state, is

reputed to be very well versed in the liberal

M. du Plessis arts and in the discovery of the most inter-
de Guénégaud esting books that can be found. With such he

adorns and enriches the magnificent library

which he has begun.[243]

If the Muses owe some gratitude to those who court them with great success, they are signally indebted to the brothers Pierre and Jacques Dupuy, sons of Claude Dupuy, a councillor

in the Paris Parlement. Pierre is a councillor
MM. Dupuy of state and Jacques is prior of Saint-Sauveur;

and besides being extraordinarily learned, they have a strong passion for good books, and fill their renowned library with them. This library consists of more than 8000 volumes, including divers ancient manuscripts which came from their father, and others which they added through their great diligence. Moreover, Pierre Dupuy has a collection of manuscript books to the number of 600 volumes, and these contain some memoirs relating to the history of France, to public affairs, and to fascinating, out-of-the-way subjects.[244]

---

[243] Henri de Guénégaud became secretary of state in 1643, keeper of the seals of the orders of the king in 1656, and died in 1676 at the age of sixty-seven (Moréri, V, Pt. 2, 426).

[244] On the contents of the magnificent Dupuy library, see Delisle, I, 262-64, III, 363, 392; Franklin, Les anciennes bibliothèques ..., II, 166-68, 171; Henri Omont, "Inventaire des manuscrits de Claude Dupuy (1595)," Bibliothèque de l'École des Chartes, LXXVI (1915), 526-31; and Léon Dorez (ed.), Catalogue de la collection Dupuy (3 vols.; Paris: E. Leroux, 1899-1928). Naudé's high regard for this library has already been indicated (nn. 152, 227). The care with which the library was built up is evident from the fact that when new books of interest appeared--in France or elsewhere--the brothers Dupuy would order two or

The Recollect fathers have established a great li-
The library of the brary in their monastery in the Saint-
Recollect fathers Martin quarter. There one finds many

---

three copies to be printed on their own special paper, or would have perfect copies made by combining the best pages of a number of less perfect copies (Peiresc, I, 270; III, 132). Primary source biographical data on the brothers Dupuy are provided by Johann Albrecht Portner, Elegia in obitum ... Jacobi Puteani (Parisiis: E. Martinus, 1657), and Nicolas Rigault, Vita Petri Puteani (reprinted in Bates, pp. 660-69). Pierre and Jacques Dupuy were the presiding geniuses of "le cabinet Dupuy," which from 1617 to 1661 "was the sturdiest of the private assemblies of Paris, and in some ways the most desirable circle into which a Parisian could obtain entry" (Harcourt Brown, p. 6). "Originating in the erudite meetings of Turnèbe, Lambin, Scaliger, Casaubon, Sainte-Marthe, Pierre and François Pithou in the famous library of président de Thou, its great reputation had already been established by 1616. After the death of its founder in 1617, the cabinet continued to function under the direction of the medieval historians, Pierre and Jacques Du Puy, who had been left in charge of his library in the rue des Poictevins. When Pierre Du Puy became intendant de la Bibliothèque du Roi in 1645, the cabinet moved with him to his new quarters in the rue de la Harpe, where it passed through the most brilliant period of its existence, over which Jacques Du Puy presided after the death of his brother in 1651. When Jacques in turn died in 1656, the meetings continued at the home of Jacques-Auguste de Thou, the son of the founder, until financial reverses forced him to leave Paris in 1661. . . . Throughout its long career, the cabinet Du Puy never lost its original purpose of providing an opportunity for scholars and writers to discuss their problems in the midst of a rich collection of precious manuscripts and books, which steadily increased in value and scope as the cabinet broadened its own connections and interests. The fine historical library of its founder was enriched in 1617 by the notable collection of Claude Du Puy, conseiller au Parlement, an authority on law and an enthusiastic student of antiquity. His sons Pierre and Jacques also built up a very unusual library of their own, which particularly served the needs of the cabinet since it had been assembled at the instigation and often with the direct aid of its members. For it was through the help of the bibliophiles Peiresc, Naudé, Bouilliau, Luillier and their own wide correspondence with foreign scholars, librarians and dealers that these keen and avid collectors satisfied their zeal for investigation not only in the medieval field but also in Greek and Latin literature, both ancient and modern. The meetings took place in this library every afternoon. At the height of its fame, the cabinet often had as many as fifty members present, although admission was strictly limited and highly prized" (de Boer, PMLA, LIII, 730-33). Among the prominent members of the Dupuy cabinet were, besides those already mentioned, Nicolas Rigault, Bignon, Deodati, Charles de Montchal, Saumaise, du Vair,

good books of theology and history.[245]

One of the large and excellent libraries of Paris is that of M. Jacques Ribier, formerly councillor of the court, and now councillor of state.[246] If one considers

M. Ribier the quality of the books, one will find that the rarest are there; if one regards their quantity, the library yields to few in Paris--for the number of books reaches 9500. This library includes the book collection of the late Guillaume du Vair, a very learned man, a first president of the Parlement of Aix in Provence, later keeper of the

Du Cange, Denis Petau, Jacques Sirmond, René Moreau, Jean Bourdelot, Nicolas Bourbon, Gilbert Gaulmin, Grotius, André Duchesne, Abel and Louis de Sainte-Marthe, Marolles, Gassendi, Mersenne, Gui Patin, de Sève, Jean Besly, Balzac, Ménage, Sarasin, La Mothe le Vayer, and our author Louis Jacob; foreign scholars who visited the cabinet included Daniel and Nicolas Heinsius, Gronovius, Holstein, Gruter, Vossius, Lambeck, Philip Pareus, Portner, Camden, Robert Cotton, Campanella (the author of The City of the Sun), and Abraham Wicquefort, to whom Jacob dedicated the last (1654) issue of his Bibliographia Gallica universalis (see ibid., pp. 731-32, 734; Harcourt Brown, pp. 1-16; Isaac Uri, Un cercle savant au XVIIe siècle. François Guyet, 1575-1655 [Paris: Hachette, 1886], pp. 1-63; and Pintard, Le libertinage érudit ..., pp. 92-101, who treats this example of "la société érudite" as one of the prime background factors for the "libertinage érudit" manifested in such avant-garde circles as that of Naudé). It was undoubtedly through the Dupuy cabinet that Jacob obtained much of his information on the private scholarly libraries of his time. Jacob's special regard for Pierre and Jacques Dupuy is indicated by the fact that he dedicated the 1649 volume of his Bibliographia Parisina (for 1647-1648) to them.

[245]The subsequent history of this library is described in Franklin, Les anciennes bibliothèques ..., II, 297-300.

[246]Jacques Ribier, brother of the better-known Guillaume Ribier, produced two works on statecraft (Mémoires et advis concernant les charges de M. les chanceliers et gardes des sceaux de France, 1629, and Discours sur le gouvernement des monarchies, 1630); contemporary testimonies to the value of his library were provided not only by Jacob, but also by Naudé and by Blanchot (see above, nn. 152 and 153 respectively).

seals of France, and ultimately bishop of Lisieux. In his will he bequeathed his library to his nephew, the Bishop de Riez, and after the latter's death the books were turned over to M. Ribier because his wife was related to these bishops.[247]

M. Nicolas Rigault, councillor in the Parlement of Metz and keeper of the royal library, has acquired great renown for

M. Rigault   his erudition and his knowledge of the Greek tongue, as his published translations and commentaries testify. The exquisiteness of his personal library is due to the selection of good books with which he has stocked it.[248]

The merits of M. Jean Riolan, first physician to the queen mother, and royal professor of medicine, are well known

M. Riolan   to all members of the medical profession by reason of the learning which he continually demonstrates through his writings. These books are not less admirable than those of his illustrious father and fellow physician, Jean Riolan. The two cooperated in the building of that noble library which the son possesses today.[249]

---

[247] Jacques Ribier's wife, the former Françoise Alleaume, was the daughter of Antoinette Alleaume, née du Vair, sister of Guillaume du Vair (Moréri, IX, Pt. 1, 173). Guillaume du Vair (1556-1621) a member of "le cabinet Dupuy" (see n. 244) and an intimate friend of Peiresc (see Peiresc, I, 5-6, and Guillaume du Vair, Lettres inédites, ed. Philippe Tamizey de Larroque [Paris: A. Aubry, 1873], pp. 22, 25), wrote a number of treatises, especially on Biblical subjects, and did some fine translations of classical authors (Jean-Pierre Nicéron, XLIII, 114-64).

[248] On Rigault, see above, nn. 49 and 71. A catalog of Rigault's manuscript collection has been provided by Philippe Labbe, Nova bibliotheca mss. librorum (Parisiis: J. Henault, 1653), p. 370. Many of these manuscripts entered the Bibliothèque du roi after Rigault's death in 1654 (Delisle, I, 261, 295).

[249] On Jean Riolan the elder (1539-1606) and younger (1577-1657), see Hirsch, IV, 822-23. Jean Riolan the younger

177

Everyone acquainted with the literary realm has high regard for the Sainte-Marthe family, which has produced those two excellent historians of France, Louis and Scévole. These twin brothers and advocates in Parlement own a delightful library of historical works, and they augment it constantly.[250]

<u>MM. de Sainte-Marthe</u>

And consider the library of M. Antoine de Sève, son of Guillaume, lord of Saint Julian, who was royal councillor and in 1625 held the post of treasurer of savings; brother of MM. Jean and Alexandre, councillors of state, etc.; abbot of the Île en Barrois under the bishop of Verdun; councillor and chaplain to the king; and a member of the distinguished family of the marquis de Sève in Piedmont, from which comes Cardinal Sève, recently created such by our holy father Pope Urban VIII. This erudite abbot Antoine de Sève is very interested in good books, and assiduously searches

<u>M. de Seve</u>

---

is remembered negatively for his bitter opposition to Harvey's demonstration of the circulation of the blood, and for betraying Marie de Médicis' confidence by spying on her for Richelieu; however, "he made some advances, describing the fat appendices of the colon, naming the hepatic duct, and observing that the common bile-duct had but one membrane which served as a valve" (Packard, p. 168). Riolan the younger was a member of Patin's circle (see above, n. 233), and the two had great personal and professional respect for each other; when in 1654, because of age and illness, Riolan gave up his professorship in the Collège royal, he resigned in favor of Patin (<u>ibid</u>., pp. 171-73; cf. also pp. 56, 91, 145, 167-69, 254, 314). The quality of Riolan's library is attested not only by Jacob, but also by Naudé, himself a physician, who considered the library to be one of the four best medical book collections in Paris (see above, n. 199).

[250]On the Sainte-Marthe family, see above, n. 74. Papers and manuscripts from the family library later entered the Oratorian seminary library in the abbey of Saint-Magloire (Delisle, II, 258).

for them to embellish his famous library of more than 6000 volumes on all varieties of subjects.[251]

The august Collège de Sorbonne is the arsenal of the Muses and the Areopagus for the world's learned men; and that

<u>The Sorbonne</u>   is why it has a very fine library, for its collection is made up of the books which many doctors of the Sorbonne have bequeathed to it as tokens of their affection. The reader, knowing this, can imagine the quality of the books, both printed and in manuscript, which are preserved there.[252]

M. Jean Tilleman Stella of Sighen in the county[253] of Hesse in Germany, son of Christopher Tilleman and grandson of

<u>M. Stella</u>   Tilemann, is known by his writings as are his father and grandfather. He is a councillor of state and royal professor of mathematics, and is widely recognized for his fine mind and for the intense passion with which he seeks out rare and interesting books to embellish his distinguished library. There one sees, besides a great

---

[251] Antoine may have been the de Sève who was a member of "le cabinet Dupuy" (see n. 244 above), although it is reported that Imbert de Sève, who became a councillor in the Paris Parlement in 1634, was "tous les jours au cabinet et a la bibliothèque de M. de Thou" (Duleau, <u>Revue nobiliaire héraldique et biographique</u>, I, 123). The "treasurer of savings" <u>(tresorier de l'epargne)</u> "received sums collected by the state and, by order of the superintendent of finances, released the funds necessary for public expenditures" (Chéruel, II, 1226). Jean de Sève is mentioned in Blanchard, Pt. II, p. 120, as having been received as councillor in the Paris Parlement on July 9, 1621.

[252] On the history of the Sorbonne library, see especially Alfred Franklin, <u>La Sorbonne, ses origines, sa bibliothèque</u> (2d ed.; Paris: L. Willem, 1875).

[253] Strictly, landgraviate.

number of printed works, more than three hundred manuscripts, some of them very rare.²⁵⁴ A portion of these rare manuscripts comes from the library of Jacob Spiegel, who was secretary to

J. Spiegel   Emperor Maximilian, and who had acquired the book collection of his uncle, Jacob Wimpheling; both Spiegel and Wimpheling were scholars famous for their publications.²⁵⁵

The reputation of the noble de Thou family is known throughout Europe, for the family has produced those great

De Thou   personnages August de Thou, president of Parlement; Christophe de Thou, first president of the same Parlement, chancellor to Henri, duke of Orléans, and later to François, duke of Anjou; and President à mortier Jacques-Auguste de Thou, who wrote in Latin that fine history

---

²⁵⁴Jean Tilleman Stella (d. 1647) "is a somewhat mysterious figure. Known under the name Stella and also bearing the title of lord of Tercy and of Morimont, Jean Tilleman, originally of Zweibrücken, made his fortune in France. Chavigny became his patron; then he served as secretary to the count of Avaux [Claude de Mesme, son of Jean-Jacques de Mesme] at Hamburg (to 1638). Three years later Richelieu sent him to Brisach to search the archives there for claims which could justify the encroachments of the Austrian house in Alsace. In 1644, he was in Strassburg as resident minister for the king, and there he died. He was intimately acquainted with the scholars of his time, and had been named professor of the mathematical sciences at the Collège royal" (Bourgeois, entry 1863; cf. entry 2850). Patin had a low opinion of his scholarly abilities, but this may have resulted simply from the fact that Stella idolized Richelieu, whereas Patin despised him (Patin, Lettres, ed. Reveillé-Parise, I, 358-59). On Tilemann Stella (1524/25-1589), see ADB, XXXVI, 32-33.

²⁵⁵Spiegel and Wimpheling have been mentioned above (see n. 198). The ADB, XXXV, 156-58, provides an excellent biographical sketch of Spiegel. Data on Wimpheling and his library are available in Joseph Knepper, Jakob Wimpfeling ("Erläuterungen und Ergänzungen zu Janssens Geschichte des deutschen Volkes," III, 2-4; Freiburg i. Br.: Herder, 1902); Richard Newald, Elsässische Charakterköpfe aus dem Zeitalter des Humanismus (Kolmar: Verlag Alsatia, 1944), pp. 55-84; and HB, III, 546-47.

of his times, and who spent forty years building the extensive and exquisite library which he left to his family.[256] At present the head of the family is his son, Jacques-Auguste de Thou, councillor of state and of the Court of Parlement, and rightful heir of his father's virtues. Jacques-Auguste the elder speaks thus of the library in his testament:

> I forbid the division, sale, or dispersion of my library, which I have collected with great diligence and at great expense for over forty years, and which it is important to preserve entire not only for my family, but also for the literary world. I declare my library, together with my ancient gold, silver, and copper coins, to be common property among those sons of mine who will work zealously at literary pursuits; but I do so with the stipulation that it be made accessible for public use to other philologians and also to foreigners. Until my sons grow up, I intrust its custody to Pierre Dupuy, my kinsman, dear to me for many reasons; he will have authority to give manuscript books for the use of those who need them-- provided that suitable care is taken for their return.[257][L]

This library contains more than 8000 of the rarest and most fascinating volumes to be obtained (at enormous expense) in Europe; they are all bound in gilded calf and morocco--still another sign of the great lavishness of that Parnassus of the

---

[256] August de Thou (d. 1544) was President Jacques-Auguste de Thou's grandfather; Christophe de Thou (d. 1582) was his father (see Jean-Baptiste de L'Hermite, Les eloges de tous les premiers presidens du Parlement de Paris [Paris: Cardin Besongne, 1645], pp. 73-76). It was to Christophe de Thou that Jacques-Auguste de Thou "owed his great love of history and of fine books" (Henry Harrisse, Le président de Thou et ses descendants, leur célèbre bibliothèque, leurs armoiries, et les traductions françaises de "J.-A. Thuani Historiarum sui temporis" [Paris: Henri Leclerc, 1905], pp. 71-72). Jean Grolier presented Christophe de Thou with four of the most beautiful books in his library; this gives some indication of the quality of Christophe de Thou's collection (Le Roux de Lincy, Researches concerning Jean Grolier, p. 69). A very full bibliography of works dealing with the de Thou library is given in Franklin, Les anciennes bibliothèques ..., II, 179. See also nn. 64, 153, and 244 above.

[257] Quoted also by Lomeier; see Lomeier, sec. "France," n. 6.

Muses.²⁵⁸ As for the library's manuscripts, it seems to have thousands, and all of high reputation; they daily serve as bases for printed editions, as one sees from the published books.

The intimate friendship between the late M. de Thou and the late M. Nicolas Lefèvre, tutor to King Louis XIII and a man of exceptional erudition, caused the latter to bequeath all his manuscripts to that library. We are told this by the learned Scévole de Sainte-Marthe in his eulogy of Lefèvre: "And though he carefully and diligently regarded them all in turn, yet there was no one he esteemed with more fondness than that remarkable ornament and embellishment of our time, Jacques-Auguste de Thou, to whom, when he was dying, he bequeathed by his last will and testament all his manuscript books (and he had brought together a most ample collection of them)"²⁵⁹[L]. François Le Bègue,

---

²⁵⁸In order to see this 8000-volume figure (which is valid for 1644) in proper perspective, it should be noted that the de Thou library was undergoing constant growth during the seventeenth century. By 1653, according to a letter from its librarian Ismaël Boulliau to Storino, it had increased to about 11,000 volumes. A catalog of ca. 1656 lists some 12,545 books. In 1659, Boulliau gives the total as not less than 13,000 volumes. Quesnel's catalog of 1679 lists some 13,178 books (Harrisse, pp. 73-74). Thus, in spite of the fact that Jacob's Traicté is the "principal source of what is generally related concerning the library of the de Thou family" (ibid., p. 217), one should not overgeneralize on the basis of his data, as has been done by writers on the subject. "As for the binding, the books were far from being all bound in gilded calf or morocco. Of a hundred de Thou volumes examined at random in the Bibliothèque Nationale, more than a third were bound in simple calf or vellum, or even in sheepskin--but all had the coat of arms and monograms of the family of de Thou de Meslay" (ibid.). It is possible, of course, that the less expensive bindings were not used until after Jacob wrote concerning the library; but it is more probable that at this point our author employs hyperbole.

²⁵⁹Scévole (I) de Sainte-Marthe, p. 275; Sainte-Marthe's text gives "observaret" and "maiore" for the impossible readings "observant" and "maior" in Jacob's quotation. Nicolas Lefèvre or Lefebvre (d. 1612) provides the historian with valuable information

royal advocate in the Court of Monies of France, speaks of this library in the life of Lefèvre which he prefaced to the <u>Opuscules</u> of that learned man: "In his leisure he provided himself with a library which was very well stocked with published books and manuscript volumes, and he collected, annotated, and surveyed with incredible care and effort all the writings of the ancients" [L]. And farther on he has more to say: "With the exception of a few books which he left to me, by his last will he bequeathed all the manuscripts in his library to Jacques-Auguste de Thou, that most honorable president of Parlement"[260][L]. Father Jean de Saint-Francis, general of the Feuillants, in his funeral oration for M. Lefèvre, also speaks of his book collecting:

> What more? As another Solon, he wished to grow old while always learning something new--preferring to learn more from others than they from him, for he

---

on the early education and character traits of Louis XIII; see, for example, Louis Batiffol, <u>Le roi Louis XIII à vingt ans</u> (Paris: Calmann-Lévy, 1910), pp. 108-109, 114-15, 132. A primary source biographical sketch of Lefèvre is given by Hilarion de Coste in his <u>Histoire catholique où sont descrites les vies, faicts, et actions heroïques & signalees des hommes et dames illustres, qui ... se sont rendus recommandables dans les XVI. & XVII. siècles</u> (Paris: P. Chevalier, 1625), pp. 699-708; see also Jean Boivin, <u>Petri Pithoei vita, elogia, opera, bibliotheca</u> (Parisiis: F. Jouenne, 1716), pp. 22, 67, 80, and Pierre-Jean Grosley, <u>Vie de Pierre Pithou</u> (2 vols.; Paris: G. Cavelier, 1756), I, 31. Delisle, I, 470, transcribes from manuscript the clauses of Lefèvre's will (October 23, 1612) in which he bequeathed his library to de Thou, and also demonstrates that Lefèvre had given some books to his friend even before that date.

[260]Two learned economic treatises by François Le Bègue are cited in Bourgeois, entries 6594 and 6601: his <u>Raisons et motifs de l'édit et règlement général des monnaies du mois de decembre 1614</u> (1615), and his <u>Consultation au fait des monnaies</u> (1627). Jacob quotes Nicolas Lefèvre, <u>Opuscula</u>, ed. François Le Bègue (Parisiis, 1614), signatures ē [sic] 3^v, and ō [sic] 2^v; in the first of Jacob's quotations, an "et," necessary to the sense of the sentence, has been restored on the basis of Le Bègue's text. On the Court of Monies, see above, n. 235.

held himself in little esteem. Thus one can gather to what high point of erudition he attained, seeing that he spent his entire life in the study of fine literature and in the preservation of the most scholarly productions of the French mind (being himself endowed with an uncommonly fine intellect). These French works were part of an extraordinary quantity of good books of all kinds, especially ancient manuscripts, which he had brought together from all quarters with unbelievable diligence and at incredible cost.[261]

With these testimonies as background, we return to M. de Thou. Numerous learned persons have praised his library, and I shall quote some of them to show the public how much they esteem it. First we have Henri Estienne, who, in his commentary on Aulus Gellius, addresses the illustrious President Jacques-Auguste as follows:[262]

> Lucian criticizes and ridicules a certain unlearned man who was buying many books; for a letter, or rather, short oration of his is extant in which he inveighs against a certain ἀπαίδευτος, πολλὰ βιβλία ὠνούμενος [ignorant fellow spending money on a great number of books].[263] Now to the same extent he held that man in derision, he would, in my opinion, have held you in honor; as much as he condemned him, he would, I maintain,

---

[261] [Jean Goulu (in religion: Jean de Saint-Francis)], Discours funèbre sur le trespas de M° Nicolas Le Febvre (2d ed.; Paris: J. de Heuqueville, 1616), pp. 31-32. On Goulu, see above, n. 143; contact between Lefèvre and Goulu is evidenced by the fact that Lefèvre presented a valuable manuscript to Goulu (Delisle, II, 252; III, 293).

[262] Henri Estienne (ed.), Auli Gellii Noctes Atticae (Parisiis, 1585), Pt. II, pp. 83-84. On Henri Estienne, see Theodore Jansson ab Almeloveen, De vitis Stephanorum (Amstelaedami: Janssonio-Waasberg, 1683); Antoine-Augustin Renouard, Annales de l'imprimerie des Estienne (2 vols., 2d ed. reprinted; New York: Burt Franklin, 1960), II, 364-477; Feugère, pp. 1-264; Louis Clément, Henri Estienne et son oeuvre française (Paris: A. Picard, 1899); and cf. Elizabeth Armstrong, Robert Estienne (Cambridge: University Press, 1954), passim.

[263] Estienne refers to the second-century satirist Lucian's diatribe, Πρὸς τὸν ἀπαίδευτον καὶ πολλὰ βιβλία ὠνούμενον ("The Ignorant Book Collector"), see Lucian, ed. and tr. A. M. Harmon, III ("Loeb Classical Library"; London: Heinemann, 1921), 174-211, especially 182-83.

have praised you--not as an ἀπαίδευτος [uneducated person], but as a πολλαχῶς εὐπαίδευτος [broadly educated man] who with all vigor applies himself zealously to collecting books from everywhere, and spares no expense in bringing together a library which will ultimately be filled full with every kind of Latin and Greek book, especially the latter. Yes indeed, the fact that you apply such careful judgment in the choice of printed editions, the fact that the more a volume costs you, the more valuable a binding (as it were, clothing) you bestow upon it--your diligence and ardor in these matters also he would not have left unpraised, unless I am badly mistaken. For my part certainly, not only do I praise that ardent passion for daily augmenting the library, but I in fact desire to yield to you in every way. . . . [L]

Also, I find that Isaac Casaubon, in writing to François Vertunien, a famous physician of Poitiers (letter 163), has the following opinion of it:[264] "I am using your Celsus; when I was recently discussing it with the great de Thou and we were in his library, he immediately took out of a bookcase comprising part of that very opulent book collection of his a codex of the archphysician Capellanus, and showed it to me" [L]. The more the acclaim comes from persons of exalted position, the more credible and well received it is. Thus the crowning praise of this library is reserved for a sovereign Roman pope, Leo XI. Before his pontificate he was a legate to France for the peace treaty drawn up at Vervins between the Catholic and the most

---

[264]This letter appears, with slight verbal variations, as No. 470 in the 2d ed. of Casaubon's correspondence: Isaac Casaubon, Epistolae, ed. Johann Georg Graevius (2d ed.; Magdeburgi: Gerlach & Beckenstein, 1656), p. 528. Vertunien (Vertunianus) was a student of Laurent Joubert in Montpellier, and produced Hippocratis Coi De capitis vulneribus liber, latinitate donatus ... commentarius in eundem (Lutetiae: M. Patissonius, 1578); see Ernst Gurlt, Geschichte der Chirurgie (3 vols.; Berlin: A. Hirschwald, 1898), II, 830. By "Capellanus" Casaubon may mean the twelfth-thirteenth century Salerno surgeon Rolando Capelluti (Hirsch, IV, 860). "Celsus" of course refers to the first-century Roman medical writer Aurelius (or Aulus) Cornelius Celsus.

Christian kings;²⁶⁵ then he came to Paris and heard about the de Thou library. He desired to visit it, and he was so pleased with it that he confessed that he had never seen a finer library in Italy. After these commendatory remarks, it is unnecessary to search for others besides, for these proceed from him who is the true oracle of the world. But note also that in 1625 the legate to France Cardinal Barberini viewed the library with admiration.²⁶⁶

We have still to say that M. Dupuy (named above in de Thou's testament) employs all his energies in enriching this library. Lately many good books have been added to it from the library of the late M. Picardet, attorney general in the

M. Picardet

Parlement of Dijon and father-in-law of the present councillor de Thou.²⁶⁷ Moreover,

---

²⁶⁵Leo XI (Alessandro de' Medici) was elected pope at age seventy and served in that capacity only twenty-seven days (d. 1605) He was completely pro-French in his sympathies. The peace of Vervins (1598) between the Spanish crown and Henry IV of France confirmed the treaty of Cateau-Cambrésis and, by restoring Spanish conquests to France, made clear that Spain no longer had the power to conquer or dismember France.

²⁶⁶I.e., Francesco Barberini (1597-1679), who served as librarian of the Vatican and collected a fine library of his own, the catalog of which was published in two folio volumes at Rome in 1681. On him, see Carlo Frati, Dizionario bio-bibliografico dei bibliotecari e bibliofili italiani dal sec. XIV al XIX ("Biblioteca di bibliografia italiana," No. 13; Firenze: Olschki, 1933), pp. 48-49.

²⁶⁷I.e., Jacques-Auguste (II) de Thou; "his love of books and of fine bindings equaled even that of his illustrious father-- so much so . . . that he doubled the patrimonial collection" (Harrisse, pp. 7-8, and see passim for detailed information on him). In the catalogs of the de Thou library only a single volume is specifically designated as coming from the library of Hugues Picardet, who died in 1641, three years before the marriage on February 5, 1644 of his only daughter to Jacques-Auguste (II); Harrisse therefore considers it very doubtful that Picardet's

President de Thou had purchased the ancient manuscripts from the library of M. Pierre Pithou, sieur de Savoye, advocate in the Paris Parlement, and celebrated jurist and historian, who died at Nogent-sur-Seine in 1596, at the age of fifty-seven.[268]

M. Pithou

The very learned Jacques Davy, cardinal Duperron, never ceased to contribute to the realm of letters, both by the outstanding works he published and by the fine library he provided for the Franciscan Tertiaries of the monastery of Picpus.[269]

The Tertiaries of St. Francis

M. du Tillet, chief clerk of the Paris Parlement, owns the famous library of the late MM. Jean du Tillet, bishop of Meaux, and Jean du Tillet, another clerk of the same Parlement; their bequest consisted of books

M. du Tillet

---

library was incorporated into the de Thou collection (ibid., pp. 8, 60, 169, 225).

[268] For further information on the dispostion of Pierre Pithou's library, see above, n. 173.

[269] Duperron (1556-1618), a convert from Protestantism who became bishop of Évreux, was a powerful opponent of the Huguenots. He was presented to the French king by Philippe Desportes, and became a royal reader and ardent supporter of the Collège de France. Later he instructed Henry IV in the Catholic faith, converted Henri de Sponde to Catholicism, and argued eloquently against Duplessis Mornay. (For general biographical information, see Pierre Féret, Le cardinal Du Perron [Paris: Didier, 1881], and fates, passim.) Duperron's library was situated at Bagnolet; he retired to his elegant mansion there toward the end of his life, and devoted himself entirely to study. His bibliophilistic interests are illustrated by the fact that he even maintained his own printing press at Bagnolet. His legacy of much of his personal book collection to the Penitents of Picpus constituted the origin of this monastic library (Jean de Burigny, Vie du cardinal Du Perron [Paris: Debure, 1768], p. 368; Franklin, Les anciennes bibliothèques ..., II, 287). It is known that not all of Duperron's books went to Picpus, for the abbey of Saint-Taurin d'Évreux received manuscripts which had belonged to him (Delisle, I, 370; II, 412).

on French history. Eulogies to both of them are provided by Scévole de Sainte-Marthe.[270]

M. de Versigni The library of M. Hector de Marle, sieur de Versigni, president of the Chamber of Accounts, is highly regarded for its good books. With great care its owner continually seeks such books for it.[271]

M. de Vic M. Dominique de Vic, archbishop of Auch in Gascony, preserves the library of his late father, M. Méry de Vic, keeper of the seals of France. Méry de Vic was a man of great diplomacy and probity, as he demonstrated in the offices he held in the kingdom; and he left children who reflect his virtues.[272]

---

[270]Scévole (I) de Sainte-Marthe, pp. 93-94. The du Tillet who was Jacob's contemporary was also named Jean; he died in 1646 (Victor Le Gris, Généalogie de la maison de du Tillet [Chartres, 1701], p. 13). After du Tillet's death, Naudé purchased for Mazarin, at a cost of 125 pounds, a quantity of "manuscripts of all kinds" from his library, but the titles of these manuscripts are not known (Delisle, I, 285). On Bishop Jean du Tillet (d. November 19, 1570), and his brother Jean du Tillet (d. October 2, 1570) who began a virtual dynasty of clerks of Parlement, see La Croix du Maine, I, 594-97, where the following statement is made concerning the Bishop: "I have heard that, as compared with any other prelate of his time, he had the best stocked library--the one best supplied with all sorts of good authors." The library interests of the two brothers are evidenced by their extensive writings (Moréri, X, Pt. 1, 188).

[271]Here Jacob adds: "It will be necessary to place this library at the letter H." Since Christophe Hector de Marle, sieur de Versigni (d. 1658) is ordinary alphabetized under neither H nor V, but under M (for Marle), it has been thought best to leave the entry where it stands to lessen confusion; in so doing, we follow the spirit rather than the letter of our author's injunction, which was certainly designed to increase the clarity of his work. On Marle, see Moréri, VII, 263, and Blanchard, Pt. I, p. 96, no. 6.

[272]On Dominique de Vic (d. 1661) and Méry (Emery) de Vic (d. 1622), see Moréri, X, Pt. 1, 580, and Le Roux de Lincy, Researches concerning Jean Grolier, pp. 85-87. The de Vic library

Everyone knows in what esteem the library of the abbey of Saint-Victor is held because of its great abundance of manuscripts.[273] It is estimated that there are up to 1500 manuscripts in a particular main building constructed expressly for the purpose in the year 1501 by Nicaise Delorme, thirty-third abbot of Saint-Victor.[274] I find that very many authors assert that the library owes the glory of its attainments to King Francis I, the patron of letters;[275] but Claude Hémeré, in his *University of Paris*, chap vi, assures us that as early as 1208, Pierre de Cambe, the bishop of Paris, when he was about to journey to the Holy Land, drew up his will and in it gave his library to that abbey: "We bequeath to the church of Saint-Victor our red chasuble, dalmatic, and tunicle, and our large library"[276][L]. Monburnus, in his *Stellarium*

The library of Saint-Victor

---

was substantially Grolier's book collection (see below, n. 298); the Grolier library "did not leave the hôtel de Vic until 1676, when it was sold" (*ibid*., p. 87).

[273] See above, n. 153. The history of this important collection is set forth by Franklin, *Les anciennes bibliothèques ...*, I, 135-85.

[274] That **Nicaise Delorme** (de Lorme, de Ulmo) began construction of a new library building in 1501 is attested by Jean de Toulouse, librarian of Saint-Victor, who died ca. 1641 (*ibid*., p. 148). The work was completed in 1508, owing in large part to the zealous efforts of Canon Guillaume Tupin or Turpin (*ibid*.).

[275] This erroneous view unhappily persisted even after the publication of Jacob's *Traicté*. One finds, for example, Pierre Le Gallois alleging at the end of the century that Saint-Victor had no library before the time of Francis I (Le Gallois, *Traitté des plus belles bibliothèques de l'Europe* [Paris: E. Michallet, 1680], p. 134). On Le Gallois, who frequently (but not in this instance) plagiarizes from Lomeier's *De bibliothecis*, see Lomeier, Editor's Introduction.

[276] Claude Hémeré, *De Academia Parisiensi* (Lutetiae:

Ecclesiae S. Victoris, after exhibiting many of the excellent merits of that order of Canons Regular and of the abbey of Saint-Victor, points to the library and records the poem of a learned and pious man named Cornelius Godensis, who thus addresses those who come to see the collection:[277]

> If you desire to see the works of grammarians,
>   rhetoricians, or poets--or the wealth of Machaon[278]--
> Or if you want to read the texts of Sophia,
>   or the deeds and accounts of the ancients, come here
>   in safety.
> Whatever a school brought forth from the grove of Academe,
>   whatever Seneca treats or the erudite Plato maintains,

S. Cramoisy, 1637), p. 59. On Hémeré, see above, n. 87. Concerning the gift of Pierre de Cambe (Chambellan, de Nemours), Jacob makes an understandable mistake. The clause in the will does indeed read, "Legamus ... Bibliothecam magnam," but by "bibliotheca magna" the bishop meant, not his "large library" (which he distributed among several monasteries), but his "large Bible," worth seventeen pounds at the time (Franklin, Les anciennes bibliothèques ..., I, 140). The use of the Latin bibliotheca for the collection of books comprising the Bible is attested in writings as early as 800 and as late as 1400 by J. H. Baxter and Charles Johnson (eds.), Medieval Latin Word-List from British and Irish Sources (London: Oxford University Press, 1934), p. 47. Franklin has been able to uncover information on book donations to Saint-Victor even earlier than Bishop Chambellan's; the earliest of the known donations was made at the beginning of the twelfth century (Franklin, Les anciennes bibliothèques ..., I, 138).

[277]These elegiac stanzas (incorrectly printed as dactylic hexameters in our text) are recorded also at the beginning of the 1513 catalog of the Saint-Victor library which was drawn up by Claude de Grandrue (de Grandivico), the first actual librarian of the collection; the first nine pages of this manuscript catalog are reproduced ibid., pp. 174-79. Following the poetical lines in this manuscript a more modern hand has added, also in Latin: "The author of this epigram is Cornelius Todensis [sic], a canon regular, as Johannes Monburnus testifies in the Stellarium S. Victoris Paris." Monburnus' Stellarium has not been located, and it is probably either a bibliographical ghost or a lost writing; in a letter of May 3, 1961, J. M. Edelstein, reference librarian, Rare Books Division, Library of Congress, writes: "I regret to say that we have been unable to identify any author with any form of the name Mon(t)burn(us)."

[278]Machaon was the son of Aesculapius; the poet alludes to medical writings.

Whatever Eratosthenes, Apuleius, or Ptolemy discusses--
   the right angle, or the finger, or the pole--
Whatever Aristotle taught on the governing of the Greeks,
   or the sacred laws proclaim, one can find here.
Hold fast in thy breast how many ideas occupy this place;
   what neither a victor nor any kingdom possesses
This Victor, full of love, here abundantly reveals--
   a treasure-store surpassing the riches of Croesus.
Now assuredly strive to give this in return for such
                              great gifts:
   carry off nothing, and let nothing be lost[279][L].

---

[279]Here in the original text follow the libraries of Isaac Habert and Jean de la Haye, with the statement: "These last two libraries came to my attention only when this sheet was being printed, and thus could not be entered in their correct order at the letter H." The paragraphs dealing with these libraries have now been moved to their proper alphabetic locations, in accord with the expressed intention of the author.

CHAPTER III (LXXXIV)

LIBRARIES OF PARIS WHICH HAVE BEEN DISPERSED[280]

M. François de Saint-André, president of Parlement, had built up a distinguished library incorporating that of G. Budé--as I remarked in discussing the library of the Jesuit fathers at the Collège de Clermont.[281] These Jesuits came into possession of the library of this president, whose son, Jean de Saint-André, was canon of Notre Dame and councillor in the Grand Chamber, and a man well versed in Greek and in sacred literature. He was no less intellectually curious than his father, and established an opulent library, which François de La Croix du Maine describes in his Bibliothèque as "full, rich, and replete with all kinds of books, especially manuscripts, many of which, previously unpublished, he causes to be printed--both Greek authors and Latin; we have this on the assured testimony of M. Feu-ardent, doctor of theology at Paris, in the prefatory letter to his

marginalia: The father of canon de Saint-André / Canon de Saint-André

---

[280] In actuality, there is no rigorous distinction of content between this chapter and the preceding one, since a number of dispersed libraries of Paris have already been treated. In the present chapter, however, our author concentrates on collections no longer in the hands of their original owners or families.

[281] See above, n. 172.

translation of Psellus, the text of which he obtained in Saint-André's library."[282] After J. de Saint-André's death, this library was sold to various persons, for M. Pétau bought many of its manuscripts, which today are still carefully preserved in the famous library of that councillor of the Court who is emulated to the same degree as was his late father.

M. Brisson

The library of President Barnabé Brisson, a great jurist of his time, was very highly thought of for its good books.[283] We are told this by Justus Sincerus, in his *Journey through France*.[284]

---

[282]La Croix du Maine, I, 586, where other testimonies to the canon's library are mentioned. François Feu-ardent (1541-1610), a prolific theological writer and controversialist, also receives biographical treatment *ibid.*, p. 217. Feu-ardent's comments on Canon de Saint-André's library appear in his preface to *Sapientiss. Michaelis Pselli, ... Dialogus de energia seu operatione daemonum e Graeco translatus, Petro Morello, ... interprete* (Parisiis: G. Chaudière, 1577). Jean de Saint-André's library has been mentioned above (see the text at n. 240).

[283]"Barnabé Brisson (1531-1591) was the writer of celebrated treatises on the terminology of the Civil Law (1557) and on the legal *formulae* of the Romans (1583). He was forced by the partisans of the League to act as first President of their Parliament in 1589, and was put to death by the faction of the Sixteen in 1591" (Sandys, II, 193); on him, see Blanchard, Pt. I, pp. 293-95; Maugis, III, 247, 275; Alfred Giraud, *La vie et la mort du président Brisson* (Nantes: A. Guéraud, [1855]); and Albert d'Herbelot, *Barnabé Brisson, jurisconsulte et magistrat* (Paris: E. Donnaud, 1877). Bibliothecally, he is perhaps best known from Joseph Scaliger's statement that during the League struggles he brought books from the Bibliothèque du roi to his home, and after his death his wife sold them for practically nothing; on this story, see Lomeier, sec. "France," n. 4, and the very full discussion in Franklin, *Les anciennes bibliothèques* ..., II, 150-52. Other more-or-less permanent borrowings by Brisson are mentioned in Delisle, II, 100, 133. Brisson was a "friend, patron, and admirer" of Jean Grolier, and he is known to have given books to Chancellor Méry de Vic (Le Roux de Lincy, *Researches concerning Jean Grolier*, pp. xxxvii, 86).

[284]Writing *ca.* 1616 of the libraries of Paris, Sincerus says: "I have looked at various libraries, both public collec-

Scholars in Paris still recall the library of
M. du Carlier. It was purchased by M. Bonzi, afterwards bishop of Béziers.[285]

M. du Carlier

When the monastery of the Cordeliers in Paris burned down, their library perished with it. In its time it had been one of the greatest and best stocked in all France, for it contained 8000 or 9000 volumes, among them numerous manuscripts. I have learned this from the Rev. Father de la Haye, who declares that he saw the catalog of the library.[286]

The library of the Cordeliers

The learned bishop of Lavaur Pierre Danès retired toward the end of his life to the abbey of Saint Germain-des-Prés. There he maintained a very famous library which was sold after his death on April 23,

P. Danès

---

tions--especially the royal library and the library of Saint-Victor's--and countless private ones--particularly Claude Depuy's, the Pithous', Nicolas Fabri's [i.e., Peiresc's], Barnabé Brisson's, as well as others, and all are filled full of the best and rarest volumes, not only printed works, but also books in manuscript" (Justus [Jodocus] Sincerus [Zinzerling], <u>Itinerarium Galliae</u> [Amstelodami: Jodocus Janson, 1655], p. 202). On this work and its author, see Lomeier, sec. "France," nn. 13, 22. A notarial inventory of Brisson's library has survived; see A. H. Schutz, <u>Vernacular Books in Parisian Private Libraries of the Sixteenth Century according to the Notarial Inventories</u> ("University of North Carolina Studies in the Romance Languages and Literatures," No. 25; Chapel Hill: University of North Carolina Press, 1955), p. 76.

[285]This library is mentioned again below; see the text at n. 421.

[286]The fire which almost completely destroyed the library of the Cordeliers occurred on November 19, 1580. However, Catherine de Médicis later donated many valuable Greek manuscripts to the monastery, and gifts of books were received from others as well (Franklin, <u>Les anciennes bibliothèques ...</u>, I, 204-205). Jean de la Haye himself, as bursar general of the Cordeliers, was to leave his rich personal library to the monastery on his death in 1661; cf. n. 159 above.

1577. His body was interred in the abbey church.[287] President de Thou mentions his library in discussing the year 1577:

> He was a man of our time who, although deeply versed in all branches of knowledge, wrote practically nothing, but left a very well-stocked book collection whose volumes he annotated with the greatest diligence throughout his long--and never inactive--life. His library was, however, sold piecemeal for the benefit of the poor, and thus perished by dispersal to the great detriment of scholarship[288][L].

The very distinguished Church of Paris[289] possessed a splendid library, which M. Claude Héméré, doctor of the Sorbonne, has described in his University of Paris, chap. vi on "The Library of the Church of Paris and of the Episcopal Schools"). He says that the books of this library were intended for the public use of the Church, and its supervision was in the hands of the chancellors, as is seen from an article in the old contract made between the chapter and the chancellor in 1215, to the effect that "the chancellor is obligated to correct, to bind, and to maintain in good condition the books of the Church of Paris,

[The Church of Paris]

---

[287]Pierre Danès (1497-1577) was one of the two original professors of Greek at the Collège royal (the other was Jacques Toussain); among their famous students were Brisson, Dorat, Amyot, Calvin, and Ignatius of Loyola (Sandys, II, 181-82, 195). Danès himself studied under Lascaris and Budé, and produced editions of Justin and Pliny. He played a significant part in the Council of Trent; and, sad to say, he was one of the judges who condemned Ramus. (See Pierre-Hilaire Danès, Abrégé de la vie du célèbre Pierre Danès [Paris: Quillau, 1731]).

[288]De Thou, III, 544.

[289]I.e., the Cathedral of Notre Dame; the previous and subsequent history of its library is given in considerable detail in Delisle, I, 426-32, and in Franklin, Les anciennes bibliothèques..., I, 1-69. During the seventeenth century this library "fell into oblivion" (ibid., p. 32).

with the exception of the antiphonaries . . . "290[L]. This library was honored with gifts from many learned persons, such as Simon de Chécy, and Stephen, archdeacon of Canterbury, who had a rich library and, according to Héméré, donated it for the use of poor scholars.291

> We come back to the last will of Stephen of Canterbury, who (as I said above) at that time bequeathed his valuable library to those in need, lest poverty often divert from the Muses the best talents, and those with the greatest aptitude for cultivating praiseworthy areas of study. He intrusted his library to the good judgment of the Paris chancellor--to be lent and distributed with the precaution that it not be broken up by sacrilegious thievery or by any other destructive means. Hence the volumes were committed to the chancellor, and he, with the aforesaid prudent caution, divided them up for the use of indigent scholars who were vigorously engaged in the most advanced studies at the University of Paris292[L].

M. Errault, lord of Chemans and son of M. de Chemans, keeper of the seals of France, left a large and very well

M. Errault
selected library. But after his death it was sold to various people, among them M. Jean Cousin,

---

290 Héméré, p. 52. This document, quoted also by Franklin, provides "irrefutable proof" that a library was in existence in the cathedral as early as October, 1215 (Les anciennes bibliothèques ..., I, 6).

291 In actuality, Simon de Chécy was treasurer of the cathedral, and received gifts of books in its behalf; he served as de facto librarian around 1268 (ibid., pp. 7-9). Franklin provides a list of the books comprising Archdeacon Stephen's donation, which was received in 1271; included was the autograph of Peter Lombard's Sentences (ibid., pp. 9-10).

292 Héméré, p. 55. Héméré asserts that the Notre Dame library was accessible to students from the time of its founding-- even before Archdeacon Stephen's gift (ibid., p. 52). Although conceding that Héméré provides the sole testimony to such very early accessibility and that his work dates only from the seventeenth century, Franklin says: "We note . . . that Claude Héméré, doctor and librarian of the Sorbonne, wrote ca. 1635, that is to say when the cathedral library was still in existence and could easily be consulted" (Franklin, Les anciennes bibliothèques ..., I, 9). On Héméré, see above n. 87.

doctor of medicine of the Paris Faculty.[293]

M. de Fontenay
The late M. Olivier de Fontenay had a good library, as one can see from Gabriel Naudé and Pierre Blanchot, who mention it in their works.[294]

However, after Fontenay's death it was sold to the bookseller Camusat.[295]

---

[293] Jacob here refers to Jean Errault (d. 1614), councillor in Parlement, abbot of Saint-Loup de Troyes, and son of François Errault, who was keeper of the seals in the chancellery and died in 1544 (Moréri, IV, Pt. 3, 173; Maugis, III, 173, 229-30). It is undoubtedly Jean Cousin whose death Gui Patin mentions in a letter of April 23, 1640 to Belin: "M. Cousin, a doctor of our company [i.e., the Paris Medical Faculty] died yesterday of dropsy" (Patin, Lettres, ed. Reveillé-Parise, I, 65).

[294] Reference is here made to François du Val, marquis de Fontenay-Mareuil/Ollivier/Lieuville/Terville (d. 1628), who is mentioned frequently in Peiresc's correspondence and was a close friend of Pierre and Christophe Dupuy; he should not be identified with François Olivier de Fontenay (1581-1636), abbot of Saint-Quentin de Beauvais--an error made in the last three volumes of the Peiresc correspondence. We learn from Peiresc that he was an active collector of medals, and that after his death some of his treasures were purchased by Antoine Coiffier, marquis d'Effiat and marshal of France (1581-1632); but (writing in 1634) Peiresc says that "only God knows" what will now become of the collection (Peiresc, V, 745). Jacob is apparently mistaken when he states that Blanchot mentions Fontenay's library (cf. n. 153 above). Naudé gives the following high praise of Fontenay: "Indeed, I may truly say that in the course of the two or three years that I have had the honor of occasionally meeting with M. de F. at the booksellers I have frequently seen him buy books so old, ill-bound, and wretchedly printed that I could not but smile and at the same time wonder--until, when later he took the trouble to tell me the cause and the circumstances for which he purchased them, his reasons seemed so pertinent that I shall never be convinced that he is not the most learned man in the knowledge of books and that he does not discourse of them with more experience and judgment than any other man, not only in France, but in all the world beside" (Naudé, Advice on Establishing a Library, pp. 12-13); see also n. 152.

[295] I.e., Jean Camusat (d. 1639), who from 1634 until his death was bookseller and printer to the French Academy; see [Jean de la Caille], Histoire de l'imprimerie et de la librairie (Paris: Jean de la Caille, 1689), p. 243.

M. Fumée A similar thing happened to the library of M. Adam Fumée, chancellor of France. It was one of the splendid collections of its time.[296]

<The library of Jacques Gopile> <Poitou has produced great and learned men, among whom Jacques Gopile deserves to be classed for having been a very distinguished physician of the Paris Faculty, and for having published scholarly works. He collected an excellent library for his own use, but it perished in a tragic way, and his sorrow over it was so great that it caused his death. The erudite Scévole de Sainte-Marthe tells us this in his eulogy:

> While civil discord was spreading in France, boisterous men from the lower class forcibly entered his museum, which was abundantly furnished with many printed as well as manuscript volumes, and violated and ravaged that holy collection with their profane hands. As a result of this, he experienced such great sorrow that his life came to an end and he left unfinished the description he was preparing of all the books of Hippocrates[297][L].>

M. Grolier Among the great losses that have come to the Muses from the dispersal of famous libraries, I may mention that of the late M. Jean Grolier of Lyon, knight, lord, viscount of Aiguisy, treasurer of Milan and of France, and king's general of finances. He was so highly regarded during his lifetime because of his rare books and

---

[296] Adam Fumée, lord des Roches (ca. 1430-1494) was physician to Charles VII and Louis XI, master of requests at the Hôtel of the king (1464), and keeper of the seals of France (1485); see Moréri, V, Pt. 1, 408. Delisle, II, 368, identifies a French manuscript which was in his library and which had earlier belonged to Étienne Pelourde, squire and cupbearer to the king.

[297] Scévole (I) de Sainte-Marthe, p. 76.

his great collection of valuable objects that his library became a marvel of its age.[298] I shall support this assertion with two authorities, and the first will be François de La Croix du Maine, who speaks of the collection in the following terms in his Bibliothèque des autheurs de France: "I understand that he owned one of the most superb and magnificent libraries of his day, filled with all kinds of book on various subjects."[299] The second authoritative testimony is taken from the great President de Thou, who wrote a noble eulogy to that patron of letters in Vol. II, Bk. LXXVIII of his history (for the year 1565); here I quote what pertains to our subject:

> Then when the French were forced out of Italy, he discharged the duties of treasurer in France with utmost fidelity and diligence, at the time when that office was not yet debased by a number of treasurers, and with the same love he had always felt for letters. He brought together a distinguished collection of ancient coins and books of highest quality. Sparing no expense, this man who was accustomed to elegance and taste in every aspect of his life, adorned and arranged these books in his home with equal taste and elegance. With such care did he preserve them that his library could be compared with Asinius Pollio's, the first to be established at Rome. Grolier had so many books

---

[298] On Grolier, see above, the text at n. 75. "Père Louis Jacob, in his Traité des plus belles bibliothèques, published in 1644, classed this collection among 'the Parisian libraries which have been dispersed.' As a matter of fact, after Grolier's death, his library was divided among several heirs; the greater part of it, that is to say, three thousand volumes, became the property, either by inheritance or by acquisition, of Méry de Vic, who was for some time Keeper of the Seals under Louis XIII, and also a bibliophile" (Le Roux de Lincy, Researches concerning Jean Grolier, p. 85). Méry de Vic has been discussed earlier (see n. 272).

[299] La Croix du Maine, I, 516, where the text reads "in various languages" rather than "on various subjects" as the concluding phrase of the sentence.

that in spite of his numerous gifts to friends and the various misfortunes by which his volumes were displaced and badly treated, the larger libraries one sees today in Paris and other parts of the kingdom are valued most highly for the embellishment which they receive from books once owned by Grolier300[L].

I have already noted, on page 92, how Grolier's collection of antiquities was incorporated into the royal museum. That illustrious Grolier family still remains in Lyons, and holds the most honorable positions in the city--for example, there is M. Charles Grolier, attorney general of the city of Lyons, and MM. du Soleil, and the commander de Servières.

Raoul Boutrays, in speaking of the Schools of Medicine in his poem about Paris, declares that all the celebrated

<u>The library of the</u>
<u>Schools of Medicine</u>

physicians in the world come to admire the true disciples of Aesculapius in that institution where his subject is so perfectly taught that today the school surpasses all the other universities of Europe.

> They all join themselves to the citizens of this populous city,
> No differently than great rivers are wont to be borne
> Through many mouths into the salt billows of the ocean
> And pay their tribute to Thetis, the queen of the waves.
> Do not search elsewhere in the world for what you could not find

---

300De Thou, II, 469 (the passage appears in Bk. XXVIII rather than in BK. LXXVIII). "In the account of Grolier written by J. A. de Thou toward the end of the XVI century, the author says that the remarkable libraries then in existence either in Paris or in the provinces, contained nothing more beautiful than the books once belonging to Grolier. By comparing this passage with the account of Père Louis Jacob written before 1644 and beginning thus: "Among the great losses that have come to the Muses from the dispersal of famous libraries, I may mention that of the late M. J. Grolier," etc., I am convinced that a notable part of this rich collection was sold or dispersed in 1565" (Le Roux de Lincy, <u>Researches concerning Jean Grolier</u>, p. 88).

> In this city; the whole world refuses what this city
> denies you.³⁰¹[L]

These Schools are honored by similar acclaim in another description of Paris, this one written by Eustathius von Knobelsdorf of Prussia, and printed in Latin by Christian Wechel in an octavo edition of 1543. There he says:

> Here under happy auspices the Paeonian arts are blooming,
> and vigor returns to minds and bodies.
> Galen is not regarded as trivial for the medical profession,
> and the erudite wealth of Hippocrates is not held back.
> What place was there like this before, where so many
> medical remedies
> for diseases were prepared, and any illness whatever was
> put to flight?
> Gaze upon the many here who can surpass Apollo,
> and who bear the powerful name of his art.³⁰²[L]

That illustrious Faculty will always be worthy of commendation for the many learned men it has produced and is continually producing, and also for a very rare and valuable library established in their Schools long before the invention of printing. The library's early existence is evidenced by the fact that Jacques Despars, first physician to King Charles VII, donated his fine book collection to these Schools.³⁰³ Now this library

---

³⁰¹Boutrays, p. 99, ll. 9-14. In the third line of the quoted passage, "influctus" and "ferii" must be corrected to "in fluctus" and "ferri" on the basis of Boutrays' text. On Boutrays, see above, n. 154.

³⁰²Knobelsdorf's *Lutetiae Parisiorum descriptio* (cited in Hauser, entry 1215) was reprinted in the same volume with Boutrays' poem; the quoted passage appears in Boutrays, p. 203, ll. 11-18. Knobelsdorf's poem consists, not of dactylic hexameters as the arrangement of lines in Jacob's text would suggest, but of elegiac stanzas. In the first line of the quoted passage, the epithet "Paeonian" signifies "medical," in that it relates to Apollo, the god of healing.

³⁰³Despars, one of the most eminent men of his time convoked the Medical Faculty on November 26, 1454, to determine means of providing better quarters for the School; he proposed acquiring a new residence and establishing a library, and he

was so highly esteemed for its famous medical books that King Louis XI gave his silver plate as security for a copy of Rhazes in it--as I remarked on page 67. Here is how Gabriel Naudé speaks of this library and of the Rhazes in his Panegyric on the Antiquity of the Paris Medical School, pp. 63-64: "The library was once so filled with a multitude and variety of rare and ancient volumes, and these were so carefully preserved, that Louis XI, wishing to have a copy made for himself of its Rhazes corpus, would never have been able to obtain it had not a vast quantity of gold been pledged by Jean de la Driesche, president of the Chamber of Accounts, and one hundred crowns been left as security with Dean Jean Loiseau"[304][L]. Claude Héméré, in his University of Paris, Chapter VI, bears this out also:

The library of J. Despars

> In the year 1471 King Louis indeed took out of the library of the Paris physicians the whole Rhazes corpus, but first they asked security for the borrowed volume

---

personally offered three hundred gold crowns, a considerable number of his best books, and even furniture; however, current war conditions prevented this plan from being realized. In 1457, the year of his death, Despars bequeathed to the Faculty his celebrated manuscript commentary on Avicenna, which comprised fifteen folio volumes, and was written on vellum. One should note, however, that the Faculty of Medicine had a library well before Despars' time--certainly as early as 1391 (Franklin, Les anciennes bibliothèques ..., II, 16, 21-22, 39-40; on the history of this library, see also Alfred Franklin, Recherches sur la bibliothèque de la Faculté de médecine [Paris: Aubry, 1864]).

[304]Gabriel Naudé, De antiquitate et dignitate Scholae Medicae Parisiensis panegyris (Lutetiae Parisiorum: J. Moreau, 1628), pp. 63-64. Naudé's text makes possible the correction of several minor infelicities in Jacob's quotation (specifically, "oppignorata" for the proper reading "oppignerata"; "Joannes" for "Joannis"; "fidei-iussione" for "fide-iussione"; and "Decani Joannis" for "Decano Joanni").

by means of a pledge of one hundred gold crowns and
twelve silver marks. That same year, Regnauld Leroi,
on asking that Faculty to allow him to borrow one
volume of Avicenna, had his request turned down because the ten silver marks he presented as security
were not equivalent to the value of the book^{305}[L].

This is taken from the archives of the Faculty of Medicine and
well shows how famous that library was for its good books; but
today the library is remembered only by writers of the past.^{306}

M. des Neuds   M. Rasse des Neuds, though a Paris surgeon, was a man
of learning and intellectual curiosity who at
his death left a large library filled with innumerable good books in divers fields of knowledge. This library was sold by his son to David Douceur, a
bookseller of Paris.^{307}

Never did a man of the past century win greater glory
for philosophy and mathematics than Pierre Ramée, or Rameau,
or Ramus, who founded the chair of mathematics at Paris.^{308}

---

^{305}Héméré, p. 54. See also Franklin, Les anciennes bibliothèques ..., II, 24.

^{306}Other testimonies to the deterioration of this library are collected ibid., p. 26.

^{307}Des Neuds, whose name is variously spelled (e.g., des Noeudz, des Noeuds, d'Esneux, Desneux, de Neus) is mentioned in Peiresc, V, 77; although a lowly barber-surgeon, he was a collector of art objects and books. In 1546 he received from one Albisse, a secretary of the king, a volume in a Grolier binding (Le Roux de Lincy, Researches concerning Jean Grolier, pp. xl, 68). David Douceur was both a bookseller and a printer; his printing activity is dated ca. 1606 (Caille, pp. 201-202).

^{308}"Toussain counted not only Rabelais, but also Ramus and Turnebus among his pupils. In 1547 (the year of the death of Francis I) Toussain was succeeded as lecturer in Greek by Turnebus, while Ramus became a professor in 1551. For a quarter of a century Ramus, or Pierre de la Ramée (1515-1572), was the most prominent teacher in Paris. He was already celebrated as the resolute opponent of the exclusive authority of Aristotle. In 1536 he had maintained the thesis that everything written by

He was concerned only with teaching this subject and with amassing all the good books which could be found

M. Ramus to perfect his magnificent library.[309] This library is held in great esteem by the authors who have written biographies of him; I shall quote two of them. First, we have Theophilus Banosius, who eulogizes it as follows:

Aristotle was false, and in 1543 he had severely attacked the Aristotelian logic. This attitude had naturally made him many enemies. Nevertheless in 1551 a special chair of 'eloquence and philosophy' was instituted on his behalf. He lectured with great success on Cicero and Virgil. He substituted humanistic methods of teaching for the scholastic methods that had long prevailed; he encouraged the study of Greek, and he improved the study of Latin" (Sandys, II, 184). On this colorful and influential figure of the French Renaissance, see especially Frank Pierrepont Graves, Peter Ramus and the Educational Reformation of the Sixteenth Century (New York: Macmillan, 1912), and Walter J. Ong, Ramus: Method, and the Decay of Dialogue (Cambridge, Mass.: Harvard University Press, 1958).

[309]Ramus' general interest in libraries is evidenced by his 1567 dedicatory epistle to Catherine de Médicis--an epistle which links the Florentine Academy to the French academies of the sixteenth and seventeenth centuries: "The Lord Cosimo de' Medici, Duke of Florence and of Siena, establishing his library in the church of St. Laurence, bringing to light the Pandects, patronising all liberal arts, what did he do but conserve the domestic patrimony of the renown of his ancestors? You see, therefore, Madame, the deeds of your family, which I propose to yourself, namely, to use their power and wealth liberally to fill their country with great benefits, to found academies, build palaces to the Muses, give due rewards to learned men, and not only profit mankind in these praise-worthy ways, but inspire other princes to do likewise" (quoted in and translated by Yates, p. 20). In this same dedication Ramus argued that the royal library ought to be moved from Fontainebleau to Paris--for, after all, "Cosimo and Lorenzo, though they possessed charming villas in Tuscany, did not establish a library there, because book collections are certainly not made for fields and woodlands; rather, these Medici placed their library at the very center of the land they ruled, that is, in the city, where its most attractive benefits would be accessible to citizens" (preface to Ramus' Prooemium mathematicum of 1567, included in his Praefationes, epistolae, orationes [Parisiis: apud D. Vallensem, 1577], pp. 182-83); this proposal was not carried out, however, until the reign of Charles IX, as we have seen (n. 47 above).

After his death his murderers destroyed all the
exquisite things he had collected, and particularly
his books; many distinguished monuments of his learning also perished, such as his commentaries on Aristotle's Republic, his book on the Roman assembly, and
many others--on ethics, physics, optics, geometry,
music, and astrology--which for certain reasons he
had not wished to publish. But several writings which
a little while before his death he had given to a particular friend to be printed will be issued shortly, as
I pointed out above 310[L].

The second author who speaks in ample terms of this library that was miserably dispersed by the ignorant is Ramus' student Nicolas de Nancel:[311]

It remains to be said that after the death, at age
fifty-seven, of this outstanding philosopher and
orator, bullies and robbers immediately directed
their frenzy against his library, and in the space
of a single hour numerous rogues thrown together
from the dregs of the people pillaged the whole
elegant collection--so that, as soon as the protec-
tive ropes, bolts, and bars had been destroyed, the
books were carried off.[312] I deplore the fact that
a library which was by far the most beautiful and
well stocked, and in whose building and organizing

---

[310] Theophilus Banosius (not "Bauosius," as in our text), Petri Rami vita (1576), prefacing his edition of Ramus' Commentaria de religione christiana (Francofurti: A. Wechel, 1577), preliminary p. [35]; in this quotation the syntactically-impossible "commentario" has been read as "commentaria," following Banosius' text. This biography is one of the basic primary sources for the life of Ramus; Banosius was one of Ramus' students.

[311] Nicolas de Nancel, Petri Rami Veromandui, eloquentiae et philosophiae apud Parisios professoris regii vita (Parisiis: C. Morellus, 1599), pp. 78-79; this is another fundamental document for biographical knowledge of Ramus. It is of interest that our Carmelite author Jacob nowhere mentions the exact circumstances of Ramus' death--as a Protestant, Ramus was one of the victims of the St. Bartholomew massacre in 1572. In the years prior to his death, when he was driven from Paris because of his Protestant view, Catherine de Médicis gave him asylum at the royal library at Fontainebleau (Johann Thomas Freige, Petri Rami vita, in his edition of Ramus' Praelectiones in Ciceronis orationes octo consulares [Basileae: P. Pernas, 1575], p. ix).

[312] A Latin manuscript with Ramus' signature on it is preserved in the Bibliothèque Nationale (Delisle, II, 396).

I had once labored hard, was so nefariously and in-
imically seized, plundered, and laid waste; but I am
even more grieved because, along with Ramus' books
and papers and αὐτόμετα [personally produced]
mathematical writings of exceeding originality, we
also lost--I do not know what thieves or booknappers
stole them--works I translated from Greek into Latin
and books in Greek copied by my own hand (in which as
a youth I had expended much effort trying to represent
the shape and beauty of the Greek letters--and not
from printed or typographical models). O that those
who unjustly hold back these things, now that they are
reminded of this grevious harvest, may either restore
them to their true owners or publish them under the
names of both their authors for the use of all. It
would be better for them to obtain praise for that
righteous act now than after death to be forced, when
they have no choice and with their conscience accusing
them, to give a reason before God, the just judge and
avenger, for so extraordinary a theft and booknapping.
In my opinion Ramus' library was worth about 1000 gold
crowns and was equal to the best. As I remember from
the catalog I myself prepared a long time ago, there
were very few theological, medical, or legal publications in the library, but it contained numerous works,
both Greek and Latin, in the humanities. Moreover, no
matter how many mathematical books were available and
whatever their languages, he bought them all and dis-
regarded the cost; and he preserved in a most scholarly manner the books collected from far and near. In
his will he had made the following provision concerning
the future heirs to his library and to the rest of his
property:[313] "I bequeath my library, my other possessions, and all my legal claims by equal division, one
half to poor scholars of the Collège de Presles,[314]
and the other half to the administrators and executors
of my testament, Nicolas Bergeron[315] and Antoine

---

[313]The complete will is printed in Nancel, pp. 80-85; in
Banosius, pp. 19-24; in C. Waddington-Kastus, De Petri Rami vita,
scriptis, philosophia (Parisiis: Joubert, 1848), pp. 163-66; and
in Charles Desmaze, P. Ramus, professeur au Collège de France, sa
vie, ses écrits, sa mort (Paris: J. Cherbuliez, 1864), pp. 113-18.

[314]On the library of the Collège de Presles, of which
Ramus became principal in 1545, see Franklin, Les anciennes
bibliothèques ..., I, 421-22.

[315]Nicolas Bergeron (d. ca. 1585), a polygraph and a
protege of Marguerite de Valois, edited the works of Jacques
Peletier, and in 1587 produced with Savigny Tableaux accomplis
de tous les arts libéraux (Roman d'Amat, in DBF, VI, 2-3).

Loisel,[316] who were formerly my students and are now advocates in Parlement." He was murdered at Paris in the Collège de Presles on August 26, 1572[L].

M. Jacques de Wicob, councillor of state and royal ambassador to Germany, was a man with a fine mind and a love both of learning and of books. He gave evident

M. Wicob proof of this by establishing an excellent library of well-chosen volumes. However, after his death it was sold to the Parisian bookseller David Douceur, and this is why many of its books are seen today in various libraries of the city.[317] In fact, all of the book collections discussed in this chapter have been incorporated into the finest extant libraries of Paris.

---

[316]Antoine Loisel (1536-1617), a student of Cujas and one of the legal luminaries of his time, published many important juridical works; his Institutes coutumières of 1607 was re-edited as late as 1846. On him, see the biography by his grandson Claude Joly, in Joly's edition of Loisel's Divers opuscules (Paris: Jean Guignard, 1656), pp. i-lxxvii; and Armand Demasure, Antoine Loisel et son temps (Paris: E. Thorin, 1876). Loisel had a fine manuscript collection of his own; he had obtained many precious volumes from the Beauvais cathedral, and he bequeathed his entire library to his grandson Joly (Delisle, I, 431). The place which libraries held in his scholarly life is clearly indicated when he "tells us that, after supper, Pithou, Cujas and himself used to meet in the library every evening, and continued to work there until three o'clock in the morning" (Sandys, II, 194).

[317]Supplementary data on Wicob have not been found. On Douceur, see above, n. 307.

CHAPTER IV (LXXXV)

LIBRARIES IN THE VICINITY OF PARIS

The library of the Minimites of Chaillot

There is a very considerable library in the monastery of the Bonshommes, or Minimite fathers of Chaillot.[318]

M. de Sourdis of Jouy

M. Charles d'Escoubleau, marquis de Sourdis & d'Alluye, knight of the orders of the king, and governor of the regions about Orléans, Chartres, Blois, Dunois, and Vendôme, so well combined the activities of Mars and of Apollo that he gained great glory in Europe.[319] All France and foreign countries admired his conduct and his courage, and today his thorough acquaintance with literature brings him renown as one of the erudite lords of France. We have entirely adequate evidence of this in his meticulous and praiseworthy search for all the best books in all fields to embellish his noble library.[320] He built it in his château Jouy, four leagues[321] from Paris, and he does not rest a moment from augmenting it.

---

[318] On this library, see Franklin, Les anciennes bibliothèques ..., III, 355-57.

[319] Charles d'Escoubleau became a knight of the orders of the king in 1633, and died at Paris in 1666 at the age of seventy-eight (Moréri, IV, Pt. 3, 189). Jacob's reference to "Mars" is based on the fact that d'Escoubleau was master of the camp of the light cavalry and marshal of the camps and armies of the king.

[320] Cf. Delisle, II, 362, 417; III, 281.

[321] I.e., ten miles.

No one is uninformed as to the high reputation of the royal French abbey of Saint-Denis, not only because it serves as the mausoleum for those eldest sons of the church, our most Christian kings, and because it possesses a rich treasury, but also because of another treasure there, one established for the Muses. I refer to a library, which was the most well-stocked and best furnished with rare books of all the libraries in France. But it did not escape the fury of the heretics during the first period of religious troubles to occur in this kingdom;[322] we are informed of this by the author of the Antiquitez de Paris, in the folio edition of 1640.[323]

<u>The library of Saint-Denis</u>

Near Melun one sees the château de la Borde. It belongs to the viscount of Melun, and contains a very good library.[324]

<u>The viscount of Melun</u>

Bishop Augustin Potier, count of Beauvais, enjoys a fine library filled with good books.[325]

<u>M. de Beauvais</u>

---

[322]Jacob refers to the conflicts between Calvinists and Roman Catholics in the sixteenth century.

[323]"The library of this abbey was the most well-stocked and best furnished with rare books of all the libraries in France, but it was dispersed by the heretics during the first period of troubles" ([Jacques Du Breul and Claude Malingre], Les antiquitez de la ville de Paris [Paris: P. Rocolet, et al., 1640], Bk. IV, p. 42; author identification in A.-A. Barbier, Dictionnaire des ouvrages anonymes [4 vols., 3d ed.; Paris: Daffis, 1872-1879], I, 221). On the library of Saint-Denis, see Delisle, I, 200-207; III, 356, 391; and passim.

[324]The complex genealogy of this ancient and distinguished French noble house is given in Moréri, X, sec. "Additions & Corrections," 32 ff.

[325]Augustin Potier (d. 1650) was grand almoner of Queen Anne of Austria; his Statuts synodaux were printed in 1646 (Moréri, VIII, Pt. 2, 519).

CHAPTER V (LXXVI)

ANJOU

The monastery of the Carmelite fathers in the city of Angers was founded through the pious liberality of René, king of Sicily and duke of Anjou. There is a very fine library in this monastery; Father Léon de Saint-Jean mentions it in the Reformed Carmelite fathers' description of the province of Touraine, when he speaks of the Angers monastery: "No less delight is afforded by the huge, rich library, filled with volumes on every possible subject, which can be seen in a particularly splendid part of the building"[326][L].

<u>The library of the Carmelites</u>

M. Claude Ménard, royal councillor and lieutenant in the provostry of Angers, is worthy of commendation not only for the books which he has written (especially the <u>History of Anjou</u>

---

[326] René I (1409-1480), though unsuccessful in most of his political dealings, earned the title "the good" because of his numerous charities; he is especially remembered as the patron of artistic endeavor in a wide variety of media (Flemish-style painting, sculpture, tapestry, and gold work). The passion plays at Angers were carried out under his auspices. On him, see Albert Lecoy de la Marche, <u>Le roi René</u> (2 vols.; Paris: Firmin-Didot, 1875), where it is printed out (II, 27-28) that René spent a considerable sum in rebuilding the Carmelite monastery (it had actually been founded in 1368); René's personal library is described in detail in II, 182-92. Jean Macé (in religion: Léon de Saint-Jean) has been mentioned above (n. 220). The Carmelite description of Touraine for which he apparently served as a contributor has not been identified.

The library of M. Ménard

now being printed), but also for a celebrated library which he built up with great care.[327]

The library at Saumur

In the town of Saumur there was once a fine library which Philippe du Plessis Mornay, the coryphaeus of the Calvinists established.[328]

The library of the Jesuits of La Flèche

The library of the Jesuit fathers of La Flèche is filled with very good books in all fields of knowledge.

The library of the Recollects

The Recollect fathers of la Baumette, near Angers, have a quite good and interesting library.[329]

---

[327] Claude Ménard (ca. 1580-1652) was appointed lieutenant of the provostry of Angers at age 33. On becoming a widower, he entered the clergy and was instrumental in reforming many monasteries in Anjou. He did considerable archival research, edited several works (e.g., Joinville's *Histoire de S. Loys*), and wrote on the history of Anjou (his general history of Anjou was never actually published, however); Ménage called him "the father of Angevin history" (Moréri, VII, 432). Some unpublished manuscripts by Ménard are listed in the *Catalogue général des manuscrits des bibliothèques publiques de France. Departements* [hereafter cited as *CMD*] (48 vols.; Paris: Librairie Plon, 1886-1933), XXXI, 786-87 and *passim*.

[328] This brief mention of Du Plessis Mornay (1549-1623), the great Huguenot statesman, does justice neither to him nor to his fine library which was destroyed when Louis XIII's officers sacked his château at Saumur in 1621 (cf. Bonnaffé, *Dictionnaire ...* p. 227). For a more adequate contemporary description, see Lomeier, sec. "France," n. 29 and corresponding text.

[329] "The Jesuit college of La Flèche, founded in 1603 by Henry IV, enjoyed a great reputation for a century and a half, and Marshal de Guébriant, Descartes, Father Mersenne, Prince Eugene of Savoy, and Séguir were all numbered among its students" (Georges Goyau, "Le Mans, Diocese of," *Catholic Encyclopedia*, IX, 144); the standard history of the college is Camille de Rochemonteix's *Un collège de Jésuites aux XVIIe et XVIIIe siècles: le collège Henri IV de La Flèche* (4 vols.; Le Mans: Leguicheux, 1889). Manuscript materials pertinent to the sixteenth-seventeenth century history of the Recollect monastery of la Baumette are preserved in the Angers library (*CMD*, XXXI, 476).

CHAPTER VI (LXXVII)

AVIGNON AND THE COMTAT VENAISSIN

Pope John XXII, whose given name was Jacques Deusa or Ossa,[330] a native of Cahors, was a very famous doctor of theology of the University of Paris, as is evidenced by the theological works he wrote. Moreover, he was a great book lover, for he had a distinguished library which he bequeathed to the Dominican monks of the city of Avignon.[331] Some ancient manuscripts from this library can still be seen, according to the

The library of the Dominicans

---

[330] Actually, Duèse or Dueze. His papacy (1316-1334) was the second of the seven Avignonese pontificates (the "Babylonian captivity") which preceded the Great Schism.

[331] This is not precisely correct. "Certain manuscripts executed by John XXII's copyists or purchased by him he generously donated to monasteries at Avignon, and especially to the Dominican monastery there. The latter received a Summa of St. Thomas Aquinas and three volumes of Bernard Gui, all of which are today in the Avignon library. The recollection of these donations gave credence to the error that John XXII had bequeathed his library to the Dominicans. . . . The truth is that in substance the library amassed by John remained with his successors, or, more precisely, with the papal see" (Maurice Faucon, La librairie des papes d'Avignon, sa formation, sa composition, ses catalogues [1316-1420], d'après les registres de comptes et d'inventaires des Archives Vaticanes ["Bibliothèque des Écoles françaises d'Athènes et de Rome," Nos. 43, 50; 2 vols.; Paris: Ernest Thorin, 1886-1887], I, 39 [cf. CMD, XXVII, 172, 204]; John XXII's remarkable activity as book collector and patron of the book arts is described in Faucon, pp. 18-39). On the manuscripts in the Dominican monastery at Avignon, see François Duchesne, Histoire de tous les cardinaux françois (2 vols.; Paris, 1660), sec. "Preuves," p. 461, and CMD, XXIX, Pt. 2, 784-85 and passim.

notes sent to me by M. Henri Suarès junior, doctor of law, a young man of wide reading and great integrity.[332]

<u>John XXII</u>   I acknowledge that I have received many notes from him for this work, and may posterity therefore recognize its debt to him for his researches.

The University of Avignon formerly possessed the library of Amédée, cardinal de Salusses,[333] who by his will gave it to them for the common use of the doctors of that University--as it appears from the cardinal's testament preserved by the above-mentioned Henri Suarès. The library was kept in the Cluniac Collège de Saint-Martial,[334] but today it exists only in memory, since, with the exception of a corpus of civil law, this collection--for which they had once refused seven hundred ducats--suffered dispersal.

<u>The University library</u>

<u>Amédée, cardinal de Salusses</u>

Cardinal Pietro Corsini of Florence was a man with a great affection for literature. Indeed, he amassed a large quantity of books to enrich his magnificent library in Avignon.

---

[332] Papers and manuscripts of Henri Suarès have been acquired by the Bibliothèque Nationale (Delisle, II, 292, 417). Henri Suarès was a cousin of Joseph-Marie Suarès, whose library Jacob mentions below, and who himself had intended to produce a work on libraries (see the text at nn. 342-45).

[333] The cardinal died in 1419 and was interred at Lyons (Moréri, IX, Pt. 2, 112). A <u>breviarium juris</u> prepared for his instruction survives in manuscript at Avignon; see <u>CMD</u>, XXVII, 410-11.

[334] "In 1379 a Collège of S. Martial (or rather a college-monastery for twelve choir-brethren and twelve students) was founded for monks of Cluny" at the University of Avignon (Hastings Rashdall, <u>The Universities of Europe in the Middle Ages</u>, ed. F. M. Powicke and A. B. Emden [3 vols.; London: Oxford University Press, 1936], II, 179).

The Augustinians

Suarès says: "His will states that his library contained a tremendous number of books which he had brought together from many places at enormous expense; but today not a volume,

Cardinal P. Corsini

and scarcely even a leaf of a volume, remains"[L]. Corsini bequeathed that library to the Augustinian fathers.[335]

In the year 1466, Giuliano della Rovere, cardinal priest with title to the parish church of St. Pierre aux Liens, and legate to Avignon,[336] determined to

Cardinal Rovere's library

leave as a testimony to posterity of his love for good literature not only the erection of a College named della Rovere,[337] but also

---

[335]Corsini, a doctor of law, became bishop of Florence under Urban V, and, in 1370, bishop of Oporto and cardinal under Gregory XI; in the Schism he followed Clement VII. He died in 1405 at Avignon, and was interred in the church of the Augustinians there (later his body seems to have been removed to Florence). He wrote lives of some popes and a treatise on ending the Schism (Moréri, IV, Pt. 1, 157). On the Augustinians' library at Avignon, see François Duchesne, Histoire de tous les cardinaux françois, sec. "Preuves," p. 461; and cf. Delisle, II, 247.

[336]The date of Giuliano's legateship is 1476 rather than 1466. Giuliano della Rovere afterwards became Pope Julius II, the papa terribile of the High Renaissance, against whom the anonymous satire Julius exclusus (attributed to Erasmus) was written, in which Julius is denied entrance to heaven (cf. Myron P. Gilmore, The World of Humanism [New York: Harper, 1952], pp. 162-63). Julius was one of the greatest art patrons in the history of the church, and commissioned the work of Raphael, Bramante, and Michelangelo.

[337]I.e., the Collège de Saint-Pierre du Roure. Giuliano was a nephew of Pope Sixtus IV, and influenced him to bestow privileges and monetary grants on the University of Avignon; indeed, "Sixtus IV also bestowed upon the Collège du Roure the papal library at Avignon" (Rashdall, loc.cit.; cf. Thomas Okey, The Story of Avignon ["Mediaeval Towns"; London: J. M. Dent, 1911], p. 262, and L. H. Labande, "Les manuscrits de la bibliothèque d'Avignon

the establishment of a very distinguished library at the Apostolic Palace. Later the library was moved to the Palais de Poitiers, as it appears from the foundation lists of this College which the above-mentioned Suarès preserves. He declares that now no trace of the library remains, except for the notice in the lists and the place where it once was located.

The library of the Cordelier fathers of the Observance was once considerable, according to Francesco Gonzaga, minister general of that order, in his Seraphic History.[338] I do not know by what misfortune this library dwindled away, but at present it contains scarcely 1500 volumes.

The library of the Cordeliers

I can say the same of the Carmelite fathers' library,

---

provenant de la librairie des papes du XIVe siècle," Bulletin historique, 1894, pp. 145-60). A catalog of the College library, drawn up at the time of the Revolution, is preserved in manuscript at Avignon (CMD, XXVIII, 566).

[338] Jacob refers here to the Franciscan Observants' monastery of Sainte-Croix, founded in 1469 (Abbayes et prieurés de l'ancienne France [hereafter cited as APAF], ed. Dom Beaunier, et al. [12 vols.; Liguge: Abbaye Saint-Martin, 1907-1941], II, 131, 140). Gonzaga concludes his discussion of the monastery as follows: "Finally, there are thirty-six Franciscan brothers in residence here, the majority of whom pay the closest attention to matters literary, and do so advantageously because of the very well-stocked library which is a delight and no little enhancement to this monastery" (Francesco Gonzaga, De origine seraphicae religionis franciscanae ejusque progressibus [Romae: D. Basa, 1587], p. 824). On Gonzaga, who was successively bishop of Cefalù, Pavia, and Mantua, see Cesare Sacco, Vita e sante attioni dell' ill' mo ... F. Francesco Gonzaga, vescovo di Mantova (Mantova: Osanna, 1624), and Ippolito Donesmondi, Vita dell'illustriss^{mo} ... F. Francesco Gonzaga, vescovo di Mantova (Venetia: G. Zarzina, 1625). The libraries of the Cordeliers and the Carmelites of Avignon receive mention in François Duchesne, Histoire de tous les cardinaux françois, sec. "Preuves," p. 461; on the manuscripts of the Carmelites, see also CMD, XXIX, Pt. 2, 763.

The library of which has greatly fallen from the splendor
the Carmelites it had two hundred years ago.

  The most magnificent and complete library of this city is that of the Celestin fathers. Besides a great number of
The library of printed books, it contains divers ancient
the Celestins manuscripts which came from the fine library of the venerable and illustrious Jean Gerson, doctor of Navarre and chancellor of the University of Paris.[339] He
J. Gerson gave his books to the monks of that house because he felt pious affection for them, due to the fact that one of his brothers was a member of that order.

  The Jesuit fathers have collected a very excellent
The library of library. It comprises all kinds of good
the Jesuits books, and there are even some old manuscripts there.[340]

---

[339] On the manuscripts of the Celestin library at Avignon, see ibid., and François Duchesne, Histoire de tous les cardinaux françois, sec. "Preuves," pp. 424, 461. "Gerson bequeathed his books to the Celestins of Avignon, in whose monastery two of his brothers were then residing. [Note that Jacob mentions only one brother.] The document containing this disposition carries the date November, 1428. In it he specifies that the donated books be placed in a press by themselves, so that they will be more convenient for those wishing to use them. He notes also that on his next birthday, the fourteenth of December, he would begin his sixty-sixth year" (A.-L. Masson, Jean Gerson, sa vie, son temps, ses oeuvres [Lyon: Vitte, 1894], p. 395); cf. n. 228 above. The Bibliothèque Nationale has one Latin manuscript which was a part of Gerson's bequest, and two other Latin manuscripts from the library of the Celestins of Avignon (both of which came by way of Colbert's library, and one of them had also belonged to President de Thou); see Delisle, II, 251.

[340] On the manuscripts of the Jesuit college at Avignon, see CMD, XXIX, Pt. 2, 766 and passim. On its history in the sixteenth and seventeenth centuries, see Henri Fouqueray, Histoire de la Compagnie de Jésus en France dès origines à la suppression (1528-1762) (5 vols.; Paris: A. Picard; Bureaux des Études, 1910-1925), I, 434-51; II, 32-34, 536.

216

That great genius of Italian poetry, Francis Petrarch, had a distinguished library at Vaucluse in the diocese of Cavaillon; Bishop Tomasini speaks of it in his *Petrarch Reborn*.[341] I do not know

<u>Petrarch's library</u>

---

[341] Jacopo Filippo Tomasini, *Petrarcha redivivus* (2d ed.; Patavii: P. Frambottus, 1650), p. 71, where mention is made of three places at which Petrarch kept books (Vaucluse, Parma, and Verona). On Tomasini (1597-1670?), who produced several works of primary-source value on Venetian and Paduan libraries of the seventeenth century, see Lomeier, sec. "Italy," n. 21 and *passim*. When Petrarch settled in Vaucluse, he moved his library there, as we see from the following passage in his unfinished autobiography, written during the last three years of his life: "Since I experienced a deep-seated and innate repugnance to town life, especially in that disgusting city of Avignon which I heartily abhorred, I sought some means of escape. I fortunately discovered, about fifteen miles from Avignon, a delightful valley, narrow and secluded, called Vaucluse, where the Sorgue, the prince of streams, takes its rise. Captivated by the charms of the place, I transferred thither myself and my books" (translated in James Harvey Robinson and Henry W. Rolfe, *Petrarch* [New York: Putnam, 1909], p. 69). The last twenty-one years of Petrarch's life were spent in Italy (chiefly at Milan, then Venice, and finally Padua and Arquà), and his books followed him wherever he went. Petrarch intended to bequeath his library to St. Mark's in Venice, and the Venetian Grand Council officially accepted the offer (September 4, 1362). Tomasini, pp. 71-73, reported that in 1634 certain stray volumes, badly affected by moisture and neglect, were discovered in a room of St. Mark's, and he assumed that these were the remnants of Petrarch's bequest. However, these books were not in fact Petrarch's. "At the time of Petrarch's death his books were on Paduan territory, and Francis of Carrara, the lord of Padua, was on bad terms with the Venetian Republic. He seems to have thrown obstacles in the way of delivering the library, which he authorized the heirs to sell, and of which he reserved for himself the lion's share. Although several of Petrarch's manuscripts may be found scattered in various Italian hands in the fifteenth century, most of them remained for a time with Carrara's at Padua. . . . Francis . . . was at last crushed by the alliance of the Venetian state with that of Gian Galeazzo Visconti. All his possessions fell to the lord of Milan, and it was this prince, an equally great friend of letters, who collected Petrarch's books in the library of the castle at Pavia. A century later, again by right of war, they passed into the hands of Louis XII, king of France. After his conquest of the Milanese, in 1499, they were transferred to the castle of Blois. And so it came about that, after so many changes, most of the books which belonged to Petrarch are to be found to-day in the Bibliothèque Nationale at Paris. . . . Twenty-seven volumes are there; seven others in the Vatican; one (the Virgil) is in the Ambrosian Library at

if this is the same library which he gave to the Venetian senate and which I discussed on page 133 [Pt. I].

The erudite and stimulating works of M. Joseph-Marie Suarès,[342] formerly provost of the Church of Avignon, then domestic[343] and librarian to Cardinal Francesco Barberini,[344] and now bishop of Vaison, have earned for him perpetual remembrance among the learned. His fame is no less due to the good and interesting library he has built up with great care; in it are kept numerous rare manuscripts which, God willing, that gentleman will publish. I should be ungrateful to this scholarly prelate if I did not inform the public that he himself has planned to work on the subject of libraries; however, the heavy responsibilities of his charge and of his more

The library of the bishop of Vaison

Milan; another (the Horace) is in the Laurentian at Florence; one is in the Marcian Library at Venice; one is at Padua, and one at Troyes in Champagne" (Pierre de Nolhac, <u>Petrarch and the Ancient World</u> [Boston: Merrymount Press (D. B. Updike), 1907], pp. 88-89; see the more detailed treatment in Nolhac's <u>Pétrarque et l'humanisme</u> [2 vols., 2d ed.; Paris: H. Champion, 1907], I, 33-122; II, 239-42, 293-96; and cf. Lomeier, sec. "Italy," nn. 11 and 44, and the corresponding text).

[342] Joseph-Marie Suarès or Suarez, who is mentioned frequently in the Peiresc correspondence, died <u>ca</u>. 1678 at the home of his friend Cardinal Francesco Barberini in Rome. A list of Suarès' works is given by Moréri, IX, Pt. 2, 604-605; Bourgeois, entry 293, cites his <u>Descriptiuncula Avenionis et comitatus Venascini, cum indice geographico</u> of 1658 (later ed., 1676). On Suarès, see Jean Columbi, <u>De rebus gestis episcoporum Vasionensium libri quatuor</u> (Lugduni: J. Canier, 1656); Louis-Anselme Boyer de Sainte-Marthe, <u>Histoire de l'église cathédrale de Vaison</u> (Avignon: M. Chave, 1731); and cf. <u>CMD</u>, XXIX, Pt. 2, 1467 and <u>passim</u>.

[343] On the seventeenth-century meaning of this word, see above, n. 164.

[344] Barberini has been mentioned previously; see n. 266.

serious studies has caused him to delay that work, and we can do no more than hope for its worthy completion. However, because of his special affection for me, he has voluntarily decided to put his notes at my disposal, as he informs me in one of his letters, written from Vaison on April 2, 1644:

> I once had a similar project, and made many notes on various libraries. If I have the spare time, I shall gather them together and send them to you. In case I cannot do it, my cousin M. Henri Suarès[345] will put himself at your service the next time you see each other.

---

[345] See the text at n. 332 for Henri Suarès' not inconsiderable contributions to Jacob's *Traicté*.

CHAPTER VII (LXXXVIII)

AUVERGNE

The library of Saint-Alire near Clermont

The Benedictine abbey of Saint-Alire, on the outskirts of the city of Clermont, is famous for its great age and for its very fine library containing a variety of ancient manuscripts.[346]

The library of the Dominicans

The library of the Dominican fathers is large and is well supplied with good books, among which some manuscripts are to be found.

As for the library of the discalced Carmelite fathers, it is well worthy of consideration for its good books on various subjects.[347] These books were acquired through the efforts of Father Seraphin de Saint-François, formerly confessor to

---

[346] Manuscripts of the Saint-Alire library are listed in Montfaucon, II, 1262-65; see also Ernst Gustav Vogel, Literatur früherer und noch bestehender europäischer öffentlicher und Corporations-Bibliotheken (Leipzig: T. O. Weigel, 1840), p. 249. On the library of the Dominicans at Clermont, see Montfaucon, II, 1353-56; François Duchesne, Histoire de tous les cardinaux françois, sec. "Preuves," pp. 487-88; and cf. Delisle, I, 465.

[347] In a letter of November 8, 1638, we find André Duchesne requesting a friend to make a list of certain manuscripts belonging to the Clermont Carmelites (ibid., I, 480-81). The manuscripts in this monastery were sufficiently valuable to arouse the envy of Baluze, and there is little doubt that they were incorporated into the Colbert library by 1690 (ibid., I, 475-76, 480-82). A catalog of this Carmelite collection was drawn up by Jacob himself; it has been reprinted in Labbe, pp. 206-210 (cf. Montfaucon, II, 1278).

The library of the discalced Carmelites M. Séguir, chancellor of France.[348] Father Seraphin was prior of this monastery at the time of his death several years ago.

The late Jean Savaron, a learned man and a Clermont president, had a library which was very noteworthy for its good books and divers manuscripts. This library is still maintained by Savaron's heirs.[349]

The library of Jean Savaron

In the town of Billom there is a Jesuit college which was founded by G. Duprat, bishop of Clermont. Formerly it possessed a celebrated library, which included that bishop's bequest of half of his own book collection. But the College library was miserably destroyed by fire.

The library of the Jesuits of Billom

The same Guillaume Duprat founded the monastery of the Minimite fathers of Beauregard. To them he bequeathed the other half of his library, which was very large and very fine.[350]

The library of the Minimites of Beauregard

---

[348] On Séguier, see above, n. 106.

[349] Several works by Jean Savaron (1566-1622), who corresponded with Peiresc, André Duchesne, and other learned book collectors of the time, are cited in Bourgeois: his treatise against venality (1615) at entry 6144; his treatises in support of absolute monarchy (1615, 1620, 1622) at entry 6085; and his letters at entry 930. Savaron's library is discussed in A. Vernière, Le président Jean Savaron, érudit, curieux, collectionneur, et ses rapports avec les savants de son temps (Clermont-Ferrand: M. Bellet, 1892), especially pp. 32-35, 62 ff.; and cf. also Joseph Meyniel, Le président Jean Savaron (Paris: Bonvalot-Jouve, 1906); and Bonnaffé, Dictionnaire ..., p. 284. Some of Savaron's books are known to have passed into the library of Charles-Maurice Le Tellier, archbishop of Reims (d. 1710), and one Latin manuscript which belonged to Savaron is today in the Bibliothèque Nationale (Delisle, I, 304; II, 415).

[350] On Guillaume Duprat, see above, n. 168. Duprat's bequest of books to the Jesuit college founded by him at Billom is confirmed in Fouqueray, I, 191. The Minimite monastery of Beauregard receives mention in AFAF, V, 95.

CHAPTER VIII (LXXXIX)

BÉARN

Pau is the principal city of this province. There King Louis XIII, to the great satisfaction of the entire Catholic Church, reestablished the Catholic faith,[351] and by his royal liberality had a Capuchin monastery erected. He bestowed upon the monastery the magnificent library of his predecessors, the kings of Navarre, and it serves as a rare ornament for this monastic community.

The library of the kings of Navarre

The cathedral chapter of the Church of Lescar deserves special praise for the glorious plan which it conceived and enacted for the establishment of a very worthy and well-stocked library for its use. This will provide all the other cathedral churches of the kingdom with an object of emulation, and will encourage them to reestablish the ancient cathedral libraries they once possessed, but which today

The library of the Church of Lescar

---

[351] By royal ordinance of June 17, 1617 (Claude de Vic, et al., Histoire générale de Languedoc [16 vols.; Toulouse: Édouard Privat, 1872-1904], XI, 937). The assertion that Louis XIII presented the Capuchins of Pau with the ancient library of the kings of Navarre is accepted as true by L. Soulice (CMD, IX, 73).

remain only in name to the great disdain of the Muses. In spite of this neglect, the example of the Lescar Church will be of value to all other cathedral chapters, for by a solemn decree made and passed in this chapter on August 3, 1637, it is declared that a chapter library will be established there.

I shall quote this decree, which is in their statutes, chap. xiv, entitled "Of the Chapter Library"[L]; Jean de Bordenave, canon of the Lescar Church, has included it at the end of his book on L'estat des églises cathédrales & collégiales, printed in folio at Paris by the widow of Mathurin du Puis, 1643, pp. 952-53:[352]

> Since it is out of the Sacred Scriptures, the writings of the saints, and other theological books that, in the public interest, the most help is provided in dealing with the numerous seductive volumes introduced by heretics especially in our time; and for the sake of upholding the truth of Catholic doctrine, exposing the temerity of our adversaries who viciously pervert those tenets, and also informing our minds by the study of the whole field of knowledge; and because the libraries of private individuals are often meager and inconsequential due to their modest means; and lest in the future we struggle with much worry and mental anxiety to regain the books we now possess--for all these reasons we very appropriately decree that a common library be set up, fully supplied with an abundance of books of all kinds, which will be as it were the armory of this spiritually-militant brotherhood, so that those books, writings, and pandects may be available to each and every canon just as if they were his own. We therefore resolve, enact, and ordain that a chapter library be established in the upper hall above the sanctuary or chapel of St. Augustine, and that this be done by a crosswise arranging of benches which should all be given

---

[352]This work is commended for its completeness by Bourgeois, entry 4859, and its companion volume (Estat des cours ecclésiastiques, first published in 1626) is "based on innumerable references, and no less useful than it is very full and scholarly" (Bourgeois, entry 4403). Bordenave (ca. 1588-1652), a convert from Calvinism, was named a canon of Lescar in 1614 (Roman d'Amat, in DBF, VI, 1076-77; see also Testament de l'historien bearnais Jean de Bordenave, ed. V. Dubarat [Pau: Vue Ribant, 1899]).

cloth coverings, and should be so positioned in relation to each other that a person can walk around the room and back and forth through it with complete freedom. At the side of the said hall a number of individual presses[353] are to be constructed, in which will be kept--not in piles but in order according to subject field--all the books, codices, and volumes which had belonged to each and every canon when he was alive (unless he otherwise dispose of them as a whole or in part in his last will and testament), as well as those now bestowed, rendered, and imparted by donation, and those already assigned to it and confirmed by virtue of the present statute.

Moreover, a catalog is to be made, in which each volume should be listed in subject categories or in alphabetical order. This catalog is to be preserved forever in a safe place, and all books added to the said library in the future, whatever their source, should be entered in it one after the other.

Tomes and volumes which are dirty because of age, decay, or neglect are to be refurbished as part of the library work; books that have come apart or are badly bound should be reglued; those lacking covers are to be bound with boards or leather; and those injured through use or in other ways should be repaired and permanently restored by new covers and fresh workmanship.

Let every canon have his own key, and when a key is handed out to any one, a particular and express oath is to be taken with one's hand on God's four holy Gospels, in a session of the Chapter before all the resident canons. The recipient must swear that he will painstakingly, diligently, and faithfully protect the said books; not remove them from the library or permit them to be withdrawn; not tear anything out of a book or cause anything to be torn out--not even the least leaf--which would do a book damage; and if he perceives that any one is committing that crime, reveal it to the Chapter immediately. But if one should depart from his oath in the aforesaid particulars, let him be censured for his theft (or more correctly, his sacrilege), and let him be obliged to make restitution for stealing what was consecrated to God's Church; thereby proper authority is upheld.

However, by this edict we are not preventing any canon from copying out particular extracts of material from a volume. Nay, if in fact he needs to read some book in private, and if it seems good to the Chapter, by all means let him have it for a time by consent of the

---

[353]Latin, _armaria_. For the history of this word as applied to library fittings, see Clark, pp. 72-88 and _passim_.

Chapter--provided that the borrower refrain from writing anything in it or marking it in any way, and provided that he give a pledge for its return.

Moreover, the Chapter is to appoint some canon who is skilled in and devoted to literature and eager to organize a library, and he shall diligently administer it. By virtue of his office this librarian is from time to time to vist, inspect, and examine the said library. If through him or through the other brothers any reason can be shown for increasing the number of theological books or works on any other acceptable subject, let this be attended to with such meticulous care that, in providing writings of this kind, consideration be given to the canonical body and to what is profitable and beneficial for the whole diocese[L].

It is thus evident from this decree how useful for the enhancement of the Muses these learned and pious churchmen consider the erecting of the library to be, and what care they take both for its establishment and for its preservation and enlargement as well--and toward the latter they all direct united effort with great zeal.

CHAPTER IX (XC)

BERRY

The capital city of this duchy is Bourges, and it is adorned not only with an ancient archbishopric and an illustrious university, but also with a rich Parnassus of the Muses--I refer to a most opulent library--which his royal highness Henri de Bourbon, prince de Condé and governor of the provinces of Burgundy, Bresse, and Berry, has collected with great energy and at lavish expense.[354] Indeed, his perfect acquaintance with all fields of knowledge and with rare and interesting books causes him to be regarded as an oracle of the Muses. It is admirable that notwithstanding his important duties in behalf of the state, his highness lets no day go by without devoting himself to study, thereby finding diversions worthy of a great

<u>The library of the prince de Condé</u>

---

[354] Jacob here refers to Henri II, 3d prince de Condé (1588-1646), who, although miserly, irascible, and profligate, became, following the death of Louis XIII, the third most important person in France (after Louis XIV and Mazarin). On him, see Roman d'Amat, in <u>DBF</u>, IX, 441-42, and Henri Chérot, "Le père du Grand Condé," <u>Études: revue fondée en 1856 par des pères de la Compagnie de Jesus</u>, LVII (September-December, 1892), 193-203. On the library of the house of Condé, which was moved to Chantilly after that town and château were given to the Grand Condé by Louis XIV in 1661, see Delisle, II, 10 (cf. I, 370), and Bonnaffé, <u>Dictionnaire ...</u>, pp. 70-71.

prince. Thus he acquires immortal glory throughout Europe --as much for surpassing all other princes in knowledge as for zealously encouraging the progress of the sciences.

The library of the Benedictine abbey of Saint-Sulpice, which is located on the outskirts of Bourges, is worth considering for the quality of its books.[355]

The library of Saint-Sulpice

The abbey of Chezal-Benoît, belonging to the same order and founded in this diocese, is very famous.[356] There one finds a highly renowned library established for the use of the monastic community.[357]

The library of Chazant-Benoist

---

[355] The library of Saint-Sulpice was later incorporated into the Bourges city library; on its manuscripts, see Montfaucon, II, 1229-30, and CMD, IV, 1-2 and passim (and cf Delisle, I, 64, 564; II, 411, 508; III, 192).

[356] Manuscripts which once belonged to this abbey are found today in the Bourges library and at the Bibliothèque Nationale (ibid., II, 354; cf. I, 564; and see CMD, IV, 1 and passim).

[357] The Appendix paragraph treating Guillaume Pellicier's library has not been added here, in spite of our author's instruction that it be inserted on "p. 626, after l. 4" of his text. Instead, the insertion has been made in the Languedoc chapter below (corresponding to p. 660, l. 4 of the original text). The "p. 626" reference is almost certainly an error, for (1) the line number for the insertion does not fit that page (though it does fit p. 660), and (2) Pellicier's city, Montpellier, is in the province of Languedoc, not in the province of Berry.

CHAPTER X (XCI)

THE DUCHY AND COUNTY OF BURGUNDY

The capital of the duchy is the city of Dijon, which received the light of the Gospel through the glorious martyr St. Benignus.[358] To his memory they erected a distinguished abbey, where a fine old manuscript library is maintained.[359] M. Paul Dumay, councillor in Parlement, has published the catalog of them under the title, Bibliotheca Janiniana Sancti Benigni Divionensis: Ope & industria P.D. (Divione, September 13, 1621, in quarto).[360] The two letters "P.D." stand for the

The library of Saint-Bénigne

---

[358]St. Benignus (Bénigne, vulg. Berin, Berain), the apostle of Burgundy, was martyred at Dijon in the second century.

[359]Manuscripts which were part of the collection at the abbey of Saint-Bénigne at Dijon have passed into the Bibliothèque Nationale, the library of the Faculty of Medicine at Montpellier, and especially the city library of Dijon. On this important collection, which contained about three hundred manuscripts in the seventeenth century, see Charles Oursel, Le bibliothèque de l'abbaye de Saint-Bénigne, et ses plus anciens manuscrits (Dijon, 1924); Delisle, II, 402-404 (cf. I, 162, 408, 564); Vogel, p. 261; and CMD V, xi, 529 and passim.

[360]This catalog, which was prepared at the request of Abbot Nicolas Janin, is wrongly attributed to Pierre Dumay by Delisle, II, 403; the eight-page catalog was drawn up by the litterateur Paul Dumay (1585-1645), as Jacob states. Both La Monnoye (in the Ménagiana, 1729 ed., II, 97-101) and Philibert Papillon, (Bibliothèque des auteurs de Bourgogne [2 vols.; Dijon: P. Marteret, 1742], I, 187) cast doubt on the existence of a printed edition of this catalog, but a unique copy of the 1621 edition survives in the Bibliothèque Nationale, and has been reprinted in CMD, V, 453-57.

228

name of that learned councillor, as I discover in his annotations to Pope Innocent III's epistle;[361] there he says that he was responsible for printing the catalog.

In the monastery of the Carmelite fathers there is a

The library of the Carmelites — large and magnificent library composed of five to six thousand excellent volumes.[362] These were put there by the very famous monk of that monastery Laurent Bureau, doctor of Paris, provincial of Narbonne province, confes-

L. Bureau — sor of Kings Charles VIII and Louis XII and of Anne of Brittany (Louis' wife), and later bishop of Sisteron, who died at Blois on July 5, 1540;[363] and especially by Didier Buffet, doctor of Paris, and vicar general

D. Buffet — of his order in France, who had great affection for good books and filled that library with them (his coat-of-arms may be seen on each). As for the modern physical

---

[361] Jacob should say "epistles" rather than "epistle." Data on this edition of the correspondence of Innocent III are provided by Delisle, I, 498; for the authorship identification referred to by Jacob, see Paul Dumay (ed.), *Innocenti III ... Epistolae ... ex cod. ms. collegii fuxensis, cum lucubrationibus* (Parisiis: N. Buon, 1625), p. 207 (Epistle 9).

[362] A Latin and a French manuscript from this Carmelite monastery are now in the Bibliothèque Nationale (Delisle, II, 360); and a fifteenth-century Ordinarium and two manuscript histories of the Carmelites (eighteenth-century) which were once in the library of the Dijon Carmelites can be seen today in the Dijon city library (CMD, V, 31, 160).

[363] The date should be 1504, not 1540. On Bureau, who wrote poetry (*l'Héliade*) and the so-called "Green Book" (*Livre vert*) containing the chronology of his episcopal predecessors and transcriptions of the old charters of Sisteron, see Scévole (II) de Sainte-Marthe, et al., *Gallia Christiana* (16 vols.; Parisiis: V. Palmé, 1865-1870), I, 500-501; and T. de Morembert, in *DBF*, VII, 687. Bureau is known to have made significant contributions to the library of Carmelites of the Place Maubert in Paris as well (Delisle, I, 286-87).

facilities of the library, the honor goes to Father François

F. Reneuey — Reneuey, prior of this monastery, and likewise a doctor of Paris.[364]

M. Bouhier — M. Bouhier, councillor in the Dijon Parlement, expends great sums to build the most sumptuous library of the duchy of Burgundy. He began it with the purchase of all the theological books from the library of the great and learned bishop of Chalon, Pontus de Tyard.

Pontus de Tyard — The latter had collected one of the finest libraries of his time, and it was divided between M. de Bissi and M. de Bragni his nephews.[365]

MM. de Bissi and Bragni — M. de Bissi obtained the theological books from the library of Cyrus de Tyard, Pontus' successor in the bishopric and likewise his nephew.[366] After the death both of Cyrus de Tyard and M. de Bissi, these books were carried to Bellegarde on account of the wars going on in the county of Burgundy, and there they were sold to the

---

[364] Collateral data on Buffet and Reneuey have not been found.

[365] Pontus de Tyard (1521-1605) was a poet and last survivor of the Pléiade, and a musical humanist related to Baïf's Academy; indeed, "there are good grounds for relying on Pontus de Tyard as the philosophical theorist of the sixteenth-century French academies" (Yates, p. 77 and passim). M. de Bissi (Pontus de Tyard) and M. de Bragni (Louis de Tyard) were, strictly speaking, grand-nephews of the poet, who bequeathed his library to them on March 20, 1601 (Jean-Pierre-Abel Jeandet, Étude sur le XVIe siècle, France et Bourgogne. Pontus de Tyard [Paris: A. Aubry, 1860], p. 107).

[366] Pontus' heirs, Louis and Pontus, gave the theological books in their grand-uncle's library to their uncle Cyrus de Tyard, and on his death (January 3, 1624), the books reverted; Louis and Pontus were, in fact, the recipients of Cyrus' entire library (ibid.). On Cyrus, who published several pastoral letters, see Papillon, II, 332.

said M. Bouhier.³⁶⁷ As for Pontus' books in the fields of history and the humanities, which M. Louis de Tyard, lord of Bragni, acquired, they were all burned in 1636, along with the Bragni mansion, by the army of the duke of Lorraine when he captured the city of Verdun-sur-Sone. This was a great pity, for I saw there some very excellent books. Now that intellectually-curious councillor M. Bouhier searches with great care for all the best books he can find to enrich his library.

M. N. de Chevanes of Autun, advocate in Parlement is

M. de Chevanes an erudite man who is absorbed with good books and has a profound knowledge of them. This is why his library is worthy of consideration.³⁶⁸

---

³⁶⁷Jean Bouhier or Boyer (d. 1671) made this acquisition in 1642. The Bouhier library was one of the glories of Dijon for over two centuries; nine generations of Bouhiers contributed to it. The history of the library was written about 1725 by the most illustrious of the Bouhiers--President Jean Bouhier (1673-1746), who was succeeded by Voltaire in the French Academy. President Bouhier describes his grandfather's book collecting activities as follows: "He maintained connections in various parts of Europe in order to ferret out good books, whether ancient or modern. Not content with printed works, he particularly sought out the most excellent manuscripts, and brought together a great quantity of them. Those which he could not obtain in the original, he had copied at great expense. He himself transcribed--with his own hand--more than fifty huge volumes, without either the tedium of such work or his infirmities reducing his indefatigable passion in that regard" (Jean Bouhier, "Mémoire de M. le président Bouhier sur sa bibliothèque," in his <u>Recherches et dissertations sur Hérodote ... avec des mémoires sur la vie de l'auteur [par François Oudin]</u> [Dijon: Pierre De Saint, 1746], Pt. 2 ["Commentarius de vita et scriptis Joannis Buherii"], p. 46. Examples of the bibliophilistic correspondence of Councillor Bouhier, contemporary testimonies to the quality of the Bouhier library, and locations of extant volumes from this collection are given in Delisle, II, 268-78.

³⁶⁸Nicolas de Chevanes (d. 1654), a celebrated advocate in the Burgundy Parlement, was chosen by Charles Févret to be one of the interlocutors in his dialogue, <u>De claris fori</u>

The great and illustrious abbey of Cîteaux was founded four leagues[369] from Dijon in the diocese of Chalon by the dukes of Burgundy. Still today[370] it possesses a splendid library, and connected with it is a room completely filled with very old and valuable manuscripts, especially writings of the church fathers. These came from the labors of the monks of that abbey, who, before the invention of printing, applied themselves at certain hours of the day to the copying of good books for their own use. They carried on this transcription in particular rooms which may still be seen in a cloister of the abbey. In olden days it was the practice of monks to copy books in the hours not occupied with divine service, and posterity is much indebted to them for this,

The library of Cîteaux

Burgundici oratoribus (Divione: P. Palliot, 1654); a eulogy of him is contained in this volume. Chevanes' writing was concerned especially with the reform of the Cistercian order (cf. DBF, VIII, 1082), and several of his productions are listed in the Catalogue général des livres imprimés of the Bibliothèque Nationale. The bibliothecal interests of Chevanes are patent from the fact that Councillor Jean Bouhier "received from the advocate Nicolas de Chevanes a Greek New Testament which Philippe de Villers of the Isle-Adam, grand master of the order of St. John of Jerusalem, had once offered to Jean Guijon as a token of remembrance for his leadership at the siege of Rhodes" (Delisle, II, 276); see also Bonnaffé, Dictionnaire ..., p. 61.

[369]I.e., ten miles.

[370]I.e., even after the great days of Burgundy's semi-independent status which ended with the defeat and death of Duke Charles the Bold (1477). Abbot Jean de Cirey's late fifteenth-century catalog of the abbey collection listed twelve hundred items, including a few printed books (this inventory has been published in CMD, V, 339-452). Today, the Dijon public library possesses over three hundred Cîteaux manuscripts; and six manuscripts from the abbey library are in the Bibliothèque Nationale (Delisle, II, 355). See also [Edmond Martène and Ursin Durand] Voyage littéraire de deux religieux bénédictins de la congrégation de Saint-Maur (2 vols.; Paris: Delaulne & Montalant, 1717-1724), I, 221-23.

since today their manuscripts serve as an exquisite ornament for all distinguished libraries.

    The town of Chalon, where I was born, was once called Orbendale because its defensive walls were triple-banded. It served as a supply depot for Emperor[371] Julius Caesar, the conqueror of the Gouls, and later it became the seat of the kings of Burgundy and one of the prime cities of that kingdom which received the Christian faith through the glorious martyr St. Marcel of Lyons.[372] Now it is quite true that this town is greatly esteemed among historians for the above characteristics and because it holds the sepulchres of two kings --the first being St. Gontran, king of Burgundy, who is interred in the priory of Saint-Marcel (where the monk Peter Abelard died), and the second, João, infante of Portugal, who became a Franciscan monk on passing through this town, and was later declared king but refused the dignity because his humility compelled him to follow Jesus Christ the King of Kings. However, the town deserves to be held in high historical regard no less with respect to the subject we are treating, for one sees there a well-stocked library established by the late M. Claude-Énoch Virey, first secretary to his Highness the Prince de Condé, and afterwards councillor, secretary, and notary to the house and crown of France.[373] He was

M. Virey

---

[371] See above, n. 88.

[372] Gotran, king of Burgundy chose Chalon-sur-Saône as his capital in the sixth century. St. Marcel preached Christianity at Chalon in the second century.

[373] Claude-Énoch Virey (1566-1636) obtained his early education at the Jesuit college in Dijon, studied philosophy at the Collège de Navarre at Paris, and received the degree of doctor of law at Padua. He was five times mayor of Chalon. A list of his

a man of great erudition, and was very well acquainted with
good books and filled his library with them. At his death on
July 25, 1636 he left his library to his son M. Jean-Christophe
Virey, royal councillor, and master of accounts for the province
of Burgundy and Bresse, who buys books daily to enlarge it.
This library is even more remarkable for its fine bindings, and
the number of its books exceeds 4000.

The duchy of Burgundy can boast of two abbeys which are
the headquarters of their orders--the monastery of Cîteaux and
that of Cluny. The latter gave many holy persons

The library to the church of God, and also many learned monks
of Cluny who honored the Muses and to a man worked to build
a splendid library.[374] This library was destroyed
by the Calvinists in the year 1562, as Michael Caspar Lundorp
remarks in his continuation of Johannes Sleidanus' history:

> Meanwhile Poncenatus took by assault the monastery of
> Cluny--the most noble in the whole world--and included
> in the sack, to the great anguish of all the studious
> in the realm of letters, its preeminently well-stocked
> library, with its entire collection of manuscript books.
> What little could be restored from this loss--and it
> was scarcely anything--perished by fire as a result of
> the wanton conduct of the soldiers[375][L].

---

works (chiefly orations) appears in Moréri, X, Pt. 1, 657. A
Latin manuscript from his library has been identified in the
Bibliothèque Nationale (Delisle, II, 424); and the Chalon public
library has a manuscript of his poetry with marginal notes apparently by the author himself--a manuscript which carries the
coat-of-arms of his son Jean-Christophe (CMD, VI, 370).

[374]On the Cluny library, see Léopold Delisle, *Inventaire des manuscrits de la Bibliothèque Nationale (Fonds de Cluni)* (Paris: Champion, 1884), pp. v-xxv; Vogel, p. 260; and James Westfall Thompson, *The Medieval Library*, reprinted with supplement by Blanche B. Boyer (New York: Hafner, 1957), pp. 224-27 (Thompson's work must, of course, be used with caution).

[375]This passage from Lundorp's continuation of Sleidanus'

The library of the Carmelites of Semur

The Carmelite fathers of Semur-en-Auxois have a considerable library of more than 4000 volumes and some 120 manuscripts. These books were placed there by numerous monks of this monastery, and the convent can pride itself on being one of the finest of its order in France. The Rev. Father Renaut de Vaulx, doctor of Paris and provincial of Narbonne, contributed much to the augmentation of this library.[376]

The library of the Minimites of Tonnerre

The imposing monastery of the Minimite fathers of Tonnerre was founded in 1611 by M. Charles-Henri de Clermont, count of Tonnerre, etc., and knight of the orders of his majesty, who, besides providing this benefit, gave these Minimites his family library. We learn this from Father François de la Noue in his *Chronicle of the Minimites*, where in speaking of this monastery he says:

> The count generously gave us an abundance of the best books he had received from his ancestors. He did this because of his conviction that provided the monks were using them, benefit would issue forth to the people whom they are accustomed to instruct in annual sermons throughout Advent and Lent[377][L].

De statu religionis et reipublicae is also referred to by Lomeier, sec. "France," text corresponding to n. 17.

[376] The Dijon public library has in its collection a seventeenth-century manuscript (dealing with the peace of the Pyrenees, 1659) which once belonged to the Carmelites of Semur (CMD, V, 204). Of 117 manuscripts in the Semur public library, no less than 25 came from this Carmelite collection (*ibid.*, VI 295, 298-301, 303, 305, 307-12, 315-17, 322). Collateral data on Vaulx have not been found.

[377] François de La Noue, *Chronicon generale ordinis Minimorum*, I (Lutetiae Parisiorum: S. Cramoisy, 1635), 449. On La Noue, see above, n. 223. The library of the Minimite monastery of Tonnerre receives mention in Martène, I, Pt. 1, 108-109.

Besançon is an imperial city in the county of Burgundy and there in the hôtel de Granvelle a noble library is maintained.

<u>Cardinal de Granvelle's library</u> It was begun by that great Cardinal Archbishop Antoine Perrenot de Granvelle, the founder of the Besançon university, who was a Maecenas of his time in his relations with scholars, as can be seen by those he promoted to higher positions and honors. Supervision of this library was in the hands of Suffridus Petri, who published numerous good books.[378]

In the Jesuit college at Besançon there is a good

---

[378] Antoine Perrenot de Granvelle (1517-1586) was one of the ablest Roman Catholic diplomats of the Counter-Reformation. He studied law at Padua and theology at Louvain, and attended the early meetings of the Council of Trent. He settled the terms of peace after the defeat of the Schmalkaldic League at Mühlberg in 1547, and drew up the treaty of Passau (1552). After the abdication of Emperor Charles V he transferred his services to Philip II of Spain, and helped to arrange the peace of Cateau Cambrésis, as well as the alliance between Spain, Venice, and the papacy which resulted in the victory of Lepanto. He is said to have spoken seven languages, and he was a generous and enlightened patron of arts and letters. Granvelle produced a tremendous diplomatic correspondence; his letters and memoirs are preserved for the most part in the Besançon archives (see CMD, XXXII and XXXIII, passim; Edwards, II, 344-45; and Vogel, p. 254), and have been the basis of the <u>Papiers d'État du cardinal de Granvelle</u>, ed. C. Weiss and C. Duvernoy (9 vols.; Paris: Imprimerie royale, 1841-1852), and the <u>Correspondance du cardinal de Granvelle, 1565-1586</u>, ed. Edmond Poullet and Charles Piot (12 vols.; Bruxelles: Hayez, 1877-1896). Suffridus Petri (1527-1597), historian and philologian, studied ancient languages at Louvain, and held the chair of belles-lettres at Erfurt prior to becoming Granvelle's librarian. Later he served as professor of law at Louvain and was given the title "historiographer of the province of Friesland." He produced many translations, editions, and original works in the fields of history, classical studies, education, and bio-bibliography; a list of his works is given in the biographical article on him in Jean-Pierre Nicéron, XXX, 123-32.

The Jesuit library library composed of books in all the academic fields.[379]

The twon of Dôle receives distinction from having a Parlement, and a university[380] where various learned persons have taught—among them Justus Lipsius.

The library of the Benedictines of Dôle No less a glory to the town has been its magnificent public library, founded in the Cluniac college of Saint-Jérôme, where a great number of manuscripts served as a marvellous ornament to it.

The library of the abbey of Luxenil was famous once,

The library of the abbey of Luxenil but today it is entirely dispersed.[381]

To the county of Burgundy also belongs the noble Cistercian abbey of Ballerne, which was founded about the year 1115. It possessed an ancient library which has deteriorated much on account of wars. However, M. Philippe Chifflet, the abbot,[382]

---

[379] A late seventeenth-century manuscript with ex-libris from the Jesuit college at Besançon is preserved in the Besançon public library (CMD, XXXII, 405). On the history of this Jesuit institution in the sixteenth and seventeenth centuries, see Fouqueray, II, 469-73; V, 212-17.

[380] In 1674 Louis XIV transferred both the university (founded ca. 1422) and the Parlement to Besançon. Some of the most valuable manuscripts in the Dôle city library today came originally from the Cluniac college of Saint-Jérôme; these manuscripts generally carry the coat-of-arms of Antoine de Roche, grand prior of Cluny, who founded the college in 1492 and supplied it with a rich library (CMD, XIII, 377-78, 499, 576 and passim).

[381] On the Luxeuil abbey library, see Delisle, Le cabinet des manuscrits, II, 380.

[382] Philippe Chifflet (1597-ca. 1663), a writer of epigrams whom Colletet called "mon frère d'alliance," took part with his friend Naudé in the mid-seventeenth century controversy over the

M. Chifflet

Pt. 2, p. 133:

> endeavors personally to restore it to its original splendor, as we learn from Anton Sander, in his <u>Library of the Manuscripts of Flanders</u>,

> Then sacred studies on the part of the monks flourished there, and Brocard, a learned and holy man, led the way. Also, a rich library was established, as certain very old catalogs of the book collection testify. Those manuscript books which remain should without doubt be considered the least part of the many volumes destroyed by war and other injurious effects of time. However, it is hoped that just as in monastic discipline, so also in library resources, a restoration to pristine splendor will be brought about by that most noble and reverend sir, Philippe Chifflet, at present the worthy abbot of the community. In the meantime, we offer to the public the catalog, given us by the pious monks, of whatever manuscripts still remain in that monastery383[L].

---

authorship of the <u>Imitatio Christi</u> (Pintard, p. 167; cf. Moréri, III, 616-17, and Bonnaffé, <u>Dictionnaire ...</u>, pp. 62-63).

383 Jacob here quotes Anton Sander's <u>Bibliotheca belgica manuscripta</u> (2 vols.; Insulis: T. Le Clercq, 1641-1644), II, 133-34; Sander's catalog of Ballerne manuscripts (pp. 134-36) was drawn up in 1641 and lists some 65 manuscripts (50 theological, 15 grammatical), including 25 of folio size. On Sander (1586-1664), a Flemish historian and bibliographer, see <u>ADB, XXX</u> 345-47. Jacob, in his chapter on libraries in the county of Flanders (chap. lxxiv) uses Sander as his chief authority. The Ballerne abbey library also receives mention in Antoine Rivet de La Grange, et al., <u>Histoire literaire de la France ... par des religieux benedictins de la congregation de S. Maur</u> (24 vols.; Paris, 1733-1862), IX, 125.

CHAPTER XI (XCII)

BRITTANY

M. Pierre de Cornulier, councillor in the Parlement of Rennes, was made bishop of Tréguier and later of Rennes because of his merits. He built a fine library, which became the property of his heirs.[384]

<small>Rennes</small>
<small>M. de Cornulier</small>

The Carmelite monastery at Rennes was founded in the year 1447. One sees there a fine and ample library composed of good books which have been put there by the Carmelite fathers of the monastery.

<small>The library of the Carmelites</small>

The library of the Dominican fathers has a reputation for being very substantial.

<small>The Dominican library</small>

---

[384] On Pierre de Cornulier (1575-1639), who held a plurality of benefices, established several foundations, engaged in liturgical reform, introduced the Minimites into Rennes, and in 1638 wrote a work entitled, Raison des États de Bretagne pour justifier que l'indult de Parlement de Paris no doit avoir lieu en la dite province, see Prosper-Jean Levot, et al., Biographie bretonne (2 vols.; Vannes: Cauderan, 1852-1857), I, 469-70; and Bulletin et mémoires de la Société archéologique du département d'Ille-et-Vilaine, LXV (1940), xxx. The Rennes public library has two late seventeenth-century manuscript catalogs of the Carmelite monastery library on the rue Vasselot at Rennes (CMD, XXIV, 231; cf. p. 46), and a manuscript inventory of the Dominican library showing 3200 volumes in its collection at the time the monastery was suppressed in the Revolution (ibid., p. 230).

M. Biré   M. Biré, who wrote several books, established a notable library through his search for good books.[385]

I find that in the city of Nantes the Oratorian fathers

The library of the Oratorians   have been concerned to build a large and excellent library which serves as a unique ornament for their monastery.

M. Jean de Rieux, marquis d'Assérac, count of Largoët, chief bearer of the name and arms of the house of Rieux,[386] and

M. d'Assérac's library   a descendant of the dukes of Brittany, is well versed in the sciences. He cultivates them daily by means of the

good books with which he has filled his exquisite library; and he labors with great effort to enlarge this collection.

---

[385] Jacob undoubtedly refers here to Pierre Biré de la Doucinière (ca. 1562-1638), royal advocate at the presidial seat of Nantes, who wrote poetry as well as works in the fields of genealogy (Alliances généalogiques de la maison de Lorraine, 1593) and heraldry (Épisemasie ... concernant l'origine, antiquité, noblesse et sainctété de la Bretaigne armorique, 1637); on him, see M. Prevost, in DBF, VI, 515; and Levot, I, 102-103. A number of manuscripts from the Oratorian library at Nantes can be seen today in the Nantes public library (CMD, XXII, 537 and passim).

[386] See Moréri, IX, Pt. 1, 201 for data on the house of Rieux. Patin calls Jean de Rieux (d. 1657) "un gentilhomme curieux et savant" and states that he financed the publication of at least one book (Gui Patin, Lettres, ed. Reveillé-Parise, II, 201 [letter of September 21, 1655]). He is included among owners of "principaux cabinets" in 1649 by Pierre Borel, Les antiquitez de Castres, ed. Ch. Pradel (Paris: Académie des Bibliophiles, 1868), Pt. 2, p. 138; on him see also Bonnaffé, Dictionnaire ..., p. 9 (cf. p. 277).

CHAPTER XII (XCIII)

CHAMPAGNE

The very illustrious Church of Reims once had as its dean Cardinal Guillaume Fillastre. He bequeathed his library to that Church, according to Pierre Frizon, who says in his Gallia purpurata: "Fillastre, dean of Reims, established a splendid library for the use of the canons of the metropolitan Church, and bestowed upon it a very great number of books"387[L]. The Cardinal of Lorraine imitated Fillastre by leaving his book collection to that Church; but it has since been dispersed.388

M. Léonor d'Étampes de Valençay, brother of the Cardinal

Reims
The library of
the Cathedral Church

The Cardinal of
Lorraine's library

387Frizon, p. 465; Frizon and his work have been discussed above (n. 144). On the library of the Cathedral Church at Reims, see the bibliographical references provided by Vogel, p. 297. Several manuscript catalogs and inventories of the Chapter library are preserved in the Reims public library (CMD, XXXIX, Pt. 2, 1019 ff.). Guillaume Fillastre (1347/48-1428) was much involved in the ecclesiastical controversies of the Great Schism, and played an important rôle at the Council of Constance (Moréri, V, Pt. 1, 158; Scévole [II] de Sainte-Marthe, IX, 174). A considerable number of manuscripts which were formerly in Fillastre's library can be seen today in the Reims public library (CMD, XXXIX, Pt. 2, 1189 and passim).

388I.e., Charles of Lorraine, cardinal archbishop of Reims (d. 1574); on him see the detailed article in Scévole (II) de Sainte-Marthe, IX, 148-54. A magnificent sixteenth-century Greek manuscript copied for him by Constantine Palaeocappa is now a part of the Reims city library collection (CMD, XXXVIII, 483-84).

de Valençay, has always had a great affection for literature. For when he was still only the abbot of Bourgueil in Anjou he had already begun that superb and admirable library which he is perfecting with such zeal; Claude Robert tells us this when he speaks of that abbey in his <u>Christian Gaul</u>.³⁸⁹ But afterwards he was made bishop of Chartres, and finally archbishop of Reims, and there he transported this treasury of the Muses which people deem the most well-stocked in France.

<u>The Archbishop's library</u>

In the diocese of Reims is the abbey of Notre Dame d'Igny. It possessed a very famous library.³⁹⁰

<u>The library of the abbey of Igny</u>

The Church of Langres has a library containing some ancient manuscripts which people hold in regard.³⁹¹

<u>The library of Langres</u>

---

³⁸⁹Claude Robert, <u>Gallia Christiana</u> (Lutetiae Parisiorum: S. Cramoisy, 1626), p. 292; "the author, grand archdeacon of Chalon-sur-Saône, recognized the incomplete nature of his work, for he engaged the brothers Sainte-Marthe to finish and perfect it; it is a first draft, which served Father [Philippe] Labbe in his <u>Pouillé royal</u> of 1648" (Bourgeois, entry 4332). On Léonar d'Étampes de Valençay (<u>ca</u>. 1589-1651), who took an active part in French ecclesiastical affairs, see Moréri, IV, Pt. 3, 246, and Scévole (II) de Sainte-Marthe, IX, 161. Anecdotes reflecting his great love of books are recounted in Bonnaffé, <u>Dictionnaire ...</u>, p. 318. Manuscript materials pertinent to the Reims archiepiscopacy of Valençay are listed in <u>CMD</u>, XXXIX, Pt. 2, 816; Pt. 3, 248

³⁹⁰A Latin manuscript from this abbey library has been identified in the Bibliothèque Nationale collection (Delisle, <u>Le cabinet des manuscrits</u>, II, 372), and a 1791 manuscript catalog of the abbey's books is preserved in the Reims public library (<u>CMD</u>, XXXIX, Pt. 2, 1023).

³⁹¹Surviving manuscripts from the Langres cathedral library which are now in the Bibliothèque Nationale are described

<u>The library at Châlons</u>   The late M. Henri Clausse, bishop of Châlons in Champagne, built a considerable library, for he was a man of great erudition.[392]

---

in Delisle, <u>Le cabinet des manuscrits</u>, II, 374-75; the Langres city library has fifteen manuscripts which originally belonged to the cathedral chapter (<u>CMD</u>, XXI, 66, 68-70, 72-74, 88-89, 91).

[392]Henri Clausse (d. 1640) became bishop of Châlons in 1624 and simultaneously administered the see of Reims during the minority of Henri of Lorraine (T. de Morembert, in <u>DBF</u>, VIII, 1397). Scévole (II) de Sainte-Marthe, IX, 899, informs us that Clausse "bequeathed his library to his [episcopal] successors."

CHAPTER XIII (XCIV)

DAUPHINÉ

Vienne
The Jesuit library
Vienne is the metropolitan city of this province; here Archbishop Jérôme de Villars founded a magnificent college for the Jesuit fathers, and they have there a very good library.[393]

The bishop of Grenoble
M. Pierre Scarron, bishop of Grenoble, has collected a library which is esteemed for its good books.[394]

M. de Boissieu
Those who are acquainted with M. Denis de Salvaing de Boissieu, knight, king's councillor in his council of state and privy council, and a first president in the Chamber of Accounts of Dauphiné, frankly admit that this lord is endowed with the most exceptional intellectual qualities of the age. If one considers his powers of memory, they are seen to be more fertile than any; if one contemplates his mental ability, its extraordinary nature

---

[393] Jérôme de Villars was canon and archdeacon of Vienne, councillor in the Paris Parlement (Maugis, III, 273, 277), and archbishop of Vienne (1599); he died on January 18, 1626 (Moréri, X, Pt. 1, 620; Scévole [II] de Sainte-Marthe, XVI, 128-30). On the early history of the Jesuit college at Vienne, founded in 1606, see Fouqueray, III, 100-103.

[394] Pierre Scarron was received as councillor in the Grenoble Parlement in 1603, subsequently became bishop of Grenoble, and died ca. 1668 (Moréri, IX, Pt. 2, 228; Scévole [II] de Sainte-Marthe, XVI, 256; CMD, VII, 528, 567, 592). His cabinet of paintings and books receives mention in Bonnaffé, Dictionnaire ..., p. 285.

makes one envious; if one observes his learning and eloquence, it is evident that they have entranced not only the French, but even the fastidious Romans when he was orator to Pope Urban VIII for our most Christian king Louis XIII.[395] The Greek language is as familiar to him as his mother tongue; moreover he can boast that there is not a single library in France that contains more Greek manuscripts and Greek printed books than his. This library was begun by his father, M. Charles de Salvaing de Boissieu.[396]

The Saint-Andrés are a distinguished family in the province of Dauphiné. From this family comes President de Saint-André, who collected a library full of good books.[397]

M. de Saint-André's library

The library of M. du Ponat, councillor in the Parlement of Grenoble, is highly regarded for the quantity of books in it;

---

[395]Denis de Salvaing (1600-1683) studied philosophy under Isaac Habert at Paris, and took his doctorate in law at Valence; his breadth of scholarly interest is evidenced by additional academic work in Greek and in mathematics. When in Rome in 1633, he visited libraries as well as delivering a Latin oration before Urban VIII which was so well received that it was published in Rome, Paris, and Grenoble that same year, and was translated into French by Pelletier and Videl. Salvaing's other publications include Latin and French poetry, editions of and commentaries on classical and medieval texts, legal works dealing with Dauphiné, and a genealogy of his own family; Vulson de la Colombière's Science héroïque (cited elsewhere by Jacob) is heavily dependent upon his scholarship. On Salvaing, see the Latin biography of him by his friend Nicolas Chorier, with an appended autobiographical Latin elegy (Nicolas Chorier, De Dionysii Salvagnii Boessii, delphinatis, viri illustris, vita [Gratianopoli: F. Provensal, 1680]), and M. Lancelot's "Memoire sur la vie & les ouvrages du président de Boissieu," Mémoires de l'Académie des inscriptions & belles lettres, XII, 316 ff.

[396]Charles de Salvaing, according to his son's biographer Chorier, had a good knowledge of Latin, Greek, Hebrew, Aramaic, Italian, Spanish, and French. He was a close friend of Cujas, and corresponded with him in Greek (Moréri, IX, Pt. 2, 106).

[397]On the libraries of the Saint-André's, see above, nn. 172, 240, 281-82, and corresponding text passages.

M. du Ponat's library and its owner adds to it every day.³⁹⁸

The late M. Claude d'Expilli, advocate general in the Dauphiné Parlement and later its president, was an erudite man, as his works attest. He was vitally interested **M. d'Expilli** in the search for good books, and from them he built his library.³⁹⁹ Today this collection is maintained by his daughter, the wife of President de Brion.⁴⁰⁰

Among those at Grenoble who are concerned with library building is M. du Vivier, sub-bailiff of **M. du Vivier** Graisivaudan in Dauphiné, for he brings together good books to furnish his collection.⁴⁰¹

M. Philippe Laigneau spares no effort in embellishing his fine library with the rarest and most inter- **M. Laigneau** esting books to be found.⁴⁰² The number of volumes

---

³⁹⁸Collateral data on M. du Ponat have not been found.

³⁹⁹Claude d'Expilli (1561-1636), statesman, orator, historian, and poet, studied at Turin, Padua, and Bourges; he obtained his doctor's degree at Bourges and was highly regarded by Cujas. He became friends with the most learned men of his time, such as the eminent book collector Gian Vincenzio Pinelli. Henry IV and Louis XIII utilized his services on important missions. He has been eulogized by Jacopo Filippo Tomasini (Elogia virorum literis & sapientia illustrium ad vivum expressis imaginibus exornata [Patavii: S. Sardus, 1644], pp. 78-98), and his biography was written by his nephew Antoine Boniel de Catilhon (La vie de messire Claude Expilly [Grenoble: F. Charvys, 1660]). A list of his works, both prose and verse, is given by Moreri, IV, Pt. 3, 336-37, and he receives mention in Bonnaffé, Dictionnaire ..., p. 102.

⁴⁰⁰Tomasini states that Expilli had only one daughter (Gasparde); he spells her husband's name "Bryon" (Moréri's spelling "Bresson" is certainly a corruption).

⁴⁰¹Possibly Jacob refers to Philippe du Vivier, president of the Chamber of Accounts of Dauphiné (CMD, AL1, 345; cf. p. 337).

⁴⁰²Philippe Laigneau is included among owners of "principaux cabinets" in 1649 by Pierre Borel, Pt. 2, p. 141.

in this collection exceeds 4000.

        The Grande Chartreuse lies in deep seclusion, but it does not lack an excellent library to provide consolation for the terrestrial angels residing there.[403]

The library of the Grande Chartreuse

        The library of M. Fromant, professor of law in the University of Valence, is highly extolled for the great number of works on jurisprudence in it.[404]

M. Fromant

        Prior to the disturbances in France caused by the religion of Calvin, there was a rich library in the abbey of Saint-Antoine, which was the motherhouse of its order. This

---

[403] The Grande Chartreuse is noted for having had one of the finest monastic libraries of the later middle ages. The Carthusians were especially devoted to book collecting and copying, and their catalogs are commendable for their fullness (P. Lehmann, "Bücherliebe und Bücherpflege bei dem Karthausern," Miscellanea Francesco Ehrle [6 vols.; Roma: Biblioteca Apostolica Vaticana, 1924], V, 364-89). The first edition of Carthusian Consuetudines, compiled by Guigo, fifth prior of the Grande Chartreuse (d. 1137), stated that each monk must have writing materials in his cell (Jacques-Paul Migne, Patrologiae cursus completus ... series Latina [221 vols.; Parisiis: Migne, 1844-1880], CLIII, 963 ff.). Raymond Lully ("doctor illuminatus"), the Spanish philosopher, mystic, and missionary, specified in his will (1313) that copies of his works were to be made and sent to the Grande Chartreuse (Léopold Delisle, "Les testaments d'Arnaud de Villeneuve et Raimond Lulle," Journal des savants, 1896, pp. 4-5). The extant fifteenth-century catalog of the Grande Chartreuse library shows its strength at the close of the medieval period (see Theodor Gottlieb, Ueber mittelalterliche Bibliotheken [Leipzig: O. Harrassowitz, 1890], No. 273). On this library, which was eventually incorporated into the Grenoble city library, see also Rivet de La Grange, IX, 119-20.

[404] Jacob apparently refers here to Gaspard Froment, doctor regent of the University of Valence, who in 1624 addressed to the King and his Council a pamphlet entitled, Advertissement pour les universitez de France contre les pères jesuites; Bourgeois considers this treatise "ecrit raisonnablement" (Bourgeois, entry 2437). Froment or Fromant also receives mention in Bonnaffé, Dictionnaire ..., p. 116.

<u>The library of Saint-Antoine</u> library was dispersed to the great sorrow of the monks, who are trying little by little to restore it.[405]

---

[405] A Latin manuscript from the abbey of Saint-Antoine-en Viennois has been identified in the Bibliothèque Nationale collection (Delisle, <u>Le cabinet des manuscrits</u>, II, 401). On this abbey and its library, see Martène, I, Pt. 1, 262; and <u>APAF</u>, IX, 25-31.

CHAPTER XIV (XCV)

GUIENNE

Bordeaux
M. de Pontac

M. de Pontac, president **à mortier** of the Parlement of Bordeaux and nephew of that learned bishop of Bazas, Arnaud de Pontac, inherited his uncle's library, and has much enlarged it.[406]

The Carthusian library

The library of the Carthusian fathers is worth commending for its good books.

M. de Fresnes

M. de Fresnes, intendant of the royal press, established a library in the city of Bordeaux, which was his birthplace; he augments this collection daily.[407]

The Jesuit library
M. de Barraut

The Jesuit fathers of Bordeaux possess a very distinguished library. This has been the case especially since they have had the book collection of the late M. Jean Jaubert de Barraut, bishop of Bazas and later archbishop of Arles,

---

[406] Arnaud de Pontac was named bishop of Bazas ca. 1572 and died on February 4, 1605. He was much devoted to academic pursuits, and had a particular interest in languages, especially Greek and Hebrew. He published, inter alia, notes on the Chronicle of Eusebius of Caesarea, and refutations of Philippe du Plessis Mornay, the great Calvinist statesman. On Bishop de Pontac, see Scévole (II) de Sainte-Marthe, I, 1211-12.

[407] On the Carthusian monastery at Bordeaux, see APAF, III, 90; the monastery was founded in 1609, but the Carthusians of Vauclaire had had a refuge at Bordeaux since 1383. Colleratal data on M. de Fresnes have not been found.

who wrote so effectively against the heretics, and whose library was already greatly esteemed while he was alive.[408]

---

[408] Jean Jaubert de Barraut was consecrated bishop in August, 1611; he became archbishop of Arles in 1630. He studied philosophy and theology at La Flèche, and wrote against Pierre du Moulin. On his death (July 30, 1643) he was buried in the Jesuit monastery at Bordeaux. Biographical data on Joubert are provided by Scévole (II) de Sainte-Marthe, I, 593, 1212. The library Joubert donated to the Jesuit community was valued at 5000 crowns (Fouqueray, IV, 200; see pp. 198-202 and V, 222-23 for the seventeenth-century history of the Jesuit monastery at Bordeaux).

CHAPTER XV (XCVI)

LANGUEDOC

Toulouse is the capital city of this province, as well as its literary center. The city, which produces fine intellects, is rendered even more praiseworthy by its abundantly flourishing libraries.

<u>Libraries at Toulouse</u>

The first which I shall discuss here is the very elegant library of the Collège de Foix. This library was founded by Cardinal Pierre de Foix, bishop of Aire, and took its name from him. He spent lavishly to stock it with the best books available at the time. Various good manuscripts from this collection have been published, and have served as the basis of printed editions.[409]

<u>The Foix library</u>

---

[409] Pierre de Foix, archbishop of Arles, was originally created cardinal by antipope Benedict XIII, but changed his allegiance at the Council of Constance. His cardinalate was confirmed, and his activities in stamping out the schism gained him the title of "the good legate." He died on December 13, 1464, in his seventy eighth year. On him, see Scévole (II) de Sainte-Marthe, I, 585-86, and Vic, XI, 55-56. The cardinal founded the Collège de Foix at the University of Toulouse in 1440, and the first statutes were drawn up in 1457; part of the College now forms the Convent of the Compassion (Rashdall, II, 172; III, 415). Foix bequeathed to the Collège his exceedingly valuable library, which had come in large part from Benedict XIII's collection and thus incorporated many books from the papel library at Avignon. In 1680 the manuscripts in the Collège library which had not been dispersed entered Colbert's collection, and thus eventually became part of the Bibliothèque Nationale (see Delisle, <u>Le cabinet des manuscrits</u>, I, 486-509; cf. Vogel, pp. 302-303). Cardinal de Foix established other

M. Charles de Montchal, archbishop of Toulouse, is a rich ornament to the French church because of his profound scholarship. He derives his learning from the excellent books that he has amassed over a long period of time to create the fine library he now possesses. Pierre Gassendi refers to the book collection of this prelate in his life of Nicolas de Peiresc.[410]

M. de Montchal

The library of the late and erudite Pierre du Faur, lord of Saint-Jory and first president in the Toulouse Parlement, was a famous one; but after his death, which occurred as a result of apoplexy, May 20, 1600, at age sixty, his library was sold by his heirs.[411]

M. de Saint-Jory's library

M. Ciron, fourth president à mortier in this Parlement, collected a library worthy of consideration for its good books.[412]

M. Ciron

---

ecclesiastical foundations as well, among them the Celestin monastery at Avignon, of which Jacob has spoken earlier (see the text at n. 339 above). Jacob is in error when he says that Pierre de Foix was bishop of Aire; it was Pierre's grand-nephew (of the same name, d. 1490) who held this bishopric (Scévole [II] de Sainte-Marthe, I, 1163-64).

[410] On the library of Charles de Montchal, see above, n. 224 and corresponding text. Gassendi made the following laudatory comment on Montchal's library: "Verily I must not forbear to name that same rare Bishop of Toulouse, Carolus Monchalius, out of whose wealthy Storehouse so many rare Manuscripts were brought" (Gassendi The Mirrour of true Nobility . . ., Bk. IV, p. 22; Gassnedi, Viri illustris ... Peiresc ... vita, p. 215).

[411] The political career of Pierre du Faur or Faber is described in considerable detail in Vie, XI, 1219 and passim.

[412] Ciron was president of the Parlement of Toulouse in 1589 (ibid., p. 784).

M. Jacques de Maussac, dean of the councillors in this Parlement and father of the learned Jacques-Philippe de Maussac,

M. de Maussac   president in the Court of Aids of Montpellier, has always had a predilection for books and literature, and has therefore established a notable library at his residence.[413]

The historical work produced by M. Gabriel de Barthellemi, lord of Grammont and president of the Inquests, testifies to his

M. de Grammont   personal scholarship. He carries on his studies in his library, which is of interest because of the good books in it.[414]

M. Guillaume de Catel, councillor in this Parlement,

M. de Catel   published histories of Languedoc and of the counts of Toulouse. These works, as well as the distinguished library he established, secure him great renown.[415]

---

[413] Jacques-Philippe de Maussac (ca. 1590-1650) has been called "one of the most able Hellenists and one of the best critics France has produced" (J.-Théodore Laurent-Gousse, et al., Biographi toulousaine [2 vols.; Paris: L.-G. Michaud, 1823], II, 34); he is cited in Sandys, II, 287 for his 1614 edition of Harpocration. He was "intimately acquainted with the brothers Dupuy, to whom in 1620 he dedicated a collection of letters written by Joseph Scaliger's father" (Tamizey de Larroque, in Peiresc, I, 11). Jacques-Philippe's father (whose name was Jean, not Jacques) published Greek and Latin poetry and a translation of Cicero's De officiis. In a letter of December 6, 1623, Peiresc wrote: "His father [i.e., Jacques-Philippe's father] showed me his very rich and excellent library" (Peiresc, I, 10-11).

[414] Grammont or Gramond (d. 1654) published in 1643 a Latin history of the reign of Louis XIII which was severely criticized by Gui Patin in a letter of September 15, 1654 to André Falconet (Patin, Lettres, ed. Reveillé-Parise, III, 39-40; cf. I, 102-103, 104, 289-90), but commended by Colomies, Bibliothèque choisie, p. 141.

[415] On Catel (1569-1626), see the biography by his nephew

M. Marand

The library of the jurist M. Raymond Marand, who wrote Paratitles of the law, is maintained by his sons, who take care of enlarging it.[416]

The libraries of the four mendicant orders

The Carmelites, Augustinians, Dominicans, and Franciscans of Toulouse have in their monasteries very large and very fine libraries. These book collections

---

which prefaces his posthumous history of Languedoc (Mémoire de l'histoire du Languedoc [Tolose: P. Bosc, 1633]), and C. Douois [ed.], "Testament de Guillaume de Catel," Revue des Pyrénées, IX [1897], 497-507). From Catel's will we learn that he was a devoted amateur of art objects as well as books, that he maintained two galleries for his collections and two studies, and that he was very concerned with the proper disposition of his library after his demise. The following clauses from Catel's testament are of interest in the latter connection: "I give and bequeath to M. de Puymisson, my son-in-law, whom I love as much as my daughters on account of his excellence and the affection he shows toward me, all of my books, both printed and manuscript, which are to be found in my large study on the top floor of my house, together with all my notes and ancient documents, or extracts therefrom which I have collected with great care, . . . and sometime in the future, when it seems best to him he is to give them to his son (and my godson) Guillaume de Puymisson, a boy of great promise. . . . I give and bequeath to my nephew, M. de Catel, advocate in the Court . . . my library in civil and canon law, which is in my small study that opens onto my large gallery, but I except from this bequest two or three books with fine illustrations which belonged to my dearly beloved second wife now deceased, which I wish to be given to Mme de Camboulas, her daughter. . . . I leave to my devout nieces, sisters Magdelaine and Constance de Catel, who have given up the world to serve God in the convent of Sainte-Catherine-de-Sienne, the sum of fifty livres, to be used for books of devotion for their convent, and I ask them to pray God for me and to retain my daughters in their affection. I also give to my godchild Madame Dulaur, a nun in the convent of Saint-Sernin, the sum of fifteen livres for the purchase of devotional books, and I pray her to remember me in their [sic] prayers" (ibid., pp. 503-504; Catel's testament was first published by Abbé Douais in 1897). On N. de Puymisson, himself a collector of paintings and medals, see Bonnaffé, Dictionnaire ..., p. 260 (cf. p. 50).

[416]Jacob apparently refers to Raymond de Maran(d), doctor regent of the University of Toulouse, who was present and acted as a signatory at the reading of Guillaume de Catel's will on October 6, 1626 (Douais, Revue des Pyrénées, IX, 507).

give them great prestige, for they include, besides printed works, numerous ancient manuscripts.

The library of the Jesuit fathers is well worth recommending for its book stock.

The Jesuit library

The monastery of the Minimite fathers of Toulouse contains one of the finest libraries in that city.[417] Not only was this library very considerable per se, but recently it was enlarged by the addition of the excellent book collection owned by Henri de Sponde, bishop of Pamiers. That learned and pious church historian died at Toulouse on May 18, 1643, and bequeathed his library to these Minimites, for whom he had always had very special affection while he was alive.[418]

The Minimite library

M. de Sponde

---

[417] The Bibliothèque Nationale possesses an unpublished catalog of the manuscripts of the Dominican monastery at Toulouse (Delisle, Le cabinet des manuscrits, II, 419). On this monastic collection and that of the Jesuits at Toulouse, see the bibliographic citations in Vogel, p. 303. In APAF, IV, 275-78 are listed materials pertinent to the general history, and, to a lesser degree, the library history, of the Carmelites, Augustinians, Dominicans, Franciscans, and Minimites of Toulouse. The history of the Jesuit monastery and college at Toulouse is discussed in Fouqueray, I, 325-28, 500-505; III, 468-69; V, 208.

[418] Henri de Sponde (1568-1643) studied Greek, Latin, and civil and canon law, and produced, inter alia, an abridgment and continuation of Baronius' Annales ecclesiastici. Himself a convert from Calvinism, Sponde made every effort to rid his diocese of this heresy, and established several religious foundations there. An excellent biography of Sponde was written by Pierre Frizon (see n. 144 above); it appears at the beginning of the first volume of Sponde's Baronius. Sponde tells us that he worked with materials in the library of the Collège de Foix at Toulouse, and that, as a result of "the negligence of the administrators of the Collège, the library today contains scarcely anything but splendid remnants of an opulent treasure" (Annalium ... Caes. Baronii continuatio [3 vols.; Lutetiae Parisiorum: D. de La Noue, 1641], II, 584 [Year 1464, No. 24]; cf. II, 21 [Year 1381, No. 3])

M. Thomas

At Montauban M. N. Thomas, a Calvinist, has formed a library which is reputed to be good.[419]

The archbishop of Narbonne

M. Claude de Rebé, formerly canon and count of the very illustrious Church of Saint-Jean at Lyons, and now archbishop of Narbonne, president of the estates of Languedoc, and knight of the Holy Spirit, has honored the city of Narbonne with an exquisite library composed of the best available books. This is his place of recreation, for he is gifted with a fine intellect and an outstanding mind.[420]

The bishop of Béziers

M. Clément de Bonzi, bishop of Béziers, possesses a good library incorporating that of M. Carlier of Paris. Carlier's library was purchased by M. Thomas Bonzi, Clément's uncle and episcopal predecessor.[421]

---

[419] In 1649, Borel included Thomas in his list of owners of "principaux cabinets"; Thomas' library is in fact the only one Borel considered worthy of specific mention at Montauban (Borel, p. 142). The "N" preceding Thomas' surname in Jacob's text need not represent his first initial, for Jacob occasionally uses an N to indicate that a person's Christian name is not known to him.

[420] Claude de Rebé's involvement in the political activities of his time is described in Vic, XI, 1353 and passim. A detailed biographical article on de Rebé (d. 1659) appears in Scévole (II) de Sainte-Marthe, VI, 119-22.

[421] Jacob has referred to this library earlier (see the text at n. 285). The Bonzi family occupied the episcopal see of Béziers for a century. Clément de Bonzi became bishop of Béziers in 1628, and though chiefly occupied with military affairs, established several important foundations in his diocese; he died in 1659. Thomas (I) de Bonzi was, strictly, Clément's great-uncle; he was born in Florence, came to France in 1550, obtained the see of Béziers in 1576 and successfully counter-reformed it; he resigned his bishopric in 1596 and died in 1603. On Clément and Thomas (I) de Bonzi, see R. Limouzin-Lamothe, in DBF, VI, 1061-63; Scévole (II) de Sainte-Marthe, VI, 368-70, 375-76; and Ernest Sabatier, Histoire de la ville et des évêques de Béziers

Cardinal Georges d'Armagnac, bishop of Rodez, was a great lover of literature, as is evidenced by his lavish expenditures to build a college in the city of Rodez for the education of the youth in the humanities. He desired to embellish this college with a most excellent library, and therefore sent into Italy Pierre Gilles, who was particularly well versed in the identification of worthwhile books.[422] Gilles made an extensive search

M. d'Armagnac, cardinal bishop of Rodez

(Béziers: Carrière, 1854), pp. 340, 363. Collateral data on M. (du) Carlier have not been found.

[422] Georges d'Armagnac (ca. 1500-1585) was one of the most prominent patrons of letters in sixteenth-century France. Early in life he entered the service of the duc d'Alençon and his wife Marguerite d'Angoulême (sister of Francis I and future queen of Navarre), and the cultural atmosphere of their court had a profound influence on him. Subsequently, he entered Francis' service and, as a result of his influence, became bishop of Rodez in 1529. In 1536 Francis sent Armagnac to Venice as his ambassador; while there he frequented the literary circles and the printing offices. Francis appointed him ambassador to the Holy See at Rome in 1539, and he found congenial company at the court of the cultured Paul III, and was elevated to the cardinalate in 1544. Addicted to the contemporary evil of holding multiple benefices, he did exercise real concern for his diocese of Rodez, as Jacob suggests. (On Cardinal d'Armagnac, see the excellent article, with full bibliography appended, by E.-G. Ledos in DBF, III, 677-79.) The cardinal's bibliothecal interests are clearly indicated by the high regard in which Peiresc held his personal library (see Peiresc's letter of December 11, 1636 to Grotius, transcribed in Delisle, Le cabinet des manuscrits, III, 367) and by the cardinal's activity in behalf of the Bibliotheque royale (see Armagnac's letter to King Henry II, published by M. Miller in the Journal des savants, 1875, p. 706). During his four year ambassadorship at Rome, Armagnac is known to have had fourteen Greek volumes copied by Christophe Awer and sent to Francis I's library at Fontainebleau in 1545 (Boivin, in Delisle, Le cabinet des manuscrits, I, 153-54, 157). The cardinal's relationship with Pierre Gilles was very strong; Gilles had been his early preceptor, and although it is doubtful that Gilles contributed directly to the growth of the Royal library (see above, n. 30), there is no reason to question his own statements with regard to manuscript hunting for the cardinal (cf. ibid., pp. 159-60).

for rare Greek and Latin manuscripts, and these caused people to look with wonder at the glorious plan of that cardinal patron of letters. I shall provide no other testimony to this than that of Pierre Gilles himself, who says in the letter addressed to the cardinal with which he prefaces his translation of the Greek commentaries of St. Theodoret, bishop of Cyrus:

> Assuredly, no other consideration induced me to travel through Italy than that I might bring back from there some books by which, on the one hand, we both might give sustenance to our leisure, and, on the other, I might, to the best of my ability, aid you in furnishing the library of that college which you are endeavoring to build. There, through your support, not only will the subject matter of the liberal arts be promoted, but also the young men will be educated from the rudiments to the full riches of scholarship[423][L].

This library is also mentioned by Jean Chenu, in his <u>Chronology of the Bishops of Rodez</u>, and by Pierre Gassendi in his <u>Life of Nicolas de Peiresc</u>.[424]

The bishop of Lodève M. Jean Plantavit de la Pause, bishop of Lodève, is very well schooled in religious and secular learning, as well as in the Hebrew, Greek, and Latin languages.

---

[423]Theodoret, <u>Explanationes in duodecim prophetas, quos minores vocant, juxta interpretationem Septuaginta, Petro Gillio, ... interprete</u> (Lugduni: S. Gryphius, 1533), p. 5.

[424]Jacob refers to Chenu's <u>Archiepiscoporum et episcoporum Galliae chronologia historia</u> (Parisiis: N. Buon, 1621), where Armagnac's library is mentioned on p. 362. This work entitles Chenu (1559-1627) to credit for being the first to have the idea of producing a "Gallia Christiana"; however, Bourgeois (entry 4350) states that only the section dealing with Bourges has real continuing value (cf. <u>ibid</u>., entries 257, 7567). On Chenu, see Jean-Pierre Nicéron, XLIX, 163, and M. Prevost in <u>DBF</u>, VIII, 995-96. For Gassendi's reference to Armagnac's book collection, see Gassendi, <u>The Mirrour of true Nobility</u> . . ., Bk. IV, p. 21; and Gassendi, <u>Viri illustris ... Peiresc ... vita</u>, p. 215.

His published works clearly evidence this; they, together with his celebrated library which is the result of his intensive search for good books, earn him great renown.[425]

M. Angelic Grimoald, cardinal bishop of Albano and brother of Pope Urban V, wished to aid the advancement of letters, and therefore founded the Collège de Saint-Ruf in the city of Montpellier. As it appears from his testament, drawn up April 11, 1388 and preserved in manuscript at Avignon by M. Henri Suarès, he embellished the Collège with a magnificent library for the use of those connected with it. The cardinal died at his bishopric Avignon in 1388.[426]

Cardinal Grimoald's library at Montpellier

<King Francis I so honored Guillaume Pellicier, whose birthplace was not far from the city of Montpellier, that he appointed him as his ambassador to the Venetians, and later rewarded him with the bishopric where he was born. This

<Guillaume Pellicier's library>

---

[425] Jean Plantavit de la Pause, who had been a Reformed minister of the church of Béziers before turning to the Catholic faith (1604), studied Roman theology under the Jesuits at La Flèche. His academic specialty was Near Eastern languages, and he produced several lexical tools for the study of Hebrew and Aramaic. On him, see Pierre Bayle, A General Dictionary, Historical and Critical, tr. and ed. John Peter Bernard, et al., VIII (London: G. Strahan, et al., 1739), 427; and cf. Vic, XI, 1023, 1059, 1098.

[426] The cardinal's name is variously spelled; the more common orthographical possibilities are: Grimoald, Grimoard, Grimouard, Grimaud. Grimoald became bishop of Avignon in 1362, and cardinal bishop of Albano (Italy) in 1366; he died on April 18, 1388 (Scévole [II] de Sainte-Marthe, I, 823-24). The Collège de Saint-Ruf was founded in 1364 at the University of Montpellier by Grimoald "for eighteen canons regular of the Monastery of S. Ruf at Valence" (Rashdall, II, 135). On the Collège library, see Charles d'Aigrefeuille, histoire ecclésiastique de la ville de Montpellier (Montpellier: Rigaud, 1739), p. 399.

good man was falsely accused by his enemies of leading a dishonest life, but by his forbearance he demonstrated his innocence; and to the end of his life he devoted himself to scholarly activity and the search for books.[427] Scévole de Sainte-Marthe informs us of this in his eulogy of Pellicier:[428] "When this abuse had produced in him a tremendous and not inappropriate distaste for the entire court, he betook himself to his Montpellier retreat, where free and unburdened he peacefully reposed in the sweet and welcome bosom of the Muses; for to this end he had a fully stocked library, provided with innumerable manuscripts of

---

[427] "Montpellier . . . had the advantage of a humanist bishop in its midst. This was Guillaume Pellicier (circ. 1490-1568), the friend and correspondent of Rabelais, a negligent bishop but a good humanist. He was a student of natural history and contemplated an edition of Pliny. He had a particularly fine library, his Greek manuscripts alone numbering 1104, and filling over 200 volumes" (Arthur Tilley, Studies in the French Renaissance [Cambridge: University Press, 1922], p. 156). On Pellicier and his library, see A. Germain, "La Renaissance à Montpellier," Mémoires de la Société archéologique de Montpellier, VI (1871), 13 ff.; Jean Zeller, La diplomatie française vers le milieu du XVIe siècle d'après la correspondance de Guillaume Pellicier (Paris: Hachette, 1880); Joseph-Xavier-Alexandre Tausserat-Radel (ed.), Correspondance politique de Guillaume Pellicier (Paris: F. Alcan, 1899); Journal des savants, 1900, pp. 78 ff.; Henri Omont, Catalogue des manuscrits grecs de Guillaume Pellicier (Paris: A. Picard, 1886); and Montfaucon, II, 1198-1202. Pellicier engaged in extensive book collecting for Francis I's library at Fontainebleau. He so decimated the Latin manuscripts of the Midi that Cujas later complained that his researches in Provence were getting nowhere, for "the late bishop of Montpellier ravaged everything" (letter of Cujas, June 20, 1571, published in Jean-Anselme-Bernard Mortreuil, L'ancienne bibliothèque de l'abbaye Saint-Victor [Marseille: V^{ue} Olive, 1854], p. 28). But the clear preference of Francis and his scholars was for Greek manuscripts, and when Pellicier succeeded Cardinal d'Armagnac as Francis' ambassador to Venice (1539-1542), he set twelve copyists to work there continually transcribing ancient Greek manuscripts for his sovereign and for himself (see two letters of Pellicier and other materials pertaining to his ambassadorship in Delisle, Le cabinet des manuscrits, I, 154-57).

[428] Scévole (I) de Sainte-Marthe, p. 35.

the ancient authors and other books on all subjects which he had brought together from far and near"⁴²⁹[L].>

In the Geneva edition of President de Thou's autobiography, Bk. I, p. 34, the president says that on passing through

The bishop of Le Puy the city of Le Puy en Velay he saw a fine library collected by M. Nectar de Senneterre,⁴³⁰ the bishop of that city:

> It required three long days of descent by almost impassable roads before Anicium (or Le Puy en Velay, as it is commonly called) appeared. . . . The city is on a very slight elevation, and its population reflects its important location. One climbs steps to reach the cathedral and its high altar. An ancient wall joins the church with the episcopal palace, where one can still read with no difficulty whatever the two initial Greek letters of the name of Christ our Lord, as we noted previously in speaking of Saint-Oren of Auch. Nectar de Senneterre, who was bishop, received de Thou with great affection, and showed him his library full of old manuscripts worth noting⁴³¹[L].

The very ancient family of the counts of Tournon does not derive its entire glory from the fact that it was one of the

The library of the Jesuits at Tournon first noble houses of France to accept Christianity, or that it gave to the Catholic church the great St. Justus; for it can pride itself on providing the last century with that mighty cardinal François de Tournon, the ornament of the sacred college of cardinals and the faithful and incorruptible

---

⁴²⁹For the position of this paragraph in our edition-translation, see above, n. 357.

⁴³⁰More properly, the bishop's name was Antoine de Senneterre (Senneterre is a contraction of Saint-Nectaire); on him, see Scévole (II) de Sainte-Marthe, II, 736-37. De Thou visited Senneterre's library in 1582, ten years before the bishop's death.

⁴³¹De Thou, <u>De vita sua</u>, Bk. II [Jacob's reference to Bk. I is erroneous], in De Thou, VII, Pt. 4, 57.

minister of our Most Christian sovereigns. He had such a love of good literature that he desired to leave to posterity a perpetual testimony to the advancement of learning, and this he did by the erection in 1542 of a celebrated college. In 1552 it was transformed into a university; he then put it under the control of the Jesuits, who maintained it as a university until 1625 when a decree was handed down to the effect that it again become simply a college. Now that generous prelate also left to the Jesuit fathers his famous library, which they have augmented so considerably that it stands as one of the most celebrated book collections in France.[432]

---

[432]François de Tournon (1489-1562) was prominent in affairs both of church and of state. In the ecclesiastical realm, he served as abbot of such key monasteries as Saint-Germain-des-Prés, as bishop and archbishop of several leading sees, and as dean of the college of cardinals. In the political sphere, he carried out delicate assignments for Francis I, Henry II, Francis II, and Charles IX; in 1525, for example, it was he who went to Spain with the first president of the Paris Parlement to secure the release of Francis I, who had been captured at the battle of Pavia. Tournon was also a patron of men of letters, and maintained close relationships with Lambin and Muret. His theological rigidity exceeded his humanistic interests, however, as can be seen by the fact the he opposed Francis I's intention to bring Melanchthon to the French court (Moréri, X, Pt. 1, 302; cf. Clyde L. Manschreck, Melanchthon, the Quiet Reformer [New York: Abingdon, 1958], p. 225). On the library of the Jesuit college founded at Tournon by the cardinal, see Lomeier, sec. "France," n. 13, where John Evelyn's commendation of the library in 1644 is quoted--a commendation corroborating our author's statements of the same year.

CHAPTER XVI (XCVII)

LORRAINE

Nancy

The library of the dukes of Lorraine

The monastery of the Franciscan Observants at Nancy has for a long time maintained the very splendid library of the dukes of Lorraine. It abounds in good and rare books which have been acquired with great care; and some manuscripts are also to be seen there.[433]

M. de Lescale

Furthermore, it has come to my attention that in Lorraine M. de Lescale has a library worthy of consideration.[434]

---

[433] The church and monastery of the Cordeliers at Nancy were founded toward the end of the fifteenth century by Duke René II of Lorraine, who had great affection for the Franciscans. The church was consecrated in 1487, and René showered rich gifts on both church and convent. "At the monastery he established a library--without doubt the oldest in Nancy--and presented numerous volumes to it. . . . René's successors continued to act generously toward the Cordeliers and to enrich them through their donations" (Christian Pfister, Histoire de Nancy [3 vols.; Paris: Berger-Levrault, 1902-1909 (Vol. II, 1909)], I, 613; see pp. 615-16 for a description of the valuable scholarly work and bibliophilistic activity carried on in this library). In 1793 the Cordeliers' library contained 3,635 volumes (2,286 works); these books became national property in that year and entered the University of Nancy (J. Favier, "Coup d'oeil sur les bibliothèques des couvents du district de Nancy pendant la Révolution," Mémoires de la Société d'archéologie lorraine, 1883, p. 26). On the manuscripts of the Franciscan library at Nancy, see Luke Wadding, Scriptores ordinis minorum (Romae: F. A. Tani, 1650), pp. 201-202, 306; and cf. CMD, IV, 128, 290-91.

[434] Jacob is apparently referring here to the Chevalier de L'Escale, who is mentioned in the correspondence of Peiresc, and who included Colletet's poetry in his Temple d'honneur, où sont compris les plus beaux et héroïques vers des plus renommez poètes

de ce tems non encor veus ny imprimez of 1622; other works by L'Escale are listed in the Bibliothèque Nationale's *Catalogue général des livres imprimés*.

CHAPTER XVII (XCVIII)

LYONNAIS, FOREZ, AND BEAUJOLAIS

The most famous library in the city of Lyons is that of the Jesuit college. In number of books it yields to few in France, for it can boast of many books

<u>The Jesuit library</u> which were provided through the liberality of the great King Henry IV and of various other persons of rank. This year, 1644, a fire started in the college which caused the destruction of some of the library books that were in the monks' private rooms.[435]

<M. Camille de Neufville, abbot of Ainay, of Ile-Barbe, etc., not only has those fine intellectual qualities character-

istic of the great men of the

<<u>M. de Neufville's library</u>> Villeroy family from whom he has

descended, but also is seen to be most zealously inclined to good literature and to the augmentation of his magnificent library. At present this library contains 4000 volumes in all fields of knowledge and in divers

---

[435]On the library of the Collège de Lyon, see Antoine-François Delandine, <u>Manuscrits de la bibliothèque de Lyon</u> (3 vols.; Paris: Renouard, 1812), I, 8-21; Léopold Niepce, <u>Les bibliothèques anciennes et modernes de Lyon</u> (Lyon: H. Georg, 1876), pp. 48 ff.; Léopold Niepce, <u>Les manuscrits de Lyon</u> (Lyon: H. Georg, [1879]), pp. xi-xii, 70-80; and Vogel, p. 268. Archbishop Camille de Neufville-Villeroy, about whom Jacob will speak in the next paragraph, bequeathed manuscripts to this library in 1692 (Delisle, <u>Le cabinet des manuscrits</u>, II, 380).

languages, especially Spanish, and the books are all richly bound in red levant morocco with that lord's coat of arms, consisting of a cheveron with three crosses anchored.[436]

The Carmelite library

The library of the Carmelite monastery on the Terreaux is very considerable with respect to the writings of the church fathers and theologians. These were donated by M. Jacques Maistret of Burgundy, a monk of this monastery who was a doctor of Paris and bishop of Damascus, and afterwards by M. Robert Berthelot, Father Maistret's nephew, and likewise a doctor of Paris and bishop of Damascus; both were suffragans of the archdiocese of Lyon and well versed in the sciences. Moreover, Father Étienne Molin, also a doctor of the Paris theological faculty, has added many good books on theology to this library.[437]

---

[436] Camille de Neufville-Villeroy (1606-1693) became archbishop of Lyons, a commander of the order of the Holy Spirit, and lieutenant general (governor) of Lyons and of Lyonnais, Forez, and Beaujolais. On his library, see Niepce, Les bibliothèques ..., pp. 590-93; and Niepce, Les manuscrits ..., pp. 7-9. Many of Neufville-Villeroy's books, bound in red morocco and bearing his coat of arms, may still be seen in the Lyons public library; these manuscripts entered the Jesuit college library at Lyons after Neufville-Villeroy's death (CMD, XXX, Pt. 2, 1339 and passim).

[437] On the library of the Carmelite monastery, cf. the manuscript catalogues cited ibid., Pt. 1, 415; Pt. 2, 915; and see Niepce, Les bibliothèques ..., pp. 24-25, and Delandine, I, 27. The Lyons public library has a manuscript Pontificalis romani epitome which belonged to Jacques Maistret and was later a part of the Carmelite collection (CMD, XXX, Pt. 1, 145; cf. p. 140), and an unfinished manuscript Pontificalis ordinis liber which was donated to the Carmelite library by Robert Berthelot, who died in their monastery (ibid., Pt. 1, 145-46). Maistret and Berthelot receive mention in Scévole (II) de Sainte-Marthe, IV, 190, 192; and also in APAF, X, 37, where we learn that Maistret was suffragan from 1574 to 1601, and Berthelot from 1602 to 1630. No other reference to Molin has been found.

As for the library of the Minimite fathers, not only does it possess a fine building, but it also has an excellent book collection.

The Minimite library

The Dominican fathers of the place de Confort once had a distinguished library; it was partly dispersed during the religious disturbances in France.[438]

The Dominican library

Étienne Charpin, a priest in the city of Lyons, was in his time a man of great intellectual curiosity, as appears from the books of highest quality which he bought for his library. He had the catalog of this library printed at Lyons in 1555, with a prefatory letter of his on the subject. I shall give the opening lines of this epistle for fear that otherwise the work may be forgotten:

Charpin's library

> "To the scholarly brothers of the Lyons church who long for God's most august and perpetual Majesty, Étienne Charpin prays that they indeed obtain perpetual salvation. For this reason I have brought together a Christian library, O upright fellow soldiers, that I might help men . . ."[439][L]

---

[438] The libraries of the Minimites and the Dominicans at Lyons are discussed briefly in Niepce, *Les bibliothèques ...*, pp. 25-28; there we learn that the Minimite library was especially strong in mathematics and natural philosophy (cf. Delandine, I, 27). On the Dominican library, which was founded by the sixteenth-century Biblical scholar Sanctes Pagninus, and was eventually incorporated into the Lyons city library, see also Lomeier, sec. "France," n. 15 and corresponding text; and cf. Delandine, I, 28. For the general history of the Lyons Dominicans and Minimites, see APaF, X, 31 and 41-42 respectively.

[439] In 1837 the Bibliothèque Nationale acquired a sixth-century manuscript (containing a portion of the Theodosian Code) which Charpin passed on to Cujas, and which later belonged to François Pithou (Delisle, *Le cabinet des manuscrits*, III, 209). Charpin edited Ausonius' *Opera* in 1558; two copies of this work

The beauty and rarity of the museum of M. Gaspard de Monconys, lord of Liergues and of Pouilly, royal councillor, and lieutenant for criminal matters at the presidial seat of Lyons, is certainly one of the fascinating sights in Europe. This is true not only with regard to its medals of gold, silver, bronze, glass, lead, and other materials, and its painted and copperplate-engraved portraits, but also with respect to the high-quality books there. The number of books, however, is only 2000, among which there are more than 200 dealing with medals, city seals, heraldic devices, and eulogies and portraits of famous men.[440] The Jesuit Father Henri Albi speaks in very respectable terms of this museum in the preface to his Parallèles des cardinaux, printed in quarto at Paris this year, 1644.[441]

M. de Liergues' library

François de La Croix du Maine, in his Bibliothèque des autheurs de France, mentions the library and museum of Antoine de

---

are in the Bibliothèque Nationale collection. Niepce (Les bibliothèques ..., pp. 571-76) supplies an exhaustive list of contemporary references to Charpin, his library, and the "extremely rare" 1555 catalog of the collection; one also finds there a careful description of a Charpin binding.

[440]The cabinet of Gaspard de Monconys, lord of Liergues, was enriched through the journeys of his brother, Balthazar de Monconys, who travelled in Spain, Portugal, England, Germany, Italy, and the Orient, and whose Journal des voyages was published posthumously by his son in 1665. Gaspard de Monconys' collection is included among the principal cabinets of Europe in 1649 by Borel, p. 141. On this collection see Bonnaffé, Dictionnaire ..., pp. 187, 222.

[441]Henri Albi, Éloges historiques des cardinaux illustres, françois et étrangers, mis en parallèle, avec leurs portraits au naturel (Paris: A. de Cay, 1644); Preface. The recency of Jacob's citation is noteworthy.

La Porte, lord of Bertha, and municipal magistrate of the city of Lyons in 1581. He was "a man very well versed in both of the activities of Pallas[442]—to use the words of M. Claude Guichard, from whom I have learned about him." He had "a most excellent museum, full of many handsome books, ancient medals, etc."[443]

<u>Antoine de La Porte's library</u>

The library of M. Henri Gras, a physician of Lyons, is one of the finest in that city both as to quality and as to quantity of books in its collection. At present it contains about eleven or twelve hundred folio volumes, and three to four thousand books of smaller size; and its owner augments it daily.[444]

<u>M. Gras' library</u>

Emperor Charlemagne, who was king of France, held such affection for the monks of the Île-Barbe near Lyons that he gave them an excellent library.[445] The post of librarian was held by Leidrade, a monk of that abbey

<u>The library of the Île-Barbe</u>

---

[442] I.e., both peace and war.

[443] La Croix du Maine, I, 49. Guichard or Guischard was a learned antiquarian who died in 1607; on him, see <u>ibid</u>., p. 143.

[444] On Henri Gras (d. 1665) and his collection of books and curiosities, see Bonnaffé, <u>Dictionnaire ...</u>, p. 129. He is mentioned several times in Gui Patin's correspondence (<u>Lettres</u>, ed. Reveillé-Parise, I, 302; II, 124, 469; III, 148, 157, 507), and his collection is listed among "principaux cabinets curieux" of Europe in 1649 by Borel, p. 141.

[445] On the history of the Île-Barbe library, which did in fact originate in the Carolingian period, but not as a repository of Charlemagne's books, see Niepce, <u>Les bibliothèques ...</u>, pp. 14-16, 19-20; Niepce, <u>Les manuscrits ...</u>, pp. vii-viii, 98; S. Tafel, "The Lyons Scriptorium," <u>Palaeographia Latina</u>, II (1923), 66 ff.;

and later bishop of Lyons. In an epistle he wrote to the emperor, Leidrade mentions books belonging to the emperor which the latter sent to the abbey:

> By order of the Emperor and Lord Charles, a royal monastery was recently founded on the Île-Barbe in the Saône river. Previously the establishment had been dedicated in honor of St. Andrew the Apostle and all the Apostles, but now it honors St. Martin. The emperor placed M. Benoît in charge as abbot, and sent his own books along with him to the abbey; and so I rearranged them . . .246[L].

Jacques Severt, doctor of Paris, says in his life of Leidrade that this library was highly esteemed at that time:

> Indeed, before he became a bishop, he was master of the sacred palace under Charles, i.e., librarian to that emperor. Due to Charles, this exceedingly learned man was afterwards created archbishop--in 799 or around that year. Many assert that at that time the very extensive library of the emperor was kept in the holy monastery on the Île-Barbe at Lyons, inasmuch as Leidrade,

---

IV (1925), 40 ff.; Vogel p. 268; and cf. APAF, X, 27, 76-77. Many of the valuable manuscripts in the library were burned in the Calvinist struggles of 1562, but a number escaped destruction and were incorporated into the library of the Cathedral chapter of Saint-Jean at Lyons. A Latin manuscript from this library has been identified in the Bibliothèque Nationale collection (Delisle, Le cabinet des manuscrits, II, 372). It was in this celebrated monastic collection that Guillaume Pellicier discovered Claudius Marius Victor's poem on Genesis (Bulletin du bibliophile, 1855, pp. 347-48).

[446] Jaffé, and Baluze before him, pointed out that this portion of Laidrade's letter of ca. 813-814 to Charlemagne is actually an interpolation, "undoubtedly by a monk of Île-Barbe" (Philipp Jaffé [ed.], Bibliotheca rerum Germanicarum [6 vols.; Berolini: Weidmann, 1864-1873], IV, 422); the genuine text reads simply, "Monasterium regale insulae Barbarae ita restauravi" ("I thus restored the royal monastery of the Île-Barbe"). But though it is uncertain that Leidrade exercised the functions of a librarian, his letters to Charlemagne do make clear that he contributed to the growth of libraries in his day through encouraging scribal and literary activity (ibid., pp. 410-13, 421; cf. Niepce, Les manuscrits ..., pp. 13-15, 80-81). On Leidrade's archiepiscopacy, which terminated in 814, see Scévole (II) de Sainte-Marthe, IV, 52-55.

who administered it before receiving papal anointing, resided there[447][L].

The next librarian after Leidrade, according to Guillaume Paradin in his Histoire de Lyon, Bk. I, and Gabriel Naudé, in his Addition à l'histoire de Louys XI and Avis pour dresser une bibliothèque, was the erudite Agobard, who was, like Leidrade, bishop of Lyons.[448]

The château of l'Abbatie, situated in Forez, belongs to the illustrious d'Urfé family. This family has given us M. Claude d'Urfé, royal ambassador to the Council of Boulogne and guardian of the princes and princesses of the blood under Henry II, and a man of great discernment and scholarship; he established a rich

---

[447] Jacques Severt, Chronologia historica successionis hierarchicae ... archiantistitum Lugdunensis (2d ed.; Lugduni: S. Rigaud, 1628), Pt. I, p. 172. Another work by Severt--the Anti-martyrologe, a somewhat trifling criticism of Protestant Jehan Crespin's Livre des martyrs--receives mention in Hauser, entry 776.

[448] Guillaume Paradin, Mémoires de l'histoire de Lyon (Lyon: A. Gryphius, 1573), pp. 98-99; the reference appears in Bk. II, chap. xix, not in Bk. I as Jacob states. (Paradin was dean of Beaujeu; Hauser, entry 772, agrees with Papillon's evaluation of Paradin's historical works: too credulous and insufficiently critical, but characterized by honesty and good faith [Papillon, II, 123]; the extent to which Paradin's works were used by later writers can be seen from Hauser, entries 768, 795, and 1253); Naudé, Addition ..., p. 338 (where Naudé cites Paradin as his source); Advice on Establishing a Library, p. 77 (where Naudé includes Leidrade and St. Agobard among twenty-three librarians of famous collections who "have considered themselves honored by appointment to such a position and have made it in turn more honorable and more to be desired by reason of their great learning and ability"). On Agobard (d. ca. 840), see Scévole (II) de Sainte-Marthe, IV, 55-59; his bibliophilistic orientation is well indicated by the fact that he "gave to the Cathedral of Saint-Étienne at Lyons--then the metropolitan Church--a vellum manuscript of the Gospels, in fine Carolingian script with initial uncial letters for each chapter. It is actually believed that the whole manuscript was transcribed by this prelate personally. At the beginning of the book, as was customary at the time, he formally dedicates it on the altar of his Church; he asks grace for those who will use the book and mercy for himself the donor, and he pronounces an anathema upon anyone who should deprive the Church of it" (Niepce, Les manuscrits ..., pp. 84-85; cf. p. viii); this manuscript eventually entered the Lyons city library.

and splendid library in that château, and put in it more than 4600 volumes, including 200 vellum manuscripts bound in green velvet. M. Honoré d'Urfé, the author of L'Astrée, wrote that work in this château, which then belonged to him. The family still exists, and is today represented in the person of the marquis d'Urfé.[449]

M. d'Urfé's library

---

[449] On the d'Urfé cabinet, see Bonnaffé, Dictionnaire ..., p. 315. Autographs of Claude and Honoré d'Urfé are preserved in the Lyons public library; Honoré's autograph appears as a detached Ex libris (1624) from one of his books (CMD, XXX, Pt. 2, 968). The Bibliothèque Nationale has a number of examples of green-velvet d'Urfé bindings in its collection (Delisle, II, 420-21; cf. I, 351; II, 315, 381). What remained of Honoré d'Urfé's splendid manuscript collection in 1777 was purchased by the bibliomaniacal duc de La Vallière (Catalogue des livres de la bibliothèque du duc de La Vallière, 1re partie [3 vols.; Paris: De Bure, 1783], I, 8; cf. Le Roux de Lincy, Researches concerning Jean Grolier, pp. xxxii-xxxiii). Honoré d'Urfé's romance, L'Astrée, was translated into English under the title Astrea in 1657-1658; on it see Auguste-Joseph Bernard, Recherches bibliographiques sur le roman d'"Astrée" (2d ed.; Montbrison: Conrot, 1861), and Norbert-Alexandre Bonafous, Études sur l'Astrée et sur Honoré d'Urfé (Paris: F. Didot, 1846). D'Urfé is known to have taken part in the "Académie de Malherbe" which met in Malherbe's room from 1610 to 1628 and concentrated on poetical technique; Jacob's friend Colletet also participated in this group (de Boer, PMLA, LIII, 740).

CHAPTER XVIII (XCIX)

LIMOUSIN

At Limoges there is a college of the Society of Jesus.

<u>The Jesuit library</u>
The Jesuits there enjoy a library which is well thought of.[450]

---

[450] On the history of the Jesuit college at Limoges, see Fouqueray, II, 510-15; IV, 246; and <u>APAF</u>, V, 183. Jacob's omission of the library of Saint-Martial at Limoges is particularly glaring (cf. Gottlieb, Nos. 314-20).

CHAPTER XIX (C)

MAINE

From his youth, François de La Croix, a native of Le Mans and a gentleman of rank, possessed great learning and demonstrated it in his search for good books in Greek, Latin, and French, with which he built his famous library in the city of Le Mans.

The library of François de La Croix of Le Mans

I cannot quote a better description of this library than the one which he himself gives in the preface to his <u>Bibliothèque françoise</u>, where he writes of it as follows:

> I can say that from my seventeenth year, that is to say, in the year of salvation 1569, when I was sent to the University of Paris to receive benefit from the liberal arts, I was so concerned to have all kinds of books--not only in Greek and Latin but also in other languages, and especially in French--that the collection I made finally became of such a size that its catalog filled more than an entire volume. As a result, from that time on I was inclined to separate the Greek and the Latin books from the books written in our French tongue--to say nothing of the Italian, Spanish, and other titles.[451]

---

[451] La Croix du Maine, II, ix (May 19, 1584). François Grudé, sieur de La Croix du Maine (1552-1592) was one of the most colorful and controversial scholarly figures of sixteenth-century France. He spent fourteen years in making historical and bibliographical compilations, and then set out for Paris with three carts filled with his notes and writings. He both impressed and bored the erudite of Paris; Scaliger considered him a rather foolish but useful drudge. He achieved his continuing reputation through his valuable biographical dictionary of French authors--a work which Jacob uses, and which Colomiès considered superior to Antoine Du

At another point he says that over a fifteen or sixteen year period he spent more than 10,000 francs for books,[452] and copied, collected, and hunted everywhere for scholarly materials from which he produced more than seven to eight hundred works in all fields of knowledge.[453] Among the latter I find that he promised an "Investigation of the most renowned libraries and museums of France (some call them chambers of wonders), with an account of the rare books, medals, portraits, statues or effigies, precious stones, and other noble objects or objects of interest to men of

---

Verdier's biobibliography of comparable scope (Colomiès, Bibliothèque choisie, p. 74). Besterman considers La Croix's bibliography "fuller and more useful" than Du Verdier's, and suggests that the latter author "May be suspected of plagiarism" (Theodore Besterman, The Beginnings of Systematic Bibliography [London: Oxford University Press, 1935], p. 25). After mentioning the fact that La Croix was murdered at age forty because he was suspected of Protestant sympathies, Besterman says: "He deserved a better fate. In his pathetic dedication and preface [to his Billiothèque françoise] Grudé describes his long-continued love of books and his accumulation of a large library. . . . At the end of his bibliography, which he eventually published from his own resources, Grudé adds a . . . petition to the king, proposing the formation of a royal library, on the lines, apparently, of his own. The library was to comprise about a hundred noble bookcases. . . . The books were to be arranged in these bookcases on what is almost a decimal classification" (ibid., pp. 24-25).

[452]La Croix du Maine, II, xvii (written May 19, 1584). La Croix has "10,000 livres," but, as we have already noted, the terms "livre" and "franc" were used synonymously at the time (see above, n. 51).

[453]Ibid., p. xii. La Croix defends this figure against charges of exaggeration and prevarication by explaining that every day for thirteen years he had spent six hours in study; three hours each day were devoted to reading, and three hours to writing, and since he was able to fill a sheet in an hour (the sheets containing at least one hundred lines and twelve words to the line), he completed over one thousand sheets per year, and thus a minimum of thirteen thousand sheets in the thirteen year period (ibid., pp. xliii-xliv). On this basis, La Croix's seven to eight hundred manuscript writings must each have averaged a little more than twenty thousand words in length.

high station, which may be seen in the houses of princes and of others who collect such splendid things."[454] His fertility of mind is admirable, for at age twenty-seven he declares that out of his personal studies he produced those seven to eight hundred volumes of scholarly materials.[455] I think that his library was dispersed after his death, for I have not heard a word as to what became of it; and the same is true of the Bibliothèque latine des autheurs de France which he promised.[456]

---

[454] Ibid., p. lxvii (November 27, 1579).

[455] Ibid., p. lxxxix. He says (at age twenty-seven) that the number of books which were then or had been in his library (excluding the seven to eight hundred personal productions, but including books he had once owned and had given away) totaled two thousand volumes, including more than three hundred manuscripts (ibid., p. lxxxii).

[456] This projected work is mentioned ibid., pp. xxi and lviii.

CHAPTER XX (CI)

MARCHE

In the town of Le Dorat in the province of Marche
near Poitou, M. Pierre Robert, lord of Ville-Martin, etc. and
lieutenant general, has collected a
<u>M. Robert's library</u>   library of interest for historical
scholarship. He is well versed in history,
particularly that of the counts of Marche, and is engaged in
writing their annals.[457]

M. Gaspar de Nuchezes, knight, lord of La Boulonnière,
etc., is very interested in
<u>M. de la Boulonnière's library</u>   hunting down books to add to
his library, which now contains
about 5000 volumes in all fields of knowledge. A part of them
came from the famous library of the late M. Pavillon, advocate
in the Paris Parlement; as for
<u>M. de Pavillon's library</u>
<u>President Fauchet's library</u>   the manuscripts to be found there,
they were formerly in the library

---

[457] Pierre Robert's numerous historical productions still remain in manuscript in the Poitiers city library. There one finds notes and transcriptions on the history of Marche, Limousin, and Poitou which he set down from 1624 to 1659; his "Histoire sommaire de l'Aquitaine"; his "Généalogies de diverses maisons de la Marche et du Poitou"; his "Marchiade, ou l'histoire de la Marche en vers"; etc. (<u>CMD</u>, XXV, 144, 146-48, 150, 167, 177).

of President Claude Fauchet, who left numerous fine works to posterity.[458]

---

[458]On Claude Fauchet and his library, see above, nn. 215 and 235. Nicolas-Georges Pavillon's <u>cabinet</u> of books and medals receives mention in Bonnaffé, <u>Dictionnaire ...</u>, p. 244; it is known that he gave a fine copy of Peter Lombard's <u>Sentences</u> to the library of Saint-Germain-des-Prés in 1584 (Delisle, <u>Le cabinet des manuscrits</u>, II, 43).

CHAPTER XXI (CII)

METZ, TOUL, VERDUN

The library of the Church of Metz

The Cathedral Church of Metz once possesed a celebrated library. It has deteriorated much from its original splendor if one considers its antiquity,[459] for I find in the history of Metz written by M. Meurisse, bishop of Dardanie and suffragan of that Church,[460] that Godegrand, the thirty-seventh bishop (fl. 753), established this library for the use of the canons, whom he had live as monks. This bishop wrote some works which are listed by Tritheim under the

---

[459] The importance of the book collections of the bishoprics of Metz and Toul in the tenth century is suggested by the fact that Bishop Abraham of Freising (957-994) secured transcripts from the libraries there to stock his own collection (Wilhelm Wattenbach, Deutschlands Geschichtsquellen im Mittelalter, I [7th ed.; Stuttgart: J. G. Cotta, 1904], 454-55, 480. In actuality, the Metz Cathedral library retained many of its manuscript treasures until modern times; Baluze was successful in obtaining some of these for Colbert at the end of the seventeenth century, and in 1802 many others of considerable interest entered the Bibliothèque Nationale (Delisle, Le cabinet des manuscrits, I, 448-51; cf. Vogel, p. 271).

[460] Martin Meurisse, Histoire des évesques de l'église de Metz (Metz: J. Anthoine, 1634), p. 163. Meurisse (d. 1644) became bishop of Madaure and coadjutor to the bishop of Metz, and was a zealous opponent of Protestantism. Bourgeois (entry 1343) states that "he wrote his history with care," and commends it particularly for its sober biographical articles and its valuable documentary inclusions.

year 760.⁴⁶¹

The library of the Cathedral Church of Verdun was held in esteem, but some years ago it was sold by the members of the chapter.⁴⁶²

The library of the
Church of Verdun

---

⁴⁶¹Johann Tritheim, Descriptoribus ecclesiasticis (Basel: [J. Amerbach], 1494), fol. 42 (entry "Ruggadus epus"). Tritheim (1462-1516) is best regarded as the "father of bibliography"; he "was not the first to compile bibliographies, but he was certainly the first genuinely bibliographically minded scholar to do so... We cannot but regard his pioneer efforts in systematic bibliography with respectful admiration" (Besterman, p. 9; see the entire section, pp. 6-10). On Godegrand, whose name is variously spelled (e.g., Chrodegangus) and who died in 766, see Scévole (II) de Sainte-Marthe, XIII, 705-708.

On the ancient library of the Cathedral of Verdun, which in the tenth and eleventh century seems to have had fewer books than Metz or Toul, see Nicolas Roussel, Histoire ecclésiastique et civile de Verdun (2 vols., rev. ed.; Bar-le-Duc: Contant-Laguerre, 1863), sec. "Notes," pp. clxi-clxii; Martène, I, Pt. 2, 93; and cf. Thompson, pp. 208-209.

CHAPTER XXII (CIII)

NORMANDY

Rouen is the capital of the province. In this city there is a metropolitan Church where numerous men of letters established a great and splendid public library through their generosity. I shall name these benefactors in the order in which they contributed their books. The one who began this glorious policy was the late M. Acarie, a son of the Blessed Carmelite Sister Marie de l'Incarnation and archdeacon of this distinguished Church; he gave his library to the Cathedral as a reminder of his love for his confrères--but on condition that they make it accessible to the public.[463] Beginnings are always imperfect; therefore the

<u>The library of the Church of Rouen</u>

<u>M. Acarie</u>

---

[463] Pierre Acarie (1587-1637) was the second son of Pierre Acarie and Barbe Avrillot (later Sister Marie de l'Incarnation, the founder of the Carmelite order in France). He held the degree of doctor of theology, and was successively a penitentiary and official of the Cathedral chapter at Rouen, archdeacon of Eu, and vicar general. He bequeathed his entire book collection, together with an annual income for its maintenance, to the library of the Rouen Cathedral, on condition that the public be allowed free access to it (August 16, 1632); his good example was soon followed by others. It was Acarie himself who first served as librarian to the Cathedral book collection. On him, see Scévole (II) de Sainte-Marthe, XI, 109; Jean-Baptiste-Antoine Boucher, <u>Vie de la bien-heureuse soeur Marie de l'Incarnation</u> (Paris: Barbou, 1800), p. 113; Pierre-Laurent Langlois, "Mémoire sur les bibliothèques des archevêques et du chapitre de Rouen," <u>Précis analytique des travaux de l'Académie des sciences, belles-lettres et arts de Rouen</u>, 1851-1852, p. 504, 523-24; Jean Saas, <u>Notice des manuscrits</u>

very learned Archbishop François du Harlay de Chanvallon, a doctor of Paris, greatly desired to contribute to the grandeur and embellishment of this treasury of the Muses by the donation of his celebrated library, and thus to render it more worthy of commendation; for this posterity will be forever in his debt.[464]

The Archbishop

---

de la bibliothèque de l'Église metropolitaine de Rouen (Rouen, 1746), p. 103. Langlois (p. 506) makes the important point that "in 1634 Rouen, thanks to its Cathedral clery, enjoyed the benefit of a public library. It is well worth noting that at this time neither the Bibliothèque du roi nor even the Mazarin library (which is considered the oldest public library in France) had yet been opened to the public." For a list of the savants who frequented this library in the seventeenth and eighteenth centuries, see ibid., pp. 512-13.

[464] François Harlay de Chanvallon (d. 1653), Archbishop of Rouen from 1615 to 1651, was very learned, but his erudition was poorly assimilated, and his writings extremely obscure; a critic described his learning as "an abyss where one couldn't make out anything at all" ([Bonaventure d'Argonne], Mélanges d'histoire et de littérature recueillis par M. de Vigneul-Marville [2 vols., 2d ed; Rouen: Maurry, 1700], II, 127-29). He was succeeded in his archbishopric by his more famous nephew of the same name, who officiated at the marriage of Louis XIV and Mme de Maintenon and was a member of the Académie française. In 1633-1634, Harley de Chanvallon the elder gave to the Rouen Cathedral the entire library in his Gaillon palais; so extensive was the collection that it was transported in six great carts. The volumes numbered 1300 (including polyglots, Hebrew and Syriac works, the best editions of the church fathers, the scholastics, and the writers of classical times, and some manuscripts); the collection was valued at 40,000 livres. Harlay also gave the Cathedral an income of 600 livres for the purchase of books and the support of a librarian --in line with his understanding that "from sunrise to sunset the library be accessible to the canons, as well as to scholars, students, and foreigners"; and in subsequent years he donated eighty folio volumes and additional income to the library. Harlay himself observed the result: "People of all classes pour into the library" (Langlois, Précis analytique ..., 1851-1852, pp. 504-506). The full text of the contract of donation (January 13, 1634) between Harlay and the Cathedral chapter has been transcribed by Langlois, "Nouvelles recherches sur les bibliothèques des archevêques et du chapitre de Rouen," Précis analytique des travaux de l'Académie des sciences, belles-lettres et arts de Rouen, 1852-1853, pp. 477-84. Langlois also provides (ibid., pp. 488-508) a list of the manuscripts once in the archiepiscopal and chapter

M. Barthélemy Hallé, a canon and archdeacon, likewise evidenced
<blockquote>his affection for this library; he bequeathed to it</blockquote>

M. Hallé   his personal book collection, which was considerable.

In remembrance of this gift, his coat of arms is emblazoned on the books he gave (azure three stars in the chief and one in the point of gold, with a fesse silver having two scallops sable thereon), and the following Latin inscription appears beneath: "From the gift of Barthélemy Hallé, priest, canon of Rouen Cathedral, and archdeacon of Eu; confidential secretary of our Most Christian King; and lord of Pittres and of Berselos" [L]. This pious canon died on September 17, 1636, and his body was interred in the Church of Louviers. An epitaph is provided for him there, and at the bottom of it one reads these words:

> The Rouen Cathedral and Its Library
> He Augmented with His Not Inconsiderable Endowment[465][L].

M. Jean Bigot, squire, sieur de Somménil & de Cleuville, dean of the councillors of the Court of Aids in Normandy, has an
<blockquote>extensive knowledge of good books, and on this basis</blockquote>

M. Bigot   has built a magnificent library comprising over 6000
<blockquote>volumes. Included are more than 500 very fine, rare</blockquote>

---

libraries at Rouen but later incorporated into the Rouen city library and into other French libraries (cf. Vogel, p. 298, and Gottlieb, Nos. 389-91, 1012-25).

[465]"A number of M. Hallé's books are still to be seen in our libraries; they are recognizable by his two initials, BH, in an interlaced monogram. His portrait is found today in the library of the [Rouen] archiepiscopal palace" (Langlois, Précis analytique ..., 1851-1852, pp. 506-507). Notable donors to the Rouen cathedral library after Jacob's time included Richard Simon, the celebrated Hebraist (1712), and Jean-Baptiste Cotton des Houssayes (1783), author of The Duties & Qualifications of a Librarian (see ibid., pp. 507-509).

manuscripts, and he readily puts them at the disposal of those who want to publish them; thus he will forever deserve praise.[466]

His Eminence Charles, the late cardinal de Bourbon (formerly cardinal de Vendôme), eighty-third archbishop of Rouen, left as a memorial the reputation of being in his time the greatest patron of men of letters and bibliophiles. We are informed of this by a statement in Pierre Frizon's biography of the cardinal: "He had a tremendous desire and love for books, and at great expense he brought them from everywhere-- from the most remote lands--to build a richly stocked library; and thus his unparalleled generosity manifested itself toward

The library of the Cardinal de Bourbon

---

[466] Jean Bigot was an ardent book collector who obtained his treasures principally from monastic libraries which were in decline at the beginning of the seventeenth century; his manuscripts came from such collections as those at Mont-Saint-Michel and the cathedral of Évreux. His relationship with the learned historian André Duchesne was very close; he loaned Duchesne manuscripts, and the latter assisted him in selecting good editions for his library. Jean's son Émeric was, if possible, an even more committed bibliophile than his father; a friend of Heinsius, Ménage, and Du Cange, he travelled throughout Europe collecting books especially Greek manuscripts, and by the time of his death in 1689 the collection was valued at forty thousand livres (Ménage, *Ménagiana*, 1693 ed., p. 76 [contributed by Galland]). Émeric attempted by his will to maintain and even enlarge the collection, and stated that if it had to be sold he wished his own books to become part of the Rouen Cathedral library (Langlois, *Précis analytique ...*, 1852-1853, pp. 459-60), but by 1706 the century-old Bigot family library was purchased by the Paris booksellers and thus dispersed (cf. *Rymaille ...*, pp. 57-58). The booksellers prepared a good catalog of the collection, however (*Bibliotheca Bigotiana* [Parisiis, 1706]; a 2d ed. of the manuscript section of this catalog was prepared by Delisle and published at Rouen in 1877), and the manuscripts (over five hundred in number, many of which are of great value for the history of Normandy) were acquired for the Bibliothèque Nationale (Delisle, *Le cabinet des manuscrits*, I, 322-29; cf. Bonnaffé, *Dictionnaire ..* p. 25). A number of manuscripts which once belonged to Jean Bigot are also to be found in the Rouen city library (*CMD*, II, 568, and *passim*).

scholars and learned men"[467][L]. He died on August 1, 1594 in Saint-Germain-des-Prés at Paris.

The Benedictine abbey of Sainte-Marie du Bec formerly enjoyed a large library. It was completely destroyed by fire about thirty years ago, and therefore hardly any vestiges of it remain today --to the great misfortune of the monks of that abbey.[468]

<u>The library of the abbey of le Bec</u>

I can state that the library of Saint-Michel-en-Ler,

---

[467]Frizon, p. 652. Cardinal Charles (II) de Bourbon-Vendôme, who held the archiepiscopate of Rouen from 1590 to 1594, succeeded to the magnificent book collection of Cardinal Georges (I) d'Amboise, archbishop of Rouen, which, as we have seen previously (n. 73), incorporated the most valuable portion of the library of the Aragonese kings of Naples. Under Charles' predecessor (Charles I) the library had suffered deterioration, and Charles II bent every effort to restore it to its previous splendor. He employed good copyists, and acquired new manuscripts which compared favorably with those of Cardinal d'Amboise. Thus contemporary inscriptions not unjustly designated him "restorer of manuscripts" and "conserver of antiquity" (Delisle, <u>Le cabinet des manuscrits</u>, I, 258-59; cf. III, 363).

[468]The fire of which Jacob speaks did not end the history of the library of the abbey of le Bec, for a manuscript catalog of printed books in the library was drawn up in 1693, and an inventory of manuscripts in 1798 (<u>CMD</u>, II, 452-53; cf. I, 308; II, 562). Bec had been one of the chief centers of Benedictine reform in the medieval period, and its library at that time was the most influential one in Normandy. Its stature was the result of such acquisitions as the fifty volumes collected under the direction of Archbishop Lanfranc in the eleventh century (J.-M.-F.-J. de Crozals, <u>Lanfranc, archevêque de Cantorbéry, sa vie, son enseignement, sa politique</u> [Paris: Sandoz & Fischbacher, 1877], p. 67; Élie Longuemare, <u>L'église et la conquête de l'Angleterre</u> [Caen: L. Jouan, 1902], p. 55), and the hundred books given to Bec in the twelfth century by Philip d'Harcourt, bishop of Bayeux (Gustav Heinrich Becker, <u>Catalogi bibliothecarum antiqui</u> [Bonnae: M. Cohen, 1885], No. 86). On the manuscripts of this library, see also Gottlieb, No. 256, 969, and Montfaucon, II, 1250-56: and cf. Delisle, <u>Le cabinet des manuscrits</u>, I, 32?, 375, 527; II, 44, 286, 340; III, 381-82; Vogel, p. 253; Thompson, pp. 239-42; and <u>APAF</u>, VII, 44-47.

The library of the abbey of Saint-Michel — in the diocese of Coutances, has had great renown because of the multitude of manuscripts there which were worthy of consideration. The Rev. Father Jacques Sirmond and many other erudite persons have assured me that they have seen that library still in existence.[469]

---

[469] On Jacques Sirmond, see above, n. 171. In speaking of Saint-Michel-en-Ler, Jacob may refer to the convent of Saint-Michel-du-Bosc in the Coutances diocese (APAF, VII, 160), or (if one assumes that "Ler" is a typographical error for "Mer") to the abbey of Mont-Saint-Michel, "au péril de la mer" (*in periculo maris*) in the neighboring diocese of Avranches, where there was a noteworthy manuscript collection (*ibid.*, pp. 95-104).

CHAPTER XXIII (CIV)

THE PRINCIPALITY OF ORANGE

Daniel Chamier, a minister of the city of Orange, collected a fine library of good books for his own use. However, I do not know who acquired that library after his death.[470]

<u>Daniel Chamier's library</u>

---

[470]Daniel Chamier (1565-1621) studied the classics at Orange and theology at Geneva. He played an active rôle in the theological controversies of his day, as is indicated by his numerous controversial works listed in the catalogues of printed books of the Bibliothèque Nationale and the British Museum. He served as professor of theology at Montauban, and was instrumental in the organization of the Protestant Academy of Dauphiné. His father (Pierre-Adrien), his son (Adrien), and his grandson (Daniel) all occupied the Protestant pulpit at Montélimar, where he himself was pastor during part of his ministry. On him, see [William Courthope], <u>Memoir of Daniel Chamier</u> (London: S. Bentley, 1852); Charles Read (ed.), <u>Daniel Chamier: Journal de son voyage à la cour de Henri IV en 1607, et sa biographie</u> [by John Quick] (Paris: Société de l'histoire du protestantisme français, 1858); Charles Read, <u>Henri IV et le ministre Daniel Chamier</u> (Paris: A. Durand, 1854); Louis Dizier, <u>Daniel Chamier, sa vie et ses écrits</u> (Strasbourg: G.-H.-E. Heitz, 1869); and Adolphe de Coston, <u>Histoire de Montélimar</u> (2 vols.; Montélimar: Bourron, 1878-1883) II, 535.

CHAPTER XXIV (CV)

THE REGIONS ABOUT ORLÉANS, CHARTRES, BLOIS, VENDÔME, ETC.

In the city of Orléans there is a famous university which has a very fine public library for its German nation.

<u>The public library of the Germans at Orléans</u>

Two members of that nation take charge of it, according to Justus Sincerus, who writes as follows in his <u>Journey through France</u>:

> Finally, there are two librarians, whose duty it is daily--except on holidays--to be present in the library from one to two o'clock, to give books to those asking for them, to require a written testimony of the transaction from those who borrow books, and to demand the return of borrowed books at the end of any procurator's term of office. Notwithstanding, the library is very well stocked with books of every kind. I understand that Hubert Gifanius, the lawyer, promoted the establishing of this library[471][L]

Amédée, cardinal de Salusses, evidenced his affection for the University of Orléans by erecting a magnificent general library for the use of those at the

<u>Cardinal Amédée's library</u>

university. This statement is based on the cardinal's testament which he drew up on June 21, 1419, and which is preserved by MM. Suarès

---

[471]This passage from Sincerus is quoted and discussed in my edition of Lomeier, sec. "France," n. 13, to which the reader is referred for further data on the Orléans University library.

of Avignon, from whom I received these notes.[472]

<The library of the Jesuit fathers is well worth noting
<The Jesuit library> for its great number of books in all fields of learning.[473]

<M. de Beauharnais, lieutenant general of that city of
Orléans, and M. de Beauharnais,
<MM. de Beauharnais' library> doctor of the Sorbonne, are the
owners of a good library which
they have built up with great care.[474]

<As for the library of the Capuchin fathers, I find that
it is esteemed as one of the fine libra-
<The Capuchin library> ries of Orléans.[475]

---

[472]On Amédée, cardinal de Salusses, see above, n. 333 and corresponding text. The Suarès copy of Salusses' will is today in the Bibliothèque Nationale, fonds Suarez 8972, fol. 14 (see Gottlieb, No. 957); since the original of the will has not been found, this copy is the basis of the printed edition in the Mémoires de la Société archéologique et historique de l'Orléannais, XII (1873), 465 ff. The early University library at Orleans, as well as the library of the German nation there, eventually became a part of the Orléans city library (Vogel, p. 276); on the ancient University library, cf. Gottlieb, No. 997.

[473]Manuscript materials relevant to the history of the Jesuits of Orléans and their library are listed in CMD, XLII, 565, 644. The basis of the collection was the personal library of Raoul de Gazil, royal councillor and chaplain ordinary, who founded the Jesuit college at Orléans in 1617 and donated his library to it the following year (Fouqueray, III, 490).

[474]Papers from 1635 relating to the Beauharnais family are preserved in the Orléans city library (CMD, XLII, 565). In the first half of the seventeenth century a M. de Beauharnais, chief treasurer of France at Orléans, served on the administrative commission of the Saint-Croix Cathedral there; this may be the lay member of the Beauharnais family referred to by Jacob (Georges Chenesseau, Sainte-Croix d'Orléans, histoire d'une cathédrale gothique, II (Paris: E. Champion, 1921), 77-78.

[475]Two sixteenth-century theological treatises, one printed and one in manuscript, which were once a part of the Capuchin library at Orléans are now in the public library there

<M. Mesmin, councillor in the bailliage, has been concerned to find good books with which to furnish his library.[476]

<M. Mesmin's library>

<A similar interest has motivated M. Destap to build his fine library. It is of considerable note because part of its books are large paper editions.[477]

<M. Destap's library>

<M. Meusnier, doctor of theology of the Sorbonne, canon and archdeacon of the Church of Orléans, and grand vicar and official of the bishop of Orléans, has also formed a significant library.[478]

<M. Meusnier's library>

<M. Boucher, subdean of Sainte-Croix, has collected a library which is not to be classed among the least in this city.[479]

<M. Boucher's library>

During the public disturbances in France caused by the religion of John Calvin and his disciples, numerous excellent

---

(CMD, XLII, 636). Two manuscript catalogs of the Capuchin library have also been preserved at Orléans--a catalog of the year 1715 and a catalog of 1783 (ibid., XII, 263, 322).

[476] Probably Florent Mismin (d. 1671), presidial councillor at Orléans, whose "Notes sur différentes coutumes et autres matière de jurisprudence" remains in manuscript at the Orléans city library (CMD, XII, 205-206).

[477] M. Destap is not known to us.

[478] M. Meusnier, later dean of Sainte-Croix at Orléans, became a clerical member of the administrative commission of the Cathedral in 1648 (Chenesseau, p. 78).

[479] M. Boucher was appointed an ecclesiastical commissioner of Sainte-Croix in 1627; later he became dean of the Cathedral (ibid.). On the Cathedral chapter library, which was eventually incorporated into the Orléans public library, see Vogel, p. 275.

libraries perished miserably. Among them was Pierre Montdoré's library, which he had established in Orléans, according to President de Thou's assertion in Bk. LII of his History (for the year 1572):

P. Montdoré's library

> Throughout that entire period, they made off with a great amount of booty. A particular example was the barbarously savage plundering of the rich library of the erudite Pierre Montedoré, who had died of grief at Sancerre two years before. This library was filled with an abundance of books of all kinds, especially Greek books on mathematics, and the majority of them manuscripts; and Montdoré himself had zealously annotated and emended them. Also, the library contained mathematical instruments which had been wrought with extraordinary skill[480][L].

If the abbey of Fleury in the diocese of Orléans is highly esteemed because it possesses the body of St. Benedict, that glorious patriarch of Western monasticism, it is not less reputed for the ancient and exquisite library which it once maintained. Abbot Jean Du Bois thus describes it in his Library of Fleury, p. 302:

The Fleury library

> The schools of the Fleury monastery were formerly considered so distinguished and famous that the number of scholars who studied there was reckoned at more than 5000. Instead of the candles or edicts which students today are accustomed to present as honorary gifts to the directors of classes at the University of Paris, the scholars at Fleury gave their teachers two manuscript books (at that time the art of printing had not yet been developed). A great number of these volumes made up the very well-stocked Fleury library which was mutilated, sacked, and dispersed as a result of Calvinist malevolence in 1561 and 1562--an incalculable loss to the realm of letters[481][L].

---

[480]Thou, III, 141. On Montdoré, see above, n. 59 and corresponding text.

[481]Jean Du Bois-Olivier (Johannes a Bosco), Floriacensis vetus bibliotheca (Lugduni: H. Cardon, 1605), Pt. I, p. 302. This work is largely a collection of historical and scholarly

The city of Chartres in Beauce is worthy of admiration because, for its size (which is not large), it has more libraries than any of the other cities of this kingdom, as will be seen from our enumeration. First place will be given to the library of M. Jacques Lescot, doctor of the Sorbonne and bishop of this city --a man whose virtues and erudition are known to all. He has always evidenced a strong tendency to hunt for good books, and he has built his fine library with them.[482]

The libraries of Chartres

Bishop Lescot's library

M. Charles Challine, squire, sieur de Messalain, and councillor and advocate of the king in the bailliage and presidial seat of Chartres, has given us the French translation of M. Naudé's *Bibliographia politica* as a unique testimony

M. Challine's library

---

writing by various authors whose manuscripts Du Bois found in the Fleury library, but he includes in the book a number of his own compositions. Du Bois (d. 1626) was called the "general of the monks" by Henry III because of his successful military exploits during the civil wars. His hatred of the Jesuits had no bounds; in his funeral oration for Henry IV he claimed that the Jesuits were responsible for the assassination, and the treatise *Anticoton*, presenting this view, has been attributed to him by Prosper Marchand and others (cf. Bourgeois, entry 1976). Du Bois spent the last fifteen years of his life imprisoned by the Inquisition, probably because of his anti-Jesuit views. On the wonderfully rich medieval library at Fleury, see HB, III, Pt. 1, 367-68 and the bibliographical citations in n. 6 on p. 367; and cf. Gottlieb, Nos. 295-97, Edwards, I, 281-86, Vogel, p. 263, and Thompson, pp. 227-30.

[482] Jacques Lescot became bishop of Chartres in 1643 and died in 1656; the Chartres public library preserves several manuscripts relating to his episcopate--including his unpublished four-volume commentary on Aquinas' *Summa* (CMD, XI, 512 and *passim*). On Lescot, see Scévole (II) de Sainte-Marthe, VIII, 1192-93.

to his love of letters. Moreover, all his mental faculties are concentrated only on performing the duties of his post and on amassing books on every subject to glorify his library, which already contains more than 3600 volumes.[483]

The library of the Dominican fathers is well worth considering because of the quantity of books there; among them are many manuscripts.

The Dominican library

The same can be said of the library in the monastery of the Cordeliers. This library is very fine.[484]

The library of the Cordeliers

M. Souchet, doctor of theology, canon of the Church of Notre Dame in Chartres, and prior of Morancez, is building a library which at present has over 3000 well chosen volumes in it, together with numerous

M. Souchet

---

[483]Charles Challine published poetry, letters, and orations, as well as his French translation of Naudé's *Bibliographia politica* (on the latter, see above, n. 227). His responsibility for this French translation may also be verified in the *Naudaeana et Patiniana*, sec. "Naudaeana," pp. 238-39. Several works of Challine remain in manuscript in the Chartres city library (*CMD*, XI, 460 and *passim*). On Challine and his bibliophilistic family, see M. Prevost in *DBF*, VIII, 213.

[484]The Chartres public library has twenty-seven manuscripts which were once in the Dominican monastery of that city, together with a manuscript commentary on Aristotle which in 1647 belonged to one Brother Vincent Mabile, a member of this monastic community (*CMD*, XI, xli, 275). The value of the books once owned by the Dominican monastery at Chartres is indicated by the fact that in 1725 the monks offered the Bibliothèque royale an original exemplar of the decrees of the Council of Basle, but the sale was not concluded because the Bibliothèque royal would not meet the price asked by the Dominicans (see Delisle, *Le cabinet des manuscrits*, I, 371; this manuscript is now in the Chartres city library--*CMD*, XI, 174-75). Note Montfaucon, II, 1364 for further data on the manuscripts of this monastery. The Chartres public library has only one manuscript which originally belonged to the Cordeliers of that city; it is a necrology of their monastery and dates from the fifteenth century (*CMD*, XI, 334).

historical manuscripts, pertaining especially to the history of illustrious families of France and of the Chartres region.[485] Souchet is very well versed in these family histories; he suc-

M. Laisné
ceeded to the notes of the late M. Laisné, prior of Mondonville, who had labored at these investigations.[4...]

The library of the Martin family was very considerable

The library of the Martins
in respect to good books, but now the collection has been broken up.[487]

M. Grenet, an advocate in the presidial seat, formed a

M. Grenet
notable library containing close to 4000 volumes in various fields.[488]

M. de Gives, secretary to the marquis de Sourdis, does

M. de Gives
not stop for a moment in accumulating books to perfect his interesting library. At present it

---

[485]Several unpublished historical works by Jean-Baptiste Souchet (ca. 1590-1654) are to be found in the Chartres library (CMD, XI, 553 and passim). Souchet was an indefatigable antiquarian and historian who utilized numerous manuscript materials and archival documents in producing such works as his (unpublished) history of the city and cathedral of Chartres. Souchet gave his precious library to the abbey of Josaphat-lès-Chartres, but the manuscripts suffered dispersal. A valuable article on Souchet by Charles-Claude-François Lérisson appears in the Biographie universelle ancienne et moderne, XLIII (Paris: L. G. Michaud, 1825), 167-71.

[486]Guillaume Laisné's (still unpublished) genealogical compilations are today in the Bibliothèque Nationale, and two extracts from them may be seen at the Chartres city library (CMD, XI, 358-59, 402-403).

[487]Further data on this Martin family of Chartres have not been found.

[488]Étienne Grenet's taste in books is evidenced by a fifteenth-century parchment book of hours containing four miniatures, which Grenet presented as a gift in 1630, and which is today in the Chartres library (CMD, XI, 252-53; cf. p. 76).

consists of more than 4000 volumes in all disciplines.[489]

The library of M. Ribier at Blois

M. Guillaume Ribier, brother of Jacques, of whom I have spoken on p. 175, was formerly lieutenant general and president at the presidial seat of Blois, and is now a councillor of the king in his Council of State and Privy Council. He is endowed with the same love of letters as his brother has, for he has established and maintains a good library in the city of Blois.[490]

The library of the kings of Navarre at Vendôme

According to François de La Croix du Maine, in his Bibliothèque françoise, the royal library of the kings of Navarre was formerly situated at Vendôme.[491]

---

[489] On the Marquis de Sourdis, an eminent book collector in his own right, see above, the text at n. 319.

[490] On Jacques Ribier, see above, nn. 246-47 and corresponding text. Guillaume Ribier (1578-1663) played an important rôle in the public life of Blois in his successive positions as lieutenant particulier, lieutenant general, and president; his oratorical powers earned him a councillorship of state from Louis XIII and Marie de Médicis (Moréri, IX, Pt. 1, 173). In 1666, Michel Belot, his nephew, published Ribier's documentary collection in two folio volumes under the title, Lettres et Mémoires d'Estat des roys, princes, ambassadeurs et autres ministres sous les règnes de François Ier, Henry II et François II, and included in it a brief biography of Ribier. Of this work by Ribier, Hauser writes: "The majority of the original documents which appear in this precious collection are preserved at the Musée Condé, . . . and they leave no doubt that Ribier more than satisfied the requirements of accuracy" (Hauser, entry 806; cf. II, 13-14, and Bourgeois, entry 2036).

[491] Unlocated in La Croix du Maine. The reference may pertain to the royal library at Blois (near Vendôme), which Francis I, brother of Marguerite, queen of Navarre, ultimately transferred to Fontainebleau.

CHAPTER XXV (CVI)

PICARDY

In the city of Amiens numerous libraries are maintained; I shall now specify them.

<u>The libraries of Amiens</u>

<u>The bishop of Amiens</u>

There is the library of M. François Le Febvre de Caumartin, bishop of the city. This library is worthy of note for the good books in it.[492]

<u>The Minimite library</u>

The library of the Minimite fathers of that city is reputed to be one of its foremost collections, owing both to the quantity and to the quality of the books there. These monks[493] enlarge their library daily.[494]

<u>The Capuchin library</u>

The Capuchin fathers also support a notable library in their monastery.[495]

---

[492] François Le Febvre (or Fèvre) de Caumartin became bishop of Amiens in 1618 and held that see until his death in 1652 (Scévole [II] de Sainte-Marthe, X, 1209-11). Cf. Delisle, <u>Le cabinet des manuscrits</u>, I, 274; II, 47, 51, 349; and Gottlieb, Nos. 239-40.

[493] In the original text, <u>il</u> must be corrected to <u>ils</u> here.

[494] A 1795 catalog of the printed books belonging to these Minimites at the time of the Revolution is preserved in manuscript at the Amiens city library (<u>CMD</u>, XIX, 303). Manuscripts which were formerly in the Minimite library and which have been incorporated into the Amiens public library are described <u>ibid</u>., pp. 45-47, 76, 154, 219.

[495] The Amiens city library has a manuscript catalog

M. Le Cat   M. Guilin Le Cat, bachelor of the Faculty of Theology of Paris and curé of Saint-Sulpice in the city of Amiens, has an excellent and interesting library which today contains more than 4000 volumes.[496]

The Jesuit library   The Jesuit fathers of Amiens possess a fine library.[497]

Saint-Martin of Laon   The abbey of Saint-Martin at Laon has a library which is held in high repute for its books.[498]

The Minimite library   The monastery of the Minimites of Laon was founded in the year 1609. Here these fathers are collecting a fine library.

---

listing the printed books which the Amiens Capucins possessed in 1795 (ibid., p. 303). Manuscripts from their library are described ibid., pp. 43, 155-58, 218.

[496] Le Cat is not known to us.

[497] An eleventh-century parchment hagiography which belonged to the Jesuit college at Amiens can be seen today in the Amiens public library (CMD, XIX, 220). On the history of this Jesuit college, see Fourqueray, III, 113-15.

[498] On the history of the abbey of Saint-Martin at Laon, see Scévole (II) de Sainte-Marthe, IX, 662-68; on its library, see Martène, II, 50. A Latin manuscript from this abbey has been identified in the Bibliothèque Nationale collection (Delisle, Le cabinet des manuscrits, II, 407).

CHAPTER XXVI (CVII)

POITOU

M. Henri-Louis Chasteigner de la Roche-Pozai, bishop of Poitiers, has given proof of his great powers and high station[499] not only in the books which he has published, but

The bishop of Poitiers

also in the magnificent library that he has built. This library is very noteworthy for its theological and historical works, and it will provide him with a blessed memorial.[500]

M. Maurivet

The library of M. Maurivet, treasurer of the Church of Saint-Hiloire at Poitiers, is very excellent, as one can see from the good and interesting

---

[499]French, condition. In the seventeenth-century, this word did not carry quite the weight of the word qualité: "The homme de condition is simply the man of noble station--one whose status is due to excellence, to nobility; the homme de qualité is the man of noble birth--the one whose noble lineage is already ancient and illustrious" (Cayrou, p. 176).

[500]Henri-Louis Chasteigner or Chataigner (1577-1651), who became bishop of Poitiers in 1611, published commentaries on a number of the books of the Bible, a work on axioms in philosophy and theology, and a book of ethico-political essays. His contact with the scholarly life of his day is evident from three letters he wrote to Sainte-Marthe with regard to the Gallia Christiana and to Besly's Évesques de Poictiers, which was dedicated to him (see below, n. 504); these autograph letters are preserved in the Poitiers library (CMD, XXV, 137). On Chasteigner, see Scévole (II) de Sainte-Marthe, II, 1206-1207, and Jacques Le Long, Bibliotheca sacra (Parisiis: F. Montalant, 1723), p. 670.

books in it.[501]

The monks of the monastery of Saint-Jean de Fontevrault have a library which is very abundantly supplied with books, especially legal publications.[502]

The library of Fontevrault

M. René Izoré, baron d'Hervaut, is deeply versed in the sciences, as he showed in the book he wrote against La Filletière, minister of Chastelrault. Also, books are his only recreation--the books in the library which he maintains at his château de Plain-Martin near Poitiers.[503]

Baron d'Hervaut

M. Jean Besly, councillor and advocate of the king at the seat of Fontenay-le-Comte in Poitou, is a man of learning and intellectual curiosity who spares no effort in the shaping of that noble library which he has established at Fontenay-le-Comte. This library excels in

M. Besly

---

[501] Additional data on M. Maurivet have not been found.

[502] Two particular manuscript treasures at Fontevrault were a finely executed book of hours believed to have been the personal copy of a duke of Brittany, and a two-volume breviary which had belonged to Madame Renée de Bourbon, the reformer of the abbey, and which she had received from the cardinal de Bourbon (APAF, III, 251). Manuscript notes and documents relating to the history of the abbey of Fontevrault are to be found in the Poitiers city library (CMD, XXV, 140, 160). Toward the close of the seventeenth century, the abbess of Fontevrault is known to have relinquished eight manuscripts to enrich Colbert's collection (Delisle, Le cabinet des manuscrits, I, 463), and Gaignières found the abbey a rich mine of documents and seals, many of which he preserved through transcription and extraction (ibid., p. 344). On this library, see also Martène, I, Pt. 2, 1.

[503] Additional data on René Izoré (or Isoré) have not been found.

history, a subject in which Besly is very well versed.[504]

Not far from the town of Fontenay-le-Comte, Baron de la Cheze has quite a notable library in his château de la Cheze.[505]

Baron de la Cheze

M. Fidoux, sieur du Challiou, lieutenant general-civil in the seneschalsy of Civray, collected a good library, but it was sold after his death.[506]

M. Fidoux

---

[504] Jean Besly (1572-1644), a member with Jacob of "le cabinet Dupuy" (see above, n. 244), was one of Ronsard's students and edited his Hymnes with commentary (1604). Besly's formal schooling was taken at Poitiers (humanities and philosophy) and at Toulouse (law). He made a career of the law, and his first marriage was to Catherine Brisson, a relative of Barnabé Brisson. Among his close friends were the brothers Sainte-Marthe (he assisted with their Histoire généalogique de la maison de France; see his autograph letters in the Poitiers library [CMD, XXV, 136]), the brothers Dupuy (his Évesques de Poictiers and L'histoire des comtes de Poictou were brought out posthumously by his son and Pierre Dupuy in 1647), Peiresc, Jacques Sermond, and André Duchesne. On Besly, see Nicolas Macquin, Joannis Beslii ... elogium (n.p., n.d.); Bulletin de la Société d'émulation de la Vendée, La Roche-sur-Yon, 1877, pp. 71-130; Apollin Briquet (ed.), Lettres de Jean Besly ("Archives historiques du Poitou," Vol. IX; Poitiers, 1880); cf. Delisle, Le cabinet des manuscrits, I, 422-23.

[505] Jacob is probably referring here to the baronial château de Chizé, of which a number of manuscript records are preserved in the Poitiers library (CMD, XXV, 100-102, 174).

[506] In the Fonteneau collection at the Poitiers public library, there are manuscript notes on the Fidoux family of Poitou (ibid., p. 183).

CHAPTER XXVII (CVIII)

PROVENCE

All who have seen the opulent library and extraordinary museum of the late M. Nicolas-Claude Fabri de Peiresc, councillor in the Parlement of Aix and abbot of Sainte-Marie d'Aquistre in Aquitaine, confess that that age produced nothing else of such a remarkable character. Indeed, apart from the printed books in this library, there are a great number of manuscripts in Eastern languages, and they are still kept today by his brother and heir M. Palamedes Fabri, lord of Valavez.[507] M. Pierre Gassendi, in writing the life of Nicolas Peiresc, speaks thus of his library in Book VI:

> Moreover, he took very great care to obtain books in large numbers and in considerable variety. I shall say nothing of manuscripts, which, if ancient and he

M. de Peiresc

---

[507]During his lifetime, Peiresc gave many of his oriental manuscripts to scholars better able than he to edit and publish them, but this did not prevent him from leaving a magnificent manuscript collection at his death. It was sold in 1647 or 1648 by Peiresc's nephew, the baron de Rians, and, though a number of manuscripts were apparently dispersed in this way, the vast majority were purchased for sixteen hundred livres by Naudé for Mazarin's library, and thus passed eventually into the Bibliothèque Nationale (Delisle, Le cabinet des manuscrits, I, 284). Peiresc's "registers" (comprising his notes, correspondence, and extracts from documents) were carried to Paris after the death of Peiresc's brother and heir M. de Valavez, and suffered much greater dispersal than the manuscripts which had been a part of his library; for the subsequent history of the "registers," see ibid., pp. 283-84.

could not procure them, he would as a matter of course
have them transcribed (and sometimes transcribed them
himself). He kept beside him catalogues of the renowned and chief libraries of the whole world, so that
if there appeared to be anything essential to his own
needs or to the work of scholars, he would have at
hand the means of ferreting it out[508][L].

And a little later on Gassendi continues:

It is truly incredible to tell how great a number of
books he gathered together; also it is incredible that
he should not therefore have left a very complete library when he died. But neither of these things will seem
strange if one realizes that he sought books not for himself alone, but for any who stood in need of them[509][L].

At another point Gassendi writes:[510]

Thus he took care of all the very old books he obtained,
whether they were printed or in manuscript. And his
care extended not only to complete copies, but even to
fragments of books and to leaves half eaten. And when
he was asked why he had them bound so sumptuously, he
answered that the best books were very often subject
to the worst treatment when they fell into unlearned
men's hands inadequately garbed, and therefore that he
did his best to have them prized at least for the beauty
of their binding, and thus not have to fear the fish-
mongers and tobacconists. On those books bound for his
own use he would have his owner's mark stamped. The
mark consisted of three Greek capital letters, N, K, and
Φ, so neatly interwoven and doubled that they could be
read as easily from the right as from the left; these

---

[508]Gassendi, The Mirrour of True Nobility . . . , Pt. 2,
pp. 193-94 (for the year 1637).

[509]The intervening passage from Gassendi is of interest:
"To pass over, I say, Manuscripts, he bought up printed Books at
Rome, Venice, Paris, Amsterdam, Antwerp, London, Lions, and other
places; and that not only after the Mart was over at Francfort,
but all the year long, his friends acquainting him with, and
sending him such, as were for his turn; for which he caused money
to be paid, either by the Bankers and Money-changers, or by friends
Also where ever any Libraries were to be sold by out-cry, he took
order, to have the rarer Books bought up, especially such as were
of some neat Edition, which he had not" (ibid., pp. 194-95).

[510]Ibid., pp. 195-96. The first sentence of the ensuing
quotation refers to Peiresc's care in having old books beautifully
bound.

initials represented the three words Νικολάος Κλαύδιος Φαβρίκιος [Nicolas Claude Fabricius].[511] As for the room containing the library, it was admittedly too small, even though, in addition to having the walls covered with precious books, he weighed down the floor--right in the middle--with bookcases, and filled them with volumes. Hence he also had books on the porch (as it were the atrium of his library) and volumes piled in heaps in several of the other rooms. And truly he often thought of building a spacious gallery, but so many things would have had to be moved, especially the library of his father and his father's father, to which he had consigned the greatest part of his rarities; also, he never had enough leisure to be able to carry out the plan, and so left the house just as he at first had found it[512][L].

This great personage died at Aix on June 24, 1637, at the age of 56 years, 6 months, 12 days, and 20 hours; his body was enterred in the Church of the Jacobins.[513] It is to be noted that by his will he left his mathematical books and instruments to M. Gassendi his biographer.[514] That library would

---

[511]This monogram may be seen today on many of the Peiresc manuscripts in the Bibliothèque Nationale.

[512]As Bonnaffé notes (Dictionnaire ..., p. 245), Peiresc's mansion presented a very bizarre appearance. Not only was it surmounted by an astronomical observatory, and filled helter-skelter with rare books and curiosities (statues, vases, medals, mummies, paintings--including a Rubens which Peiresc commissioned), but it was overrun with cats, "les conservateurs de sa bibliothèque," for whom Peiresc had special affection.

[513]For biographical data on this great amateur, who is lauded by all the savants of the first half of the seventeenth-century, and who was active, with Jacob, in "le cabinet Dupuy" (n. 244 above), see Gassendi, passim; Peiresc, passim; Pintard, passim; Paul Arbaud, Peiresc bibliophile (Aix: J. Nicot, 1871); Lomeier, sec. "France," n. 23; and Bonnaffé, Dictionnaire ..., pp. 245-47.

[514]On Gassendi, a member of the "Tétrade" (n. 229), whose philosophical studies have given him a permanent place in the history of philosophy, and who played a central role in the cultural and intellectual life of his time, see Lomeier, sec. "Italy," n. 1; and Pintard, passim. Jacob had contact with Gassendi in the Dupuy cabinet (n. 244 above). Aside from the mathematical books willed to Gassendi, the printed books in

not be too highly praised for its treasures if I should borrow a testimonial on the subject from M. Naudé--from the Latin letter he wrote to Gassendi on the death of his old friend the councillor:

> Indeed, who does not know that his mouth was the mouth not of a man, but of the Delphic Apollo, out of which oracles daily issued, touching all abstruse and hidden matters? and that his house was truly like the most renowned fair, full of the richest wares from East India and West, from Ethiopia, Greece, Germany, Italy, Spain, England, and the nearer provinces, and that no ship entered the havens of France which did not bring into the treasury of Peiresc alone some strange beast, exotic plants, marbles engraved or inscribed by the chisel of the ancients, books in the Samaritan, Coptic, Arabic, Hebrew, Chinese, and Greek tongues, or relics of greatest antiquity from the Bosporus or out of the Peloponnesus? . . .515[L].

Jean-Jacques Bouchard of Paris publicly delivered a funeral oration for Peiresc on December 21, 1637 in the Accademia degli Umoristi at Rome, in the presence of the Cardinals Barberini, Bentivoglio, La Cueva, Biscia, Pamphili, Palotta, Brancaccio, Aldobrandin, Borghese, and many other men of learning and rank; in it he says:[516]

Peiresc's library were bequeathed to M. de Valavez, and he sold them to the Collège de Navarre at Paris.

[515] Naudé's letter is printed in Gassendi, The Mirrour of True Nobility . . ., Pt. 2, p. 276, and is dated at Rome, July 16, 1637.

[516] Bouchard's oration is printed ibid., p. 258. Our above text-translation of this and other passages included in Gassendi's biography generally follows The Mirrour of True Nobility . . ., but spelling and sentence construction have been modernized, and some changes have been introduced in the interests of greater fidelity to the Latin original. Jean-Jacques Bouchard (ca. 1606-1641) was an excellent Latinist but a man of corrupt character. He went to Rome after ruining servant girls in his own household, and after disappointing Peiresc and the brothers Dupuy, whose service he had joined with high recommendations. In Rome he became a friend of Naudé, entered the clergy, became Latin secretary to Cardinal Francisco Barberini, and was received into the Accademia degli Umoristi (on this important academy, of which Naudé was

And because those men, with all their sagacious persistency, could not fully satisfy Peiresc,[217] he often sent others from his own house to all the islands of the Aegean sea, to Mount Athos, to Constantinople, Alexandria, and the pitiable remnants of Memphis and Carthage. In his name and at his expense they were to seek to procure not only things marvelous for their newness, but especially the most ancient books in the Greek, Hebrew, Arabic, Persian, Coptic, and Ethiopian languages; and finally, besides other monuments of Asiatic and African antiquity, he particularly wanted mummies of the ancient Egyptian rulers, embalmed with the most precious spices and gums. . . [L].

Robert, called the wise, king of Jerusalem and of Sicily and count of Provence, had in his day a great affection for poets and for books.[518] César de Nostredame, in his life of King Robert which appears in his Annales de Provence, affirms that he built a magnificent library in the city of Aix, and placed in it all the works of the troubadours or provençal poets, to the number of ninety.[519]

King Robert's library

---

a member, see Rice, pp. 19-21). Bouchard maintained correspondence with Peiresc until the latter's death, wrote appalling cynical and lewd Confessions, and bequeathed ancient manuscripts to Cardinals Barberini and Richelieu. On Bouchard, see Pintard, passim; Philippe Tamizey de Larroque (ed.), Les correspondants de Peiresc, III, Jean-Jacques Bouchard (Paris: A. Picard, 1881); L.-G. Pélissier (ed.), Deux lettres inédites de J.-J. Bouchard à Gabriel Naudé (Paris: Techener, 1892); and Roman d'Amat, in DBF, VI, 1184-85.

[517]I.e., men in other countries who were employed by Peiresc to send him rarities.

[518]On the bibliophilistic activities of this scholarly prince, who was greatly admired by Petrarch and Boccaccio, see Lomeier, sec. "Sicily," n. 1. Some manuscript documents from King Robert's reign can be seen today in the Aix library (CMD, XVI, 177, 182, 302-303).

[519]César de Nostredame, L'histoire et chronique de Provence (Lyon: S. Rigaud, 1614), pp. 378-79. On Nostredame (1555-1629), poet, littérateur, and gentleman of Provence, see

305

M. de Gaillard   M. de Gaillard, president of the Parlement of Aix, died in the year 1640, and left to his heirs a very good library which he had taken great care to collect.[520]

M. Viany   M. Viany, advocate in Parlement, a man of signal erudition and ability, has formed a library which is one of the finest in contemporary Provence.[521] This is true whether one considers the quantity of books of the best editions, or the quality, rarity, and interest of them, or their binding (all of them are bound in Levant morocco). One sees there all the fathers, the epistle writers, the French and foreign historians, and some rabbinic productions,

---

Philippe Tamizey de Larroque (ed.), Les correspondants de Peiresc, II, César Nostradamus (Marseille: M. Olive, 1880). César de Nostredame was a son of the prophet-astrologer Michel Nostradamus, and a nephew of Jean de Nostredame, whose notes formed the basis of his Histoire et chronique de Provence (see below, n. 521, and Jehan de Nostredame, Les vies des plus célèbres et anciens poètes provençaux, ed. Camille Chabaneau and Joseph Anglade (new ed.; Paris: H. Champion, 1913), Pt. 1, pp. 24-26, 55; Pt. 2, pp. 368-72. The list of over ninety provençal troubadours in King Robert's library is transcribed and published from Jean de Nostredame's manuscript "Chronique de Provence" (which César used) by Chabaneau and Anglade (ibid., Pt. 2, pp. 329-43, 365-67); César's statement that the list is contained in Jean's Vies des poetes provençaux is a lapsus.

[520]Jacob apparently refers here to Joseph de Gaillard, councillor in the Court of Accounts in 1622, councillor in the Provence Parlement in 1631, who was appointed president à mortier in 1638 but died before his reception in the office (Moréri, V, Pt. 2, 15). He is mentioned several times in the Peiresc correspondence (Peiresc, I, 338; VI, 774 and passim).

[521]The library of Jacques Viany, assessor at Aix in 1632 and 1648, is discussed in Chennevieres, I, 117. Viany was such an avid bibliophile that he sometimes used his wife's richest garments for book binding material. His son, Claude Viany, prior of Saint-Jean-de-Malte at Aix, founded the Palais de Malte, which is today the Aix museum (Bonnaffé, Dictionnaire ..., p. 322).

as I have been assured in letters received from M. Antoine de Ruffi, councillor at the seat of Marseilles, who has assisted me greatly with the libraries of Provence.[522]

M. Jacques Gaffarel, doctor of theology, prothonotary apostolic of the Holy See, and commendatory prior of Saint-Gilles, has collected a fascinating library of good books both in Eastern languages and in the generally-known tongues.[523] He has sought out these books with great effort, as he himself testifies in the preface which he wrote to Paolo Ramusio's History of the War of Constantinople: "Meanwhile, cultured reader, may you willingly look with favor on our labors, and welcome with a fair mind this book, indeed worthy of a prince, together with others which we have prepared to translate shortly for you from that very opulent collection which I brought together from all the regions both of Italy and of the East, by command of his eminence Cardinal Richelieu"[524][L]. This passage shows how that great cardinal esteemed Gaffarel, who was well acquainted with Eastern languages and branches of learning, as his works demonstrate.

M. Gaffarel

Jean Brognier (or Alermet, according to Claude Robert)[525]

---

[522]Antoine de Ruffi (1607-1689) published a history of Marseilles (1642) and other historical works which were highly esteemed; see Moréri, IX, Pt. 1, 429; and Bourgeois, entries 1715, 2907, 7786.

[523]Gaffarel has been mentioned previously (see above, nn. 83, 227).

[524]Jacques Gaffarel (ed.), De bello costuntinopolitano et imperatoribus Comnenis per Gallos et Venetos restitutis historia Pauli Ramnusii [sic] (2d ed.; Venetiis: M. A. Brogiolus, 1634), Preface.

[525]Robert, p. 19.

was a man honored in his time for the talents and virtues he demonstrated in high posts. He was bishop of Viviers, archbishop of Arles, and attained the dignities of cardinal bishop of Ostia, vice-chancellor of the Roman church, and president of the Council of Constance. This learned prelate had a strong inclination for letters, as he showed by building a notable library which he bequeathed to his beloved Church of Arles--notwithstanding the fact that he died at Rome (in the year 1426).[526] Pierre Frizon, in his life of the cardinal, informs us of this: "He also placed his valuable personal collection in the Church, and thereby added more than seven hundred volumes to its library"[527][L]

The library of the Church of Arles

The library of the Benedictine abbey of Saint-Pierre de Montmajour in the city of Arles was once held in such esteem

---

[526] Jean Allarmet took the name Brogníer from his place of birth in Savoy. He studied at Geneva and at Avignon, and received the degree of doctor of law at Avignon. He became bishop of Viviers in 1383, and bishop of Ostia in 1398. At the Council of Pisa and Constance he took part in the events which brought an end to the Great Schism. He administered the see of Arles from 1410 until his death in 1426. He established a number of foundations--including educational endowments--in his dioceses. (on Brogníer, see Moréri, II, pt. 2, 304; and Scévole [II] de Sainte-Marthe, I, 581-82 [where his bequest of his library to the Arles Cathedral is confirmed], and XVI, 576-77. The scholarly tradition in the Arles Church goes back to the early Middle Ages, for a school of canonists flourished there in the sixth century, and this implies an even earlier concern for document-collecting there; see F. Morin, "Les statuta ecclesiae antiqua," Revue bénédictine, July, 1913, pp. 334-42; and Louis Duchesne, Fastes épiscopaux de l'ancienne Gaule, I (2d ed.; Paris: A. Fontemoing, 1907), 144. Five Latin manuscripts formerly in possession of the cathedral and archbishops of Arles are now in the Bibliothèque Nationale (Delisle, Le cabinet des manuscrits, II, 337; III, 270-71) cf. also Gottlieb, No. 247; and CMD, XX, 347-50, 353-63, 408; XLIX, 72, 249.

[527] Frizon, p. 453.

that it attracted foreigners there to admire its splendor.

The library of Montmajour at Arles
Its glory lasted until the time of Pedro de Luna (the antipope Benedict XIII) who brought about its ruin.[528] One learns this from the extant testimonies to that famous abbey, which remains today only in memory.

The library of the Carthusians of Bon-pas
The library of the Carthusians of Bon-pas is highly regarded for its interesting books, especially historical works, which Don Polycarpe de La Rivière collected with much effort.[529]

The ancient abbey of Lérins was the first monastic academy in the West, and a seminary of saints and learned persons who have ennobled the Catholic Church by their exemplary lives and exceptional erudition. These men, with their deep

---

[528] One should not conclude from this statement that Benedict XIII was a bibliophobe; quite the contrary is true, as may be seen from n. 409 above. Manuscript materials of importance for the history of Montmajour abbey are listed in CMD, XVI, 169, 667 and passim; XX, 657-58 and passim; and XLIX, 47, 549 and passim; they show conclusively that the abbey's history did not come to an end at the time of the Schism. On the abbey library, see M. Perrier, "La bibliothèque de l'abbaye de Montmajour," Archives de la Société des collectionneurs d'ex-libris, 1904, p. 27; APAF, II, 84; and Magnoald Ziegelbauer, Historia rei literariae Ordinis S. Benedicti, ed. O. Legipontius (4 vols.; Augustae Vind.: M. Veith, 1754), I, 471.

[529] Polycarpe de La Rivière (d. ca. 1640), a Carthusian monk who corresponded with Peiresc, wrote annals of Avignon (CMD, XX, 392) and a history of the Avignon cathedral (ibid., XVI, 364), and published a work entitled, L'adieu du monde, ou le mépris de ses vaines grandeurs et plaisirs périssables, which appeared in two editions (Lyon: A. Pillehotte, 1619 and 1631). On the manuscripts of Bon-pas, see François Duchesne, Histoire de tous les cardinaux françois, sec. "Preuves," pp. 424, 461; on the history of this monastery, consult M. Gazet, "La Chartreuse de Bonpas," Mémoires de la Académie de Vaucluse, V (1886), 64-92; and cf. APAF, II, 154, and CMD, XLIX, 142.

love of study, collected a very large and splendid library for their use.[530] Jean de Nostredame gives an ample description of it in his biography of the Monge, or monk, of the Îles d'Or, one of the compilers of the lives of the provençal poets. I shall quote this description here for the light it sheds on our subject; though quite lengthy, the passage needs to be included so that the memory of the library will be retained by posterity.[531]

The library of Lérins

---

[530] On the school of Lérins and the scholars who studied there (Jean Cassian, St. Honoratus, Hilary, Lupus, Eucherius, etc.) see A. C. Cooper-Marsdin, <u>The history of the Islands of the Lerins; the Monastery, Saints and Theologians of S. Honorat</u> (Cambridge: University Press, 1913); on the library there, see Vogel, p. 266, APAF, II, 178, 182-83, Cooper-Marsdin, p. 321, and an article on the "Chapel of St. Honorat Monastery" in <u>The [London] Times</u>, October 25, 1928.

[531] Although many have taken this narrative concerning the "Monk of the Golden Isles" as a genuine account of a late fourteenth-century bibliophile, such a position can no longer be sustained. Jean de Nostredame (<u>ca</u>. 1507-<u>ca</u>. 1577), younger brother of the famous astrologer and prophet Michel Nostradamus, and uncle of César de Nostredame, the historian of Provence (see above, n. 519), included a number of fictional episodes in his <u>Vies des plus celèbres et anciens poetes provençaus</u>; by the use of anagram, analogy, and allegory he frequently depicted himself and his friends in the supposedly factual narratives. Chabaneau and Anglade (Jehan de Nostredame, Pt. 1, pp. 98-113; Pt. 2, pp. 353-54) have very effectively shown that in the story of the Monge Jean de Nostredame speaks of (1) himself (he writes of the Monge, "he was the prime reason why those superlative poets, who had been so long forgotten, were again brought into public notice"), (2) his friend Scipion Cibo (the Monge "was a descendant of the ancient and aristocratic family of Cibo of Genoa"), (3) and especially Jules-Raymond de Soliers, another close friend ("Moine des Iles d'Or" is an exact anagram of "Reimond de Soliés"; Soliers, in his "Chronographia Provinciae"--still largely unpublished--concentrates particularly on the Stecades and islands of Lérins; he was a poet, bibliophile, and author of a catalogue of provençal poets--as was the "Monge"). Thus, although the passage from Nostredame quoted <u>in extenso</u> by Jacob gives us no information on the monastic library at Lerins in the fourteenth and fifteenth centuries, it does tell us a good deal about the bibliophilistic interest of Jean de

The Monge of the Îles d'Or (in olden times called
Stecades or Îles d'Yeres) was a descendant of the
ancient and aristocratic[532] family of Cibo of Genoa.
Early in life he determined to follow the religious--
the monastic--life,[533] and therefore, led by his
noble spirit, he arrived at the monastery of Saint-
honoré on the island of Lérins in the region of
Cyagne. And because he was well-known, both for his
high birth and for the good name which he had acquired
from his youth, he was not only admitted, but strongly
beseeched, to become one of the monks of that community.
There he pursued his studies and attained facility in
poetry, rhetoric, theology, and other liberal arts.
For this reason the monks asked him to take charge of
their monastic library, which was reputed to be the
finest in all Europe. Indeed, the counts of Provence,
the kings of Naples and Sicily, and other important
persons who loved learning had enriched and endowed it
with the most excellent, rare, and exquisite works in
all languages and departments of knowledge. Thus there
was little desire that these treasures be harmfully reduced and suffer complete disorder from the wars to
which the monastery had been subjected. Hitherto such
struggles had been rife in Provence between, on the one
hand, the princes of les Baux and Charles de Duras and
Raymond de Turenne, pretenders to the county of Provence,
and, on the other, the counts and true rulers of it.

Nostredame's circle in Provence in the sixteenth century. Soliers'
biographer informs us that Soliers--who, incidentally, perpetuated
his friend's literary hoax in his own writings--"assembled a cabinet
of rarities and curiosities such as medals, paintings, prints,
antique vases, bas-reliefs, pieces of armor, inscriptions, . . .
in short, everything unusual and interesting that he could bring
together" (Joseph de Haitze, quoted in the editorial introduction
to Jehan de Nostredame, Pt. 1, p. 102). Nostredame himself was
an ardent book collector, for he tells us that he had collected
here and there "fine manuscript books both in Latin, French, and
Provençal" and that they were stolen from him in the religious
troubles of 1562 (ibid., p. 29); Chabaneau and Anglade (ibid.,
pp. 29-31) attempt a reconstruction of his library on the basis
of his reading, and note that he used the valuable materials in
the Archives of Aix and in the château of the count of Sault (Peire
esteemed the latter collection highly for its manuscripts).

[532]"And aristocratic" does not appear in the original French
text of Nostredame's Vies, but is found in Giovanni Giudici's Italian translation, published the same year, in the same place, and by
the same publisher as the French original; this Italian translation
was made from Nostredame's autograph manuscript (ibid., Pt. 2,
pp. 267, 281).

[533]Jacob drops the clause "in order to continue his studies

The Monge took the post which had been offered to him, and used his days so valuably that in a short time, by means of the good judgment consonant with his faith, he put the library in order. Not without great toil and hardship he separated the books according to subject divisions, for it was evident from the early catalog of the collection which had been drawn up by a learned monk of the monastery named Hermantere, a member of the nobility of Provence,[534] by order of King Ildefons II of Aragon, count of Provence, that many fine books had been removed and replaced by others of little worth and no scholarship.

The Monge, in attending to the catalog and in examining the books, found among them one which contained all the noble and illustrious families not only of Provence but also of Aragon, Italy, and France. In it their alliances were enumerated and their armorial bearings were described; and also included were all the works of the provençal poets in provençal rhythm (these poems the above-mentioned Hermantere[535] had collected by command of the king of Aragon). The Monge himself transcribed this book in a fine hand, and sent a copy to Louis II, father of René, king of Naples and Sicily and count of Provence;[536] and from this copy many gentlemen of the country had transcriptions made, for the contents were rare and charming. Some of these gentlemen--the same ones who were lovers of provençal poetry--had the verses copied in an elegant script and illuminated with gold and azure on parchment (the others used paper). The lives of the poets were written in red letters, and the poems, which appeared in the provençal tongue and employed many rhythmic variations, were set down in black. In doing this, the Monge found it very hard to understand the provençal language; he tells us that the difficulties arose from the variety of expressions,[537] for some of the poets had written

---

[534]"It goes without saying that along with the Monk of the Îles d'Or must also disappear from literary history Dom Hermentaire, from whom he is supposed to have transcribed the [provençal] collection. . . . The Hermentères, sieurs d'Orgon, were an old noble family of Provence. One of their descendants, Marc-Antoine de Fontèves, was councillor in the Court of Accounts at Aix in the time of César de Nostredame" (ibid., Pt. 1, p. 107, n. 3; Pt. 2, p. 354).

[535]In Nostredame's original French text the spelling is here given as "Hermentere."

[536]On René, king of Naples and Sicily, see above, n. 326.

[537]Nostredame's original French text has poemes rather than peines here, and thus reads: "he tells us that the poems contained a variety of expressions."

in their pure provençal, but others had not been as
well versed in it as in the tongue of another nation
such as Spain, Italy, Gascony, or France. Thus the
poems were interspersed with many words characteristic
of these languages, and this rendered them so obscure
and problematical that he had to go to great trouble
to discover what they meant. But finally he restored
them all completely, and his emendations were so
felicitous that he was the prime reason why those
superlative poets, who had been so long forgotten,
were again brought into public notice.[538]

Today this library is far removed from its ancient splendor,
for hardly any vestiges of it remain.

---

[538] Jehan de Nostredame, Pt. 2, pp. 148-50. In the last
sentence of the quotation, Jacob drops *mis* and substitutes
remarquez for *revoquez*, but the sense is not altered.

CHAPTER XXVIII (CIX)

TOURAINE

The library of the Church of Tours

The library of the Church of Tours was once exceedingly rich in manuscripts, for Alcuin, preceptor of Emperor Charlemagne, had the very noble library of Egbert, archbishop of York, transported there from England; we are told this by the Englishman John Bale (Century 2, chap. xvi).[539] As President de Thou notes, the Church library

---

[539] John Bale, *Scriptorum illustriū maioris Brytanniē ... Catalogus* (2 vols.; Basileae: J. Oporinus, [1557-1559]), I, 109 (Jacob's reference should be to chap. xv, rather than to chap. xvi, of Century 2). On Bale and his important bibliographical work, see Lomeier, sec. "England," n. 6. Alcuin wrote to Charlemagne: "Here I feel severely the lack of those valuable books of scholastic learning which I had in my own country, by the kind and affectionate industry of my master, and also in some measure by my own humble labors. Let me therefore propose to your excellency that I send over thither some of our youths who may collect for us all that is necessary, and bring back with them into Francia the flowers of Britain" (Ep. xxxviii; cf. epp. xl, xciii, and clxiv; and see also Edward Kennard Rand, *A Survey of the Manuscripts of Tours* [2 vols.; Cambridge, Mass.: Mediaeval Academy of America, 1929], I, 39, n. 2). The importance of Alcuin's bibliophilistic activity at Tours lies in the facts that (1) the Carolingian minuscule achieved its highest excellence in the scriptoria of Tours, and (2) it was from Tours that the multiplication of books spread to the great monastic foundations throughout the Frankish empire--thus carrying on the tradition begun by Cassiodorus and continued by Benedict Biscop, Bede, Egbert of York, and Alcuin. In this connection, see Alcuin's well-known hexameters on library and scriptorium (Ernst Duemmler [ed.], *Poetae latini aevi Carolini* ["Monumenta Germaniae historica"; 2 vols.; Berolini, 1880-1884], I, 320; Alcuin's metrical catalog is given in Latin and in English translation

was begun by Saint Perpetuus, who had been bishop of that cathedral: "Saint Perpetuus, bishop of Touraine, set up a copious library near his episcopal palace as an aid in upholding the Catholic faith"⁵⁴⁰[L].

In the monastery of the Minimite fathers of Le Plessis-lez-Tours, there is a well supplied library of more than 6000 volumes.⁵⁴¹

<u>The Minimite library</u>

M. N. de Voyer, knight, viscount of Paulmy in Touraine, owns a fine library which was already worthy of consideration when it belonged to M. René de Voyer, viscount of Paulmy and of La Roche de Genes, knight of the order of the king, bailiff of Touraine, etc. René was a man with a great love of letters, as François de La Croix testifies in

<u>The viscount of Paulmy's library</u>

---

in Dorothy May Norris, <u>A History of Cataloguing and Cataloguing Methods</u> [London: Grafton, 1939], pp. 8-10). Delisle describes some interesting (and unsuccessful) attempts on the part of Baluze at the end of the seventeenth century and Bignon in the eighteenth century to persuade the Cathedral chapter to part with its manuscripts (<u>Le cabinet des manuscrits</u>, I, 461-63). See also the manuscript lists in Montfaucon, II, 1273-74, and <u>CMD</u>, XXXVII, Pt. 2, 1055-63, 1077-78, 1080-82; and cf. Vogel, p. 303.

⁵⁴⁰Perpetuus was sixth bishop of Tours, and held the see in the latter half of the fifth century (Scévole [II] de Sainte-Marthe, XIV, 12-14).

⁵⁴¹This Minimite monastery was founded in 1482 by St. Francis of Paola, who died there in 1507. The Tours city library preserves manuscript materials of value for the monastery's history, and eleven manuscripts which were once a part of its library--including the autograph manuscripts of Gassendi's <u>Syntagma philosophicum</u> (<u>CDM</u>, XXVII, Pt. 2, 1079, 1158 and passim) For printed works dealing with the history and bibliothecal activity at Le Plessis-lez-Tours, see the bibliographical citations given in <u>APAF</u>, VIII, 20, n. 15.

his Bibliothèque françoise (see the letter R). La Croix assures us that his library contained numerous good manuscripts, and that among them were many excellent and learned books of the late Guillaume Postel, including his confession of faith written and signed by his own hand.[542]

G. Postel

---

[542] La Croix du Maine, II, 373-75. La Croix informs us that René de Voyer, lord of Argenson (d. ca. 1585) supplied much material on the antiquities of Touraine for François de Belleforest's Cosmographie (cf. n. 34 above), wrote Latin and French poetry, and engaged in some translating of Latin into French. We are also informed by La Croix (ibid., I, 607) that René's father, Jean de Voyer (d. 1571), was a man of literary tastes who was able to translate literary Spanish into French. When Jacob speaks of "N." de Voyer, he is not necessarily giving the first initial of René's successor; Jacob on occasion uses the initial N to indicate that he does not know an individual's Christian name. On Guillaume Postel, see above, n. 30; the Bibliothèque Nationale received a number of his manuscripts when it acquired the excellent library of Philibert de la Mare of Dijon in 1687 (Delisle, Le cabinet des manuscrits, I, 361). Postel's books suffered dispersal even while he was alive, as we learn from his recent biographer Bouwsma: "He was badly in need of money [in 1555]. He was finally forced even to sell his beloved books. Masius arranged their purchase by the Elector Palatine, and eventually Postel's manuscripts were to play an important role in the beginnings of German oriental study. But the loss of his treasures almost broke his heart; he felt again, he wrote, all the labors and suffering they had cost him, journeying through the deserts of Asia and the mountains of Europe. . . . Early in 1562 he appeared in Lyons. . . . Then he left for Paris itself just before the Huguenots took over Lyons; they seized and destroyed books and papers he had left behind. . . . His library, once so rich in rare volumes, was reduced to a single Psalter" (Bouwsma, pp. 22, 25-26; cf. p. 28). Bouwsma devotes a chapter of his biography to "Postel's Reading" (Chapter II, pp. 30-63).

CHAPTER XXIX (CX)

SAVOY

The library of Geneva

Theodore Beza

In spite of all my efforts to obtain notes on the libraries of this province, I have been unable to uncover any information except that in the city of Geneva, which is situated in the province, one finds an ample public library incorporating the highly-reputed book collection of Theodore Beza.[543]

---

[543] Although the private book collections of Calvin and his fellow reformer Peter Martyr Vermigli formed the basis of the Geneva public library (HB, III, Pt. 1, 582-84; Edwards, II, 499-500; Lomeier, sec. "France," n. 22), Beza's personal library apparently suffered dispersal. We know that in 1581, when he sensed the decline of his scholarly powers, Beza presented the University of Cambridge with the famous sixth-century New Testament codex from his library--the codex (D) which has come to be designated "Codex Bezae" (A. T. Robertson, An Introduction to the Textual Criticism of the New Testament [Nashville, Tenn.: Broadman Press, 1925], pp. 86-87; Frederic G. Kenyon, Handbook to the Textual Criticism of the New Testament [2d ed.; Grand Rapids, Mich.: Eerdmans, 1953 (reprint of 1912 ed.)], pp. 88-97). When the young Francis de Sales attempted to convert Beza to Roman Catholicism toward the end of his life, a Geneva manuscript tells us that "he pointed to his library shelves empty of books; for these had been sold to defray the expenses of the support of a number of French refugees" (quoted in Henry Martyn Baird, Theodore Beza, the Counsellor of the French Reformation, 1519-1605 [New York: Putnam, 1899], p. 339). Beza in fact sold the substance of his library for six hundred gold crowns to a George Sigismond of Zastrisell, one of his students who boarded in his Geneva home (see Charles Borgeaud, in Bulletin historique et littéraire de la Société de l'histoire du protestantisme français, XLVIII [1899], 64). Many of Beza's letters are preserved in the libraries of Geneva, Zurich, and Basel.

Now this library concludes my _Traicté des plus belles bibliotheques, qui sont dans le monde_, in the research of which I have expended great effort. The honor and the glory be to God, and the utility to the public; this is all the recompense I desire from you, O equitable reader.[544]

---

[544] Jacob adds: "I give you this further word of advice, that during the printing of this book many notes came into my hands concerning matters already dealt with; this necessitates my adding an appendix, so that nothing will remain imperfect, and so that if there should be a second edition, everything will be put in its proper order." In the present edition-translation, the appendix material has been integrated into the text in accordance with our author's specific instructions. All integrations are set off from the text proper by triangular brackets (<, >).

SELECTED BIBLIOGRAPHY

SELECTED BIBLIOGRAPHY

Abbayes et prieurés de l'ancienne France. Edited by
    Dom Beaunier, et al. 12 vols. Ligugé: Abbaye
    Saint-Martin, 1907-1941. (Cited as APAF.)

Albrich, Eva. "Der avis pour dresser une bibliothèque von
    Gabriel Naudé." Unpublished Ph.D. dissertation,
    Friedrich-Alexander Universität, Erlangen, Germany, 1949.

Allgemeine deutsche Biographie. 56 vols. Leipzig: Duncker,
    1875-1912. (Cited as ADB.)

Auberoche, Pierre d'. Eminentissimo principi Julio cardinali
    Mazarino. Parisiis: A. Coulon, 1644.

Backer, Augustin de. Bibliothèque de la Compagnie de Jésus.
    Edited by Carlos Sommervogel. 10 vols. Bruxelles:
    O. Schepens, 1890-1909.

[Bates, William (ed.).] Vitae selectorum aliquot virorum.
    Londini: George Wells, 1681.

Bayle, Pierre. Dictionnaire historique et critique. 8 vols.
    5th ed., with supplement by de Chauffepié. Amsterdam:
    Bounel, et al., 1740-1756.

Besterman, Theodore. The Beginnings of Systematic Bibliography.
    London: Oxford University Press, 1935.

Biographie nationale de Belgique. Edited by the Académie Royale
    des Sciences, des Lettres, et des Beaux-arts de Belgique.
    28 vols. Bruxelles: Bouylant-Christophe, 1866-1944.
    (Cited as BNB.)

Blanchard, François. Les presidens au mortier du Parlement de
    Paris ... ensemble un catalogue de tous les conseillers
    selon l'ordre des temps & de leurs receptions. Paris:
    Cardin Besongne, 1647.

Blanchot, Pierre. Idea bibliothecae universalis. Parisiis:
    S. Cramoisy, 1635.

Boer, Josephine de. "Men's Literary Circles in Paris 1610-1660," Publications of the Modern Language Association of America, LIII (September, 1938), 730-80.

Bonnaffé, Edmond. Les collectionneurs de l'ancienne France. Paris: A. Aubry, 1873.

_____. Dictionnaire des amateurs français au XVIIe siecle. Paris: A. Quantin, 1884.

Borel, Pierre. Les antiquitez de Castres. Edited by Ch. Pradel. Paris: Académie des Bibliophiles, 1868.

Bouchel, Laurent. La bibliothèque ou thresor du droict françois. Paris: J. Gesselin, 1615.

Bourgeois, Émile, and André, Louis. Les sources de l'histoire de France: XVIIe siècle (1610-1715). 8 vols. Paris: A. Picard, 1913-1935.

Boutrays, Raoul. Lutetia. Lutetiae Parisiorum: R. Thierry, 1611.

Bouwsma, William J. Concordia Mundi: The Career and Thought of Guillaume Postel, 1510-1581. Cambridge, Mass.: Harvard University Press, 1957.

Brice, Germain. Nouvelle description de la ville de Paris. 4 vols. 8th ed. Paris: J. M. Gandouin, 1725.

Bridge, John S. C. A History of France from the Death of Louis XI. 5 vols. Oxford: Clarendon Press, 1921-1936.

Brown, Harcourt. Scientific Organizations in Seventeenth Century France, 1620-1680. Baltimore: Williams & Wilkins, 1934.

Bury, Richard de. The Philobiblon. Edited by Archer Taylor. Berkeley: University of California Press, 1948.

[Caille, Jean de la.] Histoire de l'imprimerie et de la librairie. Paris: Jean de la Caille, 1689.

Cantor, Moritz. Vorlesungen über Geschichte der Mathematik. 4 vols. 2d ed. Leipzig: Teubner, 1894-1908.

Catalogue général des manuscrits des bibliothèques publiques de France. Departements. 50 vols. Paris: Librairie Plon; Bibliothèque Nationale, 1886-1954. (Cited as CMD.)

Catholic Encyclopedia. 16 vols. New York: Appleton, et al., 1907-1914.

Cayrou, Gaston. Le Français classique: lexique de la langue du XVIIe siècle. Paris: Didier, 1948.

Chenesseau, Georges. Sainte-Croix d'Orléans, histoire d'une cathédrale gothique. Vol. II. Paris: E. Champion, 1921.

Chennevières-Pointel, Charles-Philippe de. Recherches sur la vie et les ouvrages de quelques peintres provinciaux. 4 vols. Paris: Dumoulin, 1847-1882.

Chéruel, A. Dictionnaire historique des institutions, moeurs et coutumes de la France. 2 vols. 5th ed. Paris: Hachette, 1880.

Clark, John Willis. The Care of Books. 2d ed. Cambridge: University Press, 1902.

Collinson, J. The Life of Thuanus. London: Longman et al., 1807.

Colomiès, Paul. Bibliothèque choisie. 2d ed. Amsterdam: G. Gallet, 1699.

Coste, Hilarion de. Les éloges de nos rois, et des enfans de France, qui ont este daufins de Viennois. Paris: S. Cramoisy, 1643.

Cotton des Houssayes, Jean-Baptiste. The Duties & Qualifications of a Librarian. ("Literature of Libraries in the Seventeenth and Eighteenth Centuries.") Chicago: A. C. McClurg, 1906.

Delandine, Antoine-François. Manuscrits de la bibliothèque de Lyon. 3 vols. Paris: Renouard, 1812.

Delisle, Léopold. Le cabinet des manuscrits de la Bibliothèque Impériale. 3 vols. Paris: Imprimerie Impériale, 1868-1881.

Devauchelle, Roger. La reliure en France, de ses origines à nos jours. Paris: J. Rousseau-Girard, 1959--.

Dibdin, Thomas Frognall. Bibliomania; or Book-Madness. New ed. London: Chatto & Windus, 1876.

Dictionnaire de biographie française. Edited by J. Balteau et al. Paris: Letouzey, 1933--. (Cited as DBF.)

Dorat, Jean. Poematia. 3 vols. Lutetiae Parisiorum: G. Linocerius, 1586.

Du Breul, Jacques. Le théâtre des antiquitez de Paris. Paris: C. de La Tour, 1612.

[Du Breul, Jacques, and Malingre, Claude.] Les antiquitez de la ville de Paris. Paris: P. Rocolet, et al., 1640.

Duchesne, François. Histoire de tous les cardinaux françois. 2 vols. Paris, 1660.

Duleau, A. (ed.). "Portraits des membres du Parlement de Paris et des maîtres des requêtes vers le milieu du XVIIe siècle," Revue nobiliaire héraldique et biographique, I (1862), 105-190.

Dutcher, G. M., et al. Guide to Historical Literature. New York: Macmillan, 1931.

Edwards, Edward. Memoirs of Libraries. 2 vols. London: Trübner, 1859.

Enciclopedia biografica e bibliografica "Italiana." Milano: Istituto ed. Ital., Bernardo Carlo Tosi, 1936-.

Esdaile, Arundell. National Libraries of the World. 2d. ed. revised by F. J. Hill. London: The Library Association, 1957.

Espiner-Scott, Janet Girvan. "Note sur le circle de Henri de Mesmes et sur son influence," Mélanges offerts à M. Abel Lefranc. (Paris: E. Droz, 1936), pp. 354-61.

Evelyn, John. Diary. Edited by E. S. de Beer. 6 vols. Oxford: Clarendon Press, 1955.

Feugère, Léon. Essai sur ... Henri Estienne, suivi d'une étude sur Scévole de Sainte-Marthe. Paris: Delalain, 1853.

Fouqueray, Henri. Histoire de la Compagnie de Jésus en France des origines à la suppression (1528-1762). 5 vols. Paris: A. Picard; Bureaux des Études, 1910-1925.

Franklin, Alfred. Les anciennes bibliothèques de Paris. 3 vols. Paris: Imprimerie Impériale, 1867-1873.

_____. Histoire de la Bibliothèque Mazarine et du Palais de l'Institut. 2d ed. Paris: H. Welter, 1901.

Frati, Carlo. Dizionario bio-bibliografico dei bibliotecari e bibliofili italiani dal sec. XIV al XIX. Firenze: Olschki, 1933.

Frizon, Pierre. Gallia purpurata. Lutetiae Parisiorum: S. Le Moine, 1638.

Gassendi, Pierre. The Mirrour of true Nobility & Gentility. Being the Life of the Renowned Nicolaus Claudius Fabricius Lord of Peiresk. Translated by W. Rand. London: H. Moseley, 1657.

_____. Viri illustris Nicolai Claudii Fabricii de Peiresc ... vita. Parisiis: S. Cramoisy, 1641.

Gottlieb, Theodor. _Ueber mittelalterliche Bibliotheken._
    Leipzig: O. Harrassowitz, 1890.

Guérard, Albert. _France, A Modern History._ Ann Arbor:
    University of Michigan Press, 1959.

Hamel, Frank. "The Librarians of the Royal Library at Fontainebleau," _The Library_, 3d series, I, No. 2 (April, 1910), 190-99.
    Though very useful, this article must be used with caution, since in several instances it keeps alive traditions whose falsity had already been demonstrated by other writers.

Handbuch der Bibliothekswissenschaft. Edited by Fritz Milkau and Georg Leyh. 2d ed. Wiesbaden: Harrassowitz, 1952--. (Cited as _HB_.)

Harrisse, Henry. _Le président de Thou et ses descendants, leur célèbre bibliothèque._ Paris: H. Leclerc, 1905.

Hassall, Arthur. _Mazarin._ London: Macmillan, 1903.

Hauser, Henri. _La prépondérance espagnole (1559-1660)._ 3d ed. ("Peuples et Civilisations.") Paris: Presses Universitaires de France, 1948.

────. _Les sources de l'histoire de France, XVIe siècle (1494-1610)._ 4 vols. Paris: A. Picard, 1906-1915.

Héméré, Claude. _De Academia Parisiensi._ Lutetiae: S. Cramoisy, 1637.

Herbet, Félix. "La librairie royale de Fontainebleau," _Bibliographe moderne_, XXIV (1928-1929), 141-52.

Hessel, Alfred. _A History of Libraries._ Translated, with supplementary material, by Reuben Peiss. Washington, D.C.: Scarecrow Press, 1950.

Huxley, Aldous. _Grey Eminence._ New York: Meridian Books, 1959 [c1941].

Labbe, Philippe. _Nova bibliotheca manuscriptorum librorum._ Parisiis: J. Henault, 1653.

La Croix du Maine, François de, and Du Verdier, Antoine. _Les bibliothèques françoises de La Croix du Maine et de Du Verdier._ Edited by Rigoley de Juvigny. 6 vols. New ed. Paris: Saillant & Nyon, 1772-1773.

Lenoble, Robert. _Mersenne, ou la naissance du mécanisme._ Paris: J. Vrin, 1943.

Leprince, Nicolas-Thomas. Essai historique sur la bibliothèque du Roi. Paris: Belin, 1782. (A new edition by Louis Paris was published at Paris: Bureau du Cabinet historique, 1856.)

Le Roux de Lincy, Antoine-Jean-Victor. Researches concerning Jean Grolier, His Life and His Library, with a Partial Catalogue of His Books. Translated and revised by Carolyn Shipman. New York: Grolier Club, 1907.

L'Estoile, Pierre de. Registre-Journal de Henri III, Henri IV et Louis XIII. ("Nouvelle collection des mémoires," edited by J.-F. Michaud and J.-J.-F. Poujoulat, Vol. XIII.) Lyon: Guyot, 1851.

l'Hospital, Michel de. Oeuvres complètes. Edited by P. J. S. Duféy. 5 vols. Paris: Boulland, 1824-1826.

Lomeier, Johannes. A Seventeenth-Century View of European Libraries. Lomeier's De bibliothecis, Chapter X. Translated and edited by John Warwick Montgomery. ("University of California Publications in Librarianship," Vol. III.) Berkeley: University of California Press, 1962.

Lough, John. An Introduction to Seventeenth Century France. London: Longmans, Green, 1954.

Mader, Joachim Johann, and Schmidt, Johann Andreas (eds.). De bibliothecis atque archivis. 3 vols. Helm[e]stadi[i]: G. W. Hammius, 1702-1705.

Malclès, Louise-Noëlle. "Le fondateur de la bibliographie nationale en France, le R. P. Louis Jacob de Saint-Charles (1608-1670)," Mélanges d'histoire du livre et des bibliothèques, offerts à Monsieur Frantz Calot (Paris: Librairie d'Argences, 1960), pp. 243-55.

Manzoni, Alessandro. The Betrothed. Translated by Archibald Colquhoun. ("Everyman's Library," No. 999.) London: Dent, 1956.

[Martene, Edmond, and Durand, Ursin.] Voyage littéraire de deux religieux bénédictins de la congrégation de Saint-Maur. 2 vols. Paris: Delaulne & Montalant, 1717-1724.

Maugis, Édouard. Histoire du Parlement de Paris de l'avènement des rois Valois à la mort d'Henri IV. 3 vols. Paris: Picard, 1914-1916.

Mazarin, homme d'état et collectionneur, 1602-1661. Exposition organisée pour le troisième centenaire de sa mort. Paris Bibliothèque Nationale, 1961. (Review by John Warwick Mogomery in the Library Quarterly, XXXII [April, 1962], 174

Ménage, Gilles. Ménagiana. Amsterdam: A. Braakman, 1693. (This edition specifies by symbol the contributors of Ménage's remarks.)

_____. Ménagiana. 4 vols. New ed. Paris: Delaulne, 1729.

Mersenne, Marin. Correspondance. Edited by Mme. Paul Tannery and Cornelis de Waard. 3 vols. Paris: G. Beauchesne (Vols. I and II), Presses Universitaires de France (Vol. III), 1932-1946.

Meyer, R. W. Leibnitz and the Seventeenth-Century Revolution. Translated by J. P. Stern. Cambridge, England: Bowes & Bowes, 1952.

Molinier, Auguste. Les sources de l'histoire de France dès origines aux guerres d'Italie (1494). 6 vols. Paris: A. Picard, 1901-1906.

Montfaucon, Bernard de. Bibliotheca bibliothecarum manuscriptoru nova. 2 vols. Parisiis: Briasson, 1739.

Moreau, C. (ed.). Bibliographie des Mazarinades. 3 vols. Paris J. Renouard, 1850-1851.

_____. Choix de Mazarinades. 2 vols. Paris: J. Renouard, 1853.

Moréri, Louis. La grand dictionnaire historique. 10 vols. Paris: Libraires Associés, 1759.

Mowery, Bob L. "Gabriel Naudé, Librarian." Unpublished Master's thesis, University of Chicago, 1951.

Naudé, Gabriel. Addition a l'histoire de Louys XI. Paris: F. Targa, 1630.

_____. Advice on Establishing a Library. Edited by Archer Taylor. Berkeley: University of California Press, 1950.

_____. Jugement de tout ce qui a esté imprimé contre le cardinal Mazarin. [2d ed.]. [Paris, 1650]. (Cited as Mascurat.)

Naudé, Gabriel, and Patin, Gui. Naudaeana et Patiniana. 2d ed. Amsterdam: F. vander Plaats, 1703.

The New Schaff-Herzog Encyclopedia of Religious Knowledge. Edite by Samuel Macauley Jackson. 13 vols. plus 2 supplementar vols. Reprint ed. Grand Rapids, Michigan: Baker Book House, 1958. (Cited as New Schaff-Herzog.)

Nicéron, Jean-Pierre. Mémoires pour servir a l'histoire des hommes illustres dans la république des lettres. 43 vols Paris: Briasson, 1727-1745.

Niepce, Léopold. Les bibliothèques anciennes et modernes de Lyon. Lyon: H. Georg, 1876.

──────. Les manuscrits de Lyon. Lyon: H. Georg, [1879].

Nostredame, Jehan de. Les vies des plus célèbres et anciens poètes provençaux. Edited by Camille Chabaneau and Joseph Anglade. New ed. Paris: H. Champion, 1913.

Packard, Francis R. Guy Patin and the Medical Profession in Paris in the XVIIth Century. New York: Hoeber, 1925.

Papillon, Philibert. Bibliothèque des auteurs de Bourgogne. 2 vols. Dijon: P. Marteret, 1742.

Patin, Gui. Correspondance. Edited by Armand Brette. Paris: A. Colin, 1901.

──────. Lettres. Edited by J.-H. Reveillé-Parise. 3 vols. Paris: J.-B. Baillière, 1846.

Pattison, Mark. Isaac Casaubon. London: Longmans, Green, 1875.

Peiresc, Nicolas Claude Fabri de. Lettres. Edited by Philippe Tamizey de Larroque. 7 vols. Paris: Imprimerie Nationale, 1888-1898.

Perkins, James Breck. France under Mazarin, with a Review of the Administration of Richelieu. 2 vols. New York: G. P. Putnam, 1886.

Petit-Radel, Louis-Charles-François. Recherches sur les bibliothèques anciennes et modernes, jusqu'à la fondation de la Bibliothèque Mazarine. Paris: Rey et Gravier, 1819.

Pintard, René. Le libertinage érudit dans la première moitié du XVIIe siècle. Paris: Boivin, 1943.

Rashdall, Hastings. The Universities of Europe in the Middle Ages. Edited by F. M. Powicke and A. B. Emden. 3 vols. London: Oxford University Press, 1936.

Retz, Cardinal de. Oeuvres. Edited by Alphonse Feillet, et al. 11 vols. Paris: Hachette, 1870-1920.

Rice, James V. Gabriel Naudé, 1600-1653. ("Johns Hopkins Studies in Romance Literatures and Languages," No. 35.) Baltimore: Johns Hopkins Press, 1939.

Rivet de La Grange, Antoine, et al. Histoire literaire de la France ... par des religieux benedictins de la congregation de S. Maur. 24 vols. Paris, 1733-1862.

Robert, Claude. Gallia Christiana. Lutetiae Parisiorum: S. Cramoisy, 1626.

Ronsard, Pierre de. *Oeuvres complètes*. Edited by Paul Laumonier. Paris: Hachette, et al., 1914--.

Rubens, Peter Paul. *Letters*. Translated and edited by Ruth Saunders Magurn. Cambridge, Mass.: Harvard University Press, 1955.

Rymaille sur les plus célèbres bibliotières de Paris en 1649. Edited by Albert de La Fizelière. Paris: A. Aubry, 1868.

Sainte-Marthe, Scévole (I) de. *Lucubrationum pars altera, qua continentur, Gallorum doctrina illustrium, qui nostra patrumque memoria floxuerunt, elogia*. Lutetiae: P. Duru 1616. (Vol. II of Sainte-Marthe's *Opera*.)

Sainte-Marthe, Scévole (II) de, et al. *Gallia Christiana*. 16 vols. Parisiis: V. Palme, 1865-1870.

Sandys, John Edwin. *A History of Classical Scholarship*. 3 vols. Cambridge: University Press, 1903-1908.

Scaliger, Joseph Juste. *Epistolae*. Lugduni Batavorum: Elzevir, 1627.

Stankiewicz, W. J. *Politics & Religion in Seventeenth-Century France*. Berkeley: University of California Press, 1960.

Tallemant des Réaux, Gédéon. *Les historiettes*. 6 vols. 3d. ed. Paris: Techener, 1862.

Taylor, Archer. *Book Catalogues: Their Varieties and Uses*. Chicago: Newberry Library, 1957.

————. *A History of Bibliographies of Bibliographies*. New Brunswick, N.J.: Scarecrow Press, 1955.

Thou, Jacques-Auguste de. *Historia sui temporis*. 7 vols. Londini: Buckley, 1733.

Tilley, Arthur. *The Dawn of the French Renaissance*. Cambridge: University Press, 1918.

Van Dyke, Paul. *Catherine de Médicis*. 2 vols. London: John Murray, 1923.

Vic, Claude de, et al. *Histoire générale de Languedoc*. 16 vols. Toulouse: Édouard Privat, 1872-1904.

Villiers de Saint-Étienne, Cosme de. *Bibliotheca carmelitana*. 2 vols. Orléans, 1752.

Vogel, Ernst Gustav. *Literatur früherer und noch bestehender europäischer öffentlicher und Corporations-Bibliotheken*. Leipzig: T. O. Weigel, 1840.

Wedgwood, C. V. *The Thirty Years War*. 2d ed. Harmondsworth, Middlesex: Penguin Books, 1957.

Wickelgren, Florence L. *La Mothe le Vayer, sa vie et son oeuvre*. Paris: E. Droz, 1934.

Yates, Frances A. *The French Academies of the Sixteenth Century*. London: Warburg Institute of the University of London, 1947.

TRAICTE'
DES
BIBLIOTHEQVES.
Seconde Partie.

CHAPITRE LXXXII.

Du Royaume de France.

A France excede au-jourd'huy tous les autres Royaumes en *sçauans hommes, & en Bibliotheques* ; car quant aux hommes de lettres il sera facile à le voir dans *nostre Bibliotheque Vniuerselle des Autheurs François*, qui ont illustrés le public par leurs escrits. Et pour ce qui est des Bi-

Ee iiij

bliotheques le denombrement que l'on en verra cy-apres, fera bien cognoistre, que noſtre France excelle par deſſus toutes les autres nations. Ie donneray donc le commencement des Bibliotheques par celles de Paris, & celles-cy par la Royale. Quoy qu'en tout le reſte des Prouinces, ie les diſtribueray par l'ordre alphabetique.

CHAPITRE LXXXIII.

De la Prouince de France.

De la ville de Paris.

QVoy que l'Empereur Charlemagne, aye eſté le premier de nos Roïs à dreſſer des Bibliotheques : toutefois nous ne

des Bibliotheques. 441

treuuons point que ce fut à Paris, ains à Aix la Chapelle, comme i'ay remarqué en la p. 201. & à Lyon, ainsi qu'il se verra en son lieu: c'est pour quoy ie treuue que le Roy Charles V. a esté le premier qui a donné le fondemét à la tres-manifique Bibliotheque Royale, qu'il erigea à Fontaine-bleau; car il fit rechercher auec vn grád soin les meilleurs liures, qui se pouuoient treuuer de son temps pour l'enrichir. Et iaçoit que ce Monarque n'eust la cognoissance de la langue Latine : il estoit neantmoins naturellement enclin aux sciences, & vsoit d'vne eloquence merueilleuse en ses discours, comme le témoignent ceux qu'il fit pour appaiser les seditions de Paris & respondre aux inuectiues

Biblioth. Royal. erigée à Fontaine-bleau par Charles V.

de Charles Roy de Nauarre, dit le Mauuais, selon la remarque qu'en fait Hilarion de Coste Minime, *en ses Eloges Des Dauphins de France pag.* 223. Ce Sage Roy portoit vn grand amour aux gens de lettres; lesquels il employoit à faire diuerses traductions. Il commanda à *Nicolas Oresme* Docteur de la Faculté, grand Maistre du College de Nauarre, Chanoine de la saincte Chapelle, puis Euesque 28. de Lisieux, qui estoit fort intelligent en la Theologie & Philosophie, de faire les versions *de la Bible, des Ethiques, Politiques, & des liures du Ciel & du monde,* d'Aristote, auec *les Dialogues* de François Petrarque de l'vne & de l'autre Fortune. Par le commandement du mesme; *Iean Golain* Docteur de Paris & Prouincial des Carmes, de la Prouince de France, traduisit *le Rational des diuins Offices*, ou *Ceremonies de l'Eglise*, & *les Collations des sainct Peres*, traduites de Grec en Latin par Cassiodore; *Iean Corbichon* Docteur de l'Ordre des Augustins, trauailla aussi sur *le grand Proprietaire de toutes choses*, de Barthelemy Langlois; *Simon de Hesdein*, pareillement Docteur, donna la version de *Valere* le Grand; *Rodolphe de Presles* eut le mesme employ pour les liures de S. Augustin *de la Cité de Dieu*. Plusieurs autres sçauans personnages luy presenterent diuers ouurages qu'il receuoit tres volontiers, en témoignage de l'inclination qu'il auoit pour les lettres.

Charles VI Le Roy Charles VI. son fils & son successeur, eut cognoissance des sciences, comme remarque Charles de Louuiers *au songe du Verger*; & plusieurs autres, qui asseurent qu'il aimoit fort les Mathematiciens, & qu'il auoit vne belle Bibliotheque au Louure, à laquelle il joignit celle de son Pere, qui estoit à Fontaine-bleau; la charge de laquelle fut donnée à Antoine des Essarts, puis apres à Garnier de S. Yon, pour lors Escheuin de la ville de Paris, selon la remarque qu'en fait Iacques du Brüeil Benedictin, dans le 3. *liure des Antiquitez de Paris*, *pag.* 1049. où il rapporte vn extrait tiré du 8. *liure des memoriaux de la Chambre des Comtes.* Cotté H, P, S. lequel i'infereray icy pour vn authentique témoignage de l'antiquité de la Bibliotheque de nos Roys *Garnerius de S. Yon*, dit-il, *Scabinus villæ Parisiensis, commissus ad custodiam Librariæ Regis in Lupara, & aliorum etiam librorum, quocúmque loco fuerint, loco Antonij de Essartis, causis certis ad hoc ipsum Regem mouentibus exonerati, per eius litteras datas octauo Maij, 1412. sic signatas*, par le Roy presens Messire Gerard de Graneual, & autres: Calot. *Duodecimóque mensis eiusdem præstititit solitum iuramentum.* Et peu apres. *Garnerius de S. Yon, cui Rex per litteras datas Parisiis 21. Iulij 1418. sic signatas*, par le Roy Messire Iacques Denté, & autres presens I. Milet *commiserat custodiam librorum suorum in Lupara existentium, & ad dicti Garnerij reque-*

stam commissum erat certis personis de Camera compotorum faciendo inuentorium fuit hodie traditum ad Burellum per dictos Commissarios duplicatum fecit, & præstitit iuramentum de benè & fideliter custodiendo dictos libros, & nemini reuelare dicta Librariæ secretum. Quo iuramento præstito, reddita fuit ei clauis, altera dicta Libraria in camera existente, vna cum inuentorio prælat. cum duplicato suo manuali signo signato commisit in camera eum similibus. Voila comme ces Roys ont esté curieux à eriger & conseruer cette Bibliotheque. ausquels a succedé Loüys XI. qui eust vne parfaite cognoissance de la Politique, au rapport de son fidel historien Philippe de Comines, Seigneur d'Argenton; lequel l'appele *le Maistre en science d'Estat*;

Loüys XI.

des Bibliotheques. 447
le plus sage qu'il ait cognu pour se tirer d'vn mauuais pas ; celuy qui a mieux entendu l'art de separer les gens. Nonobstât ce grand estude à la Politique, il ne negligeoit pas les autres sciences : veu que Iean Bouchet Autheur des Annales d'Aquitaine, dit de luy, *qu'il auoit de la science acquise tant legale que historiale, plus que les Roys de France n'auoient accoustumez.* Ce que confirme Robert Gaguin son Historien, & Bibliothecaire *au liu.* 10. de l'Histoire de France. *Callebat litteras,* dit-il, *& supra quam Regibus mos est, erat eruditus.* Or cette cognoissance des sciences, ne luy estoit pas moins vtile, que celle des liures. Car comme il n'appliquoit son esprit qu'à de grandes choses, non seulement pour la police de son

Royaume, mais encore pour l'aduancement & progrez des bon-
nes lettres; cela fut cause qu'il per-
fectionna la Bibliotheque Royale du plus grand nombre de volumes qui se pouuoient treuuer, se
seruant pour cét effet *de Robert Gaguin*, Religieux de la Trinité, homme tres sçauant en son temps, qui
depuis merita d'estre Ambassadeur sous Charles VIII. & enfin
Ministre General de son Ordre:
la grãde cognoissance qu'il auoit
des bons liures luy fit meriter cette dignité de Bibliothecaire du
Roy Loüis XI. & non XII. comme s'est trompé Aubert le Mire
dans l'Eloge dudit Gaguin, où il
dit. *Cúmque facundiâ & rerum vsu
eximiè valeret, sæpe Regum* Gallia-
rum nomine, in Italia, Germania, *ac*
Britan-

des Bibliotheques. 449

Britanniæ publicas legationes obiuit. Ludouico XII. *in primis carus, qui cùm librorum studio colligendorum teneretur, ingentem ei pecuniæ vim eo nomine appendit, Regiæque suæ Bibliothecæ præfecit.* Or il est tres constant que ledit Gaguin mourut au cômencement du regne de Louys XII. lequel tenoit sa Bibliotheque à Blois, comme l'a iudicieusement remarqué M. Naudé *au chap.* 4. *des Additions à l'Histoire de Louys XI.* qui déduit les raisons, pour monstrer l'erreur dudit le Mire, où ie renuoy le Lecteur.

* al. XI.

Plusieurs ont treuuez estrange ce qui se lit dans *les Registres des Escholes de Medecine* de ce Roy : lequel donna en gage sa vaisselle d'argent ausdites escho=

F f

les pour auoir vne copie *du Rasis*, qui estoit dans leur Bibliotheque, qu'il fit demander par Messire Iean de la Driesche : mais ceux qui auront leu ce que ledit Gabriel Naudé en dit en son chap. 4. de l'Addition à l'histoire de ce Roy, verront & cognoistront l'affection de ce Prince enuers les liures.

Le Roy Louys XII. n'a pas seulement merité l'honneur d'auoir esté vnanimément proclamé *le Pere du peuple*; pour la bonté & affection qu'il portoit à ses sujets : mais encore pour la grande inclination qu'il auoit pour les bonnes lettres, puis qu'vn docte Historien l'appelle *le Ptolomée* de son temps, à cause de la grande recherche de liures, qu'il fit auec vne grande despence pour enrichir sa Bibliotheque qu'il tenoit à Blois: C'est Symphorien Champier, Lyonnois, Medecin du Duc de Lorraine, qui a escrit la vie de nostre Roy, sous lequel il viuoit, dans son 3. *liure des Trophées des François*, où l'on verra de quel amour ce Monarque cherissoit les Muses. *Eius animi*, dit-il, *sapientia, consilium atque reliquæ virtutes omnibus sunt admirationi: adeò vt difficillimum sit diiudicare in qua earum præstet; vel ob quam maiorem promereatur laudem. Est etiam bonarum litterarum amantissimus: ac virorum doctorum obseruantissimus; & librorum cupidissimus instar Ptolomæi Philadelphi, qui Demetrium Phalerium Bibliothecæ suæ præfecit; grandem pecuniam ei tradens i vt vn-*

dique ad Bibliothecam Regis, vel emendo, vel transcribendo libros congregaret. Et cùm eum interrogasset quotnam libri iam in Bibliothecis essent. Respondit plures quam ducenta millia: sed breui tempore ad quingenta millia posse peruenire putabat. Sic item Ludouicus noster Christianissimus libros vndique non minori diligentia perquiri atque ornari iubet. Nec minus sumptuosam, quam ipse Philadelphus Bibliothecam extruxit, vir certè prudentissimus: & tanto principatu dignissimus, qui regio diademate suscepto: omnia quæ ad Reipublicæ statum pertinere arbitrabatur: maxima animi prudentia disposuit. Que la Grece ne se vante plus d'auoir esté l'vnique en honneur, pour la splendide Bibliotheque de Ptololomée? mais qu'elle se souuienne,

des Bibliotheques. 453

que la Gaule luy a esté aussi bien Sœur pour les Bibliotheques, que pour les lettres : & que nos Roys ont esté les vrais imitateurs des leurs, en l'erection de leur Bibliotheque. L'vne des principales augmentatiós de cette Bibliotheque, qui fut faite sous ce Roy, furét les liures d'vn grand nombre de Docteurs du Droict, qui furent pris à Milan, & apportez en celle-cy : Or elle estoit en telle reputation, qu'vn Ambassadeur nommé *Bologninus*, la voyant à Blois, l'estima pour vne merueille de son temps ; ainsi qu'il se peut voir dans *son curieux liure*, qu'il a fait des quatres plus remarquables singularitez, qu'il auoit trouué en France, où il ne craint point de luy donner le premier lieu.

Ff iij

Le Grand Roy François I. a esté en son temps *le Parnasse des Muses, & vn Cabinet des sciences.* Car bien que les lettres eussent esté fleurissantes sous les regnes de ses predecesseurs : toutefo s leurs perfections parurent par ses soins & diligences. Il ordonna l'an 1527. le restablissement de la Bibliotheque Royale de Fontaine-bleau, qui en auoit esté transportée du temps de Charles VI. comme il a esté remarqué cy-dessus; & ce par les conseils & aduis que luy en auoient donnez *Ianus Lascaris*, Grec de nation & *Guillaume Budé* : voulant pouruoir à sa perfection, & augmentation, il enuoya *Iuste Tenelle, Guillaume Postel, & Pierre Gille* en Orient, afin de rechercher soi-

des Bibliotheques.

gneusement les liures rares de cette langue, tant pour enrichir cette tres magnifique Bibliotheque : que pour faire enseigner ces langues publiquement par douze Lecteurs Royaux, qu'il ordonna l'an 1531. pour les langues Latines, Grecques & Hebraïques; & pour les sciences de Mathematique, Philosophie, Art d'Oratoire, & de Medecine. Il est à remarquer, que les liures, qui furent mis dans cette Bibliotheque, furent tous tres bien reliez; car les relieures en ce temps là commencerent à estre fort belles. Auparauant que de sortir de cette Bibliotheque, j'en donneray la description, qui se retreue dans le *Thresor des Merueilles de Fontaine-bleau*, qu'a depuis peu imprimé *Pierre Dan*, Religieux de la Redemption des Captifs, Miniſtre de leur Conuent dudit Fontaine-bleau. *Ie viens au au dernier eſtage*, dit-il, liu. 2. chap. 7. n. 4. pag. 98. & 99.) *de ce departement, qui eſt la gallerie où a eſté autrefois la Libraire, que le grand Roy François auoit dreſſé en cette maiſon Royale, auec vn grand ſoin & curioſité, dont il en donna la charge au docte Pierre* Gillius: *& tout ce qui s'en peut dire de preſent, eſt que le malheur de nos guerres Ciuiles a eſté la cauſe, que pour ne la voir diſſipée, l'on en tranſporta les liures à Paris, où ils ſont encore. C'eſtoit bien vne des choſes plus conſiderables de ce lieu, où ce Prince n'auoit rien eſpargné pour recouurer tous les liures & tous les Manuſcrits les plus rares, & les plus curieux, qui fuſſent point ailleurs; ayant*

des Bibliotheques. 457

pour cet effet enuoyé ledit Gillius & plusieurs autres personnages, en Asie, Grece & en diuerses parties du monde pour en chercher; & où l'on ne pouuoit auoir les propres Manuscrits, il fit en sorte par sa faueur de les faire transcrire. (Belleforet Cosmograp. fol. 333.) Il se lit que quelques Princes & Seigneurs estrãgers venans en Frãce, ont infiniment plus desiré de venir icy visiter ce thresor des liures, que toute autre chose, que l'on put admirer ailleurs. Voyla la gloire que s'est acquis ce grand Monarque, pour auoir restably les sciences, qui estoient descheuës de leur premiere splendeur, par le barbarisme, qui s'estoit coulé dans nos Gaules: ce qui fera que son nom sera à iamais en benediction parmy les peuples, & particulierement les gens de lettres, defquels il eftoit le Mœcenas; & lefquels il aymoit fi tendrement, qu'il appelloit les Efcholiers fes enfans.

Catherine de Medicis. Paſſons de ce Roy à la Reyne Catherine de Medicis ſa belle fille, qui eſpouſa Henry II. ſon fils & ſon ſucceſſeur à la couronne. Cette Reïne en ſon bas aage eſchappa de la ſedition des Florentius, qui arriua l'an 1529. contre la maiſon de Medicis, qui furent chaſſez de Florence : puis apres elle fut mariée à noſtre Roy Henry II. auquel elle apporta entre autres choſes, les Manuſcrits de la celebre Bibliotheque des Medicis qui furent mis dans la Bibliotheque Royale, où ils ſont iuſqu'à preſent conſeruez. Les lettres doiuent vne perpetuelle memoire à

des Bibliotheques. 459
cette Reine, qui leur causa vn grad aduancemét, comme le remarque le P. Hilarion de Coste en son *Éloge*, duquel i'emprúteray le tesmoignage pour orner ce discours. *Durant la paix*, dit-il, *la Reine Catherine fit fleurir les lettres & les arts mechaniques, l'Architecture, la Peinture, & la Sculpture; mais on ne sçauroit assez la loüer pour auoir à l'exemple des Princes de sa maison (qui ont serui de refuge aux Muses de la* Grece *chassées & bannies de Constantinople & de l'Orient, par la barbarie des Ottomans) fauorisé les hommes doctes & sçauans, & d'auoir auec vne Royale despence digne de la belle fille du grand Roy François, le Pere & le Restaurateur des lettres, enuoyé querir en* Grece *& par tout le Leuant les plus rares Manuscrits en toute sor-*

te de langues, outre ceux de la Bibliotheque des Medicis, qu'elle fit venir d'Italie, qui seruent maintenant d'ornement à la Royale Librairie de nos Monarques.

Cette Reine d'honneur des Medicis issuë,
Ainçois que Calliope à son ventre à conceuë,
Pour ne degenerer de ses premiers ayeux,
Ronsard. Soigneux a fait chercher les liures les plus vieux,
Hebreux, Grecs, & Latins traduits & à traduire :
Et par noble despence elle en a fait reluire
Le haut Palais du Louure, afin que sans danger
Le François fut vaincueur du sçauoir estranger.

Ce n'est pas sans raison, que ce grand Poëte *Pierre Ronsard* Gentilhomme Vendosmois a si dignement loüé cette Reine, pour le progrez des sciences: car à vray dire, elle merite vne gloire eternelle, par les nourrissôs des Muses. La mort ayant rauy cette Princesse; ces liures ont esté quelques années en la garde de *Iean Baptiste Benciregni*, Abbé de Bellebranche, iusques au témps que le Roy Henry IV. par Lettres Patentes du 14. Iuin 1594. ordonna que tous les anciens liures tant Hebreux, Grecs, Latins, Arabes, François, Italiés & autres quels qu'ils soient nommez entre les meubles de la defuncte Reine, soient joints à la Bibliotheque Royale ; & fut enjoint audit Abbé *Benciregni*, de mettre tous lesdits liures és mains de feu *Iacques Auguste de Thou*, pour lors nommé par sa Majesté pour Maistre de sa Librairie, afin de demeurer tousiours meublés de la Couronne de France, sans en pouuoir estre distraits. C'est vne chose digne de remarque, que la plus grande partie de ces liures, sont reliez en marroquin incarnat:& la despence qui fut faite pour cela, fut prise sur quelques rentes, qui appartenoient aux Iesuites, desquelles le Roy iouïssoit pendant leur expulsion du Royaume.

Charles IX.   Charles IX. fils de Henry II. & de Catherine de Medicis, fut esleué dans les lettres, ainsi qu'il se peut voir par les liures *De la Venerie & de la Chasse*, qu'il a composé, & qui ont esté imprimez l'an 1625. quoy qu'imparfaits. Aussi ce Roy fit de beaucoup augméter la Bibliotheque Royale, par vne partie de tres excellents Manuscrits Latins, qui auoient esté au President *de Ranconnet*, qui mourut dans la Bastille sous ledit Roy.

Du temps du Regne d'Henry IV. cette Bibliotheque fut transportée à Paris, & mise dans le College de Clermont, pendant l'exil des Peres Iesuites de France, qui arriua l'an 1595. mais apres leur rétablissement, elle fut transportée en vne grande sale, dans les Peres Cordeliers, par le soin & l'Ordre de Monsieur le Presidét de Thou, où elle a esté quelques années, & depuis mise en vne maison par-

Henry IV.

ticuliere, que le Roy loüe à cét effet, laquelle appartient ausdits Cordeliers, & là le Garde de cette Bibliotheque, a son logement. Monsieur Rigaut, par ses amys, traicta cét cccommodement.

LoüysXIII. Ce iuste Roy Loüys XIII. d'heureuse memoire, ne ceda à aucuns de ses Predecesseurs, pour faire enrichir ce thresor des Muses. Car de son regne; sur ce qu'il fut representé qu'entre les liures de feu *Philippes Huraut*, Euesque CVIII. de Chartres, fils de Philippes Comte de Chiuerny, Chancelier de France, il y auoit grand nombre de Manuscrits anciens Grecs & Latins, qui auoient esté soigneusement amassez par M. *de Boistaillé Huraut*, Ambassadeur pour sa Majesté à Venise. Il fut don-

des Bibliotheques. 465

donné arrest au Conseil le 8. Mars 1622. par lequel MM. *Pierre Du Puy* & Nicolas *Rigaut*, furent nommez, pour auec deux autres personnages, & nommément les heritiers & creanciers dudit Euesque, conuenir du prix desdits liures, ce qui fut executé. Car MM. *Oliuier de Fontenay, & Henry de Sponde*, depuis Euesque de Pamiers, & lesdits sieurs *Du Puy & Rigaut* aprecierent lesdits liures à *douze mille francs*, qui furent payez à l'espargne, & les liures transportez à la Bibliotheque Royale. Si cette Bibliotheque fut comparée à celle de Ptolomée sous Loüys XII. en quelle estime à presét doit elle estre, puis qu'elle a receu de si notables augmentations par la liberalité de nos inuincibles Monarques. Qui ne sçay que toutes les nations ont en grande estime cette incomparable Bibliotheque, pour ses anciens & rares Manuscrits en toute sorte de langues, qui y sont conseruez? De plus, quant aux liures imprimez, il est facile à cognoistre combié elle en doit estre garnie, puis qu'il ne s'imprime point de liure dans ce Royaume auec priuilege de sa Majesté, qu'il n'y en soit mis deux exemplaires; outre la diligence que les Gardes font d'achepter tous les meilleurs liures qui s'imprimét dans l'Europe: par ainsi cette Bibliotheque est reputée pour l'vne des plus splendides & plus celebres de l'Vniuers.

Apres auoir remarqué tous les progrez de cette Bibliotheque,

des Bibliotheques. 467

qui ont efté faits iufqu'à prefent, *Maiſtres de*
ie donneray icy vn Catalogue des *la Librairie*
Maiſtres de la Librairie de nos *Royale.*
Roys, depuis François I. iufqu'à
noſtre ieune Monarque Loüys
XIV. tel qu'il m'a eſté donné par
M. *Du Puy.* Conſeiller d'Eſtat,
homme duquel la probité & doctrine eſt cognuë par toute l'Europe. Ce mot de *Maiſtre de la Li-*
brairie leur eſt ainſi donné, plu-
ſtoſt que celuy de Bibliothecaire.
Bien que i'aye remarqué fous
Charles VI. *Antoine des Eſſarts, &*
Garnier de ſainct Yon, & fous Loüis
XI. *Robert Gaguin,* Religieux Tri-
nitaire pour Maiſtres de la Librairie de nos Roys, toutefois ie ne
donneray ce Catalogue que depuis le reſtabliſſement fait par ledit François I.

Gg ij

G. Budé. Guillaume Budé Parisien, Maistre des Requestes, fut nommé à cette charge par le Roy François I. pour ses merites, & particulierement pour sa grande doctrine, qu'il a tesmoiné dans ses ouurages, entr'autres de celuy de *Asse*. Il deceda à Paris l'an 1540. le 22. Aoust, âgé de 73. ans.

P. du Chastel ou Castellanus. Pierre du Chastel ou Chastelain, de Langres, succeda à Budé, par la nomination du Roy François I. qui se seruoit de luy pour l'entretenir des sciences dans ses discours familiers; car il estoit hóme d'vn grand sçauoir; ce qui luy fit acquerir l'amitié de ce Prince, qui l'honnora de cette dignité: puis luy donna l'Esuesché de Tulles, apres il fut pourueu de celuy de Mascon, & en fin de celuy d'Or-

des Bibliotheques.

leans, où il mourut en preschant l'an 1558. ainsi que le remarque Michel de l'Hospital Chancelier de France, dans l'Epitaphe qu'il luy a dressé.

Apres celuy-cy fut pourueu de cette charge *Pierre de Mont-doré* ou *Montaureus*, natif d'Orleans, Maistre des Requestes, homme de grands merites, au rapport du susdit Chancelier de l'Hospital.

P. de Mont-doré.

totus fuit aureus intus;
Aureus ingenio, doctrina, & moribus aureis.
Omneis præterea linguas, & nouerat artes,
Scribebat dignos vobis & Apolline versus.
Tantum illum talémque virum si Roma tulisset,
Aureus in summa staret Montaureus arce,

Aureus inque foro & roſtris, tota aureus vrbe :

Iacques Amiot. — Iacques *Amiot*, de Melun merita par ſa ſcience d'eſtre Precepteur de nos Roys Charles IX. & Henry III. lequel fut pourueu de cette dignité par le meſme Charles, apres la mort de Mont-doré; puis il fut Eueſque d'Auxerre & Grand Auſmonier de France : ſa mort arriua l'an 1593. le 7. de Feurier âgé de 79. ſes doctes verſions de Plutarque, ont aſſez fait cognoiſtre l'experiéce qu'il auoit dans les ſciences & les langues Grecques.

I. A. de Thou. — Ce ſçauant Hiſtorien, *Iacques Auguſte de Thou*, Preſident au Parlement de Paris, ſucceda audit Amiot en la charge de Maiſtre de la Librairie de nos Roys; qui

des Bibliotheques. 471

prit vn grand soin pour cette Bibliotheque, non seulement pour la faire transporter à Paris; mais encore pour la garnir des meilleurs liures qui se pouuoient treuuer de son temps: son deceds arriua à Paris l'â 1617. au mois de May. Voy plus amplement, ce que ie diray de luy dans la Bibliotheque de MM. de Thou cy-apres, & passons à son successeur qui fut;

François Auguste de Thou, son fils, Conseiller d'Estat, qui auoit de tres belles parties d'esprit. *F. A. de Thou.*

Les merites de *Hierosme Bignon*, Conseiller au Conseil d'Estat, l'ont fait choisir par le defunct Roy Loüys XIII. l'an 1642. pour excercer cette dignité, de laquelle il s'acquitte auec vn merueilleux soin : Ie remarqueray que les ga- *H. Bignon.*

Gg iiij

ges du Maiſtre de la Librairie Royale ſont de 1200. liures & qu'il y a des Gardes ſous eux, qui ont leurs logemens proche de cette Librairie auec 400. liures d'appointemens; deſquels ie rapporteray le Catalogue, comme il m'a eſté communiqué.

1. *Iean Goſſelin.*, fut pourueu de cette charge, pour la grande cognoiſſance, qu'il auoit des liures; il eſt decedé à Paris fort âgé.

2. *Iſaac Caſaubon*, natif de Geneve, eſt cognu de tous les gens de lettres, en conſideration de ſon ſçauoir; ce qui luy a fait exercer quelques années cette charge: Mais eſtant paſſé en Angleterre, il euſt pour Succeſſeur:

3. *Nicolas Rigaut*, Conſeiller au Parlement de Mets; qui a don-

des Bibliotheques. 473

né au public les œuures *de Tertulien*,& autres autheurs Grecs auec des doctes Annotations, qui ne luy acquerront pas vne moindre gloire, que les peines qu'il prend à augmenter des meilleurs liures, qui se peuuent treuuer la Bibliocque de nos Monarques; & de dresser vn'exact Catalogue de cette Librairie ; assisté des Sieurs *Claude de Saumaise* & *Hautin*, personnages tres intelligens aux liures MSS. Grecs & Latins.

Quoy que nos Roys possedét cette tres-opulente Bibliotheque publique: toutefois ils en ont vne particuliere dans le Louure, pour leur vsage ; où sont conseruez plusieurs bons liures, entr'autres tous ceux qu'on leur presente : de laquelle à present M. *Chau-* *Bibl. du Louure.*

mont Conseiller d'Estat, a le soin. Il y en a encore vne autre petite à Fõtaine-bleau, pour diuertir nos Roys, quand ils y font leur sejour dont *Abel de sainɫte Marthe*, fils de Sceuole, & frere aisné de Loüys & Sceuole Historiographes de France, Conseiller d'Estat; est Bibliothecaire, par les letres qui luy en furent donnez par le feu Roy Loüys XIII.

Bibl. de Fontaine-bleau.

Le Cabinet de nos Roys passe pour vne merueille du monde, pour ses raretez & antiquitez, outre ses pierreries. Car ie treuue que pour vne seule fois, l'on achepta le Cabinet de *Iean Grolier*, natif de Lyon, Cheualier, Vicomte d'Aguisi, Thresorier de Milan & de France, l'honneur des lettres de son temps, & le plus grand

Le Cabinet Royal.

I. Grolier.

des Bibliotheques. 475

rechercheur d'antiquitez, que de long-temps euſt paru dans ce Royaume; lequel apres ſa mort auoit eſté porté iuſqu'à Marſeilles pour eſtre tranſporté à Rome, afin d'y eſtre vendu : Ce qui fut dit au Roy Charles IX. qui commanda que l'on euſt à faire rapporter ce Cabinet, pour eſtre joint auec le ſien, faiſant payer la valeur aux heritiers d'iceluy Grolier, ainſi que le remarque le docte Preſident de Thou au 38. liu. de ſon Hiſtoire l'an 1565. dans l'Eloge dudit Grolier *Numi ærei, qui optimi*, dit-il, *cum Lutetia in Prouinciam migraſſent, iamque in eo eſſent vt in Italiam exportarentur regis Chriſtianiſsimi cura effectum eſt, ne tanto theſauro Gallia defraudaretur, eoſque grandi pretio redemptos in Muſæum suum cum aliis prisci æui monumentis inferri mandauit*, M. de Chaumont a aussi la charge de ce Cabinet Royal.

M. le Duc d'Orleans. Monseigneur Iean Baptiste Gaston de France, Duc d'Orleans & de Chartres, fils d'Héry le Grand, frere de Loüys le Iuste, & Oncle de Loüys XIV. Lieutenant General du Royaume de France & Gouuerneur du Languedoc; donne de l'estonnement & de l'admiration à toute l'Europe, pour la parfaite congnoissance qu'il a des medalles anciennes: & ie puis dire de ce Prince sans flatterie, que ny Alexandre Seuere Empereur des Romains, ny Atticus grand amy de Ciceron, ny le tres-docte Varron, n'ont eus vne cognoissance desdites Medalles comme

des Bibliotheques. 477

luy : & sa curiosité ne se termine pas en icelles, mais encore dans la recherche des bons liures, desquels il orne sa tres riche & splendide Bibliotheque, qu'il a dressé depuis peu dans son hostel de Luxembourg, au bout de cette admirable gallerie, où toute la vie de la feuë Reine Marie de Medicis a esté depeinte par l'exellent ouurier Rubens. Or cette Bibliotheque n'est pas seulement remarquable pour l'ornement de ses tablettes, qui sont toutes couuertes de velours verd, auec les bandes de mesme estoffe, garnies de passemens d'or, & les crespines de mesme : pour toute la menuserie qui se void, elle est embellie d'or & de riches peintures : Mais outre cela les liures sont de toutes les meilleurs editions qui se peuuent treuuer; & quant à leur relieure, elle est toute d'vne mesme façon, auec les chiffres de son Altesse Reale. Ce Prince fait tous les iours vne grande recherche des meilleurs liures qui se peuuent treuuer dans l'Europe ; donnant des memoires pour ce sujet, par la solicitation de Monsieur Bruneau & Bibliothecaire, qui trauaille continuellement à la perfection de ce thresor des liures & des Medalles.

M. Bruneau

Feu Monseigneur Armand Iean du Plessis de Richelieu, Cardinal Duc, auoit esté esleué auec vn grand soin dans les bonnes lettres ainsi qu'il appert par les liures, qu'il a donné au public. Ce qui a esté cause qu'il les a tou-

Du Card. de Rich.

sieurs honoré & chery : & mesme qu'il leur a dressé des superbes monumens, qui eternizeront sa memoire, aussi bien que le Gouuernement de l'Estat, qu'il a fait en ce Royaume sous nostre trespieux Roy Loüys XIII. Le somptueux College de Sorbonne, en est vn tesmoignage irreprochable, auquel i'adjouteray cette tres-magnifique Bibliotheque, qu'il auoit dressé auec vne grande despence : Car il n'espargnoit rien, pour ce qui pouuoit concerner son embellissement, & augmentation : puis qu'il enuoya les doctes *Iacques Gaffrel* en Italie & *Iean Tileman Stella* en Allemagne pour ramasser les meilleurs liures manuscrits & imprimez qui se pouuoient treuuer: ce qu'ils executerent si heureusement, que cette Bibliotheque en a esté admirée de tous ceux qui ont la cognoissance des bons liures. Lors que nostre inuincible Monarque Loüys XIII. d'heureuse memoire, dompta l'heresie en la prise de la Rochelle l'an 1628. il conceda audit Cardinal la Bibliotheque publique de cette ville, qu'il fit apporter à Paris, & colloquer dans la sienne pour y estre conseruée. Enfin Ce grand Cardinal & Protecteur des Muses, ne voulant souffrir que cette Bibliotheque vint à deperir, la substitua par son testament au Duc de Richelieu, chef de son nom & de ses armes. Quoy que son testament aye esté imprimé, toutefois ie ne lairray d'en rapporter les clauses

Bibl. de la Rochelle.

des Bibliotheques. 481

ſes qui concernent cette Bibliotheque.

Item, *ie donne audir* Armand
de Vignerot *mon petit neueu aux
clauſes & conditions des inſtitutions
& ſubſtitutions, qui ſerontcy-apres
appoſées ma Bibliotheque; non ſeulement enl'eſtat auquel elle eſt à preſent,
mais en celuy auquel elle ſera lors de
mon deceds. Declarant que ie veux
qu'elle demeure au lieu, où i'ay commencé de faire batir l'Hoſtel de Richelieu joignant le Palais Cardinal: &
d'autant que mon deſſein eſt de rendre
ma Bibliotheque la plus accomplie
que ie pourray, & la mettre en eſtat
qu'elle puiſſe non ſenlemẽt ſeruir à ma
famille, mais encore au public. Ie veux
& ordonne qu'en ſoit fait inuentaire
general lors de mon deceds par telles
perſonnes que mes executeurs teſta-*

Hh

mentaires iugeront à propos, y ap-
pellans deux Docteurs de la Sorbone,
qui seront deputez par le corps, pour
estre presens à la confection dudit
inuentaire, lequel estant fait, ie veux
qu'il en soit mis vne coppie en ma
Bibliotheque, signée de mes executeurs
testamentaires & desdits Docteurs de
Sorbone; & qu'vne autre coppie soit
pareillement mise en ladite maison de
Sorbone signée ainsi que dessus : &
afin que ladite Bibliotheque soit conseruée en son entier, Ie veux & ordonne, que ledit inuentaire soit recollé &
verifié tous les ans par deux Docteurs,
qui seront deputez de la Sorbone, &
qu'il y ait vn Bibliothecaire qui en aie
charge aux gages de mille liures par
an, lesquels gages & appointemens ie
veux estre pris par preference à toutes
autres charges de quartier en quartier,

& par aduance sur le reuenu des arrentemës des maisons basties & à bastir à l'entour du Palais Cardinal : lesquelles ne sont point part du Palais & ie veux & entend que moyennant lesdits 1000. liures d'apointement, il soit tenu de conseruer ladite Bibliotheque ; la tenir en bon estat, & y donner l'entrée à certaines heures du iour aux hommes de lettres & d'erudition pour voir les liures & en prendre communiquation dans le lieu de ladite Bibliotheque, sans transporter les liures ailleurs ; & en cas qu'il n'y eust aucun Bibliothecaire lors de mon deceds, ie veux & ordonne que la Sorbonne en nomme trois audit Armand de Vignerot, & à ses successeurs, qui seront Ducs de Richelieu, pour choisir celuy des trois qu'ils iugeront le plus à propos, ce qui sera tousiours obserué, lors qu'il sera necessaire de mettre vn nouueau Bibliothecaire.

Et d'autant que la conseruation du lieu des liures de ladite Bibliotheque, il sera besoin de nettoyer souuent : j'entend qu'il soit choisi par mondit neueu vn homme propre à cet effet, qui sera obligé de ballaier tous les iours vne fois ladite Bibliotheque, & d'essuier les liures ou les armoires dans lesquelles ils seront ; & pour luy donner moyen de s'entretenir & de fournir les ballets & autres choses necessaires pour le nettoiement : Ie veux, qu'il ait quatre cent liures de gages par an, à prendre sur le mesme fond, que ceux du Bibliothecaire, & en la mesme ferme ; ce qui sera fait ainsi que ce qui concerne ledit Bibliothecaire par les soins & par l'authorité de mondit neueu & ses successeurs en la possession dudit Hostel de Richelieu.

des Bibliotheques.

Et d'autant qu'il est necessaire pour maintenir vne Bibliotheque en sa perfection, d'achepter de temps en temps les bons liures, qui seront imprimez de nouueau, ou ceux des anciens, qui y peuuent manquer : ie veux & ordonne qu'il soit employé la somme de mille liures par chacun an, en achapt de liures par l'aduis des Docteurs, qui seront deputez tous les ans par la Sorbone pour faire l'inuentaire de ladite Bibliotheque, laquelle somme de mille liu. sera pareillement prise par preference à toutes autres charges, excepté celles des deux articles cy-dessus sur le reuenu desdits arrentemens des maisons, qui ont esté & seront basties à l'entour du parc du Palais Cardinal.

L'on void par là le grand soin qu'il a eu pour la conseruation de cette Bibliotheque ; la charge

de laquelle il donna peu auant sa
sa mort à M. *Claude Hemeré*, Docteur de Sorbonne: neantmoins à
present c'est M. *Geoffroy*, qui exer-
ce la charge de Bibliothecaire:
La mort de ce Cardinal arriua à
Paris dans son Palais Cardinal,
l'an 1642. le 4. Decembre sur le
midy, estant âgé de 58. ans.

L'Empereur Iules Cæsar honora autrefois la ville de Rome d'v-
ne tres-belle Bibliotheque, qu'il
auoit destiné au public : Et à present nous auons ce grand Cardi-
Du Card. nal Romain, *Iules Mazarini*,
Mazarini. Ministre d'Estat de leurs Maje-
stez, qui n'honore pas moins la
ville de Paris par cette tres-somptueuse & tres-exquise Bibliotheque, qu'il a erigé depuis vn an,
sur celle de feu M. Iean Des-Cor-

des Chanoine de Limoges, vn autre Varron de son temps en la recherche des bons liures, qui auoit acheptécelle de Simon Bofius, qui a composé des liures: il est vray neantmoins que cét Empereur Romain n'auoit que destiné sa Bibliotheque au public : mais nostre Cardinal, luy a donné en effet, puis que tous les Ieudys, depuis le matin iusqu'au soir, elle est commune à tous ceux qui y veulent aller estudier au grand contentement des doctes: & nonobstant que i'aye desia remarqué en la pag. 94. que la Bibliotheque, que son Eminéce a dans son Palais Quirinal de Rome, est tresconsiderable ; toutefois celle-cy est bié en autre estime, puis qu'elle est l'vne des plus accomplie de

H h iiij

l'Europe , pour l'abondance de ses liures imprimez, & des meilleures editions qui se peuuent treuuer; outre que sans cesse on la remplis de tous les plus rares qui s'impriment tant dedans que dehors le Royaume de France. Quát aux Manuscrits il y en a prés de quatre cens volumes infolio, couuerts de maroquin incarnat, auec des filets d'or. Ainsi quoy que son Eminence trauaille continuellement pour le bien & le repos de ce Royaume, auec vne approbation vniuerselle de toute la France & des Estrangers : elle ne perd toutefois aucune occasió de faire fleurir les sciences : soit en recognoissant les merites des gens de lettres; soit en ordonnant la perfection de ce Parnasse des Muses, à l'honneur duquel Pierre d'Aulberoche Docteur en Theologie, a fait plusieurs Epigrames Latines, desquels ie remarqueray seulement la suiuante.

Iulius ingenij mirandi dotibus actis
   Tot sparsa in libros continet ingenia.
Et quoniam ingenium illius res publica totum
   Poscit, in his, hospes, vult potiare libris.
O certè Herois factum inuentúmque benigni
   Qui sua sic cunctis dona patere cupit.

Or bien que son Eminence merite vne gloire immortelle pour l'erection de cette Bibliotheque: il est tres certain qu'elle n'en doit pas auoir vne moindre pour l'election qu'elle a fait de son tres-vigilant & tres-laborieux Bibliothecaire M. *Gabriel Naudé*, Chanoine de Verdun en Lorraine, & Prieur d'Artige, lequel possede vne parfaite cognoissance des liures; ce qui fait que tous ceux qui ont l'honneur de le cognoistre, l'estiment pour vn autre *Demetrius Phalæreus*. La crainte que i'ay d'offencer sa modestie me fera emprunter des témoignages de ses loüages d'autruy, plustost que de moy. L'vn des eloquents de ce siecle, sera mon oracle, c'est M. *François de la Mothe le Vayer*, Parisien iadis Conseiller du Roy & substitut de M. le Procureur General au Parlement de Paris, qui luy dedie son second volume *des Opuscules*. Voicy donc com-

des Bibliotheques. 49**1**

me il parle à luy en son Epistre dedicatoire au moins sur nostre sujet. *J'ayme mieux vous faire le trait d'amy, dont parle Pline le ieune, m'abstenant de toute loüange que vous pourriez nommer onereuse. Et i'en vseray* de la sorte d'autant plus volontiers, que le choix connu de tout le monde qu'a fait de vostre personne ce grand Cardinal, qui vous confie non moins pour le bien public, que pour sa propre satisfaction, ce qu'il a de plus à cœur apres le bon-heur de cét Estat, est le cõble de tous les Eloges que ie vous sçaurois donner. Il faut pourtant que vous nous permettiez de faire vn peu de reflexion sur la prudente eslection de son Eminence, lors qu'il a commis cette fameuse Bibliotheque à celuy qui est regardé luy mesme comme vne Bibliotheque viuante, ou comme vne estude ani-

Hoc ipsũ amātis est non onerare laudibus l. 1. ep. 14.

mée & ambulatoire, selon les termes
dōt Eunapius tāsche d'exprimer le merite du Sophiste Longinus. Et neātmoins
cette vaste connoissance que vous auez
de toute sorte de litterature, n'estoit pas
seulement suffisante pour vous faire
preferer à tout autre. Si vostre science eust esté de celles dōt parle l'Apostre,
qui enflent & qui remplissent de vani-
té, elle ne se fust pas treuuée propre à
vostre employ. C'est la douceur de vos
mœurs, auec l'affabilité de vostre nature, qui vous donne de l'auantage sur la
pluspart des sçauans. Et ce que l'Empereur Antonin admiroit au Philoso-
phe Sextus, vne profonde doctrine
exempte de toute ostentation, vn τό πο-
λυμαϑὲς ἀνεπιφάντως qu'il estime si
fort, sont des dons du Ciel qui ont esté
iudicieusement considerez en vous,
par celuy qui vous a comme trié entre

In vita
Porph.
c. ςλοτικὸν
ἡ ψιχος,
ϰ πεϱιπα-
τὸν μυ-
σιων.

l. 1. de vi-
ta sua.

des Bibliotheques. 493
tant d'hommes de lettres, auec la mesme clair-voyance qui esclatte dans toutes ses actions. Outre cét Eloge, ie donneray en suitte l'Epigrame que luy a fait M. d'Aulberoche, comme Bibliothecaire de son Eminence.

Quisquis in hoc sacri Musæum Principis intras,
Audi Palladios qui tibi monstrat opes.
Vt rapiunt oculos tot lecta volumina, mulcet
Aures Naudæus Bibliotheca loquens.

Ie remarqueray encore que le Pere Marin Mersenne Minime, homme d'vne grande estude, parle de cette Bibliotheque dans son traicté Latin *de Magnete*, qu'il a dedié au sieur Naudé.

M. le Duc d'Angoulesme.

Monseigneur Charles de Valois, fils naturel de Charles IX. Roy de France, Duc d'Angoulesme, Prince vaillant & sçauant, lequel a tousiours eu en recommandation la gloire des armes, & le lustre des lettres, ainsi que le remarque le Pere Hilarion de Coste *en son Traicté des Gouuerneurs du Dauphiné*, auquel i'ay de grandes obligations, pour m'auoir assisté de beaucoup de memoires pour cét ouurage, & duquel i'ay appris, que ce Prince auoit dans son Palais vne belle Bibliotheque, qui possede de tres-bons liures. Ce Seigneur vit à Paris cette année 1644. âgé de 72. ans.

M. le Mareschal de Bassompierre.

Monseigneur de Bassompierre Mareschal de France, est en esti-

des Bibliotheques. 495

me d'vn esprit tres accomply pour les sciences; car son estude est continuelle, aussi bien que le soin qu'il a de rechercher les meilleurs liures pour enrichir sa celebre Bibliotheque, où sont conseruez plus de *quatre milles volumes*.

Entre les Bibliotheques, qui sont en grande consideration dans la ville de Paris, celle de Monseigneur Pierre Seguier Cheualier, Comte de Gien, Chancelier de France, en est vne; non seulement pour la beauté du lieu, mais encore pour les bons liures en toutes les sciences & langues, qui y sont mis continuellement par ce Seigneur, qui esclaire aujourd'huy l'Europe par ses rares merites, & grande doctrine : qualité vrayment essentielle à la tres- *M. Seguier, Cheu. de France.*

illuſtre famille des Seguiers, comme on le pourra voir dans *noſtre Bibliotheque Vniuerſelle des Autheurs de France*, où ie ſpecifieray les œuures de ceux de cette famille qui ont eſcrits. En fin cette Bibliotheque poſſede encore diuers bons & anciens Manuſcrits, qui luy donnent vn grand luſtre. Le ſieur *Pierre Blaiſe*, a le ſoin de cette Bibliotheque, pour laquelle il trauaille à ſon augmentation auec vn grand zele.

M. Molé I. Preſident. L'integrité, la probité, & l'erudition de Monſeigneur Matthieu de Molé, Cheualier & Premier Preſident de cetres auguſte Parlement de Paris, l'ont eſleué à cette dignité par noſtre victorieux Monarque Loüis XIII. d'heureuſe memoire. Or ſon affection

fection est si grande enuers les liures, que sa Bibliotheque se peut esgaller aux plus belles de nostre France, pour les liures rares & curieux qui s'y mettent auec vne grande despence, par les soins de ce Seigneur, qui en a vne parfaite cognoissance.

Cher Lecteur, *Ie t'aduoüe ingenument que i'ay esté fort en peine, comme ie pourrois colloquer toutes les Bibliotheques de Paris, selon l'ordre des qualitez de tous ces Seigneurs & autres, qui les possedent, lesquelles m'estant incognües, ie me suis resolu (auec le conseil des plus doctes & intelligens) de les mettre cy-apres par ordre alphabetique: coniurant ces Messieurs de ne le treuuer mauuais, afin que ie n'encoure le blasme de ne les auoir pla-*

I i

cez selon leurs merites. I'espere que leur bonté, supplera à mon defaut, & qu'ils approuueront mon procedé, puis qu'il est estimé legitime. Ie commenceray donc par cét ordre proposé, comme le plus conuenable.

De M. Amelot.

M. Iacques Amelot de Beaulieu, premier President à la Cour des Aydes, a fait vne celebre Bibliotheque, qui est garnie, non seulement de liures Grecs, Latins & François des meilleures impressions, mais aussi de diuers anciens & modernes Manuscrits, & de beaucoup de recueils, traictez & memoires Politiques & Historiques des derniers siecles, escrits à la main. L'on y remarque encore plusieurs Manifestes imprimez, & autres discours du temps depuis quatre-vingt ans. Cette Bibliotheque a esté augmentée premierement par celle de M. *De M.* Chenard Aduocat en Parlement, *Chenard.* puis de celle de feu M. Gilles de Souuré Euesque d'Auxerre, qui a *M.de Sou-* esté fort versé dans les lettres sa- *uré.* crées, comme on le pourra voir dans *nostre Bibliotheque Vniuerselle des Aucteurs de France*, où ie remarqueray les liures, que ce docte Prelat a laissé à la posterité, lesquels toutefois sont conseruez MSS. iusqu'à present par ses heritiers.

La Reyne Marguerite, premie- *Des petits* re femme du Roy Henry le Grād, *Augustins.* a esté doüée d'vn bon esprit pour les sciences. C'est pourquoy elle estoit la Protectrice des hommes de lettres, qu'elle affectionnoit grandement : entre lesquels les Peres Augustins furent des premiers, comme il se peut voir, par

Ii ij

ce noble Conuent, qu'elle leur erigea dans le faux-bourg de S. Germain, où il y a vne Bibliotheque assez considerable, puis qu'elle possede enuiron *quatre mille volumes*.

De M. de Barillon. M. Le President de Barillon, est porté d'vne loüable curiosité à rechercher les bons liures pour garnir vne belle Bibliotheque, qu'il fait auec de grands soins.

De M. Bignon. Bien que i'ay parlé en la pag. 471. de M. Hierosme Bignon, iadis Aduocat general, & à present Conseiller d'Estat, comme Maistre de la Librairie de nostre Roy tres-Chrestien ; toutefois icy il est à remarquer qu'il a vne insigne Bibliotheque en son particulier, où se conseruent des meilleurs liures en toutes les sciences qui se

des Bibliotheques. 501

retreuuent à present; desquels il a puizé cette grande doctrine, qu'il fait paroistre dans ses ouurages, dont il a honoré le public.

M. Bluet Aduocat en Parlement a dressé vne Bibliotheque; qui est considerable, pour la qualité de ses liures de Droicts, Histoires & autres sciences. *M. Bluet.*

Ie puis dire le mesme de la Bibliotheque de M. Bordier Secretaire du Conseil, qui recherche auec vn grand soin les bons liures pour luy seruir d'ornemens. *M. Bordier.*

La cognoissance des liures, qu'a M. Henry du Bouchet Seigneur de Bournonuille, Conseiller en Parlement; est vne preuue suffisante de l'exacte recherche qu'il en fait pour embellir son excellente Bibliotheque, laquelle *M. De Bournonuille*

Ii iij

possede enuiron six mille volumes des mieux choisis en toutes les sciences & langues.

M. Bourdelot. Entre les hommes doctes & curieux, qui ont esté en ce siecle, feu M. Iean Bourdelot en a esté l'vn, car il auoit vne grande cognoissance des langues Orientales, & des bons liures, qu'il ramassa auec vn grand labeur pour enrichir sa Bibliotheque, qui consiste en liures imprimez & diuers Manuscrits Arabes, Hebreux, Grecs & Latins; laquelle est aujourd'huy conseruée par M. Pierre Bourdelot son neueu, Medecin de Monseigneur le Prince de Condé, qui l'augmente des meilleurs liures du temps.

M. Brodeau. Quoy que M. Iulien Brodeau Aduocat en Parlement, soit en reputation pour sa doctrine qu'il a fait paroistre dans ses beaux Arrests de la Cour qui sont entre les mains de tous ceux de sa profession : toutefois l'erection, qu'il a fait d'vne curieuse Bibliotheque, ne luy cause pas vne moindre gloire à la posterité.

La Bibliotheque des Peres Capucins du faux-bourg de S. Honoré, est de consideration pour la quantité & qualité de ses liures. *Des Capucins de S. Honoré.*

Quant à celle de ces Peres du faux-bourg S. Iacques, elle n'est pas de moindre nature que la precedente. *Des mesmes de S. Iasques.*

Le Conuent des Peres Carmes Deschaussez du fauxbourg sainct Germain, a esté fondé l'an 1611. par la permission de la Reine Marie de Medicis; dans lequel est *Des Carmes Deschaussez.*

Ii iiij

conferué vne infigne Bibliotheque, où font de bons liures.

Des Celeftins.

Les Peres Celeftins ont vne confiderable Bibliotheque, dans laquelle eft foigneufement conferuée vne grande Bible en velin MS. qui leur a efté donnée par Loüis d'Orleans, Comte de Valois, de Blois & de Beaumont, fecond fils de Charles V. Roy de France, qui eft fignée des mefmes Princes. Ce Duc d'Orleans donna encore vne autre grande Bible en quatre volumes in folio, efcrite fur le velin, qui a toufiours feruy & fert à prefent pour lire durant la refection de ces Religieux.

Des Chartreux.

La gloire de nos Roys tres-Chreftiens S. Loüys, fonda le Conuent des Peres Chartreux, où la pieté & erudition ont toufiours esté en credit: leur vies solitaires en est vne marque infaillible ; aussi bien que leur celebre Bibliotheque, leur sert de diuertissemens apresleur assiduité à la priere.

Si la mort a iamais esté fatale *De M. du* aux hommes de lettres de nostre *Chesne.* temps, il faut aduoüer que ç'a esté à ce tres fameux Historiographe du Roy M. André du Chesne, Tourangeau, duquel la memoire sera eternelle parmy les Muses, pour tant de beaux ouurages, qu'il a donné au public ; & qu'il esperoit encore de donner, par les grandes recherches qu'il faisoit continuellement. Aussi sa Bibliotheque est tres-exquise pour les histoires de toutes les nations qu'elle possede ; & de laquelle jouït son fils M. Fráçois du Chesne, Aduocat au Priué Conseil, & Historiographe du Roy, qui a des-ja fait voir, comme les qualitez de son pere reuiuent en luy, & qu'il sera doüé d'vne pareille inclination au bien public.

M. Chrestien.
Nostre inuincible Monarque Henry IV. eut pour Precepteur le sçauant Q Septime Florent Chrestien natif d'Orleans, qui a laissé pour fils M. Claude Chrestien, Aduocat en Parlement, puis Conseiller du Roy & Lieutenant en la Conestablie & Mareschaussée de France; qui a fait vne considerable Bibliotheque, où sont les liures des meilleures editions qui se retreuuent, & quantité en langue Orientales comme Arabes, Syriaques, Chaldaiques, & Hebraiques

des Bibliotheques. 507

& quelques Manuscrits, entre lesquels est vne traduction des Commentaires de Iules Cesar faite par le Roy Henry IV.

Monsieur Clement Conseiller aux Enquestes a vne grande curiosité à rechercher les liures, pour fournir sa Bibliotheque, qui est en estime, pour ceux des Emblemes, deuises, & entrées. *M. Clement.*

Les escrits de M. Iacques Corbin Aduocat en Parlement, sont dès témoignages de l'affection qu'il a pour les bons liures, desquels il est soigneux de remplir sa Bibliotheque. *M. Corbin*

M. Iacques Cordeau Aduocat au Parlement, est dans la recherche des liures pour parfaire sa Bibliotheque. *M. Cordeau*

La Bibliotheque de M. Elie *M. Deodati*

Deodati, aussi Aduocat en Parlenent, est garnie de liures curieux de diuerses sciences & langues.

M. l'Escuyer.

Le grand amas de liures que fait M. Sebastien l'Escuyer, Conseiller Cler au Parlement: est digne de loüange : car sa belle Bibliotheque est aussi bien fournie de bons liures, que plusieurs autres de cette ville, n'espargnant aucune despence pour ramasser, ceux qui peuuent seruir à sa perfection.

M. d'Espeisses.

L'Illustre famille des Fayes, Seigneurs d'Espeisses, se peut vanter d'auoir eu de sçauans personnages, comme Barthelemy Conseiller de la Cour, qui a eu pour fils Iacques, Conseiller du Roy en ses Conseils d'Estat & Priué,

Aduocat dudit Seigneur, puis President au Parlement; & celuy-cy a eu aussi pour fils Charles, Coseiller du Roy en ses Conseils, & Ambassadeur en Hollande, qui tous ont escrits & trauaillez à laisser vne bonne Bibliotheque, qui se conserue encore dans cette famille.

Les Peres Feüillans de la ruë S. Honoré, ont dressez vne exquise Bibliotheque pour leur vtilité: de laquelle les PP. Iean de S. François, Eustache de S. Paul, Pierre de S. Ioseph, & autres sçauans personnages, ont puisez ces beaux ouurages, qu'ils ont donnez au public. *Des Feüillans.*

M. Pierre Frizon, Docteur de Nauarre, a fait vne Bibliotheque assez côsiderable, pour les bons li- *M. Frizon.*

ures en toutes les sciences, qu'il y met auec vne grande recherche. C'est de luy que le public ioüyt de la *Gallia Purpurata*.

M. Gaumin. La grande cognoissance des langues & des sciences, qu'a M. Gilbert Gaumin natif de Moulins en Bourbonnois, Maistre des Requestes de l'Hostel du Roy, luy a acquise cét honneur & reputation d'y estre tres-experts; comme il appert par les œuures Latines & Grecques qu'il a composé: Aussi il se peut vanter d'auoir vne excellente Bibliotheque en bons liures, particulierement en ceux des langues Grecques, Arabiques & Hebraïques.

S. Germain des Prés. La Bibliotheque de l'Abbaye de S. Germain des Prés de l'Ordre de S. Benoist, est tres opulen-

des Bibliotheques. 511

ce par la multitude de ses liures imprimez & manuscrits, qui y ont esté mis en partie par Guillaume Briçonnet Euesque de Meaux, Abbé de ce Monastere ; & en partie par plusieurs Religieux. De plus il est à remarquer, que les Manuscrits de la Bibliotheque de S. Pierre de Corbie, y ont esté apportez, depuis quelques temps, afin d'y estre conseruez : ce qui rend cette Bibliotheque l'vne des plus considerable de Paris, aussi bien que la grande & continuelle recherche, que ces Religieux font tous les iours des meilleurs liures qui se peuuent treuuer. Laurent Bouchel Aduocat en Parlement, fait vne ample description de cette Bibliotheque au 1. Tome de sa Bibliotheque du Droict François

De S. Pierre de Corbie.

V *Bibliotheque*, où il remarque entre autre choses, que le Roy Childebert premier de ce nom, apporta des despoüilles de la ville de Tolede en Espagne le *Pseautier* du glorieux Euesque S. Germain enuiron l'an 542. lequel est escrit en lettres d'argent sur du parchemin pourpré ou violet, où les noms de DEVS ET DOMINVS, selon l'occurrence du texte, sont escrits en or, aussi resplendissant que le temps passé : plusieurs autres liures anciens, mesme tablettes de cire, ou iadis l'on escriuoit, y sont aussi conseruez. La Bible qui seruit au Colloque de Poissy, se void en ce mesme lieu. Le Pere Iacques du Brüeil Religieux de ce Monastere en fait aussi vne mesme descriptió dans le second liure

liure des Antiquitez de Paris.

M. Hallé Conseiller du Roy *M. Hall.*
& Maistre des Comptes a vne Bibliotheque bonne & curieuse, de laquelle font mention Gabriel Naudé *en son Aduis pour dresser vne Bibliotheque*, Pierre Blanchot Minime, *en l'idée de sa Bibliotheque Vniuerselle*, & Rodolphe Boteray Aduocat au grand Conseil en sa description de Paris.

similique accensus amore.
Neustriæ honos Hallæus habent sibi,
  mole stupenda
Librorum precium tribuit quibus ipsa
  vetustas,

Quant à la Bibliotheque de *M. Hardy.* M. Hardy Conseiller au Chastelet, elle fait bien voir la cognoissance qu'il a dans les bons liures, particulierement des Mathematiques, & dans les langues Hebraïques & Arabiques.

M. de Harlay. M. Achilles de Harlay, Maistre des Requestes de l'Hostel du Roy, possede vne belle Bibliotheque: dans laquelle est conseruée celle de feu M. Achilles du Harlay son grand pere, premier President au Parlement de Paris.

M. Hautin. La Bibliotheque de feu M. Iean Baptiste Hautin Conseiller au Chastelet, decedé l'an 1640. se conserue encore par MM. Hautin ses fils, & Chandelier son Gendre, auec le soin de l'augmenter des liures nouueaux; ayant esté composée de plus de *dix mille volumes*, mais à present elle est diuisée en trois, sçauoir en ses fils MM. Hautin Conseiller au Chastelet, & l'Ecclesiastique, comme aussi

des Bibliotheques. 515

M. Chandelier Aduocat en Parlement, lesquels tous en leur particulier, ont plus de *quatre mille volumes*, sans le Cabinet des Medalles ; que ledit sieur Hautin auoit recueillis auec vne grande curiosité, car il estoit sçauant dans les Histoires domestiques & estrangeres, & mesme dans les Genealogies, ce qui l'a fait fort estimé par les Escriuains de ce temps, entre autres des Sieurs André du Chesne *en diuers de ses ouurages*, sainct Amand *en ses memoires Historiques*, & Pierre Gassendi *en la vie de Nicolas de Peresc Conseiller au Parlement d'Aix*.

Le pieux & docte M. Iacques Henequin, Docteur & Professeur Royal au College de Sorbône, a employé & employe la plus

M. Henne-quin.

K k ij

grande partie de son reuenu en bons liures, pour augmenter sa Bibliotheque tres considerable pour la Theologie.

M. Hesselin. La curiosité des liures & des choses rares & antiquitez, se treuue autant en M. Hesselin, qu'en homme qui soit en France, au rapport du P. Iean François Niceron Minime, *en son 3. liu. de la Perspectiue curieuse pag. 77.* qui fait vne ample description de la Bibliotheque & du Cabinet dudit sieur Hesselin, duquel ie rapporteray le témoignage. *Ceux qui auront veu* (il parle de quelques machines) *vne semblable machine, qui est à Rome à la vigne de Borghese, n'auront pas de peine à le croire: & à Paris, que l'on peut appeller le Cabinet de l'Europe, pour les merueilles de nature & de l'art, qui s'y voyent, &*

des Bibliotheques.

qu'on y apporte encore de tous costez ; nous ne sommes pas despourueus de cette curiosité, depuis que M. Hesselin Conseiller du Roy & Maistre de sa Chambre aux deniers en a fait dresser vne d'importance, ne voulant pas permettre que quelque chose de curieux manquast à son Cabinet de ce qui se peut recouurer à quelque prix que ce soit : i'appelle son cabinet toute sa maison : car veritablement elle est ornée & remplie de tant de raretez ; on y void tant de belles glaces, d'excellens miroirs, tant de rares peintures & de pieces à rauir pour les rondes, bosses & les reliefs ; tant de bons liures en toute sorte de sciences, qu'on la peut dire l'abbregé des Cabinets de Paris, & que les rares diuersitez, qui sont ça & là en tous les autres, se retrouuent en celuy-cy soigneusement assemblez, qui monstrent assez que l'esprit du maistre est tout à fait vniuersel en ces cognoissances.

Tous ceux qui ont cognoissan-
M. de l'Ho- ce des lettres, admirent le grand
ſpital Chāc. esprit de M. Michel de l'Hospital, Chancelier de France, sous le regne de François II. duquel la Bibliotheque estoit tellement estimée, qu'il la recommande par son testament, qui est rapporte dans le troisiesme Tome de la Bibliotheque du Droict François, de Laurent Bouchel, dont voicy les clauses. *Ie laisse & legue par testament toute ma Librairie & Bibliotheque à Michel Hurault de l'Hospital, qui me semble plus idoine, & affectionné aux bonnes lettres, que les autres petits enfans. Toutefois ie veux que ma femme & fille gardent ma Librairie, afin que personne n'en puisse rien*

des Bibliotheques. 419

souſtraire, & qu'ils la donnent audit Michel, quand il ſera en âge, ſous condition qu'elle ſera ouuerte, pour la commodité de ceux de la famille, enſemble des domeſtiques, & ceux qui frequentent la maiſon. Et plus bas; Mon gendre prendra garde & aura le ſoin, que les liures du Droict Ciuil que i'ay redigé en art par methode, eſtant ieune, ne ſoyent deſchirez ou bruſlez. Mais qu'ils ſoient donnez à vn de mes petits fils des plus capables, & qui les pourra à l'imitation de ſon ayeul par auanture acheuer. La mort de ce Chancelier arriua l'an 1573. âgé de 75. ans.

Les Peres Iacobins Reformez de la ruë S. Honoré ont dreſſé vne Bibliotheque tres-ſomptueuſe en ſon edifice; mais beaucoup de moindre qualité en liures, veu

Des Iacobins de S. Honoré.

K k iiij

qu'à present elle ne possede qu'à trois ou 4000. volumes, entre lesquels il y en a de fort considerable de la Medecine, qui viennent de la Bibliotheque d'vn Medecin Allemand, qui a vn fils Religieux de cét Ordre.

Des mesmes de S. Iac-

La Bibliotheque des mesmes Religieux de la ruë S. Iacques, est bien plus belle pour ses liures imprimez & Manuscrits ; mais non pas quant à la structure.

Maison professe des Iesuites.

La Maison professe de sainct Loüys des Peres Iesuites de la ruë S. Antoine, estoit anciennement

M. le Card. de Bourbon.

l'Hostel d'Anuille, que leur achepta M. Charles Cardinal de Bourbon, qui leur donna aussi enuiron l'an 1580. sa Bibliotheque excellemment reliée en marroquin : mais comme il arriua que ces Peres furent chaſſez hors de la France, toute cette Bibliotheque fut diſſipée. Toutefois le Roy Henry IV. les ayans reſtablis dans tous les lieux du Royaume, ils ont dreſſez vne autre tres opulente Bibliotheque, laquelle ils augmentent tous les iours.

Les meſmes Peres du College de Clermont de la ruë ſainct Iacques, ont eus pour Fondateur Guillaume du Prat, Eueſque de Clermont en Auuergne, qui affectionnoit fort les gens de lettres. C'eſt pourquoy recognoiſſant l'amour de ces Peres enuers les ſciences, il les protegea, & procura leur aduancement par la fondation de ce College, où ils eſtablirent vne Bibliotheque, qui receut vne notable augmen-

Du College de Clermõt,

tatio par celle que leur legua *Hie-*
rofme de Varade, illuftre Medecin
de la Faculté, puis Efcheuin de la
ville, en confideration d'vn fien
fils, qu'il auoit dans cette compagnie, qui fut Recteur de ce College : Iefçay que Pierre Bonfons
dans *fes Antiquitez de Paris*, parlant de la Bibliotheque que le
Cardinal de Bourbon donna à la
maifon profeffe de S. Loüys, qu'il
parle auffi de cette Bibliotheque
de Varade en fuitte; mais elle doit
eftre colloquée dans celle-cy, felon que me l'a dit le R. P. Iacques
Sirmond, Confeffeur du feu Roy
Loüys XIII; duquel i'ay encore
appris, que ce College a auffi autrefois poffedé vne bonne Bibliotheque, qui venoit de feu M. François de S. André, Prefident au Par-

H. de Va-
rade.

F. de S.
André.

lement, qui deceda le 6. Ianuier
1571. lequel auoit achepté celle de G. *Budé*,
feu *Guillaume Budé* auec ses manuscrits. Lesquelles Bibliotheques furent conseruées, iusqu'à ce
que ces Peres furent chassez hors
de France, qu'elles furent dissipées au grand dommage des lettres; neantmoins apres leur restablissement, ils en ont redressez
vne tres exquise par l'vnion de
plusieurs autres, qui leur ont esté
données ; sçauoir le *Cardinal* Card. de
François de Ioyeuse, Archeuesque *Ioyeuse*.
de Roüen, qui ordonna que sa celebre Bibliotheque, qui auoit este
composée de trois autres, entre
lesquelles estoit celle de ce sçauant Pierre Pithou, natif de P. *Pithou*.
Troyes en Champagne, seroit
partagée entre les Iesuites de Pon-

toife, & ceux de ce College. Le Pere Antoine Poffeuin, loüe la Bibliotheque de ce Cardinal dans fon Aparat Sacré. *Francifcus de Ioyeufe*, dit-il, *non potuit non habere vberrimam Bibliothecam, & in prima commendatione ponendam, qui fuam fecit ex tribus, quarum vna fuit Pithæi.*

La feconde augmentation qu'a receu cette Bibliotheque, c'eft encore par vne partie de celle de *Philippes Des-Portes*, Chartrain, Abbé de Tyron, qui en auoit vne tres confiderable, au rapport de Sceuole de fainéte Marthe en fon Eloge. *Nullus enim*, dit-il, *eum vel hofpitalis menfæ liberalibus epulis, vel inftaurandæ Bibliothecæ fumptu, & ftudio, vel omni denique ciuilis vitæ fplendore fupe-*

Ph. des Portes.

des Bibliotheques. 525

rauit. Cette Bibliotheque a à prefent diuers bons & anciens Manufcrits Grecs & Latins, qui viennent en partie de la Bibliotheque d'vn Abbé de Lorraine, fort curieux de ces Manufcrits, lefquels apres fa mort furent negligez par fes heritiers, qui les vendirent à vn relieur pour feruir à l'vfage de fes relieures; mais Dieu difpofa autrement de ces liures, car le tres docte Pere *Iacques Sirmond*, paffant pour lors dans la Lorraine, euft aduis de ce peril des Mufes, à quoy il obuia, ne perdant point de temps pour aller à ce relieur, duquel il les achepta *cinquante efcus*; puis les fit conduire à Paris fur vne charette, & mettre dans ce College; où ils font conferuez dans vne chambre au

P. Iacques Sirmond.

fond de leur Bibliotheque.

Du Nouitiat. La Bibliotheque des mesmes Peres du Nouitiat du faux-bourg de sainct Germain est aussi fort considerable ; car elle contient à *quatre* ou *cinq milles volumes* de bons liures.

M. Ioubert. Monsieur Ioubert Aduocat en Parlement, a fait sa Bibliotheque auec de grands soins pour la recherche des bons liures.

M. Iouuin. De semblable curiosité a esté porté M. Iacques Iouuin, Docteur de la Faculté de Medecine de Paris, lieu de sa naissance pour eriger sa Bibliotheque.

M. Iustel. Iaçoit que M. Christophle Iustel Secretaire du Roy, soit cognu par ses beaux ouurages qu'il a donné, & qu'il donne à present,

des Bibliotheques. 527

entr'autres l'Histoire des Dauphins d'Auuergne, & de la maison de la Tour, toutefois sa curieuse Bibliotheque le rendra encore recommandable à la posterité.

Quoy qu'il y aye plusieurs Bibliotheques dás cette ville plus grádes, que celle de M. Iacques Keruer Conseiller Secretaire du Roy maison & Couronne de France, Receueur general de ses Finances à Paris; toutefois ie treuue qu'il n'y en a point de mieux recherchée pour les liures, les bonnes editions & les grands papiers que celle-cy; laquelle il augméte tous les iours auec vn grand soin & despence. De plus il a encore vn beau cabinet de medalles & pieces d'antiquitez; car il a vne grande co-

M. Keruer

gnoiſſance des liures & de ces raretés.

M. Labbé. M. Charles Labbé Aduocat de la Cour a depuis long-temps commencé ſa Bibliotheque, qu'il rend conſiderable.

M. Leſné. La Bibliotheque de M. Leſné, Seigneur de la Marguerie, Maiſtre des Requeſtes de l'Hoſtel du Roy, eſt en eſtime d'eſtre belle.

M. de Longueil. M. René de Longueil Cheualier Seigneur de Maiſon, cy-deuant premier Preſident en la Cour des Aydes de Paris, & à preſent Preſident au Mortier au Parlement, eſt yſſu de l'illuſtre famille des Longueils, qui a donné à l'Egliſe Romaine vn Cardinal nommé Richard Oliuier de Longueil, Eueſque de Porto, Legat de l'Vmbrie, & Miniſtre d'Eſtat du

Roy

des Bibliotheques. 529

Roy Loüys XI. lequel mourut à Peruse, & depuis son corps fut porté à S. Pierre de Rome dont il estoit Archiprestre. Ce qui fait voir combien cette famille a esté & est encore en reputation, non seulement pour sa noblesse, mais aussi pour vne notable Bibliotheque, que ce Seigneur possede dans son Hostel, de laquelle il a herité de feu Messire Nicolas Cheualier, premier President de la Cour des Aydes, & qu'il augmente tous les iours. Ie puis dire que cette Bibliotheque est l'vne des plus excellentes de Paris pour la relieure, qui est toute en veau parsemée de fleurs de Lys, & dorée sur la tranche. Il y a aussi quelques manuscrits bien rares, couuerts de velours, & qui seroient bien vtiles

M. Cheualier.

pour le public, & particulierement pour les anciennes familles de noblesse.

M. de Lozon. M. le President de Lozon a erigé vne Bibliotheque, qui est entre les considerables de Paris, selon les tesmoignages que i'en treuue dans *l'Aduis de dresser vne Bibliotheque* de Gabriel Naudé, & *l'Idée de la Bibliotheque Vniuerselle* de Pierre Blanchot.

M. Mangot. M. de Mangot Abbé de saincte Colombe, fils de M. Claude de Mangot Garde des Sceaux de France, a vne grande cognoissance des bons liures, qu'il a recherché & recherche continuellement pour orner sa celebre Bibliotheque, qui a pour le present enuiron six mille volumes bien choisis & des meilleurs impressions.

des Bibliotheques. 531

Ie me sens icy obligé de remar- *M. Mente.*
quer qu'enuiron l'an M.CCCC-
XLII. (quelques fables qu'ils
vueillent conter des Chinois)
l'on trouua à *Strasbourg*, ville d'Alsace en Allemagne, cét admirable secret & ce riche tresor des
sciences, l'Imprimerie. *L'image &*
le mirouer (comme dit vn de nos *Blanchon*
Poëtes) *de tous les ornemens* : en *l.3. de ses*
quoy l'on douteroit volontiers, *Meslanges.*
qui a plus donné de peine à en ré-
cognoistre l'Inuenteur: ou la te-
merité des vns de ceux qui en ont
escrit, poussez de vaine gloire
pour leur famille ou païs: ou bien
la negligence des autres, qui se
sont reglés, sur ceux-là, sans en rechercher curieusement l'origine.
Or il n'est pas raisonnable que la
verité soit toufiours inconnuë, &

Ll ij

que *Guttemberg Fuſt*, & *Scoëffer*; ou ce tard auiſé *Coſter*, emportent la loüange de cette diuine Inuention; de laquelle ils ne meritent au plus, que celle d'en auoir trauaillé des premiers: De meſmes que Maïence ſe pourroit preualloir ſur les autres lieux, en ce que Guttemberg, Orféure de ſon premier meſtier, s'y retira auec Fuſt; & là par le moyen d'vn des domeſtiques de *Iean* Mantel de Straſbourg, vray & legitime autheur de ce noble artifice, que ledit Guttemberg luy auoit beſbauché, commencerent d'imprimer le *Durandus de Ritibus Eccleſiæ* l'an 1461. & là *Bible in fol. en deux volumes*, l'an 1462. qui ſe trouue encore aujourd'huy en la Bibliotheque des RR. PP. Carmes de la pla-

Bibliotheq. des PP. Carmes.

ce Maubert, & en celle de saincte Croix de la Bretonnerie à Paris, où Fuſt & Scoëffer ſont ſeulement qualifiez *Miniſtres*. Et neantmoins eux & leurs succeſſeurs ont voulu par apres inſinüer qu'ils eſtoient les veritables Autheurs de l'impreſſion des liures: de ſorte que ledit *Mentlen* (ainſi parlent-ils dans le païs) fut contraint & neceſſité de leur faire voir le contraire: meſmes par l'authorité de l'Empereur Frederic III. qui l'aduoüaſt & recognuſt pour Autheur & Inuenteur de la *Typographie* l'an 1466. l'honnorant & ſa Poſterité de prerogatiues & Titres de nobleſſe à ce ſujet, ainſi que nous rapporte M. de la Colombiere *en ſon Traicté de la Science Heroïque*. Vvimphelinge,

Iacques Spiegel, H. Guebuilier, André Althamer & autres celebres autheurs florissans fort peu apres les premiers Temps de cette Inuention, luy en rendent les mesmes tesmoignages dans leurs escrits. Si bien que l'excellence & la richesse des Bibliotheques estant deuës à cet Art, i'ay pris occasion d'en parler en ce lieu suiuant la verité de l'histoire, pour monstrer l'obligation que nous auons à ce grand Personnage, la memoire duquel doit estre à iamais cherie des gens de lettres, & sa posterité recognuë & honorée; laquelle subsiste encore aujourd'huy en quelques endroits d'Allemagne & ailleurs, comme en France vers la Champagne, d'où vient M. Iacques Mentel Do-

des Bibliotheques. 535

-cteur en Medecine en la Faculté de Paris, homme de grande probité & de doctrine, comme il est tres-curieux en bons liures, en ayant au nombre de quatre à cinq mille volumes, bien conditionnez & bien reliez; dont plusieurs viennent des Bibliotheques de feu M. Iean Passerat & de M. Iean Grangier, autrefois Professeurs du Roy en Eloquence Latine à Paris. *Iean Passerat. Iean Grangier.*

Feu M. Guillaume Marescot Conseiller du Roy en ses Conseils & Maistre des Requestes ordinaire de son Hostel a trauaillé auec vn grand soin par l'espace de cinquante ans à faire sa riche & belle Bibliotheque, qui possede plus de six milles volumes, contenans principalement les Histoires par- *M. Marescot.*

ticulieres de France, & Royaumes Eſtrangers de toute l'Europe: Car ledit ſieur Mareſcot auoit en ſa ieuneſſe voyagé dans les Prouinces d'Eſpagne, Italie & Allemagne, où il auoit apris les langues, ce qui luy cauſa la volonté de faire la recherche de tous les meilleurs liures de ces païs: & de plus ayant eu pluſieurs employs dans ces Prouinces pour le ſeruice du Roy, il n'eſpargna ny ſoin ny diligence pour perfectionner ſon genereux deſſein de rendre ſa Bibliotheque tres conſiderable, ce qui luy fut facile de faire, à cauſe de la grande cognoiſſance qu'il auoit des liures, qu'il a curieuſement aymez iuſques en l'âge de quatre vingt ans qu'il a veſcu. Il a laiſſé ce precieux monument des Muses à M. Marescot son fils, Maistre des Requestes, vray heritier de ses vertus & de sa doctrine, ayant desiré qu'elle demeurast à luy seul & à ceux de son nom apres luy sans estre diuisée, pour laisser en vn seul corps ce grand trauail, qu'il a iugé ne deuoir estre separé, mais deuoir demeurer entier dans sa famille autant qu'il plairroit à Dieu la conseruer dans les honneurs & dignitez, qui sont possedez par ceux de cette maison.

M. Claude Martin Bachelier en la Faculté de Medecine de Paris, a vne Bibliotheque considerable pour les liures de Medecine & Mathematique. *M. Martin.*

La Bibliotheque de M. Michel le Masle, Abbé des Roches, *M. des Roches.*

Chanoine & Chantre de noſtre Dame, eſt fort eſtimée pour la bonté & multitude de ſes liures, qu'il a ramaſſé de long-temps: laquelle il veut qu'elle ſoit conſeruée apres ſa mort dans le College de Sorbonne, en vn lieu ſeparé de la commune de cette maiſon, pour ſeruir à ceux qui voudront y eſtudier; laiſſant pour cét effet des gages pour vn Bibliothecaire particulier.

M. de Meſ-me. Seuerin Boëce, Senateur Romain, grand homme d'eſprit & d'Eſtat, tiroit ſon extraction d'vne tres noble & ancienne famille de Rome. Ie puis dire le meſme de M. Henry de meſme, Cheualier & Preſident au Mortier de ce tres-auguſte Parlement des Pairs, lequel outre ſon rare eſprit eſt iſſu de cét illustre Amané de Mesme Escossois, Pere de Iean Iacques, qui fut grand amateur des lettres, comme le tesmoigne Sceuole de S. Marthe en son *Eloge*; auquel succeda dans la mesme affection Henry de Mesme son fils, Seigneur de Roissy & de Malasisse, Maistre des Requestes, Ambassadeur pour le Roy Henry II. vers les Sienois en Italie, puis Chancelier de Nauarre, lequel commença la tres-opulente Bibliotheque de cette famille, où il mit outre les liures imprimez, vn grand nombre de manuscrits, Grecs, Latins, François, & autres Idiomes, selon la remarque qu'en fait François de la Croix, en la *Bibliotheque des Autheurs François*, v. H. Ce que confirme Denys Lambin, en vne *Epistre Liminaire* qu'il addresse audit Henry, où il parle de cette Bibliotheque en ces termes, *Tu verò (vt cætera tua in remp. merito hoc loco sileam) quam habes omni librorum & calamo descriptorum, & typis impressorum genere instructissimam ac refertissimam, impensóque emptam Bibliothecam, eam ita omnibus nostri ordines hominibus patefacis, vt non tibi, sed omnibus comparasse videaris. Ex ea enim antiquissima & fidelissima deprompta exemplaria cū iis libenter ac iucundè communicas, quos exploratum habes & posse & velle fructus inde decerptos Reip. impertire.* Iean Passerat, Professeur Royal de l'eloquence, rend vn pareil témoignage de cette Bibliotheque, en vn *Poëme* qu'il a escrit sur ce sujet, l'an 1571. que ie rapporteray.

Hæc tot codicibus Graiis, Latiisque
 superbit
Pœta voluminibus, quot vel mirentur
 Athenæ
Incolumes, vel Barbarico nondum ar-
 dua Roma
Pressa pede.hic florent populorum fa-
 cta ducûmque:
Socraticæ hic secreta domus, Coïque
 reperta
Clara senis, fama & linguæ ventosa
 disertæ
Parnassûsque Helicônque, æquataque
 gloria Pindo:
Puluisque & radius, magno & glo-
 bus æmulus orbi:
Cuncta omnis monumenta æui : pars
 optima certis
Scripta notis: &c.
 Voilà comme du viuant de ce
Seigneur, cette Bibliotheque

estoit en grande reputation : car outres ces Autheurs citez , plu- plusieurs sçauans personnages en ont aussi fort honorablement parlé, comme le President Claude Fauchet , André Turnebe & Marsil. M. Iean Iacques de Mesme fils de Henry, President au mesme Parlement, n'a pas esté vn moindre ornement de cette famille, puis qu'il a merité d'auoir de grands employs par nos Rois, pour les grandes qualitez d'esprit qu'il possedoit ; car son affection fut aussi admirable enuers les bónes lettres , veu qu'il n'espargna aucun soin ny despence à augmēter cette Bibliotheque paternelle. Nous apprenons du Roy Salomon que, *gloria Patris est Filius sapiens*, ce sacré axiome, se treuue ve-

des Bibliotheques. 543

ritablement en M. Henry de Mefme, fils de Iean Iacques, auſſi Preſident au mortier : ſi vous iettez les yeux ſur ſon eſprit, il eſblouyt les plus ſçauans : ſi vous contemplez ſon integrité, ſa vie eſt vne perle ſans tache : ſi vous peſez ſa dignité, il eſt des premiers du plus Auguſte Parlement du monde: bref la cognoiſſance qu'il a des ſciences, le rend l'vn des plus conſiderables du Royaume. Or dóc toutes ces qualités, auec l'affectió qu'il a pour les liures, le rendent amateur des ſciences & des liures, & ainſi il a fait ſa Bibliotheque l'vne des plus accomplies de Paris, de laquelle autrefois ce Genie des Bibliotheques, M. Naudé a eu la charge; & pour le ſujet de laquelle nous iouyſſos de ſon docte & curieux liure, intitulé, *Aduis pour dresser vne Bibliotheque*, qu'il dedie à ce Seigneur. Vn autre rare esprit de ce temps, non moins pieux que sçauant, le R. P. Leon de S. Iean, Predicateur du Roy, & Prouincial des Peres Carmes Réformez, de la Prouince de Touraine, a fait aussi par le commandement du mesme Seigneur vn liure Latin sur ce sujet, qu'il nous donnera bien-tost dans ses *Opuscules*, soubs le tiltre de *Idea Bibliothecæ viuentis & mortuæ, ad Henricum Memmium*, &c.

M. de Metz. M. de Metz Commissaire des guerres, employe toute son industrie à faire vne curieuse Bibliotheque, qui excelle pour les Mathematiques.

Des Minimes. La Bibliotheque des Peres Minimes

Minimes de la place Royale est veritablement vn riche cabinet des Muses de Paris, puis qu'elle possede de huit milles volumes de liures en toutes les sciences, qui y ont esté mis en partie par les soins du P. Robert Renaud, qui en auoit vne grande cognoissance & de plusieurs sçauans autres Religieux de ce Monastere, qui ont honorez & honorent tous les iours le public, comme sont les Peres Marin Mersenne, François de la Noüe, Hilarion de Coste, Iean François Niceron, & autres.

M. de Monchal, Maistre des Requestes ordinaire de l'Hostel du Roy, frere de M. de Monchal Archeuesque de Tolose, témoigne au public l'affection qu'il

M. d. Monchal.

a pour les sciences, par le ramas qu'il fait des bons liures pour rendre illustre sa Bibliotheque.

M. Morand. La diuersité des Bibliotheques de cette ville, est vn extréme contentemét pour les gens de lettres, & vn témoignage comme les sciences y sont cultiuées. La doctrine & la curiosité de M. Morand Conseiller au grand Conseil, le portent à faire vne notable Bibliotheque.

M. Moreau. Quoy que M. René Moreau Docteur de la Faculté de Paris, & Professeur Royal en Medecine, se soit acquis vne grande reputation pour sa doctrine: toutefois ie treuue que son excellente Bibliotheque ne luy en cause pas vne moindre; car elle est tres-accomplie pour les liures de Medecine, &

des Bibliotheques. 547

Philofophie. Auſſi quelques Autheurs en parlét auec eloge, comme Gabriel Naudé en ſon *Addition à l'Hiſtoire de Loüis XI. pag.* 91. où il l'appelle, *riche & bien aſſortie.* Le meſme parlant dans *ſa Bibliographie Politique*, des Bibliotheques bien remplies de Paris, nombre celle-cy pour l'vne : le P. Pierre Blanchot Minime, la met auſſi entre les celebres & magnifiques de cette ville, dans ſon *Idée d'vne Bibliotheque Vniuerſelle.* Ce ſçauant Medecin prend vn ſoin particulier de faire rechercher en Allemagne, Flandre, Hollande, Angleterre & Italie, tous les meilleurs liures, qui concernent ſes loüables deſſeins.

Le Royal College de Nauarre, a touſiours eſté vn ſeminaire de

Nauarre.

Mm ij

tres celebres Docteurs, qui ont illuſtrez l'Egliſe de Dieu par leur bonne vie; & le public par leurs ſciences, comme Pierre d'Ailly Cardinal, & le venerable Iean Gerſon, & pluſieurs autres, leſquels ont laiſſé leurs ouurages dans ce College pour honorer cette magnifique Bibliotheque, qui a eſté conſtruite par la liberalité du Roy Charles VIII. dans laquelle ſont conſeruez diuers anciens Manuſcrits.

M. Naud.   Ce n'eſt pas ſans raiſon que M. Gabriel Naudé, eſt appellé vne Bibliotheque viuante pour la grande cognoiſſance qu'il a des ſciéces & des liures, puis que pour ces meſmes raiſons il a eu l'honneur d'exercer la charge de Bibliothecaire des plus celebres Bi-

des Bibliotheques. 549

bliotheques de l'Europe, comme premierement de celle de M. le Président de Mesme, puis de celle de M. le Cardinal Bagny à Rome, apres la mort duquel M. le Cardinal Antonio Barberin luy donna la charge de la sienne, qu'il fit quelques mois, iusques à ce qu'il fut appellé par M. le Cardinal Mazarin pour estre son domestique & Bibliothecaire, à quoy il s'occupe si dignement, qu'il ne pense plus à augmenter sa rare & curieuse Bibliotheque qui possede plus de huit milles volumes, tant en ce qu'il a encore à Rome que ce qu'il conserue en cette ville : mais comme il ne se soucie plus qu'à enrichir la Bibliotheque de son Eminence de tout ce qu'il y a de meilleur & de plus rare en Europe, il

M m iij

a librement renoncé à ses propres interests pour mieux & plus facilement executer sous la faueur d'vn si bon maistre, ce dont il y a plus de dix-sept ans qu'il nous auoit donné le dessein en *son Aduis pour dresser vne Bibliotheque accomplie.*

Des PP. de l'Oratoire. La memoire du Cardinal Pierre de Berulle, sera à iamais en benediction, pour auoir esté l'Autheur de la pieuse Congregation des Peres de l'Oratoire de Iesvs, qui a donné diuers sçauans personnages pour la gloire de cet Ordre, & de leur maison de Paris, qui ont tous contribuez à l'establissement d'vne insigne Bibliotheque, qui possede plus de six mille volumes; entre lesquels se void toute la Theologie & Phi-

des Bibliotheques.

losophie des Hebreux manuscrits qui a esté apportée de Constantinople par M. de Sancy, pour lors *M. de Sancy.* Ambassadeur de nostre Roy tres-Chrestien vers le grand Seigneur, lequel depuis mesprisant les grädeurs de ce monde, pour acquerir plus parfaitemét les eternelles, print l'habis & maniere de viure de ceux de cette Congregatió, où il a demeuré iusqu'à ce que le Roy Loüis XIII. d'heureuse memoire l'a pourueu de l'Euesché de S. Malo en Bretagne, où il vid auec vn grand exemple.

M. Guy Patin natif de Beau- *M. Patin.* uaisis, Docteur en la Faculté de Medecine de Paris, & Censeur des Escholes, est digne de loüange, non seulement pour sa viuacité & bonté d'esprit, mais encore pour vne singuliere recherche qu'il fait des bons liures pour augmenter sa belle Bibliotheque, qui excede six milles volumes en toutes les sciences.

M. Petau. M. Paul Petau Conseiller au Parlement de Paris, a donné le commencement à la Bibliotheque de cette famille, qui est tres-opulente & tres-remarquable pour les manuscrits qu'elle possede, qui sont en grande quantité, qu'il auoit recherché auec vn grand soin & vne notable despence; lesquels prouiennent en partie des Bibliotheques de feu *M. de Fauchet.* M. Claude Fauchet President de la Cour des Monnoyes, & de Pier- *P. Bailly.* re Daniel Bailly de S. Benoist sur Loire. Or l'on peut iuger la rareté de ces manuscrits, pour ce que plusieurs ont seruis aux editions des grands ouurages que le Pere Iacques Sirmond a donné au public, & particulierement feu M. du Chesne en son corps des Historiens de France. La mort qui rauit trop tost les gens de lettres, priua le public de ce docte Senateur l'an 1614. apres auoir laissé à la posterité diuers beaux & curieux ouurages, qui sont entre les mains des studieux. Nicolas Bourbon luy a consacré vn Epitaphe dans ses poëmes, qui rend vn particulier témoignage de ses liures & curiositez, que ie rapporteray icy, puis qu'il fait à nostre sujet.

PIIS MANIBVS MEMORIÆQVE SACRVM.

Auli Petauii Senatoris Parisiensis, integritate vitæ cum primis suspiciendi rerum diuinarum humanarúmque scientia editis ingenii fœtibus per Europam clarissimi: nec tantum antiqui moris retinentissimi, sed & omnis antiquitatis priscorum rituum, signorum archetyporum & numismatum in elegantioris doctrinæ vsum studiosissimi : cui vero præmatura morte extincto Pallas & Astræa pari damno ac dolore affectæ iuerunt exequias; coniux vero, gener in purpura successor, & liberi superstites, marito, socero, parentique carissimo, paruum hoc æterni sui desiderij monumentum posuere.

Ossa solo linquens, animóque Petauius astris
Insitus, ad meritos æui melioris honores
Maturauit iter cœlo, corrupta perosus
Sæcula, quamquam illo visa est sub Iudice, sese

des Bibliotheques. 355

Reddita damnatis Astræa ostendere
 terris
Ordinis eximii robur, virtúsque Ca-
 toni
Æmula, Palladias, sed enim conuer-
 sus ad artes
Multus in antiqui latebras penetra-
 uerat æui.
Quicquid longa dies alia caligine te-
 xit
Nouerat. Ecce viri tam cana scientia,
 vanam
Decepit Lachesim, qui tantum limina
 lustri
Pulsarat decimi, quæcumque fuêre
 capacis
Illi notitiæ, falso est rara tempora vi-
 tâ.
Obiit 15. Kal. Octobris anno Domini 1614. Vixit annos 46. mens. 4. dies
2. M. Alexandre Petau son fils

Conseiller au mesme Parlement, imite les vertus & desseins de son pere, lequel augmente tous les iours cette Bibliotheque des meilleurs liures imprimez, & manuscrits, entre autres il a achepté plusieurs manuscris de la Bibliotheque de feu M. Iean de S. André Chanoine de nostre Dame & Conseiller de la grande Chambre, qui sont bien rares, car le Cardinal Sirlet luy en auoit enuoyé quelqu'vns Grecs de Calabre.

M. Philippeaux. M. Loüis Philippeaux Cheualier Seigneur de la Vreliere, Conseiller du Roy en ses Conseils Secretaire de ses commandemés, & Grand Maistre des Ceremonies de l'Ordre des Cheualiers du S. Esprit, outre ses grandes occupations aux affaires d'Estat, ne laisse pas de faire rechercher les bons liures pour embellir sa somptueuse Bibliotheque, qu'il a erigé dans son Palais.

La Bibliotheque de M. du Plessis, Baron de Monbart en Bourgongne, & Conseiller d'Estat, est composée des meilleurs liures de toutes les sciences qui se peuuent treuuer; ce qui fait voir combien est grande la cognoissance qu'il en a & ie puis dire qu'il a l'vne des heureuses memoires, & vne viuacité d'esprit des plus accomplies de ce temps.

M. Du Plessis de Guenegaud, Secretaire d'Estat, est en estime d'estre tres-bien versé dans les sciences & la recherche des liures les plus curieux, qui se peuuent retreuuer, desquels il orne & enrichit vne magnifique Bibliotheque, qu'il a commencé.

MM. du Puy. Si les Muses doiuent quelques recognoissances à ceux qui les courtisent auec vn grand fruit, elles en doiuent vne signalée à MM. Pierre & Iacques du Puy freres, fils de Claude du Puy Conseiller au Parlement de Paris: le premier est Conseiller d'Estat, & l'autre Prieur de S. Sauueur; lesquels outre leur singuliere science, ont vne extréme passion pour les bons liures, desquels ils remplissent leur fameuse Bibliotheque, qui est composée de plus de huit milles volumes, y comprenant diuers anciés manuscrits qu'ils ont eu dudit sieur du Puy le Pere & autres qu'ils

des Bibliotheques.

y ont adjouſtez par vne grande diligence; outre cela ledit ſieur du Puy Conſeiller d'Eſtat a vn cabinet de liures eſcrits à la main en nombre de ſix cens volumes qui contiennent quelques memoires touchant l'Hiſtoire de France & affaires Publiques & matieres curieuſes.

Les Peres Recolets ont erigez vne grande Bibliotheque dans leur Conuent du faux-bourg de S. Martin, où ſont pluſieurs bons liures de Theologie & d'Hiſtoire. *Des PP. Recolets.*

Entre les grandes & excellentes Bibliotheques de Paris, celle de M. Iacques Ribier iadis Conſeiller de la Cour, & à preſent Conſeiller d'Eſtat en eſt vne : car ſi l'on conſidere la bonté des li- *M. Ribier* ures, il se treuuera que les plus rares y sont, si quant à la multitude, elle ne cede à gueres de Paris, puis que le nombre se monte iusques à neuf mille cinq cens; y comprenant les liures de la Bibliotheque de feu le tres docte Guillaume du Vair premier President au Parlement d'Aix en Prouence, puis Garde des Sceaux de France, & en fin Euesque de Lisieux; qui la legua par son testament à M. l'Euesque de Riez son nepueu, apres la mort duquel ils sont retournez à M. Ribier à cause de Madame sa femme, parente desdits Euesques.

M. Rigaut. M. Nicolas Rigaut Conseiller au Parlement de Mets, & Garde de la Bibliotheque Royale, a acquis vne grande renommée pour son

son erudition & cognoissance de la langue Grecque, ainsi que le tesmoignent les versions & commentaires qu'il donne au public. Sa Bibliotheque est exquise pour le choix des bons liures, desquels il l'a garnie.

Les merites de M. Iean Riolan, *M. Riolan.* premier Medecin de la Reyne Mere, & Professeur Royal en Medecine, sont assez cognus de tous ceux de sa profession, à raison de sa doctrine, de laquelle il donne tous les iours des preuues par ses liures, qu'il a composé, non moins admirables que ceux de cét illustre Iean Riolan son Pere, aussi Medecin; lesquels tous deux ont concouru à l'erection de cette noble Bibliotheque, que possede auiourdhuy ce cher fils.

MM. de S. Marthes.

Il n'y a personne qui aye cognoissance des lettres, qui n'aye en estime la famille de MM. de saincte Marthes, qui a donné ces deux excellents Historiographes de France, Louys, & Sceuole, freres iumeaux, Aduocats en Parlement, lesquels possedent vne rauissante Bibliotheque pour l'histoire, qu'ils augmentent tous les iours.

M. de Seue.

M. Antoine de Seue, fils de Guillaume sieur de sainct Iulien, Conseiller du Roy en ses Cóseils, & qui en l'année 1625. exerça la charge de Thresorier de l'Espargne, frere de MM. Iean & Alexandre, Conseillers d'Estat, &c. Abbé de l'Isle en Barrois, soubs l'Euesché de Verdun, Conseiller & Aumosnier du Roy, issu de l'Il-

des Bibliotheques. 563
luſtre famille des Marquis de Seue en Piedmont, de laquelle eſt le
Cardinal Seue, creé nouuellemét
par noſtre S. Pere le Pape Vrbain
VIII. Or ce docte Abbé eſt fort
curieux en bons liures, qu'il recherche ſoigneuſement pour embellir ſa fameuſe Bibliotheque,
qui poſſede plus de ſix milles volumes en toute ſorte de ſcience.

Le tres-Auguſte College de *Sorbonne,*
Sorbonne, eſt l'Arſenal des Muſes
& l'Areopage des ſçauans hommes de l'vniuers : ce qui fait qu'il
y a vne tres-belle & tres-bonne
Bibliotheque, qui a eſté faite des
liures de pluſieurs Docteurs, de
cette maiſon, qu'ils y ont laiſſez
pour gages de leur affection : c'eſt
pourquoy ie laiſſe à preſumer le
Lecteur la bonté des liures qui y
Nn ij

sont conseruez, tant imprimez que Manuscrits.

M. Stella. M. Iean Tileman Stella de Sighen au Comté en Hesse en Allemagne, fils de Christophle Tileman, & petit fils de Tileman, tous cognus par leurs escrits, Conseiller d'Estat, & Professeur Royal aux Mathematiques, est assez cognu pour son grád esprit, & pour l'extréme passion qu'il a pour la recherche des liures rares & curieux, pour orner cette insigne Bibliotheque qu'il fait, où se voyent (outre vne grande quantité de liures imprimez,) plus de trois cents Manuscrits, dont il y en a des tres-rares, qui prouiennent en partie

I. Spiegel. de la Bibliotheque *de Iacques Spiegel*, Secretaire de l'Empereur Maximilien, qui auoit eu la Bibliotheque de Iacques VVimphiling son oncle, qui tous deux ont esté sçauans personnages, & reputez par leurs ouurages.

La reputation de la noble fa-*De Thou.* mille de MM. de Thou est cogneuë dans toute l'Europe, pour auoir donné ces grands personnages, Augustin President au Parlement, Christophle I. President au mesme Parlement, & Chancelier d'Henry Duc d'Orleans, puis de François Duc d'Aniou, & Iacques Auguste President au mortier, qui a escrit cette belle histoire Latine de son temps, & qui a consommé XL. ans à eriger cette nombreuse & exquise Bibliotheque, qu'il a laissé à sa famille, de laquelle est chef à present M. Iacques Auguste de Thou son fils, Conseiller d'Estat, & de la Cour de Parlement, legitime heritier des vertus de son pere; de laquelle il parle en son Testament en cette sorte : *Bibliothecam meam XL. amplius annorum spatio magna diligentia ac sumptu congestam (quam integram conservari non solum familiæ, sed etiam rei litterariæ interest) diuidi, vendi ac dissipari veto. Eámque communem cum numismatis antiquis, aureis, argenteis, & æreis inter filios qui litteris operam nauabunt facio : ita vt etiam exteris aliisque philologis ad vsum publicum pateat. Eius custodiam Petro Puteano cognato meo & multis nominibus mihi charo, donec filij adolescant, committo, qui & libros MSS. iis qui opus habebunt, vtendos dare poterit, modo de illis restituẽdis idonea cauetur.* Cette Bibliotheque possede plus de 8000. volumes des plus rares & curieux, qui ont esté recherchez dans l'Europe, auec vne despence excessiue, lesquels sont tous reliez en marroquin & veau dorez, qui est encore vne autre grande sumptuosité de ce Parnasse des Muses. Quant aux Manuscrits, il y en peut auoir milles tous de grande consideration, lesquels seruent iournellemét aux impressions, comme il se void par le, liures. L'estroicte amitié qui estoit entre feu M. de Thou, & feu M. Nicolas le Febure, Precepteur du feu Roy Louys XIII. homme d'vne rare doctrine, obligea ce dernier à leguer tous ces Manuscrits à cette Bibliotheque, comme le remarque le sçauant Sceuole de saincte Marthe, en l'Eloge de Nicolas le Febure. *Cùmque vi-cißim (dit-il) eos omnes curiosé ac diligenter obseruant, nullum tamen coluit maior studio, quam Iacobum Augustum Thuanū singulare nostri sæculi Decus & ornamentum, cui & moriens omnes suos codices manuscriptos (horum enim amplißimam supellectilem collegerat) supremo testamento legauit.* François le Begue Aduocat du Roy, en la Cour des Monnoyes de France, parle de la Bibliotheque du mesme en sa vie qu'il a donné au deuant des Opuscules de ce sçauant homme. *Hoc in otio Bibliothecam editis MSS. Codicibus instructißimam sibi parauit, ac pleráque omnia veterum scripta incredibili diligentia & labore contulit, notauit, recensuit.* Et plus bas il dit encore. *Iacobo Augusto Thuano amplißimo senatus*

Præsidi omnes MSS. Codices, mihi verò paucis exceptis cæteros Bibliothecæ libros suprema voluntate reliquit. Le P. Iean de S. François general des Feuillans, en l'oraison Funebre qu'il a fait de M. le Febure, parle aussi de sa recherche dans les liures en ces termes. *Mais quoy? comme vn autre Solon, il vouloit vieillir en apprenant tousiours quelque chose de nouueau, aymant mieux apprendre des autres, que les autres apprinssent de luy, tant il faisoit peu d'estime de soy-mesme, d'où l'on peut colliger iusqu'à quel haut degré d'erudition & de science il est paruenu, veu qu'il a consumé tout le temps de sa vie en l'estude des bonnes lettres, en la conseruation des plus doctes esprits de la France, estant luy mesme doüé d'vn esprit rarement bon, entre vne quantité extréme* de toutes sortes de bons liures qu'il auoit recueilly de toutes parts, & specialement d'anciens manuscrits, qu'il ramaſſoit par tout, auec vne diligence & deſpence incroyable. Apres ces témoignages reuenons à M. de Thou. Pluſieurs doctes perſonnages ont rendus des témoignages de loüange à cette Bibliotheque, deſquels i'en rapporteray quelqu'vns, pour faire voir au public l'eſtime qu'ils en font; le premier ſera d'Henry Eſtienne, ſur l'*Aulugelle*, où il parle ainſi à cét illuſtre Preſident Iacques Auguſte. *Indoctum quendam multos tamen libros ementem irridet & inſectatur Lucianus. Eius enim extat epiſtola ſine oratiuncula qua inuehitur in quendam* ἀπαίδευτον, πολλὰ βιβλία ἀνούμροι. *Quantum autem illum ludibrio habuit, tanto*

des Bibliotheques. 571

te, vt opinor honore profequeretur: Quantum illum vituperauit, tantum te laudaret, te inquam, non ἀπαιδευτον, ſed πολλαχῶς ἐνπαιδευτον huic libros vndique conquerẽdi ſtudio acerrimè incumbentem, atque vt omni librorum genere Græcorum præſertim & Latinorum, tua tandem Bibliotheca poſsit eſſe referta nullis ſumptibus parcentem. Quin etiam quod in delectu editionum Typographicarum tãtum iudicij adhibes, quod quanto maiore in pretio tibi eſt aliquod volumen, eo pretioſiore integumento & velut indumento ornas: tuum in iis quoque ſtudium, tuamque diligentiam, non illaudatam, (ni fallor) relinqueret: Ad me quidem certè quod attinet non tantum ardens illud amplificandæ in dies Bibliothecæ deſiderium laudo, ſed etiam omnimodis gratificari cupio, &c. Ie treuue encore que

Isaac Casaubon escriuant à François Vertumien celebre Medecin de Poictiers, en son Epistre 163. en fait cas ainsi : *Vtor tuo Celso, de quo nuper cũ verba facerem magno Thuano essemúsque in eius Bibliotheca, ille statim à forulis suæ illius opulentissimæ librorum supellectilis codicem Capellani Archiatri prompsit & mihi ostendit*; Plus les loüanges partent dès personnes releuées en dignités ; plus sont elles plausibles & receuës, ce qui fera que le couronnement de cette Bibliotheque, est reserué par vn souuerain Pontife Romain, qui est *Leon XI*. lequel auparauant son Pontificat fut Legat en France, pour la paix entre les Roïs tres-Chrestien & Catholique, au traicté qui se fit à Veruins; apres lequel estant venu

des Bibliotheques. 573

à Paris, il oüyt faire recit de cette Bibliotheque, qu'il voulu visiter; ou il treuua tant de satisfaction, qu'il aduoüa qu'il n'en auoit point veu de plus belle dans l'Italie : apres ces loüanges il n'en faut plus chercher d'autres, puis qu'elles prouiennent de celuy qui est le vray oracle du monde. Le Cardinal Barberin Legat en Fráce, l'an 1625. visita ladite Bibliotheque auec admiration. Il est encore à remarquer que *M. du Puy*, cy-dessus denommé dans le testament, employe tous ses soings à enrichir cette Bibliotheque, à laquelle nouuellement ont esté mis plusieurs bons liures de la Bibliotheque de feu *M. Picardet*, Procureur General au Parlement de Dijon, beau-pere de M. le Con-

M. Picardet.

seiller de Thou, d'apresent. De plus feu M. le President de Thou, achepta les manuscrits anciens de

M. Pithou. la Bibliotheque de M. Pierre Pithou, sieur de Sauoye, Aduocat au Parlement de Paris, celebre Iurisconsulte & Historien, qui deceda à Nogent sur Seine, aagé de 57. ans l'an 1596.

Les Religieux du Tiers Ordre de S. François. Le tres-sçauant Iacques Dauy Cardinal du Perron, n'a iamais cessé de faire du bien aux lettres; tant pour ses rares ouurages qu'il a donné au public, que pour l'erection d'vne belle Bibliotheque qu'il a fait aux Religieux du Tiers Ordre de S. François du Conuent de Picquepusse.

M. du Tillet. M. du Tillet Greffier en chef du Parlement de Paris, est possesseur de la celebre Bibliotheque de

des Bibliotheques. 575
feu MM.Ieans du Tillet Euesque de Meaux, & l'autre Greffier au mesme Parlement, qui ont laissez des liures de l'histoire de France; desquels Sceuole de saincte Marthe fait les Eloges.

La Bibliotheque de M.Hector de Marle, sieur de Versigny President en la Chambre des Comptes, est estimée pour les bons liures qu'elle possede, & qu'il cherche tous les iours auec vn grand soin; il faudra rétablir cette Bibliotheque en la lettre H. *M. de Versigny.*

M. Dominique de Vic Archeuesque d'Ausch en Gascogne, conserue la Bibliotheque de feu M. Emery de Vic son pere, garde des Sçeaux de France, homme grand Politique & de probité, comme il l'a tesmoigné dans les *M. de Vic.*

charges qu'il a exercé dans ce Royaume, qui a laissé des enfans qui sont imitateurs de ses vertus.

De S. Victor.   Il n'y a personne qui ne sçache en quelle estime est la Bibliotheque de l'Abbaye de S. Victor, pour la grande abondance des MSS. qu'elle possede; puis que l'on estime qu'il y en a iusques à 1500. dans vn corps de bastiment particulier, qui fut fait expressément pour ce sujet, l'an 1501. *par Nicaise de Lorme*, Abbé xxxiii. dudict S. Victor. Ie treuue que plusieurs Autheurs affirment que cette Bibliotheque doit la gloire de ses progrez au Roy François I. le Protecteur des lettres; neantmoins *Claude Hemeré* en son Academie de Paris *chap.* 6. nous asseure que Pierre de Câbe Euesque de Paris allant

des Bibliotheques. 577

allant au voyage de la Terre saincte fit son testament l'an 1208. par lequel il donna sa Bibliotheque à cette Abbaye. *Legamus Ecclesiæ S. Victoris insulam dalmaticã, & tunicã rubeas, & Bibliothecã magnã.*

Monburnus en son *Stellarium Ecclesiæ S. Victoris*, apres auoir estalé plusieurs belles aduantages de cét Ordre de Chanoines Reguliers, & de cette maison de sainct Victor, venant à la Bibliotheque, il rapporte les vers d'vn docte & pieux personnage nommé *Cornelius Godensis*, qui abordent celuy qui la vient voir de cette sorte :

Qui tibi Grammaticos qui Rhetora quique Poëtas
Siue Machaonis visere quæris opem ;
Siue libet Sophiæ textus ; seu gesta priorum.

O o

Et legere historias, hûc sine fraude
veni.
Quicquid academij quondam schola
protulit horti.
Seneca quicquid agit, seu Plato doctus
habet
Quicquid Erastothenes, Apuleius &
Ptolomæus
Disserit orthogono, tùm digito atque
Polo.
Quicquid Aristoteles frenandis tradi-
dit argis
Seu sacra iura docent ; hic reperiri li-
cet,
Quid multis teneor fixum tibi pectore
serua,
Quod non Victor habet nec Regio
vlla tenet
Cresi diuitias. Vincentem Victor
abundé
Hic aperit Gazam plenus amore suã

des Bibliotheques. 579
Hoc vel pro tantis contende repedere donis
Vt nihil abripias nilque perire sinas.

M. Isaac Habert, Chanoine & *M. I. Habert.* Theologal de l'Eglise de Paris, Abbé de saincte Marie des Alleües, Docteur de Sorbonne, Conseiller, & Predicateur ordinaire du Roy, est cognû de tous, pour la grande cognoissance qu'il a dans les bonnes lettres & la langue Grecque, qui luy ont fait donner cette belle version du Pontifical des Grecs, dont iouyt le public: La Bibliotheque qu'il a erigé, est digne de consideration, pour la Theologie & l'Histoire Ecclesiastique.

Le R.P. Iean de la Haye, Parisien, Religieux de S. François, *Du P. de la Haye.* Predicateur du Roy, & Procureur

O o ij

General de son Ordre en France, fait voir tous les iours au public la grande affection qu'il a pour les bonnes lettres, tant par ses doctes commentaires qu'il a donné sur la Genese & Exode : la grande Bible, qui est sortie nouuellement en lumiere, en cinq volumes in-folio, auec annotations litterales: les œuures de S. François, celles des Saincts Antoine de Padoüe, & Bernardin de Siene, corrigez & augmentez sur manuscrits en III. volumes ; outre lesquels il a à present soubs la presse III. volumes sur l'Apocalypse : que pour vne celebre Bibliotheque, qu'il a dressé pour son vsage, auec permission de ses Supérieurs au Monastere Royal de S. Claire du faux-bourg de S. Marceau lez Paris, où

des Bibliotheques. 581

il fait sa residence ordinaire ; laquelle contient prez *de quatre milles volumes*, dont la pluspart concernent la Theologie Positiue & Scholastique; & de plus, c'est qu'il y a encore de tres-bons & anciens manuscrits, qui n'ont point esté imprimez; mais l'inclination qu'il a pour le public, faira qu'il donnera ces thresors à la posterité.

Ces deux dernieres Bibliotheques n'estant venuës à ma cognoissance que lors que l'on imprimoit cette feüille ; par ainsi elles n'ont peu entrer dans leur ordre, qui est en la lettre H.

Chapitre LXXXIV.

Des Bibliotheques de Paris, qui ont esté dissipées.

<small>M. de S. André Pere.</small>

M. François de sainct André President au Parlement, auoit erigé vne insigne Bibliotheque, dans laquelle auoit esté mise celle de G. Budé, comme ie l'ay remarqué dans celle des Peres Iesuites du College de Clermont, qui ont eu la Bibliotheque de ce President, qui eust vn <small>M. de S. André Chanoine.</small> fils Iean de sainct André Chanoine de Nostre Dame, & Conseiller en la grande Chambre, homme bien versé dans le Grec, & dans les lettres sacrées, qui non moins curieux que son pere, dressa vne opulente Bibliotheque, que Fráçois de la Croix du Maine appelle en sa Bibliotheque : *ample & riche, remplie de toute sorte de liures, & principalement des escrits à la main, desquels il en fait imprimer plusieurs, tant des Autheurs Grecs que Latins, lesquels n'auoyent point encore esté mis en lumiere parcy-deuant*, ce qu'a bien tesmoigné monsieur Feu-ardent Docteur en Theologie à Paris, en son Epistre mise au deuant de la traduction de Psellus, pris de la Bibliotheque du sieur de sainct André. Apres la mort de ce I. de S. André, cette Bibliotheque fut venduë à diuerses personnes ; car M. Petau achepta beaucoup de ses Manuscrits, qui sont encore aujourdhuy soigneusement conseruez dans la fameuse Bibliotheque de ce Conseiller de la Cour, qui a la mesme emulation qu feu son pere.

M. Brisson. Celle du President Barnabé Brisson, grand Iurisconsulte de son siecle, estoit tres-recommandable pour ses bons liures, ainsi que le tesmoigne Iosse Sincer, en son voyage de France.

N. du Carlier. La memoire de la Bibliotheque de M. du Carlier, est encore parmy les studieux de Paris. Le sieur Bonzy depuis Euesque de Beziers l'achepta.

Des Cordeliers. Lors que le Conuent des Peres Cordeliers de cette ville fut bruslé, leur Bibliotheque y perit, qui estoit en ce temps-là vne des plus grandes & plus accóplies de toute la Fráce; car il y auoit 8000. & 9000. *volumes*, & entre autres plusieurs manuscrits, ainsi que ie l'ay appris du R. P. *de la Haye*, qui asseure qu'il en a veu le Catalogue.

Le docte Euesque de la Vaut, *P. Danes.*
Pierre Danes, se retira sur la fin de
ses iours, dans l'Abbaye de sainct
Germain des Prés, où il auoit vne
tres-celebre Bibliotheque, qui fut
venduë apres sa mort, qui arriua
l'an 1577. le 23. Auril; son corps
est inhumé dans l'Eglise de ladite
Abbaye. Le President de Thou
fait mention de cette Bibliotheque, l'an 1577. *Is vir nostra ætate
(dit-il) in omni scientiarum genere
doctißimus nihil ferè scripsit, sed instructißimam librorum supellectilem
reliquit à se summa diligentia toto longißimæ vitæ nec vnquam otiosæ tempore notatorum, quæ tamen diuendita in vsus pauperum ac dißipata magno rei litterariæ detrimento periit.*

La tres-illustre Eglise de Paris, *L'Eglise de Paris.*
a possede vne splendide Biblio-

theque, de laquelle M. Claude Hemeré Docteur de Sorbonne, a donné la description dans son Academie de Paris, *chap. 6.* de la Bibliotheque de l'Eglise de Paris, & des Escholes Episcopales, & dit que les liures de cette Bibliotheque, estoient destinés aux vsages publiques de l'Eglise, & le soin en estoit donné aux Chanceliers; comme il se void dans vn article du vieil concordat, fait entre le Chapitre & le Chancelier, l'an 1215. qui porte, que: *Libros quidem Parisiensis Ecclesiæ sine cantu Cancellarius corrigere, ligare, & bono in statu tenetur conseruare*, &c. Plusieurs sçauans personnages ont honorez cette Bibliotheque de leurs bien-faits; comme Simon de Chery ; Estienne Archidiacre de

des Bibliotheques. 587

Canterbury, qui auoit vne riche Bibliotheque, qu'il donna pour l'vsage des pauures escholiers, au rapport dudit Hemeré. *Reuertimur ad testamentum* (dit-il) *Stephani Cantuariensis, qui, ne paupertas, optima plærumque ingenia, & excolendis laudabilibus disciplinis aptissima à Musis auocaret, legauit, vt dixi, prætiosam illa ætate Bibliothecam egenis & prudentiæ Cancellarij Parisiensis tradidit ea ratione, cautionéque distribuendam, commedandámque, vt nec sacrilego furto, nec quauis alia iactura distraheretur. Quare Cancellario commendabantur, quæ in vsus indigentium scholasticorum, qui in Parauisi Auditorio nauarent operam supremis disciplinis, prudenti, quod dixi, cautione diuideret.*

M. Errault.

M. Errault Seigneur de Chemans, fils de M. de Chemans, Garde des Seaux de France, laiſſa vne grande Bibliotheque fort bien choiſie; mais apres ſa mort elle fut venduë à diuerſes perſonnes, entre autres à M. Iean Couſin Docteur en Medecine de la faculté de Paris, qui en achepta vne partie.

M. de Fontenay.   Feu M. Oliuier de Fontenay auoit vne bonne Bibliotheque, comme il ſe peut voir dans Gabriel Naudé & Pierre Blanchot, qui en font mention dans leurs ouurages: toutefois apres ſa mort elle fut venduë au Libraire Camuſat.

M. Fumée.   Pareille choſe eſt arriué à la Bibliotheque de M. Adam Fumée, Chancelier de France, qui eſtoit l'vne des ſplendides de ſon temps.

M. Grolier.   Entre les grandes pertes qui

font arriuées aux Muses du debris des fameuses Bibliotheques, ie puis mettre celle de feu M. Iean Grolier, Lyonois, Cheualier, Seigneur, Viconte d'Aguisy, Thresorier de Milan & de France, & General des Finances du Roy, qui estoit en telle estime de son viuant pour la rareté de ses liures, & le grand amas de ses curiositez, qu'elle estoit vne merueille de son siecle, ce que ie confirmeray par deux authoritez; la premiere sera de François de la Croix du Maine, qui en parle en ces termes dãs la Bibliotheque des Autheurs de Fráce. *I'entends qu'il auoit l'vne des plus superbes & magnifiques Bibliotheques de son tẽps, remplie de toute sorte de liures en diuerses sciences.* La secõde authorité est prise de ce grand

President de Thou, qui a fait vn noble Eloge à ce Protecteur des lettres, au Tome 2. de son Histoire, liure 88. année 1565. duquel i'emprunteray ce qui fait à nostre sujet. *Exclusis dein Italia* (dit-il) *Gallis, in regno quæsturam, cùm id munus nondum numero viluisset, summa fide ac diligentia exercuit, & in eodem litterarum amore perseuerauit, insigni numorum antiquorum & optimè notæ librorum supellectile comparata; quos nullis sumptibus parcens, vir munditiæ & elegantiæ in omni vita assuetus, pari elegantia ac munditia ornatos ac dispositos domi tam curiosè asseruabat, vt eius Bibliotheca Asinij Pollionis quæ prima Romæ instituta est, componi potuerit : tantaque copia librorum fuit, vt post tot eius in amicos largitiones, tot varios casus, quibus illi*

des Bibliotheques.

iactati ac malé habiti sunt, instructiores Bibliothecæ, quæ hodie Lutetia & aliis regni locis visuntur, non alio maiore, quam à Grolerianis libris ornamento commendentur. I'ay desia remarqué dans la page 474. comme le cabinet de ce Grolier a esté mis dans celuy du Roy. Cette illustre famille des Groliers subsiste encore à Lyon, laquelle possede des plus honorables charges de la Ville, comme M. Charles Grolier, Procureur General de la maison de Ville de Lyon, & MM. du Soleil, & Commandeur de Ceruieres freres.

Rodolphe Bouteray, parlant des Escholes de Medecine dans son *Poëme* de Paris, asseure que tous les celebres Medecins de l'vniuers, viennent admirer les vrays

Des Escholes de Medecine.

Sectateurs d'Esculàpe, où sa science s'enseigne auec tant de perfection, qu'auiourd'huy elle emporte la palme sur toutes les autres Vniuersitez de l'Europe.

Illi omnes populosæ addunt se ciuibus vrbis,

Non aliter quàm magna solent vt flumina, salsos

Oceani influctus, numerosa per ostia ferij,

Reginæ vndarum, & Thetidi pendere tributum,

Non alibi quæras nec in orbe, quod vrbe nequisti

Inueniffe, negat quóque quod negat integer orbis.

De pareilles loüanges sont honorées ces Escholes, dans vne autre *Description* de Paris, qui a esté faite par Eustache de Knobelsdorf

des Bibliotheques. 593
belsdorf, de Prusse, imprimée en Latin par Chrestien VVechel, l'an 1543. in 8. où il dit :

Pæoniæ auspiciis vernant felicibus artes,

Quīs animis remeat, corporibúsque vigor.

Tractatur medica non vilis in arte Galenus,

Hippocratis doctæ nec reticentur opes.

Quis locus hîc morbis vbi pharmaca tanta parantur,

Et medica quoduis pellitur ante malũ?

Pæona conspicias multos qui vincere possint,

Phœbeáque potens nomen ab arte ferant.

Cette illustre Faculté sera à iamais recommandable pour tant de sçauans hommes qu'elle à produit, & produit continuellement :

P p

& encore pour vne bien exquife & bien rare Bibliotheque, qui auoit eſté erigée dans leurs efcholes, long-temps auparauant l'Imprimerie, ainſi qu'il ſe peut remarquer par le don, que *Iacques des Pars*, premier Medecin du Roy Charles VII. fit de ſa belle Bibliotheque à ces Efcholes. Or cette Bibliotheque a eſté en telle eſtime pour ſes fameux liures de Medecine, que le Roy Louys XI. donna en gage ſa vaiſſelle d'argent, pour auoir vne copie du *Raſis*, comme i'ay remarqué en *la page* 449. Voicy comme Gabriel Naudé parle de cette Bibliotheque, & de ce Raſis en ſon *Panegyrique* de l'Antiquité de l'Efchole de Medecine de Paris, pag. 63. & 64. *Non Bibliotheca multitudine, antiquitate.*

De I. des Pars.

varietate & raritate voluminum olim ita referta, & diligenter conseruata, vt Ludouicus XI. continentis Rasis ex ea copiam sibi fieri, non nisi oppignorata Ioannes de la Drieshe summi Cameræ Computorum Præsidis multa supellectile aurea, & 100. *scutorum fidei-iussione Decani Ioannis Auis relicta, potuerit vnquam obtinere.* Claude Hemeré, en son Academie de Paris *chap.* 6. confirme encore le mesme. *Ludouicum Regem* (dit-il) *eduxisse quidem Bibliotheca Parisiensium Medicorum, totum continens Rasis, sed prius esse quæsitam securitatem traditi voluminis, pignore centum scutorum auri, & duodecim marcarum argenti, anno* 1471. *Eodem anno Reginaldum Regis, postulantem sibi ab cadem facultate mutuo concedi, volumen vnum Auicennæ, passum esse repulsam* petitionis, quia oblatum decem marKarum argenti pignus pretio libri non responderet. Cecy est tiré des Archiues de la Faculté de Medecine, & fait bien voir, comme cette Bibliotheque estoit reputée pour ses bós liures, de laquelle à presét il n'é reste que la memoire dás les Autheurs.

M. des Neuds.   M. Rasse des Neuds Chirurgien à Paris, mais homme sçauant & curieux, qui laissa apres sa mort vne grande Bibliotheque, remplie d'vne infinité de bons liures en diuerses sciences, qui fut vendue par son fils, à Dauid Douceur Libraire de Paris.

M. Ramus.   Iamais homme du siecle passé ne s'est acquis vne plus grande gloire pour la Philosophie & les Mathematiques, que Pierre la Ramée, ou Rameau ou Ramus,

des Bibliotheques. 597
qui a fondé la chaire des Mathematiques de Paris. Tout son som n'estoit que d'enseigner ces sciences, & d'amasser tous les bons liures qui se pouuoyent treuuer pour accomplir sa magnifique Bibliotheque, qui est en grande reputation chez les Autheurs, qui ont escrits sa vie, entre lesquels i'en rapporteray deux ; le premier sera Theophile Bauosius, qui en parle auec cét eloge : *Post eius obitum direpta est à siccariis bonorum omnium, præsertim librorum supellex exquisitissima : perierunt etiam multa Rami egregia doctrinæ monumenta, vt commentarios in libros Aristotelis de Rep. Liber de comitiis Romanorum, & pleraque alia, Ethica Physica, Optica, Geometrica, Musica, Astrologica, quæ certis quibusdam de causis in lucem*

edere noluerat, nonnulla verò quæ paulo ante mortem amico cuidam tradiderat excudenda, breui vt supra admonui excudentur. Le second qui parle amplement de cette Bibliotheque dissipée miserablement par des ignorans, c'est Nicolas Nancel son disciple, qui a aussi escrit sa vie. *Illud superest* (dit-il) *dicere, post extinctum anno ætatis* 57. *Philosophum oratoremque præstantissimum illico in Bibliothecam grassatores ac prædones suam rabiem conuertisse, permultósque de fæce populi permistos fures totam lautem suppellectilem intra horæ vnius momentum expilasse: ita vt seræ, & vectes & repagula auulsa raperentur. Doleo autem Bibliothecam longè pulcherrimam instructissimámque tam nefariè, támque hostiliter direptam, expilatam, depopulatam; in*

des Bibliotheques. 599
qua instruenda & dirigenda quondam
grauiter laboraueram : sed eo magis
doleo, quòd cum Rami libris & moni-
mentis & αὐτομάτοις Mathematicis
per quàm eximiis, simul etiam libri à
me de Gręco in Latinum conuersi, &
mea manu Gręcè de scripta volumina
(in quo me puer studio multum exer-
cueram, characterum Gręcorum for-
mam & elegantiam conatus manu ty-
picis vel excusis haud ab simile refer-
re & exprimere) à nescio quibus pi-
ratis vel plagiariis rapta nobis perierunt. V tinam verò qui ea iniustè deti-
nent, pungente synteresi commoniti, aut
veris Dominis restituant : aut in communes vsus sub nominibus geminorum
authorum emitant : plus laudis ex ista
iustitia reportaturi, quam si arguente
conscientia, coram Deo iusto iudice ac
vindice post mortem de plagio furtóque

P p iiij

tam insigni rationem reddere, vbi necesse erit cogantur. Rami Bibliotheca meo quidem iudicio, circiter mille aureorum coronatorum vallorem, ad summum equabat, libris quidem plurimis Humanioribus & Grecis & Latinis exornata : sed perpaucis Theologicis, Medicinalibus, Legalibus vt ex indice memini, quem ipse pridem confeceram. Quotquot autem in Mathematicis extabant, in omni linguarum genere, hos omnes quantocumque pretio redimebat, studiosissiméque vndique conquisitos asseruabat. De cuius Bibliothece futuris olim heredibus & facultatum reliquarum ita testamento cauerat. Bibliothecam & supellectilem reliquam nomináque omnia lego, semisse altero pauperibus alumnis Prælei Gymnasij. Altero Procuratoribus Executoribúsque mei testamenti Nicolao Bergero-

des Bibliotheques. 601
nio & Antonio Loyſello diſcipulis quondã meis modò Aduocatis inSenatu. Pariſiis 1572. die 26. Auguſti necatus fuit à Sicariis in Collegio Prelco.

M. Iacques de Vuicob Con- *M. Vulcob.*
ſeiller d'Eſtat, & Ambaſſadeur pour le Roy en Allemagne, eſtoit homme d'vn bon eſprit, & amateur des ſciences, auſſi bien que des liures : le teſmoignage en eſtoit euident pour auoir dreſsé vne belle Bibliotheque de liures bien choiſis : mais apres ſa mort elle fut venduë à Dauid Douceur Libraire de Paris ; ce qui eſt cauſe que pluſieurs de ces liures ſe voyent en diuerſes Bibliotheques de cette Ville. Or toutes ces Bibliotheques ſpecifiées dans ce Chapitre ont eſté miſes dans les plus belles de cette Ville.

Chapitre LXXXV.

Des Lieux circonuoisins de Paris.

Des Minimes de Challiot.

DAns le Conuent des bons hommes ou Peres Minimes de Challiot, il y a vne Bibliotheque assez considerable.

M. de Sourdys à ioin.

M. Charles Descoubleau, Marquis de Sourdis & d'Alluye, Chevalier des Ordres du Roy, Gouuerneur du Pays Orleanois, Chartrain, Blesois, Dunois & Vendosmois, a si bien ioint les exercices de Mars & d'Apollon, qu'il en reçoit vne grande gloire dans l'Europe : car toute la France & les Prouinces estrangeres ont admirez sa conduite & son courage : & à present cette grande cognoissance qu'il a dans les bonnes lettres, le fait estimer pour l'vn des sçauans Seigneurs de la France : nous en auons des tesmoignages assez suffisans par la curieuse & loüable recherche qu'il fait de tous les meilleurs liures en toutes les sciences, pour embellir cette noble Bibliotheque, qu'il a dressé dans son Chasteau de Ioüy à quatre lieuës de Paris, laquelle il ne cesse d'augmenter tous les iours.

Personne n'ignore l'estime en laquelle est la Royalle Abbaye de S. Denys en France ; non seulement pour seruir de Mauzolez aux fils aisnez de l'Eglise nos Roys tres-Chrestiens, & pour posseder vn riche thresor : mais encore pour vn autre thresor, qui y auoit esté erigé pour les Muses, sçauoir vne Bibliotheque, qui

De S. Denys.

estoit la plus remplie & mieux fournie de rares liures, que pas vn autre de la France : laquelle toutefois n'a pas eschappé de la furie des Heretiques durant les premiers troubles, qui arriuerent dâs ce Royaume pour le fait de la Religion, ainsi que le remarque l'Autheur *des Antiquitez* de Paris, dans l'edition de 1640. in fol.

M. le Visc. de Melun.
Prez de Melun se void le Chafteau de la Borde, qui appartient à M. le Viscomte de Melun, où il possede vne assez bonne Bibliotheque.

M. de Beauuais.
M. Augustin Potier Euesque & Comte de Beauuais, iouyt d'vne belle Bibliotheque garnie de bons liures.

CHAPITRE LXXXVI.

D'Anjou.

LE Conuent des Peres Car- *Des Carmes.*
mes de la ville d'Angers, a
esté fondé par la pieuse liberalité
de René Roy de Sicile & Duc
d'Anjou, dans lequel il y a vne
tres-bonne Bibliotheque, de laquelle
fait mention le P. Leon de
sainct Iean, en la description de la
Prouince de Touraine des Peres
Carmes Reformez en celle du
Conuent d'Angers. *Nec minori
oblectamento* (dit-il) *Bibliotheca diues
& perampla, cuiusuis disciplinæ voluminibus
instructa, datur conspici in
ædium parte nobiliori.*

 M. Claude Menard Conseil- *De M. Menard.*
ler du Roy & Lieutenant en la

Preuosté d'Angers, est digne de recommandation tant pour les liures qu'il a donné au public, particulierement pour *l'histoire d'Anjou* qu'il fait imprimer à present; que pour vne celebre Bibliotheque, qu'il a fait auec de grands soings.

De Saumur. Dans la ville de Saumur il y a eu autrefois vne belle Bibliotheque, qui auoit été dressée par Philippes du Plessis Mornay, le Coriphé des Caluinistes.

Des Iesuites de la Flesche. La Bibliotheque des Peres de la Compagnie de IESVS de la Flesche, est garnie de tres-bons liures en toutes les sciences.

Des Recolets. Les Peres Recolets de la Baumette proche d'Angers, ont vne Bibliotheque assez bonne & curieuse.

Chapitre LXXXVII.

D'Auignon & du Comté de Vezim.

LE Pape Iean XXII. nommé auparauãt Iacques Deufa ou Offa natif de Cahors estoit tres-celebre Docteur en Theologie de l'Vniuersité de Paris, comme le tesmoignent les ouurages qu'il a composé sur la Theologie, & de plus il fut grand amateur de liures, veu qu'il auoit vne insigne Bibliotheque, qu'il legua aux Religieux de l'Ordre de S. Dominique de la ville d'Auignon, de laquelle il se void encore quelques anciens MSS. de cette Bibliotheque, selon les memoires que m'a enuoyé *M. Henry Suares* fils Docteur és Droicts, ieune homme de

Des Dominicains.

Iean XXII.

grande lecture & probité, duquel i'aduoüe auoir receu quantité de memoires pour ce trauail, afin que la posterité luy soit redeuable de ses estudes.

De l'Vniuerfité. L'Vniuersité d'Auignon eust autrefois la Bibliotheque d'Amedé Cardinal de Saluces, qu'il leur donna par testamét pour le commun vsage des Docteurs de cette *Amedé Cardinal de Saluces.* Vniuersité, comme il appert par le testament du mesme Cardinal, qui est conserué par ledit Henry Suares: laquelle estoit conseruée dans le College de S. Martial de l'Ordre de Cluny, mais à present il ne reste que la memoire de cette Bibliotheque, qui a esté dissipée à la reserue d'vn corps Ciuil, duquel autrefois on a refusé *sept cent ducats.*

Pierre

des Bibliotheques. 609

Pierre Cardinal Corsin Florentin fut homme fort affectionné aux lettres, car il auoit fait vn grand amas de liures pour orner vne magnifique Bibliotheque qu'il auoit en cette Ville : *in qua (dit-Suares) ingens librorum copia, quam multis ex locis ingentibúsque sumptibus conquisiuerat ; verba sunt ipsius testamenti, hodie non volumen modo, sed vix etiam voluminis folium superest.* Or il legua cette Bibliotheque aux Peres Augustins.

L'an 1466. Iulian de Ruuere, Prestre Cardinal du tiltre de S. Pierre aux Liens, Legat d'Auignon, voulut laisser ce temoignage à la posterité de l'amour qu'il auoit pour les bonnes lettres, par l'erection non seulement qu'il fit d'vn College nommé de Ruuere,

Augustin.

P. Corsin Cardinal.

Du Cardinal Ruuere.

Qq

mais auſſi d'vne tres-celebre Bibliotheque au Palais Apoſtolique, laquelle depuis fut tranſportée dans le Palais de Poiƈtiers; ainſi qu'il appert par les Tables de la fundation de ce College, qui ſont conſeruées par ledit Suares, lequel aſſeure qu'à preſent il ne reſte aucun veſtige d'icelle, que par le lieu ou elle eſtoit autrefois & par les Tables.

Des Cordeliers. La Bibliotheque des Peres Cordeliers de l'Obſeruance, a eſté autrefois conſiderable, ſuiuant la remarque qu'en fait François de Gonzaque, Miniſtre General de cét Ordre, en ſon Hiſtoire Seraphique: mais ie ne ſçay pas par quel malheur cette Bibliotheque eſt deperie, qu'à preſent il ne ſi void pas 1500. volumes.

des Bibliotheques.

Ie puis dire le mesme de celle *Des Carmes.* des Peres Carmes, laquelle est bien descheuë de sa splendeur qu'elle auoit il y auoit deux cens ans.

La Bibliotheque la plus splen- *Des Celestins.* dide & la plus entiere de cette ville, est celle des Peres Celestins, qui outre vn grand nombre de liures imprimez, possede encore diuers anciens Manuscrits, qui prouiennent de la bonne Bibliotheque de ce venerable & celebre Iean *I. Gerson.* Gerson, Docteur de Nauarre & Chancelier de l'Vniuersité de Paris, qui leur donna ses liures pour la pieuse affection qu'il auoit aux Religieux de cette maison, à cause d'vn frere qu'il auoit de cét ordre.

Les Peres Iesuites ont faits vne *Des Iesuites.* fort belle Bibliotheque, en toute forte de bons liures, mesme il y a quelques anciens manuscrits.

De Petrarque.

Ce grand Genie de la Poësie Italienne François Petraque, auoit vne insigne Bibliotheque à Vaut clause au diocese de Cauallion, de laquelle l'Euesque Tomasin parle dans son *Petrarque renaissant*. Ie ne sçay si c'est la mesme qu'il a donné au Senat de Venise, comme ie l'ay remarqué dans la page 133.

De M. l'Euesque de Vaison.

Les doctes & curieux ouurages de M. Ioseph Marie Suares, iadis Preuost de l'Eglise d'Auignon, puis Domestique & Bibliothequaire de M. François Cardinal Barberin, & à present Euesque de Vaison, luy ont acquis vne memoire eternelle parmy les sçauans; aussi bien que la curieuse &

des Bibliotheques. 613

bonne Bibliotheque qu'il a fait auec de grands foings, où font conferuez plufieurs rares manufcrits, que ce Seigneur donnera, Dieu aydant, au public. Ie ferois ingrat enuers ce tres-fçauant Prelat, fi ie ne tefmoignois au public, le deffein qu'il a eu de trauailler fur le fujet des Bibliotheques; mais les grandes occupations de fa charge & de fes eftudes plus ferieufes, luy font retarder cét ouurage, que l'on ne peut efperer qu'auec vne admirable perfectió, quoy que par vne particuliere inclination qu'il à enuers moy, il aye voulu volontairement me donner la communication de fes memoires, comme il me le tefmoigne par vne de fes lettres, qu'il m'efcrit de Vaifon le ij. iour d'Auril 1644. *I'ay eu* (dit-il) *autrefois semblable dessein, & fait beaucoup de remarques sur diuerses Bibliotheques; si i'ay le loisir ie les ramasseray, & vous les addresseray, M. Henry Suares mon cousin, en cas que ie ne puisse le faire, à la premiere entreueue vous seruira.*

CHAPITRE LXXXVIII.

D'Auuergne.

De S. Allire de Clermont.

L'Abbaye de S. Allire, de l'Ordre de S. Benoist, au fauxbourg de la Ville de Clermont est en reputation pour son antiquité, & pour vne tres-bonne Bibliotheque qui si conserue, dans laquelle il y à diuers anciens manuscrits.

Des Dominicain.

La Bibliotheque des Peres Do-

des Bibliotheques. 615

minicains est grande & bien garnie de bons liures, entre lesquels sont quelques manuscrits.

Quant à la Bibliotheque des Peres Carmes Deschauffez, elle est bien considerable pour ses bons liures en diuerses sciences, qui y ont esté mis par les soings du Pere Seraphin de S. François, iadis Confesseur de M. Seguier Chancelier de France, qui est mort Prieur de ce Conuent ces années passées. *Des Carmes Deschauffez.*

Feu le docte Iean Sauaron President de Clermont, auoit vne Bibliotheque assez considerable pour les bons liures, & diuers manuscrits; laquelle est encore conseruée par ses heritiers. *De Sauaron.*

Dans la ville de Billon, est vn College des Peres Iesuites, fondé *Des Iesuites de Billon.*

Qq iiij

par G. du Prat Euefque de Clermont, où autrefois eſtoit conſerué, vne celebre Bibliotheque, qui a eſté miſerablemét bruſlée, dans laquelle cét Euefque auoit legué la moitié de la ſienne.

Des Minimes de Beauregard. Le meſme Guillaume du Prat Euefque de Clermont a eſté le fondateur du Conuent des Peres Minimes de Beauregard, où il a legué l'autre partie de ſa Bibliotheque, qui eſtoit tres-belle, & tres-grande.

Chapitre LXXXIX.

De Bearne.

Des Roys de Nauarre. LA Ville de Pau eſt la principale de cette Prouince, où le Roy Louys XIII. a reſtablis la Religion Catholique au grand contentement de toute l'Eglise Catholique, & par sa Royalle liberalité y a fait eriger vn Conuent de Capucins, ausquels il a concedé la tres-magnifique Bibliotheque des Roys de Nauarre ses Predecesseurs, qui sert d'vn rare ornement à ce Conuent.

Le Chapitre de l'Eglise Cathe- *De l'Eglise* drale de Lascar, merite vne gloire *de Lascar.* particuliere pour le glorieux dessein qu'elle a formé & decreté, pour l'establissement d'vne tresdigne & tres-accomplie Bibliotheque destinée pour son vsage, Ce qui seruira d'emulation à toutes les autres Eglises Cathedrales de ce Royaume, pour restablir ces anciennes qu'elles ont possedées; desquelles à present il n'en reste à la posterité que le nom, au grand mespris des Muses. Mais toutefois l'exemple de celle-cy sera vtile à toutes les autres, puis que par vn solemnel decret fait & passé dans leur Chapitre l'an 1 6 3 7. 3. iour d'Aoust, il est porté que l'on erigera vne Bibliotheque pour le Chapitre, dont ie rapporteray le decret, qui est dans leurs Statuts, ch. 14. intitulé, *De Bibliotheca Capituli*, que Iean de Bordenaue Chanoine de l'Eglise de Lascar a inseré à la fin de son Liure de l'*Estat des Eglises Cathedrales & Collegiales*, imprimé à Paris chez la vefue Mathurin du Puis 1 6 4 3. in folio. pag. 952. & 953. *Cùm ex sacris Scripturis* (dit-il) *voluminibúsque Sanctorum, & aliis Ecclesiasticis Codicibus in tanta librorum corruptela, his præsertim temporibus per hæreticos in-*

des Bibliotheques. 619

troducta, plurimum adiumenti rebus publicis afferatur, & ad Cathólicæ doctrinæ veritatem tuendam, & ad coarguendam aduersariorum vitiosè illa deprauantium temeritatem; vel etiam ad animos nostros vniuersæ disciplinæ studio informandos: cúmque identidem pauper sit & tenuis libraria singulorum ob modicas cuiúsque priuati facultates; & ne posthac in recuperandis libris tanto solicitudine & animi anxietate elaboremus: peropportunè decretum est nobis, communem Bibliothecam conficere librorum omnium copia refertißimam, quæ sit tanquam armamentarium sodalitatis huius spiritualiter militantis, vt Codices illi, scripta & pandectæ singulis Canonicis pateant, non secus ac si peculiares essent. Volumus itáque statuimus & ordinamus, quòd Capituli Bibliotheca in superna aula, quæ extat supra capellam seu sacellum diui Augustini, constituatur, per ordinem scamnorum quæ sint transuersa, omniáque stragulis operta atque inter se ita disposita, vt ambitus transitúsque liber vndequaque sit. Aut ad latus dictæ aulæ armaria aliquot extruantur, eaque sitibus distincta, in quibus Codices, libri, & volumina cuiusuis generis, quæcúmque extant, ad omnes singulos Canonicos pertinentia, post cuiúsque obitum (nisi de his aliter testamento, vel vltima voluntate sua, ex parte siue in totum disposuerint) tanquam donatione ex nunc facta, concessa, relicta, eique iam addicta & virtute præsentis statuti obfirmata, reponantur, non aceruatim, sed ordine suo, secundum cuiusque scientiæ facultatẽ.

Index prætereà fiat, in quo per disciplinarum genera, aut pro alphebi ra-

des Bibliotheques. 621

tione, volumina singula notentur. Isque index certo loco in perpetuum asseruetur; notatis deinceps aliis libris, quicumque in posterum eidem Bibliothecę quáuis modo accesserint.

Tomi ac volumina quæ pro vetustate, carióue; situ´ve ob sorde scunt, librario opere polliantur; dissoluta & male compacta, conglutinentur : nuda seu operculo destituta, asseribus corióve tegantur: vsu, alióve modo consumpta, reconcinnentur, & ad perpetuitatem opere recenti nossíque integumentis restaurentur.

Habeántque singuli Canonici singulas claues : & cùm clauis cuique tractetur, præstet iuramentum specialiter & expresse, ad quatuor sancta Dei Euangelia corporaliter tacta, in sessione Capituli, coram omnibus Canonicis residentibus; quòd dictos libros fideliter accuratè, & diligenter custodiet, neque extra Bibliothecam defert, neque auferri permittet, aut aliquid euellet seu euellendum curabit, ne minimum quidem folium, ex quo liber deterior fiat: & si hoc commissum ab aliquo sciuerit; id Capitulo subinde reuelabit. Si quis verò in præfatis defecerit, sit furti seu verius sacrilegij notatus, teneaturque ad restitutionem ablatorum Dei Ecclesiæ dicatorum, & iura disponunt.

Hoc tamen edicto nulli Canonicorum inhibemus, quin possit exempla quædam tabularum ex apographo describere: imo etiam si libro aliquo ad legendum priuatim indigeat, quominus, si Capitulo visum fuerit, planè valeat, de eiusdem consensu, illum ad tempus recipere; dùm in eo nec scribat quidquam, nec notam vllam inprimat, data cautione de restituendo.

des Bibliotheques. 623

Capitulum autem constituat Canonicum aliquem vsu peritum, literarum studiosum, instruendæque Bibliothecæ cupidum, qui illius curæ diligenter præsit : & tanquam Bibliothecarius dictam librariam interdum ex officio visitet, inspiciat ac recognoscat : sique per eum, & per cæteros fratres, ratio aliqua miri potest, quà in Bibliotheca librorum Ecclesiasticorum ac reliquorum omnium probatorum copia augeatur ; id sollicitè curetur, vt eiusmodi scriptorum apparatu, publico Canonicali totiúsque diœcesis commodo atque vsui consultum sit.

L'on voit donc par ce decret combien ces Doctes & pieux Ecclesiastiques iugent l'erection de cette Bibliotheque vtile pour l'accroissement des Muses : & quels soings ils prennent non seule ment à son establissement; mais encore pour sa conseruation & augmentation, pour laquelle ils concourent tous auec vn grand zele.

CHAPITRE LXXXX.

Du Berry.

De M. le Prince de Condé.

BOurges est la ville capitale de ce Duché, qui est non seulement ornée d'vn ancien Archeuesché, & d'vne illustre Vniuersité: mais aussi d'vn riche Parnasse des Muses ou bien d'vne tres-opuléte Bibliotheque, que Monseigneur Henry de Bourbon Prince de Condé & Gouuerneur des Prouinces de Bourgongne, Bresse & Berry, a fait auec de grands soings soins & somptueuse despente; car la parfaite cognoissance qu'il a de toutes les sciences & des liures rares & curieux, le font estimer pour vn oracle des Muses. Chose admirable en cette Altesse, que nonobstant les grandes affaires qu'il a pour l'Estat, il ne pert aucun iour sans s'addonner a l'estude, où il treuue des diuertissemens dignes d'vn grand Prince; ce qui luy acquiert vne gloire immortelle par toute l'Europe; tant pour surpasser en sciences tous les autres Princes, que pour le grand zele qu'il a à les faire fleurir.

La Bibliotheque de l'Abbaye de S. Sulpice, de l'Ordre de S. Benoist au faux-bourg de Bourges, est en consideration pour la bonté de ses liures.

De S. Sulpice.

De Cha-zautt-Be-nuift.

L'Abbaye de Chazaut-Benoift du mefme Ordre de S. Benoift, eft tres-fameufe, laquelle a efté fondée dans ce diocefe, où il y a vne fort celebre Bibliotheque pour l'vfage des Religieux.

CHAPITRE LXXXXI.

Du Duché & Comté de Bourgongne.

De S. Beni-gne.

LA Ville de Dijon eft la Capitale du Duché, laquelle a receu la lumiere de la foy Euangelique par le glorieux martyr S. Benigne, à l'honneur duquel on a erigé vne infigne Abbaye, où eft conferué vne ancienne & bonne Bibliotheque pour les manufcrits, defquels *M. Paul du May*, Confeiller au Parlement a donné au public le Catalogue fous ce ti-

des Bibliotheques. 627

tre. *Bibliotheca Ianiniana ſincti enigni Diuionenſis : Ope & induſtria P. D. Diuione eid. Sept.* CIƆ. IƆ CXXI. *in* 4. les deux lettres P. D. ſignifient le nom de ce docte Conſeiller, ainſi que ie le remarque dans les notes, qu'il a donné ſur l'Epiſtre du Pape Innocét III. où il dit auoir imprimé ce Catalogue.

Dans le Conuent des Peres Carmes il y a vne grande & magnifique Bibliotheque composée de cinq à ſix mille volumes d'excellens liures, qui y ont eſté mis par le tres-celebre *Laurent Bureau* Religieux de ce Monaſtere, Docteur de Paris, Prouincial de la Prouince de Narbone, Confeſſeur des Roys Charles VIII. Louys XII. & Anne de

Des Carmes.

L. Bureau.

Rr ij

Bretagne femme de ce dernier Roy, puis Euesque de Sisteró, qui decedaà Blois l'á 1540. le 5. Iuillet,

D. Buffet. & particulierement *Didier Buffet*, Docteur de Paris & Vicaire General de son Ordre en France, qui auoit vne grande affection pour les bons liures, desquels il a remply cette Bibliotheque, où se voyent ses armes sur chaques liures. Quant à la structure moderne de cette Bibliotheque, l'honneur en

F. Reneuey. est deu au P. *François Reneuey*, aussi Docteur de Paris & Prieur de ce Conuent.

M. Boyer. M. N. Boyer Conseiller au Parlement de Dijon, fait vne grande despence à dresser la plus somptueuse Bibliotheque du Duché de Bourgongne, qu'il a commencé par l'achapt de tous les liures de

des Bibliotheques. 629

Theologie de la Bibliotheque de ce grand & docte Euesque de Châlon *Pontus de Thyard*, qui en auoit fait vne des plus belle de son temps, qui toutefois a esté partagée entre MM. de Bissy & de Bragny ses neueus: le premier a eu les liures de Theologie, qui prouenoyent de la Bibliotheque de *Cyrus de Thyard*, neueu aussi de Pontus & son successeur en l'Euesché, apres la mort duquel M. de Bissy estant aussi decedé ces liures furent portez à Bellegarde à cause des guerres du Comté de Bourgongne, où ils furent vendus audit sieur Boyer. Quant aux autres liures de l'Histoire, & des Humanitez qu'auoit M. Louys de Thyard Seigneur de Bragny, ils furent tous bruslez l'an 1636. auec

Pontus de Thyard.

MM. de Bissy & Bragny.

Rr iij

sa maison de Bragny par l'armée du Duc de Lorraine, lors qu'il prit la Ville de Verdun sur Sone, dequoy il a esté grand dommage; car i'y ay veu de tres-excellens liures. Or ce curieux Conseiller recherche auec de grands soings tous les meilleurs liures qu'il peut trouuer pour enrichir sa Bibliotheque.

M. de Cheuanes. M.N. de Cheuanes, natif d'Autun, Aduocat en Parlement, est homme docte & curieux des bons liures, desquels il a vne grande cognoissance; ce qui a fait que sa Bibliotheque est digne de consideration.

De Cisteaux Cette grande & illustre Abbaye de Cisteaux a esté fondée à quatre lieues de Dijō au diocese de Châlon par les Ducs de Bourgongne, laquelle possede encore à present vne splendide Bibliotheque, à laquelle est joincte vne chambre, qui est toute garnie & remplie de tres-bons & anciens Manuscrits, particulierement des Peres de l'Eglise, qui y ont esté mis par le labeur des Religieux de cette Abbaye, qui autrefois s'appliquoient à certaines heures de la iournée, à descrire les bons liures pour leurs vsages, dans des chambres particulieres, qui se voyent encore dás vn Cloistre de cette Abbaye auparauant l'impression : car anciennemét s'estoit l'exercice des Moynes que d'escrire les liures aux heures, qui leur restoyent apres le seruice diuin ; en quoy la posterité leur est beaucoup redeuable, pource que leurs manuscrits à present seruent d'vn exquis ornement à toutes les excellentes Bibliotheques.

M. Virey. La Ville de Châlon, lieu de ma naissance, a esté autrefois appellée *Orbendale*, pource que ses murailles estoyent ornez de trois bandes d'orées, laquelle a seruy de magasin à l'Empereur Iules Cesar le conquerant des Gaules, & depuis a esté le siege des Roys de Bourgongne, & l'vne des premieres Villes de ce Royaume, qui aye receu la foy Chrestienne par le glorieux martyr S. Marcel Lyonnois. Or nonnobstant que cette Ville soit fort recommandable chez les historiens pour ces qualitez & pour les sepulchres de deux Roys; le premier est de S. Gontrant Roy de Bourgongne, qui est enterré

des Bibliotheques. 633

dans le Prieuré de S. Marcel, où iadis mourut le Moyne *Pierre Abailard*: le second est de Iean Infant de Portugal, qui se fit Religieux de l'Ordre de S. François passant par cette Ville, lequel depuis fut declaré Roy : mais son humilité luy fit refuser cette dignité pour suiure le Roy des Roïs IESVS-CHRIST : elle n'est toutefois pas encore des moindres pour le sujet que nous traictons; veu qu'il se void vne bien accomplie Bibliotheque, qu'a erigé feu M. Claude Enoch Virey premier Secretaire de Monseigneur le Prince de Condé, puis Conseiller, Secretaire & Notaire de la maison, & Couronne de France, qui estoit homme d'vne grande doctrine, & qui cognoissoit tres-bien les bons liures, desquels il l'a garnie, & l'a laissé apres sa mort qui arriua l'an 1636. le 25. Iuillet, à M. Iean Christophle Virey son fils Conseiller du Roy & Maistre des Comptes de la Prouince de Bourgógne & Bresse, qui achepte tous les iours des liures pour l'augmenter; de plus cette Bibliotheque est encore remarquable pour la belle relieure de ses liures, qui sont à plus de 4000. volumes.

De Cluny. Le Duché de Bourgongne se peut váter d'auoir deux Abbayes chefs d'Ordre, celle de Cisteaux & l'autre de Cluny, qui a donné tant de SS. personnages en l'Eglise de Dieu, & tant de doctes Religieux, qui ont honorez les Muses, & qui auoyent tous trauaillez à faire vne splendide Bibliotheque,

des Bibliotheques. 635

qui fut ruinée par les Caluinistes l'an 1562. comme le remarque Michel Gaspard Lundorp en la continuation de l'histoire de Iean Sleidan: *Interea Poncenatus* (dit-il) *Cluniacum nobilissimum toto orbe Cænobium impetu capit, in cuius direptione longè copiosissima & omni librorum manuscriptorum suppellectile Bibliotheca magno studiosorum omnium dolore Reipublicæ litterariæ. Quod vix vnquam sarciri poterit detrimento militari licentia incendio periit.*

Les Peres Carmes de Semur en l'Auxois, ont vne considerable Bibliotheque, qui a plus de 4000. volumes & quelques CXX. Manuscrits, qui y ont esté mis par plusieurs Religieux de ce Conuent, qui se peut vanter d'estre l'vn des beaux Conuents de son

Des Carmes de Semur.

Ordre en France. Le R. P. Renaut de Vaulx Docteur de Paris, & Prouincial de la Prouince de Narbonne, a beaucoup contribué pour l'augmentation de cette Bibliotheque.

Des Minimes de Tonnerre. Le sumptueux Conuent des Peres Minimes de Tonnere a esté fondé l'an 1611. par M. Charles Henry de Clermont Comté de Tonnere, &c. Cheualier des Ordres de sa Majesté, lequel outre ce bien-fait, a donné à ces Peres la Bibliotheque qu'il auoit eu de ses ancestres, selon la remarque qu'en fait le P. François de la Noüe en sa Chronique des Minimes, où parlant de ce Monastere, il dit. *Optimorum librorum, quos à maioribus D. Comes accepit, copiam nostris liberaliter fecit, vt dum iis vtuntur ad populos vtilitas promanet, quos annuis per Aduentum & Quadragesimam concionibus solent instituere.*

Besançon, est Ville Imperiale dans le Comté de Bourgongne, où est conserué vne noble Bibliotheque dans l'Hostel de Granuelle, qui a esté dressée par ce grand Cardinal Antoine Perrenot de Granuelle, Fondateur de l'Vniuersité de cette Ville, & Archeuesque, qui fut vn autre Mæcenas de son temps enuers les hommes d'estude, ainsi qu'il se peut voir par ceux de cette condition qu'il a aduancé dans les charges & honneurs. La charge de cette Bibliotheque a esté exercée par Suffridus Petrus, qui a donné plusieurs bons liures au public. *Du Cardinal de Granuelle.*

Des Iesui-tes. Dans le College des Peres Iesuites de Besançon, il y a vne bonne Bibliotheque, composée de liures en toutes les Facultez.

Des Bened. de Dole. La Ville de Dole, est honorée d'vn Parlement & d'vne Vniuersité; où ont enseignez diuers sçauans personnages, entre autres Iuste Lipse: ce qui n'a pas esté vne moindre gloire à cette ville, qu'vne magnifique Bibliotheque publique, qui auoit esté erigée dās le College de S. Hierosme des Religieux de l'Ordre de Cluny, où il y auoit vne grande quantité de Manuscrits qui luy rendoyent vn merueilleux ornement.

De l'Abbaye de Luxeuil. La Bibliotheque de l'Abbaye de Luxeul a esté autrefois celebre, mais à present elle est entierement dissipée.

versé dans les sçiences diuines &
humaines, comme aussi dans
les langues Hebraïques, Grecques & Latines;les ouurages qu'il
a donné au public,en sont des euidents tesmoignages, lesquels luy
acquerét vne grande reputation,
aussi bien qu'vne celebre Bibliotheque qu'il a fait,par vne grande
recherche de bons liures,dont elle
est composée.

M. Angelic Grimaldi, Cardi-
nalEuesque d'Albane,frere du Pape Vrbain V. voulant contribuer à
l'aduancemét des lettres, fonda le
College de S.Ruf,dans la Ville de
Montpellier, auquel il adiousta
pour ornement vne magnifique
Bibliotheque,pour l'vsage de ceux
de ce College, comme il appert
par son testament, fait l'an 1380.

Tt ij

bello aliisque temporum iniuriis deperditorum minima pars existimari debet. Spes tamen est fore vt quemadmodum disciplina Cœnobitica, ita etiam supellex Libraria à nobilißimo ac Reuerendo admodum Domino Philippo Chiffletio, Domus illius hodierno Antistite dignißimo, pristino splendori restituatur. Interim qualescumque ij sunt, qui etiammum supersint Libri Manu exarati, eorum indicem ad nos à piis Cœnobitis transmissum, luci damus.

Chapitre LXXXXII.

De Bretagne.

Rennes. M. de Cornuiller.

M. Pierre de Cornuiller, Conseiller au Parlement de Rennes, fut fait par ses merites Euesque de Treguier, puis de Rennes,

Rennes, lequel auoit erigé vne belle Bibliotheque, qui est demeurée à ses heritiers.

Le Conuent des Peres Carmes de Rennes a esté fondé l'an 1447. dans lequel se void vne ample & bonne Bibliotheque composée de bons liures, qui y ont esté mis par les Peres de ce Monastere. *Des Carmes.*

La Bibliotheque des Peres Dominicains est reputée pour tres-considerable. *Des Dominicains.*

M. Biré Autheur de quelques liures a dressé vne notable Bibliotheque, par la recherche qu'il a fait des bons liures. *M. Bire.*

Ie treuue que dans la ville de Nantes les Peres de l'Oratoire ont esté curieux a faire vne grande & excellente Bibliotheque, *Des PP. de l'Oratoire.*

qui sert d'vn singulier ornement à leur maison.

De M. d'Asserac. M. Iean de Rieux, Marquis d'Asserac, Comte de Largouel, Chef du Nom & des armes de la Maison de Rieux, issu des Ducs de Bretagne, est bien versé dans les sciences, qu'il cultiue iournellement par le moyen des bons liures, desquels il a remply son exquise Bibliotheque, pour l'augmentation de laquelle il trauaille auec vn grand soin.

CHAPITRE LXXXXIII.

De Champagne.

Rheims. De l'Eglise Cathedrale. LA tres-illustre Eglise de Rheims, a eu autrefois pour Doyen Guillaume Philastre Cardinal, qui legua à cette Eglise sa

des Bibliotheques. 643

Bibliotheque, comme le remarque Pierre Frizō en sa *Gallia Purpurata,* où il dit : *Philasterio Decano Rhemis præclara in Metropolitanæ Ecclesiæ Canonicorum vsum instructa est Bibliotheca, cui maximam Codicum copiam est largitus.* Le Cardinal de Lorraine imita celuy-cy, par le legs qu'il fit à cette Eglise de sa Bibliotheque, qui depuis a esté dissipée

M. Leonor D'estampes de Valancey, frere du Cardinal de Valancey, a esté tousiours fort affectionné aux bonnes lettres ; car n'estant encore qu'Abbé de Bourgueil en Anjou, il auoit des-ia doné le commencement à cette superbe & admirable Bibliotheque, qu'il perfectionne auec tant de soins, comme le remarque Clau-

Du Cardinal de Lorraine.

De M. l'Archeuesque etc.

S s ij

de Robert, lors qu'il parle de cette Abbaye en sa *Gaule Chrestienne*; mais depuis ce Seigneur a esté fait Euesque de Chartres, & en fin Archeuesque de Rheims, où il a porté ce thresor des Muses, que l'on tient estre le plus accomply de la France.

De l'Abbaye d'Igny. Dans le Diocese de Rheims, est l'Abbaye de nostre Dame d'Igny, qui auoit vne assez notable Bibliotheque.

De Langres. L'Eglise de Langres à vne Bibliotheque, où il y a quelques anciens Manuscrits, desquels on fait estime.

De Chaalons. Feu M. Henry Clausse, Euesque de Chaalons en Champagne, auoit erigé vne considerable Bibliotheque, estant homme d'vne grande doctrine.

Chapitre LXXXXIV.

Du Dauphiné.

Vienne, est la Ville Metropolitaine de cette Prouince, où Hierosme de Villars Archeuesque, a fondé vn magnifique College pour les Peres Iesuites, qui y ont vne assez bonne Bibliotheque.

Vienne. Des Iesuites.

M. Pierre Scarron Euesque de Grenoble, a fait vne Bibliotheque, qui est en estime pour ses bons liures.

M. l'Euesque de Grenoble.

Ceux qui ont la cognoissance de M. Denys de Saluaing de Boissieu Cheualier, Conseiller du Roy en ses Conseils d'Estat & Priué, & premier President en la Cham-

M. de Boissieu.

Ss iij

bre des Comptes de Dauphiné, aduoüent ingenuëment que ce Seigneur est doüé des plus rares qualitez d'esprit de ce siecle : si l'on considere sa memoire, il ne s'en treuuera vne plus fertile : si son esprit, la rareté en donne de l'enuie : & si sa doctrine, & eloquence, il n'en n'a pas seulement rauy les François; mais mesme ces delicats Romains, lors qu'il estoit Orateur pour nostre Roy tres-Chrestien Louys XIII. vers le Pape Vrbain VIII. La langue Grecque luy est aussi commune que sa maternelle, aussi se peut-il glorifier, qu'il n'y a point de Bibliotheque en France, qui conferue plus de liures Grecs imprimez & Manuscrits que la sienne, qui a esté commencée par M. Charles de Saluaing de Boiffieu son Pere.

La famille de MM. de S. André, *De M. de S. André.*
est illustre dans la Prouince du
Dauphiné, de laquelle est issu M.
le President de S. André, qui a fait
vne Bibliotheque, garnie de bons
liures.

La Bibliotheque de M. du Po- *De M. du Ponat.*
nat, Conseiller au Parlement de
Grenoble, est estimée pour la
quantité de ses liures, laquelle il
augmente tous les iours.

Feu M. Claude d'Expilly, Ad- *M. d'Expilly.*
uocat General au Parlement du
Dauphiné, puis President, estoit
homme sçauant, comme le tesmoignent ses œuures; & curieux
en la recherche des bons liures,
desquels il auoit fait sa Bibliotheque, qui est à present cõseruée par
M. la Presidente de Brion sa fille.

Ss iiij

M. du Vi-
nier.
  Entre ceux qui sont curieux à Grenoble pour eriger des Bibliotheques, M. du Viuier, Vibally du Graisiuodan en Dauphiné en est l'vn ; car il fait vn ramas de bons liures pour garnir la sienne.

M. Lai-
gneau.
  M. Philippes Laigneau, n'espargne aucuns soings à embellir sa bonne Bibliotheque des liures les plus rares & curieux qui se peuuent treuuer, le nombre d'iceux excedant quatre mille volumes.

De la grã-
de Char-
treuse.
  Cette vaste solitude de la grande Chartreuse, n'est pas despourueuë d'vne excellente Bibliotheque, pour la consolation de ces Anges terrestres.

M. Fromat
  La Bibliotheque de M. Fromant, Professeur en Droit en l'Vniuersité de Valance, est reputée pour tres-celebre, à cause de la

multitude de ses liures en la Iuris-
prudence.

Auparauant les troubles de *De S. An-toine.* France pour la religion de Caluin, il y auoit vne riche Bibliotheque dans l'Abbaye de S. Antoine chef de son Ordre; mais elle fut dissipée au grand regret de ces Religieux, qui tâchent peu à peu de la restablir.

Chapitre LXXXXV.

De Guienne.

M. de Pontac President au *Bourdeaux.* Mortier du Parlement de *M. de Pontac.* Bourdeaux, neueu du docte Arnaud de Pontac Euesque de Bazas, a herité de la Bibliotheque de son oncle, qu'il a de beaucoup augmenté.

Des Char-treux. La Bibliotheque des Peres Chartreux est recommandable pour ses bons liures.

M. de Fres-nes. M. de Fresnes, Intendant de l'Imprimerie Royale, a fait vne Bibliotheque en cette Ville de Bourdeaux, lieu de sa naissance, qu'il augmente tous les iours.

Des Iesui-tes. Les Peres Iesuites de Bourdeaux possedent vne tres-insigne Bibliotheque, notamment depuis qu'ils ont eu celle de feu M. Iean *M. de Bar-raut.* Iaubert de Barraut Euesque de Bazas puis Archeuesque d'Arles, qui a si dignement escrit contre les Heretiques, laquelle estoit des-ia de grande consideration.

CHAPITRE LXXXXVI.

Du Languedoc.

LA ville de Tolose est la Ca- *De Tolose.*
pitale de cette Prouince, aussi bien que le siege des bonnes lettres, dans laquelle (outre les beaux esprits qu'elle produit) il y a de tres-fleurissantes Bibliotheques, qui rendent encore cette Ville plus recommandable. La premie- *De Foix.*
re que ie colloqueray icy sera la tres-exquise du College de Foix, fondée par le Cardinal Pierre de Foix Euesque d'Aire, d'où elle tire son Nõ, lequel fit vne sumptueuse despence pour la garnir des meilleurs liures, qui se pouuoient treuuer pour lors, de laquelle ont esté tirez diuers bons manuscrits, qui

ont feruy au public pour les impreſſións.

M. de Monchal. M. Charles de Monchal Archeueſque de Toloſe, fert d'vn riche ornement à l'Egliſe Gallicane par ſa grande erudition, laquelle il puize de ces excellens liures qu'il a depuis long-temps ramaſſez, pour dreſſer cette belle Bibliotheque qu'il poſſede. Pierre Gaſſendi fait mention de la Bibliotheque de ce Prelat, en la vie de Nicolas de Pereſc.

De M. de S. Ioyre. La Bibliotheque de feu le docte Pierre Faber, Seigneur de S. Ioyre, premier Preſident au Parlement de Toloſe, eſtoit celebre; mais apres ſa mort (qui arriua d'vne apoplexie l'an 1600. 13. des Kal. de Iuin, âgé de 60. ans,) elle à eſté venduë par ſes heritiers.

M. Ciron quatriesme President au mortier en ce Parlement, a fait vne Bibliotheque digne de consideration, pour les bons liures qu'il y a mit. *M. Ciron*

M. Iacques de Mauſſac, Doyen des Conſeillers de ce Parlement, & Pere de ce ſçauant Iacques Philippes de Mauſſac, Preſident en la Cour des Aydes de Montpellier, ayant touſiours eſté affectionné pour les lettres & les liures, il a dreſſé vne notable Bibliotheque, qu'il conſerue dans ſa maiſon. *M. de Mauſſac.*

L'hiſtoire que M. Gabriel de Barthelemy, Seigneur de Grammont, Preſident aux Enqueſtes, a donné eſt vn témoignage de ſes eſtudes particulieres, qu'il fait dás ſa Bibliotheque, qui eſt curieuſe pour les bons liures. *M. de Grãmont.*

M. du Catel.

M. Guillaume du Catel, Conseiller du Parlement, a donné au public les Histoires du Languedoc & des Comtes de Tolose, lesquelles luy acquerent vne grāde reputation; aussi bien que cette insigne Bibliotheque qu'il a erigé.

M. Marand.

Pour la Bibliotheque de M. Raymond Marand Iurisconsulte, qui a escrit des Paratitles du droict, elle est conseruée par MM. ses enfans, qui ont le soin de l'augmenter.

Des quatre mendians.

Les Carmes, Augustins, Dominicains & Franciscains, de cette Ville de Tolose, ont dans leur Monasteres de tres-grandes & tres-belles Bibliotheques, qui leur donnent de grands lustres, car outre les liures imprimez, il y a plusieurs anciés MSS. dans icelles.

La Bibliotheque des Peres Ie- *Des Iesuites.*
suites, est fort recommandable
pour ses liures.

Entre les belles Bibliotheques *Des Minimes.*
de Tolose, celle du Conuent des
Peres Minimes en est l'vne ; car
nonobstant qu'elle fut bien considerable de soy ; neantmoins depuis peu de temps elle a esté augmentée de l'excellente Bibliotheque de ce sçauant & pieux Annaliste Ecclesiastique Henry de Spó- *M. de Sponde.*
de Euesque de Pamiers, qui deceda audit Tolose l'an 1643. le 18.
May, laquelle il legua par son testament ausdits Peres Minimes,
lesquels il auoit tousiours pendant sa vie vniquement aymé &
chery.

A Montauban M. N. Thomas *M. Thomas.*
Caluiniste a fait vne Bibliothe-

que, qui est en estime d'estre bône

M. l'Archeuesque de Narbone.

M. Claude de Rebé, iadis Chanoine & Comte de la tres-illustre Eglise de S. Iean de Lyon, & à present Archeuesque de Narbone, President des Estats du Languedoc, & Cheualier du S. Esprit, a honoré la Ville de Narbonne d'vne exquise Bibliotheque, composée des meilleurs liures, qui se peuuent treuuer, où il prent ses diuertissemens, comme estant doüé d'vn excellent esprit, & d'vne singulier doctrine.

M. l'Euesque de Beziers.

M. Clement de Bonzi, Euesque de Beziers, possede vne bonne Bibliotheque, dans laquelle est conseruée celle de M. Carlier Parisien, qui fut acheptée par M. Thomas Bonzi son oncle & Predecesseur.

M. Georges

des Bibliotheques. 657

M. Georges d'Armagnac Euesque de Rhodez & Cardinal, fut grand amateur des lettres, ainsi que le tesmoigne la sumptueuse despence qu'il fit à eriger vn College en la Ville de Rhodez, pour faire instruire la ieunesse dans les lettres humaines, lequel il voulut decorer d'vne tres-excellente Bibliotheque, pour lequel sujet il enuoya en Italie Pierre Gilles, qui auoit vne particuliere intelligence en la cognoissance des bons liures, lequel fit vne grande recherche des exquis manuscrits Grecs & Latins, qui ont fait admirer le glorieux dessein de ce Cardinal Protecteur des lettres: ie n'en rendray autre tesmoignage que celuy du mesme Pierre Gilles, qui se lit dans l'Epistre Liminaire de sa

T t

version, des Commentaires Grecs de S. Theodoret Euesque de Cyr, sur les petits Prophetes, qu'il addresse à ce Cardinal : *Neque verò* (dit-il) *aliud quicquam me induxit ad lustrandam Italiam, quàm vt aliquos libros illinc reportarem, à quibus partim otium viriusque nostrum aleremus, partim pro meis viribus te ad instruendam Bibliothecam adiuuarem istius Gymnasij, quod moliris ædificare, vbi tùm liberalium artium doctrinæ, tùm etiam à necessariis in opes pueri tuo sumptu alantur & erudiantur.* Iean Chenu dans sa *Chronologie des Euesques de Rhodez*, fait aussi mention de cette Bibliotheque, & Pierre Gassendi dans *la vie de Nicolas de Peiresc*.

M. l'Euesque de Lodeue.

M. Iean Plantauy de la Pause Euesque de Lodeue, est tres-bien

des Bibliothèques. 659

versé dans les sciences diuines &
humaines, comme aussi dans
les langues Hebraïques, Grecques & Latines,les ouurages qu'il
a donné au public,en sont des euidents tesmoignages, lesquels luy
acquerét vne grande reputation,
aussi bien qu'vne celebre Bibliotheque qu'il a fait,par vne grande
recherche de bons liures,dont elle
est composée.

M. Angelic Grimaldi, Cardinal Euesque d'Albane,frere du Pape Vrbain V. voulant contribuer à
l'aduancemét des lettres, fonda le
College de S.Ruf,dans la Ville de
Montpellier, auquel il adiousta
pour ornement vne magnifique
Bibliotheque,pour l'vsage de ceux
de ce College, comme il appert
par son testament, fait l'an 1380.

T t ij

le 11. Auril, qui est conserué MSS. en Auignon, par M. Henry Suares. Ce Cardinal mourut en Auignó, d'où il estoit Euesque l'an 1588.

M. l'Euesque du Puy.   M. le President de Thou, dit au 1. liure de sa vie pag. 34. de l'Impression de Geneue, que passant par la ville du Puy en Vellay, il vid vne belle Bibliotheque, qu'auoit fait M. Nectar de Seneterre Euesque de ladite ville. *Inde per impedita* (dit-il) *maximè itineraria triduo exacto longè descendentibus apparet Anicium seu Podium Velaunorum vulgò dictum, &c. Vrbs ab imo in altum paullatim quoque assurgit, pro ratione loci popul:sa & ad templum vsque ad altare maius per gradus itur, quod muro antiqui operis cum Episcopi ædibus coniungitur, in quo adorandi Christi duæ priores litteræ Græcæ, sicu-*

ti ad S. Oren ij Augustæ Aufciorum diximus, adhuc integræ leguntur à præ-fule, is erat Nectarius Senetarius, peramanter exceptus Thuanus, etiam Bibliothequam antiquis bonæ notæ libris MSS. refertam lustrauit.

La tres-ancienne famille des Comtes de Tournon, ne tire pas seulement sa gloire d'auoir esté des premieres nobles maisons de France illuminée du Christianisme, & d'auoir donné ce grand S. Iust à l'Eglise Catholique : mais encore elle se peut vanter d'auoir donné au siecle passé, ce grand Cardinal François de Tournon, l'ornemeut du sacré College des Eminentissimes Cardinaux ; fidel & incorruptible Ministre de nos Roys tres-Chrestiens, qui estoit tellement amoureux des bonnes

Des Iſuites de Tournon.

lettres, qu'il voulut laisser ce perpetuel tesmoignaga à la posterité pour l'accroissement des sciences, que d'eriger l'an 1542. vn celebre College, qui fut couerty l'an 1552. en Vniuersité, laquelle puis apres il donna aux Peres Iesuites, qui l'ont conserué sous ce titre *d'Vniuersité* iusques à l'an 1625. qu'il fut dit par Arrest qu'elle seroit reduite en simple College. Or ce genereux Prelat laissa encore à ces Peres, sa fameuse Bibliotheque, laquelle ils ont tellement augmentée, qu'elle est l'vne des plus celebres de la France.

Chapitre LXXXXVII.

De Lorraine.

Dans le Conuent des Religieux de l'Obseruance de S. François de Nancy, est conseruée la tres-splendide Bibliotheque des Ducs de Lorraine, depuis vn long-temps; laquelle est abundante en bons & rares liures, qui y ont esté mis auec de gráds soings. On y void aussi quelques MSS. *Nancy.*

Des Ducs de Lorraine.

M. de Lescale possede aussi en Lorraine vne Bibliotheque de consideration, à ce que ici'ay appris. *M. de Lescale.*

Chapitre LXXXXVIII.

Du Lyonnois, Forest & Baujolois.

Des Iesui-tes.

LA plus celebre Bibliotheque de la ville de Lyon, est celle du College des Peres Iesuites, qui pour la quantité de ses liures ne cede à beaucoup de France; car elle se peut vanter d'auoir plusieurs liures, qui viennent de la liberalité du grand Roy Henry IV. & de diuerses autres personnes de condition. Cette année 1644. le feu s'estant pris dans ce College, quelques liures de cette Bibliotheque, qui estoyent dans des chambres particulieres y sont peris.

Des Carmes.

La Bibliotheque du Conuent

des Bibliotheques. 665

des PP. Carmes sur les Terreaux, est tres-considerable pour les Peres & Theologiens, qui y ont esté mis par M. Iacques Maistret Bourguignon profez de cette maison, Docteur de Paris, & Euesque de Damas, puis par M. Robert Berthelot, neueu du P. Maistret aussi Docteur de Paris & Euesque de Damas, tous deux Suffragans de l'Archeuesché de Lyon, & hommes bien versez dans les sciences: le P. Estienne Molin, Docteur de la mesme Faculté de Paris, l'a de beaucoup augmentée en bons liures de Theologie.

Quant à la Bibliotheque des PP. Minimes, elle est non seulement belle pour son edifice ; mais encore bonne pour ses liures. *Des Minimes.*

Les Peres Dominicains de la *Des Dominicains.*

place de Confort, ont eu autrefois vne insigne Bibliotheque, laquelle a esté en partie dissipée durant les troubles de la France, pour la Religion.

De Charpin.

Estienne Charpin, Prestre de la ville de Lyon, a esté homme fort curieux en son temps, comme il appert par les meilleurs liures qu'il achepta pour former sa Bibliotheque, de laquelle il fit imprimer à Lyon le Catalogue l'an 1555. en suitte d'vne Epistre qu'il escrit de ce sujet, dont voicy le titre de peur que la memoire ne s'en perde. *Studiosis tantum Lugdunensis Ecclesiæ Fratribus qui augustißimam eius Maiestatem perennem expetunt, Stephanus Charpin etiam perennem illis optat salutem. Bibliothecam ideo Christianam comparaui candidißimi commili-*

tones, vt pro viri adiuuarem, &c.

La beauté & la rareté du cabinet de M. Gaspard de Monconys, Seigneur de Liergues & de Poüilly, Conseiller du Roy & Lieutenant Criminel au Siege Presidial de Lyon, est bien l'vne des curieuses pieces de l'Europe, tant pour les medailles d'or, argent, airain, verre, plomb & autres matieres, & pour les pourtraits en taille douce, & peinture; que pour la bonté des liures qui si treuuent, quoy qu'en nombre seulement de deux milles, entre lesquels il y en a plus de 200. de medailles, entrées de villes, deuises, eloges & pourtraits d'hommes illustres. Le P. Henry Alby Iesuite, parle fort honorablement de ce cabinet, dans la Preface des Parallelles des

De M. de Liergues

Cardinaux, imprimées à Paris cette année 1644. in 4.

D'Antoine de la Porte. François de la Croix du Maine, fait mention dans sa *Bibliotheque des Autheurs de France*, de la Bibliotheque & du cabinet d'Antoine de la Porte, Seigneur de Bertha Escheuin de la ville de Lyon, l'an 1581. lequel estoit homme fort bien versé en l'vn & l'autre exercice de Pallas (à fin d'vser des mots du Seigneur Claude Guichard, duquel ie l'ay apris.) Il auoit vn cabinet fort excellent, remply de plusieurs beaux liures, & de medailles antiques, &c.

De M. Gras. La Bibliotheque de M. Henry Gras Medecin de Lyon, est l'vne des plus belles de cette ville, tant pour la qualité des bons liures, que pour la quantité: car à present il possede enuiron vnze ou douze cens volumes in folio, & trois à quatre mille plus petits volumes; & la continuë tous les iours.

Charlemagne Empereur & *De l'Isle Barbe.* Roy de France, auoit vne telle affectió pour les Religieux de l'Isle Barbe prez de Lyon, qu'il leur donna vne excellente Bibliotheque; de laquelle ont eu la charge de Bibliothecaire Leidrard Moine de cette Abbaye, puis Euesque de Lyon, qui fait mention des liures de cét Empereur, qu'il enuoya en cette Abbaye *Monasterium Regale* (dit-il en l'Epistre qu'il escrit à cét Empereur) *Insulæ Barbaræ situm in medio Araris fluuij, antiquitus dicatum in honorem S. Andreæ Apostoli & omnium Apostolorum, nunc autem in honorem S. Martini re-*

cens est fundatum, iussu Domini Caroli Imperatoris, qui ibidem præfecit D. Benedictū Abbat. cum quo simul ibi direxit suos Codices, ita restauraui, &c. Iacques Seuert Docteur de Paris, dit en la vie de Leidrat, que cette Bibliotheque estoit en grande estime en ce temps-là. *Ante Episcopatum* (dit-il) *verò habitus est Magister sacri Palatij sub Carolo, seu Bibliothecarius eiusdem Imperatoris: quo postea procurante creatus est Archiepiscopus valdè doctus ad annum 799. aut circiter. Permulti ferunt, quòd tunc amplissima Caroli Bibliotheca asseruabatur in sacro Insulæ barbaræ Cœnobio Lugdunensi: vt poteouam regebat Ledradus nondum Pontificia vnctione delibutus, & ibidem commorans.* Apres Leidradus le docte Agobardus aussi Euesque de Lyon, a

des Bibliotheques. 671
eu le soin de cette Bibliotheque
selon Guillaume Paradin *liu.1.* de
l'histoire de Lyon, Gabriel Naudé en son *Addition à l'histoire* de
Louys XI. & en son *Aduis pour
dresser vne Bibliotheque.*

De M. d'Vrfé.
Le Chasteau de l'Abbatie, situé
dans le Forest appartient à l'Illustre famille d'Vrfé, de laquelle est
issu M. Claude d'Vrfé, Ambassadeur pour le Roy tres-Chrestien,
au Concile de Boulogne, & Gouuerneur des Enfans de Fráce, sous
Henry II. homme d'vn grand
iugement & doctrine : car il dressa vne splendide & riche Bibliotheque dans ce Chasteau, où il
mit plus de 4600. volumes, entre
lesquels il y auoit deux cens manuscrits en velin, couuerts de velour verd. M. Honoré d'Vrfé Au-

theur de l'Astrée, composa cét ouurage en ce chasteau qui luy ap-
partenoit, & cette famille subsiste encore à present en la personne de M. le Marquis d'Vrfé.

CHAPITRE LXXXXIX.

Du Limosin.

Des Iesui-
tes.
LEs Iesuites du College de la ville de Limoges, iouyssent d'vne Bibliotheque de conside-ration.

CHAPITRE C.

Du Maine.

De Fran-
çois de la
Croix du
Mans.
FRançois de la Croix natif du Mans, Gentilhomme de condition, a fait paroistre la gran-
de

de cognoissance qu'il auoit dés son ieune âge, à la recherche des bons liures Grecs, Latins, & François, desquels il auoit composé sa fameuse Bibliotheque dans la ville du Mans. Ie ne puis emprunter vne meilleure description de cette Bibliotheque, que celle qu'il en donne luy mesme, en la Preface de sa *Bibliotheque Françoise*, où il en parle en ces termes. *Ie diray que dés l'an de mon âge dix-septiesme, sçauoir est, en l'an de salut 1569. estant enuoyé en l'Vniuersité de Paris, pour faire profit aux lettres, i'estois si curieux d'auoir toutes sortes de liures non seulement en Grec, Latin & autres langues, & sur tout en François, qu'enfin l'amas que i'en fais estoit si grand, que le Catalogue d'iceux se monstroit tenir plus d'vn iuste volume. De façon qu'il* me prit dés-lors vne enuie de mettre à part les Grecs & les Latins, & d'vn autre costé les François, où Autheur qui auoyent escrit en nostre langue, sans parler des Italiens, Espagnols & autres. En vn autre endroit, il dit auoir achepté en quinze ou seize ans, pour plus *de dix mille francs* de liures, & d'auoir escrit, recueilly & recherché, de toutes parts des memoires, desquels il auoit fait & composé plus de *sept à huict cens volumes* en toute sorte de sciences, entre lesquels ie treuue qu'il promettoit *La recherche des Bibliotheques, ou cabinets les plus renommez de France,* (qu'aucuns appellent chábres de merueilles) *auec la declaration des liures rares, medailles, pourtraits, Statues ou effigies, pierreries ou autres gentilesses, ou gentilles curiositez*

des Bibliotheques. 675
qui se voyent és maisons des Princes, & autres qui font amas de telles magnificences. C'est vne chose digne d'admiration de voir sa fecondité d'esprit, veu qu'en l'âge de vingt-sept ans, il asseure auoir fait de ses particulieres estudes, ces sept à huict cens volumes de memoires. Ie pense que cette Bibliotheque a esté dissipée apres sa mort; car ie n'ay iamais peu apprendre qu'elle estoit deuenuë, non plus que sa *Bibliotheque Latine, des Autheurs de France,* qu'il promettoit.

Chapitre CI.

De la Marche.

Dans la ville du Daurat, en la Prouince de la Marche, prés le Poictou, M. Pierre Robert, *De M. Robert.*

Seigneur de Ville-Martin, &c. Lieutenant General, a fait vne Bibliotheque curieuse, pour l'histoire en laquelle il est bien versé, particulierement en celle des Comtes de la Marche, desquels il prepare l'histoire.

De M. de la Brulonniere.

M. Gaspar de Nuchezes, Cheualier, Seigneur de la Brulonniere, &c. est fort curieux en la recherche des liures pour la composition de sa Bibliotheque, qui est remplie d'enuiron 5000. volumes en toutes les sciences; vne partie desquels vient de la celebre Bibliotheque de feu M. Pauillon,

De M. de Pauillon.

Aduocat au Parlement de Paris; & quant aux manuscrits qui si treuuent, ils prouiennent de la Bibliotheque du President Clau-

Du President Fauchet.

de Fauchet, qui a laissé à la poste-

des Bibliotheques.
rité plusieurs bons ouurages.

CHAPITRE CII.

De Mets, Tou & Verdun.

L'Eglise Cathedrale de Mets, *De l'Eglise de Mets.* a eu autrefois vne celebre Bibliotheque, laquelle est beaucoup descheuë de sa splendeur, pour son antiquité; car ie treuue dans l'histoire de Mets, de M. Murisse Euesque de Dardanie, & Suffragant de ladite Eglise, que Godegrand Euesque 37. qui viuoit l'an 753, l'auoit erigee pour l'vsage de ses Chanoines, lesquels il faisoits viure comme Religieux. Cét Euesque a escrit quelques ourages qui sont specifiés par Trithemius l'an 760.

Quant à la Bibliotheque de *De l'Eglis de Verdun*

l'Eglife Cathedrale de Verdun, elle a efté en eftime, mais depuis quelques années elle a efté venduë par Meſſieurs du Chapitre.

Chapitre CIII.

De Normandie.

De l'Eglife de Roüen.

LA ville de Roüen eſt la Capitale de cette Prouince, dás laquelle il y a vne Eglife Archiepifcopale, où l'on a erigé vne grande & fplendide Bibliotheque publique, par la liberalité de pluſieurs perſonnes de lettres, que ie nommeray felon l'ordre qu'ils ont donnez les liures. Le premier qui commença ce glorieux deſ-

M. Accarie. fein, fut feu *M. Accarie*, fils de la B. Sœur Marie de l'Incarnation

Carmeline, Archidiacre de cette insigne Eglise, à laquelle il donna sa Bibliotheque, pour memoire de l'amour qu'il portoit à ses Confreres, à la chage toutefois qu'elle seruiroit au public. Mais comme les commancemens sont tousjours imparfaits, ce tres-sçauant Archeuesque *M. François du Harlay de Chaualon*, Docteur de Paris, a voulu beaucoup contribuer à la grãdeur & à l'ornement de ce tresor des Muses, par le don qu'il a fait de sa celebre Bibliotheque, afin d'accompagner celle-cy, pour la rendre plus recommandable, en quoy la posterité luy en aura eternelle obligation. *M. Barthelemy Hallé*, Chanoine & Archidiacre à pareillement tesmoigné son affection à cette Bibliotheque, à

M. l'Arch.

M. Hallé.

laquelle il a laiſſé celle qu'il poſſe-
doit, qui eſtoit conſiderable, & en
memoire du don des liures qu'il a
laiſſé, l'on void ſes armes deſſus,
qui ſont d'azur à trois eſtoilles en
chef & vne en pointe d'or, à vne
feſſe d'argent de deux coquilles
de ſable, auec cette inſcription
Latine. *Ex Dono Bartholomæi Hallé Presb. in Ecclesia Rotho mag. Canonici & Archidiaconi de Augo Chri-
ſtianiſſ. Regis à Secretis; Dom. de Pittres & de Berſclos.* La mort de ce
pieux Chanoine arriua l'an 1636.
le 17. de Septembre : ſon corps eſt
enterré en l'Egliſe de Louuiers
auec vn Epitaphe, au bas duquel
ce liſſent ces mots.

Eccleſiam Roth. ſua fundatione
Eiuſque Bibliothecam ſuâ non te-
nui auxit.

des Bibliotheques. 681

M. Iean Bigot, Escuyer, sieur *M. Bigot.*
de Sommeuil & de Cleuuille,
Doyen des Conseillers de la Cour
des Aydes de Normandie, a vne
grande cognoissance des bons liures, desquels il a fait vne magnifique Bibliotheque composee de
plus de 6000. volumes, entre lesquels il y a plus de 500. manuscrits
tres-bons & bien rares, lesquels il
communique facilement à ceux
qui en ont besoin pour le public,
en quoy il sera à iamais loüable.

Feu Monseigneur Charles, Car- *Du Card.*
dinal de Vendosme, puis de Bour- *de Bour-*
bon, Archeuesque 83. de Roüen, *bon.*
a laissé cette memoire à la posterité, d'auoir esté le plus grand
amateur des gens de letrres &
de liures, qui fut en son temps,
suiuant la remarque qu'en fait

Pierre Frizon en sa vie. *Amor & desiderium* (dit-il) *ipsi ingens librorum, quos vndequaque ad Bibliothecam locupletem, extruendam à disiunctissimis regionibus magno sumptu extrahebat, vndè erga eruditos doctósque homines singularis beneuolentia prodiit.* Il mourut à Paris à S. Germain des Prez, l'an 1594. le 1. d'Aouſt.

De l'Abbaye du Bec. L'Abbaye de ſaincte Marie du Bec, de l'Ordre de ſainct Benoiſt, a ioüy autrefois d'vne grande Bibliotheque, laquelle fut entierement brûlée il y a enuiron 30. ans; c'eſt pourquoy à preſent il n'en reſte que fort peu de veſtiges, au grand dommages des Religieux de cette Abbaye.

De l'Abbaye de S. Michel. Ie puis dire de la Bibliotheque de S. Michel en Ler, au dioceſe de Coutances, qu'elle a eſté fort renommée pour la multitude de ſes manuſcrits, qui eſtoient tres-conſiderables: car le R. P. Iacques Sirmond & pluſieurs autres ſçauans hommes, m'ont aſſeurez d'auoir veu encore ſur pied cette Bibliotheque.

CHAPITRE CIV.

De la Principauté d'Oranges.

Daniel Chamier Miniſtre de cette ville, auoit fait vne belle Bibliotheque, pour ſon vſage, où il auoit mis de bons liures: mais ie ne ſçay qui a eu cette Bibliotheque apres ſa mort.

De Daniel Chamier.

CHAPITRE CV.

De l'Orleanois, Chartrain, Blesois & Vendosmois, &c.

Publique à Orleans des Allemans.

DAns la ville d'Orleans, il y a vne celebre Vniuersité, dans laquelle il y a vne tres-bonne Bibliotheque publique pour la nation Allemande, de laquelle deux de cette nation ont la charge, comme le tesmoigne Iosse Sincer en son Itineraire de France, où il en parle en cette sorte. *Bibliothecarij tandem sunt duo, quorū vnus est quotidiè diebus profestis ab hora prima ad secundam in Bibliotheca comparere, libros petentibus indulgere, ab ipsis commodato eos sumunt notam reiteftem exigere: finito cuiusuis Pro-*

des Bibliotheques. 685
curatoris officio commodatos libros reposcere. Cæterùm Bibliotheca omnis generis libris est instructißima. Intellexi Hubertum Giphanium I.C. authorem fuisse eius instituendæ.

Amedé Cardinal de Saluces, *Du Cardinal Amedé.* tesmoigna l'affection qu'il portoit à l'Vniuersité d'Orleans, par l'erection qu'il fit d'vne magnifique Bibliotheque commune pour l'vsage de ceux de cette Vniuersité, ainsi qu'il appert par le testament de ce Cardinal, qu'il fit l'an 1419. le 21. de Iuin, qui est conseruée par MM. Suarez d'Auignon, desquels i'ay receu ces memoires.

Durant les troubles de la Fran- *De P. Montauré.* ce, pour le fait de la Religion de Iean Caluin & ses Sectateurs, plusieurs belles Bibliotheques perirent miserablement, entre lesquelles fut celle de Pierre Montauré, qu'il auoit dressé en cette ville selon la remarque qu'en fait le President de Thou au liu. 52. de son histoire l'an 1572. *Magna præda* (dit-il) *toto illo tempore abacta, & locuples in primis illa Petri Montaurei viri doctississimi ante biennium Sancerræ ex animi mœrore extincti Bibliothecâ omnium librorum copia instructa, præcipuè mathematicis Græcis maiorem partem manuscriptis, & ipsius Montaurij studio emendatis & illustratis, instrumentis item ad eas scientias raro artificio elaboratis, barbara immanitate direpta est.*

De Fleury. Si l'Abbaye de Fleury au Diocese d'Orleans, est en grande estime pour posseder le corps du glorieux Patriarche des Moines

des Bibliotheques.

d'Occident S. Benoist : elle n'est pas encore en moindre reputation pour le sujet de son ancienne & exquise Bibliotheque qu'elle a autrefois conserué, de laquelle l'Abbé Iean du Bois fait la description dans sa Bibliotheque de Fleury pag. 302. *Scholæ* (dit-il) *quondam adeo insignes & celebres in Cænobio Floriacensi habebantur vt scholasticorum in eis numerus plus quinque millibus recenseretur. Hi didascalis suis muneris honorarij gratia pro candelis edictisve in Parisiensi Academia nostra ætate claßium moderatoribus exhiberi consuetis bina manuscripti (eo quod necdum Typographica ars emerserat) offerebant volumina, quorum numerositas locupletißimam Floriacensem conflarat Bibliothecam, quam annis Domini 1561.*

& 1562. diritas Caluinica inæstima-
bili litteraria rei iactura dirīpuit, dis-
sipauit, lacerauit.

De Char-   La ville de Chartres en Beausse,
tres.   est digne d'admiration en ce que
pour sa petitesse elle possede plus
de Bibliotheques qu'aucunes autres villes de ce Royaume, comme on le verra par le denombrement. Le premier lieu sera donné
De M. Les-   à la Bibliotheque de M. Iacques
cot Euesq.   Lescot, Docteur de Sorbone &
Euesque de cette ville, duquel les
vertus & la doctrine sont cognus
de tous: il a tousiours tesmoigné
vne grande inclination à la recherche des bons liures, dont il a
composé sa belle Bibliotheque.

De M.   M. Charles Challigne, Escuyer,
Challigne.   sieur de Messalain, Conseiller &
Aduocat du Roy, au Baillage &
siege

des Bibliotheques. 689

siege Presidial de Chartres, nous a donné la traduction Françoise de la Bibliographie Politique de M. Naudé, pour vn singulier tesmoignage de son affection aux lettres: aussi toute l'aplication de son esprit n'est que dans l'exercice de sa charge, & dans le ramas des liures en toutes les sciences pour rendre sa Bibliotheque celebre, laquelle a des-ia plus de 3600. volumes.

La Bibliothoque des Peres Iacobins est de grande consideration, pour le nombre de ses liures, entre lesquels il y a beaucoup de manuscrits. *Des Iacobins.*

Le mesme se peut dire de la Bibliotheque du Conuent des Peres Cordeliers, qui est fort belle. *Des Cordeliers.*

M. Souchet Docteur en Theo- *M. Souchet*

logie, Chanoine de l'Eglife noftre Dame de Chartres, & Prieur de Morancez fait vne Bibliotheque, où à presét il y a plus de trois mille volumes bien choifis, qui font accompagnez de plufieurs Manufcrits qui concernent l'hiftoire, & principalement celle des familles illuftres de France & du Chartrain, dans lefquelles il eft fort intelligent; ayant fuccedé aux

M. Laifné. memoires de feu M. Laifné Prieur de Mondonuille, qui auoit trauaillé à ces recherches.

De MM. les Martins. La Bibliotheque de MM. les Martins eftoit affez confiderable, pour les bons liures, mais elle eft à prefent diuifée.

M. Grenet. M. Grenet Aduocat au fiege Prefidial, a dreffé vne notable Bibliotheque, où il y a prés

des Bibliotheques. 691

de 4000. volumes de diuerses professions.

M. de Giues Secretaire de M. le Marquis de Sourdis, ne cesse continuellement à ramasser des liures pour accomplir sa curieuse Bibliotheque, laquelle à present est composée de plus de 4000. volumes en toutes les Facultés. *M. de Giues.*

M. Guillaume Ribier frere de Iacques, duquel i'ay parlé en la page 559. iadis Lieutenant General & President au siege Presidial de Blois, & à present Conseiller du Roy en ses Conseils d'Estat & Priué est doüé d'vne pareille affection pour les lettres que M. son frere : car il a erigé vne bonne Bibliotheque dans la ville de Blois, où il la conserue. *De M. Ribier à Blois.*

La Royale Bibliotheque des *Des Rois de Nauarre à Vend.*

Xx ij

Roys de Nauarre, estoit autrefois cóseruée a Vendosme, au rapport de François de la Croix du Maine, en sa Bibliotheque Françoise.

CHAPITRE CVI.

De Picardie.

D'Amiens M. l'Euesque d'Amiens.

DAns la ville d'Amiens y sont conseruées plusieurs Bibliotheques, sçauoir celle de M. François le Févre de Caumartin, Euesque de cette ville, qui est considerable pour les bons liures qu'elle contient.

Des Minimes.

La Bibliotheque des Peres Minimes de cette ville est reputée pour l'vne des principales, à cause de la quantité & bonté de ses liures, laquelle il augmentent tous les iours.

des Bibliotheques. 693

Les Peres Capucins conseruent aussi vne notable Bibliotheque en leur Conuent. *Des Capucins.*

M. Guilin le Cat Bachelier en la Faculté de Theologie de Paris, & Curé de S. Sulpice de la ville d'Amiens, fait vne Bibliotheque bonne & curieuse, laquelle à present contient plus de quatre mille volumes. *M. le Cat.*

Les PP. Iesuites d'Amiens ont vne belle Bibliotheque. *Des Iesuites.*

L'Abbaye de sainct Martin de Laon, a vne Bibliotheque, qui est en reputation pour ses liures. *S. Martin de Laon.*

Le Conuent des Peres Minimes de Laon a esté fondé l'an mil six cens neuf, dans lequel ces Peres font vne belle Bibliotheque. *Des Minimes.*

X x iij

Chapitre CVII.

De Poictou.

M. l'Euesque de Poictiers.

M. Henry Louys Chastenier de la Rochepozay Euesque de Poictiers, n'a pas seulement donné des preuues de sa grande vertu & condition dans les liures qu'il a communiqué au public : mais encore il a erigé vne magnifique Bibliotheque, qui est tres-notable pour les Theologiens, & historiens, qui luy causera vne memoire de benediction.

M. Maurinet.

La Bibliotheque de M. Mauriuet Thresorier en l'Eglise de S. Hilaire de Poictiers, est fort excellente en bons & curieux liures.

De Fontenerrux.

Les Religieux du Monastere

de S. Iean de Fonteuraux, ont vne Bibliotheque tres-abundante en liures, principalement de Droict.

M. René Izoré Baron d'Heruaut, est tres-bien instruit dans les sciences, comme il a fait paroistre dans le liure qu'il a escrit contre la Pilletiere Ministre de Chastelrault: aussi ses diuertissemens ne sont que parmy les liures, qui sont dans sa Bibliotheque, qu'il conserue dans son Chasteau de Plain-Martin pres de Poictiers. *M. le Ba-d'Heruaut.*

M. Iean Besly Conseiller & Aduocat du Roy au siege de Fontenay le Côte en Poictou, est homme sçauant & curieux, & qui n'espargne aucun soin à former cette noble Bibliotheque qu'il a erigé a Fontenay le Comte, qui ex- *M. Besly.*

celle pour l'histoire en laquelle il est fort bien versé.

M. le Baron de la Cheze.

Prés de la ville de Fontenay le Comte M. le Baron de la Cheze a vne Bibliotheque assez notable dans son Chasteau de la Cheze.

M. Pidoux.

M. Pidoux sieur du Challiou Lieutenant General Ciuil en la Seneschaussée de Ciuray, auoit fait vne bonne Bibliotheque, qui a esté venduë apres sa mort.

CHAPITRE CVIII.

De Prouence.

M. de Peresc.

TOus ceux qui ont veus la tres-opulente Bibliotheque, & le rare cabinet de feu M. Nicolas Claude Fabry de Peresc, Conseiller au Parlement d'Aix & Abbé de saincte Marie d'Aquilstre,

des Bibliotheques. 697

en Aquitaine, aduoüent qu'il n'y auoit rien de si rare en ce siecle; car outre ses liures imprimez, il y a vn grand nombre de Manuscrits en langues Orientales, qui sont encore aujourd'huy coseruez par M. Palamedes Fabry Seigneur de Valaues son frere & heritier. M. Pierre Gassendy, escriuant la vie dudit de Peresc, en parle en cette sorte au liu. 6. *Ad hæc impenso fuit studio ad librorum copiam, varietatémque comparandam. Nam de MSS. vt nihil dicam, quos nisi habere antiquos potuit, escribi certè procurauit (ex scripsítque interdum ipse) præhabitis indicibus Bibliothecarum celebrium, ac toto orbe præcipuarum, vt si quid sibi, studiosísve necessarium occurreret, vnde erui posset, in promptu haberet.* Et vn peu apres il poursuit.

Et incredile quidem dictu, quantam copiam congesserit; incredibile etiam, quorsùm nō propterea completissimam Bibliothecam reliquerit: sed neutrum videbitur mirum, si quis considerauerit quæsisse eum libros non sibi solum, sed etiam quibus suis opus illis foret. En vn autre endroit il dit: *Sic curauit etiam quoscunque est nactus peruestutos Codices, seu impressos, seu MSS. Neque ipsos integros modò; sed illorum etiam fragmenta, semesáque folia. Et cùm ex eo quæreretur, cur tam sumptuosas ea in re foret, causam dixit, quòd persæpè libri optimi facta peßima paterentur, cùm in manus ineruditas parum culti inciderent; ac se ideò operam dare, vt, vel ex decôre pretium obtinentes, nec scombros metuerent, nec thus. Quos sibi verò compactos habuit, proprio charactere insignitos voluit. Constitit*

des Bibliotheques. 699

ille ex tribus Græcis maiusculis litteris N, K, Φ, eâ elegantiâ inter se commissis, vt geminatæ tam dextrorsùm, quam sinistrorsùm legi possent; ipsísque initialibus exhiberentur tres illæ voces Νικολάος Κλαύδιος Φαβρίκιος. Quantum ad Bibliothecæ locum, is fuit sanè nimis angustus, quantumuis præter parietes supellectile pretiosâ ornatos, tabulatum quoque medium forulis onerauerit, ex eadémque instruxerit. Hinc libros quoque habuit tam in promusæo, seu quasi Bibliothecæ atrio, quàm per diuersa conclauia, columnatim cumulatos. Et sæpe quidem cogitauit de prolixa quadam pergula ex ædificanda; sed tam multa mouenda fuerunt, potissimùm verò paterna, atque auita Bibliotheca, in quam aliunde maximam partem cimeliorum coniecerat; tam etiam parùm otij sibi semper fecit, ac *habuit, vt exsequi non valuerit, ipsás-que ędeis, vt ab initio se habuerant reliquerit.* Ce grand personnage mourut à Aix l'an 1637. le 24. Iuin, âgé de 56. ans, 6. mois, 12. iours, & 20. heures: son corps est enterré dans l'Eglise des Iacobins. Il est à remarquer, que par son testament il a legué ses liures de Mathematiques auec ses instrumens, à M. Gassendi Autheur de sa vie. Cette Bibliotheque ne seroit estre trop loüée pour les raretés qu'elles contient, ce qui faira que i'emprunteray encore vn tesmoignage de M. Naudé pour ce sujet, c'et de l'Epistre Latine, qu'il escrit audit sieur Gassendy, sur la mort de ce Conseiller son ancien amy. *Quis enim nescit* (dit-il) *os eius non hominis, sed Apollinis Delphici*

des Bibliotheques.

fuiſſe, ex quo oracula de rebus omnibus abſtruſi, & incognitis quotidie reddebātur? Domum verò inſtar celeberrimi emporij, mercibus pretioſiſſimis ex vtráque Indiâ, Æthiopiâ, Græciâ, Germaniâ, Italiâ, Hiſpaniâ, Angliâ. vicinioribúſque Prouinciis refertam extitiſſe; nullámque nauem Galliẹ portus intraſſe, quæ non aliquod animal peregrinum, non plantas exoticas, non marmora priſcorum cœlo ſculpta, aut exarata, non codices Samaritanos, Coptos, Arabas, Hebræos, Sinenſes, Græcos, non erutas ex Boſphoro, aut Peloponeſo antiquitatis penitiſsimæ reliquias in vnius Pereſcij Cimeliarchium inferet? &c.

Iean Iacques Bouchard Pariſien dans l'Oraiſon funebre dudit de Pereſc, qu'il dit publiquement, le 21. Decembre 1637. dans l'Academie des Humoristes à Rome en presence des Cardinaux Barberins, Bentiuoglio, la Cueua, Biscia, Pamphili, Palotta, Brancaccio, Aldobrandin, & Borghese: & plusieurs autres personnes de qualité, & d'erudition. *Et cùm isti (dit-il) homines, sua quantumuis arguta sedulitate, Peresciocumulatùs satisfacere nequirent, sæpiùs ipse alios domo misit, ad omnes maris Ægei insulas, montem Atho, Bysantium, Alexandriam, & ad miserandas illas Memphis, atque Carthaginis reliquias qui suo nomine, atque ære conquirerent, preter res alias nouitate mirabiles, præcipuè vetustissimos Codices, Græcos, Hebraïcos, Arabicos, Persicos, Coptos, Æthiopicos: denique cùm cętera Asiaticę, atque Africanę antiquitatis monumenta, tum maximè priscorum*

Principum Ægyptiorum corpora, pretiosissimis odoribus, medicaminibusque condita, &c.

Robert Roy de Hierusalem & de Sicile, & Comte de Prouence surnommé le Sage, fut en son temps grand amateur des Poëtes & des liures; car Cesar Nostradamus tesmoigne dans ses *Annales de Prouence*, en la vie de ce Roy qu'il auoit erigé vne magnifique Bibliotheque dans la ville d'Aix, où il auoit mis tous les ouurages des Trobadours ou Poëtes Prouençaux, qui estoyent en nombre de 90. *Du Roy Robert.*

M. de Galliard, Président au Parlemét d'Aix, deceda l'an 1640. & laissa à ses heritiers vne assez bonne Bibliotheque, qu'il auoit fait auec vn grand soin. *M. de Galliard.*

M. Viany.

M. Viany Aduocat en Parlement, personnage de grand sçauoir & merité, a dressé vne Bibliotheque, qui est l'vne des plus belles de la Prouence pour le present, soit pour la quantité de liures des meilleurs editions, soit pour la bonté, rareté & curiosité d'iceux, soit pour la relieure, qui est toute en marroquin deleuant: L'on y void tous les Peres, les Epistoleres, les Historiens François & Estrangers, & quelques Rabins, selon le tesmoignage que m'en donne par ses lettres M. Antoine de Ruffi, Conseiller au siege de Marseille, qui m'a beaucoup assisté pour les Bibliotheques de Prouence.

M. Gaffarel.

M. Iacques Gaffarel Docteur en Theologie, Protonotaire du S. Siege

des Bibliotheques.

S. Siege Apostolique & Prieur Commandataire de sainct Gilles, a fait vne tres-curieuse Bibliotheque en bons liures, tant en langues Orientales, qu'en communes, qu'il a recherché auec de grands soins, cóme luy mesme le tesmoigne dans la preface qu'il a mit deuant l'histoire de la guerre de Constantinople de Paul Ramnusio : *Interim Lector humanissime* (dit-il) *Librum hunc verò Principe dignum, cum aliis, quos tibi propediem ex illa supellectile ditissima, quam Eminentissimi Cardinalis Richelÿ iussu, ex omnibus tùm Italiæ, tùm Orientis partibus conquisiui, vertendos instituimus, æquo exspectes animo, nostrísque libenter faueas laboribus.* Ce passage fait voir comme ce grand Cardinal auoit en estime ledit sieur Gaffarel, qui a vne grande cognoissance des sciences & langues Orientales, ainsi que ses œuures le tesmoignent.

De l'Eglise d'Arles. Iean Brognier, ou selon Claude Robert, Alermet fut homme de son temps honoré pour ses merites & vertus en de grandes charges ; premierement il fut Euesque de Viuiers, puis Archeuesque d'Arles ; & enfin Cardinal Euesque d'Ostie, Vice-Chancelier de l'Eglise Romaine & President au Concile de Constance. Ce sçauant Prelat auoit de grandes inclinations pour les lettres, cóme il le tesmoigna par l'erectió qu'il fit d'vne notable Bibliotheque, qu'il laissa par son testament à sa chere Eglise d'Arles ; nonobstant qu'il deceda à Rome l'an 1426. au rapport de Pierre Frizon. *Supellectilem* (dit-il en sa vie) *quoque in templo pretiosam, librorum in Bibliotheca plusquam septingenta volumina posuit.*

La Bibliotheque de l'Abbaye de S. Pierre de Mont-maiour de l'Ordre de S. Benoist en la ville d'Arles, estoit autrefois en telle estime, qu'elle attiroit les estrangers pour aller admirer sa splendeur, qui subsista iusqu'au temps de Pierre de Lune Antipape nommé Benoist XIII. qui la fit ruïner, comme on l'apprent des monumens de cette celebre Abbaye, de laquelle à present il n'y reste plus que la memoire. *De Mont-maiour d'Arles.*

La Bibliotheque des Chartreux de Bon-pas est en reputatió pour ses liures curieux particulierement *Des Chartreux de Bon-pas.*

Yy ij

en histoire, que Don Policarpe de la Riuiere, auoit recueilly auec beaucoup de soin.

De Lerins.

L'ancienne Abbaye de Lerins a esté la premiere Academie Monastique de l'Occident &, vn seminaire de Saincts & doctes personnages, qui ont illustrez l'Eglise Catholique par leurs vies exemplaires, & singulieres doctrines; lesquels comme fort affectionnez à l'estude auoyent faits vne tres-somptueuse & tres-grande Bibliotheque pour leur vsage, de laquelle Iean Nostradamus fait vne ample description dans la vie du Monge ou Moyne des Isles d'or, l'vn des Compilateurs des vies des Poëtes Prouençaux, que ie rapporteray icy pour seruir à nostre sujet, quoy qu'assez prolixe; mais neantmoins necessaire pour en conseruer la memoire à la posterité. Le Monge des Isles d'or, dites anciennement Stecades ou les Isles d'Yeres, descendu de l'ancienne & noble famille de Cibo de Gennes, s'estant resolu en ses premiers ans de suiure la vie Religieuse & Monacale, conduit par son bon esprit paruint au Monastere de S. Honoré en l'Isle de Lerins dans la plaige de Cyaqne: y ayant esté cognu, tant pour la noblesse de son sang, que pour sa bonne renommée que dés sa ieunesse auoit acquise, non seulement fut receu, mais grandement prié d'estre du nombre des Religieux de ce Monastere, auquel suiuant ses estudes paruint facond en la Poësie, Rhetorique, Theologie & autres Arts liberaux: parquoy fut prié des Religieux prendre la charge de la Librairie de leur Monastere, qu'estoit renommée la plus belle de toute l'Europe, pour auoir esté enrichie & doüée par les Comtes de Prouence, & Roys de Naples & de Sicile & autres grands personnages amateurs des sciences, des plus belles & rares œuures & des plus exquises en toutes langues & facultez qu'on eust peu desirer, qu'estoyent mal reduites & sans nul ordre pour raison des guerres esquelles ledit Monastere auoit esté suiect, qu'auoyent eu cours par le passé en Prouence, entre les Princes des Baux & Charles de Duras & Raymond de Turene, pretendans droicts en la Comté de Prouence, & entre les Comtes & vrais possesseurs d'icelle. Le Monge donc ayant pris la charge qui luy auoit esté donnée, fist si bien par ses iournées qu'en brief de temps par le moyen de son beau iugement, conforme à son esperance, mis en ordre la Librairie, separant les liures selon la faculté des sciences non sans grand peine & fatigue : pour autant que selon le Catalogue d'iceux qu'vn sçauant Religieux du Monastere nommé Hermantere, descendu de la noble famille de Prouence, auoit fait par le passé par commandement d'Ildefons Roy d'Arragon deuxiesme du nom, Comte de Prouence, plusieurs beaux liures en auoyent esté ostez & au lieu d'iceux mis d'autres de peu de valeur & de nulle doctrine. Ce Monge vacquant au Catalogue & à la visite des liures, entre autres en trouua vn, auquel estoyent escrits toutes les nobles & illustres familles tant de Prouence que d'Arragon, Italie & France, où estoiēt deduites leurs alliances auec leur armoiries, ensemble toutes les œuures des Poëtes Prouençaux en rithme Prouençale, recueillies par ledit Hermantere par le commandement dudit Roy d'Arragon, que luy mesme transcriuit en belle lettre, desquelles enuoya coppie à Louys II. du Nom, pere de René Roy de Naples & de Sicile, & Comte de Prouence, de laquelle plusieurs Gentilhommes du pays en firent faire des coppies, comme estans œuures rares & plaisantes : aucuns desquels Gentilhommes, mesme ceux qui estoyent amateurs de la Poësie Prouençale les firent transcrire en belle lettre de forme, & illuminer d'or & d'azur sur parchemin, les autres sur de papier : les vies des Poëtes estoyent escriptes en caracteres rouges, & les Poëmes en lettre noire en langue Prouençalle, de plusieurs sortes & façons de rithmes : quoy faisant il eust grande peine d'entendre la langue Prouençalle, pour autant (dit-il) que leurs peines estoyent de diuerses phrases : car les vns auoyent escrit en leur pure langue Prouençalle & des autres qui n'estoyent si bien versez en icelle qu'estoient d'autre nation, cōme Espagnolle, Italienne ou Gascongne & Françoise, les Poëmes estoyent entremeslez de plusieurs mots de leurs Idiomats, qui les rendoit si obscurs & difficile qu'à grand peine en pouuoit-il tirer le sens. Finalement il les restaura tous en leur entier, & eust tant de grace en son entendement qu'il fut le premier cause que ces souuerains Poëtes, qu'auoyent esté si long-temps en oubly furent remarquez en lumiere. Cette Bibliotheque à present est bié esloignee de cette ancienne splendeur, car il en reste fort peu de vestiges.

Chapitre CIX.

De Touraine.

<small>De l'Eglise de Tours.</small> LA Bibliotheque de l'Eglise de Tours, a esté autrefois tres-riche en Manuscrits; car Alcuin Precepteur de l'Empereur Charlemagne, fit transporter d'Angleterre icy la tres-noble Bibliotheque d'Egbert Archeuesque d'Yorck, au rapport de Iean Balé Anglois *Cent. 2. chap. 16.* sainct Perpetue Euesque de cette Eglise a donné le commancement à cette Bibliotheque, comme le remarque le President de Thou, *S. Perpetuus* (dit-il) *Episcopus Turonensis, Bibliothecam tuendæ Catholicæ fidei præsidio instruxit copiosam propè Episcopium.*

<small>Des Minimes.</small> Dans le Conuent des Peres

des Bibliotheques. 715

Minimes du Plessis les Tours, il y a vne copieuse Bibliotheque de plus de 6000. volumes.

M. N. Le Voyer, Cheualier, Viscomte de Paulmy en Tourai-ne, possede vne belle Bibliotheque, qui estoit des-ia en consideration, sous M. René le Voyer, Viscóte de Paulmy & de la Roche de Genes, Cheualier de l'Ordre du Roy, Bailly de Touraine, &c. qui estoit homme fort affectionné aux lettres, comme le tesmoigne François de la Croix en sa Bibliotheque Françoise, V. R. qui asseure qu'il y auoit plusieurs bós Manuscrits dans icelle, & entre autres plusieurs beaux & doctes liures, de feu Guillaume Postel, entre lesquels se void sa confessió de foy, escrite & signé de sa main.

Et M. le Viscomte de Paulmy.

G. Postel.

Chapitre CX.

De Sauoye.

De Geneue. NOnobſtant toutes les diligences, que i'ay peu faire pour auoir des memoires de cette Prouince, ie n'ay peu en recouurer, ſinon que dans la ville de Geneue ſize en icelle, l'on y conſerue vne ample Bibliotheque publique, à laquelle a eſté ioincte *Theodore de Beze.* la Bibliotheque de Theodore de Beze, qui eſtoit en reputation. Or cette Bibliotheque faira la fin du Traicté des plus belles Bibliotheques, qui ſont dans le monde, que i'ay recherché auec vn grand ſoin; l'honneur & la gloire en ſoit à Dieu, & l'vtilité au public: c'eſt toute la recompenſe que i'en desire de toy (Lecteur equitable) te donnant encore aduis que pendant l'impression de ce liure, plusieurs memoires me sont tombez entre les mains sur les matieres des-ia passées, ce qui causera que ie donneray vn *Appendix*, afin de ne rien laisser imparfait, & que si l'on vient à vne seconde edition, toutes choses soyent remises selon leur ordre.

APPENDIX.

resies de son temps, ce qui causa, que du temps de Iean d'Autriche, il fut pendu à Bruxelles enuiron l'an 1578. pour le fait de la Religion.

Pag. 423. apres la ligne 11. adjoustez

Le Senat a tesmoigné l'affection qu'il a pour l'auancement des bonnes lettres, non seulement pour l'erection d'vn celebre College pour y faire enseigner la ieunesse: mais aussi pour vne insi-gne Bibliotheque pour l'vsage du public ; de laquelle fait mention Iean Niportius en l'Oraison qu'il fit à l'ouuerture de ce College, qui a esté imprimée à Vtrech l'an 1634. in 4. chez Abraham ab Hervuiick & Hermam Ribbius, *Tacco*, dit-il, *de publicis Bibliothecis, quas habemus hic varias optimorum librorum copia instructißimas, inter quas insignior illa, quæ à viris amplißimis Bucchelio & Pollione Reip. nostræ legata est ; quam multorum insuper librorum accessione auctam, magis ac magis instruere ac locupletare Senatui nostro animus est.* I'aurois bien souhaité que cét Autheur nous eust donné la cognoissance des autres Bibliotheques publiques, qui n'ornent pas moins cette ville, que cette sçauante Anne Marie de Schurman l'honneur du sexe feminin pour les sciences & les langues, qui luy sont tres familieres : Elle vid en grande reputation cette année 1644.

A. M. de Schurman.

Pag. 463. lig. 9. apres ledit Roy, *adjoustez*,

APPENDIX.

Iean d'Aurat de Limoges excellent Poëte de son temps, fit vne Epigrame au Roy Charles sur cette Bibliotheque, qui seruira d'ornement à cette description liu.1. pag.6. de l'impression de Paris 1586. chez Guillaume Linocier in 8. lequel Epigrame porte pour titre. *Ad Carolum IX. Galliæ Regem de Bibliotheca Regia.*

Et Ptolemæorum palatia clara fuerunt,
   Et Ptolemææ littora nota Phari.
Littora nocturna fulgente per æquora flamma
   Conspicua & longo prospicienda mari.
Quæ dubium per iter nautis vice syderis essent
   Et regerent grata nautica vela face.
Sed non ille vagis nautarum cursibus ignis
   Gratior in dubio dux erat ante freto.
Clara palatina quam quæ fulgebat ab arce
   Artera doctorum Bibliotheca Pharos.
Vnde per innumeras dispersa volumina terras
   Ingeniis nitidas exeruere faces.
Illa sed vt rerum mortalia cætera fato
   Functa suo Regum munera pressa iacent.
Nulli que nunc Pharos est, emersaque culmina terris
   Extinctique iacent & sine luce foci.
Nec minus ipsa iacet Musæi nomine dicta
   Obruta cum libris Bibliotheca suis.
Sed pia Regis aui Francisci, Carole, cura
   Conquirens doctæ diruta saxa Phari,

APPENDIX.

Muſæúmque nouum Muſis ſacrauit & illis:
Fontis Aquæ-bellæ riuè dicauit aquam.
Cedat Alexandrina Pharo Pharos inclyta Gal-
læ:
Cedat Francisco vis Protomæe tua.
Doctorum tua non habuit plus aula libro-
rum:
Et plus doctorum nostra habet aula vi-
rum.

Pag. 501. apres la 14. ligne, adioutez.

De M. Boſ-
ſu.

M. Boſſu, Aduocat General de la Cour des Aydes, a fait vne Bibliotheque, qui est en recommendation pour les bons liures.

Pag. 502. apres la 3. ligne, adioutez.

De Gilles
Bourdin.

La memoire de ce tres-sçauant Gilles de Bourdin, Procureur General du Roy du Parlement de Paris, n'est pas seulement recommendable pour les grandes qualitez d'esprit qu'il possedoit, ny pour les doctes obseruations sur la coustume de Moulins qu'il a laissé au public: mais elle le doit encore estre pour vne tres-exquise Bibliotheque, qu'il auoit erigé auec de grandes despences & de grands soins: laquelle a merité beaucoup de loüanges par deux excellens Poëtes de son temps, sçauoir Pierre Ronſard dans le 5. liu. des Odes en la 23. qu'il oscrit à Pierre Belon, où il dit:

Il est abordé dans le port
Du docte Bourdin, son support,
Qui comme vn sçauant Ptolomée

APPENDIX.

A de tous costez amassez
Les liures des siecles passez
Empanez de la Renommée.
  Qui garde en son cœur l'equité
L'innocence & la verité,
Ennemy capital du vice,
Aymé des peuples & de Dieu,
Et qui du Palais au milieu
Paroist l'image de Iustice.
  Qui doit sur tous auoir le prix,
Comme aux trois langues bien appris ?
Qui seul fait cas des doctes hommes,
Qui par son sçauoir honoré
A presque tout seul redoré
Cét âge de fer où nous sommes.

Le second Autheur, qui a rendu des honneurs à cette Bibliotheque, est Iean d'Aurat, lequel escriuant vn Epigrame à Bourdin, en laisse vn beau tesmoignage.

Nam Græcam, Latinam iuuenis callebat, Hebræam
  Iam senior linguam, Chaldaicámque simul.
At varias artes cognouerat, omnibus vsus
  Per quos spes aliquid discere posse noui.
Sumptibus & parcens nullis librisque parandis,
  Aut, per quos posset proficere ipse, viris.
Testis & his fuerit sua Bibliotheca superstes;
  Qua non Parrisia clarior vrbe patet.

Pag. 528. apres la lig. 6. adioutez.

M. Iacques Lambin Aduocat en Parlement, homme vray imitatur des belles qualitez de feu son grand Oncle Denis Lam- *De M. Lambin.*

APPENDIX.

bin, qui a laissé de si beaux & doctes ouurages à la posterité: cét eloquent Aduocat n'a espargné aucuns soins à rechercher les liures en toutes les sciences pour faire sa Bibliotheque.

Pag. 544. à la 15. ligne *apres* Memmium, *&c. adioutez.* M. Florent Docteur en l'Vniuersité d'Orleans, à auiourdhuy le soin de cette Bibliotheque, lequel en à vne assez curieuse en son particulier.

De M. Florent.

Pag. 588. *apres* la 20. ligne, *adioutez.*

De Iacques Gopile.

Le Poictou a produit de grands & sçauans personnages, entre lesquels Iacques Gopile merite cette qualité, pour auoir esté tres-celebre Medecin de la Faculté de Paris, & pour les doctes ouurages qu'il a donné au public. Il auoit fait vne excellente Bibliotheque pour son vsage, laquelle perit miserablement, dequoy il en eust vn tel regret, qu'il en mourut, comme le tesmoigne le docte Sceuole de saincte Marte en son Eloge. *Verum gliscentibus* (dit-il) *in Gallia ciuilibus discordiis, cùm turbulenti de plebe homines in Musæum, quod pluribus voluminibus tum impreßis, tum manuscriptis ornatum habebat, inuolassent, sacrámque illam supellectilem profanis manibus violassent ac diripuissent, tantum inde mœrorem collegit, vt extremum vitæ diem clauderet & Ecphrasin, quam in omnes Hippocratis libros meditabatur, inchoatam relinqueret.*

Pag. 626. *apres* la 4. ligne *adioutez.*

APPENDIX.

Le Roy François I. honora tellement *De Guillau-* Guillaume Pellicier, natif d'auprés de la *me Pellicier,* ville de Montpellier, qu'il le fit son Ambassadeur prés les Venitiens, puis le recompensa de l'Euesché du lieu de sa naissance. Ce bon homme ayant esté faussement accusé par ses ennemys d'vne vie des-honneste : fit par sa patience recognoistre son innocence, & vescut iusques à la mort dans l'exercice des sciences, & la recherche des liures, ainsi que le remarque Sceuole de saincte Marthe en l'Eloge de Pellicier. *Quâ ex contumelia* (dit-il) *concepto ingenti næ inani totius aulæ fastidio abdidit se in Monspeliensem illum secessum, vbi liber solutúsque in dulci & optato Musarum sinu placidè ac lubenter acquieuit. Cùm in hunc vsum Bibliothecam haberet locupletissimam innumerísque veterum manuscriptis, & aliis omnium generum codicibus vndique conquisitis adornatam.*

Pag. 664. apres la 17. ligne, *adioutez.*   *De M. de*
M. Camille de Neufville, Abbé d'Ai- *Neufville.*
nay, de l'Isle Barbe, &c. ne possede pas seulement ces belles qualitez d'esprit de ces grands hommes des Villeroys, desquels il est yssu : mais aussi le voyons nous porté d'vn grand zele aux bonnes lettres, & pour l'augmentation de sa magnifique Bibliotheque, qui a prés de quatre mille volumes en toutes les sciences, & en diuerses langues, particulierement des liures Espagnols,

APPENDIX.

lesquels sont tous richement reliez de maroquin incarnat de leuant, auec les armes de ce Seigneur, qui sont vn cheuron à trois Croix ancrées.

Pag. 685. apres la 17. ligne, *adioutez.*

Des Iesuites. La Bibliotheque des Peres Iesuites est fort considerable pour la multitude de ses liures en toutes les sciences, qui y sont conseruez.

Des MM. de Beauharnois. MM. de Beauharnois Lieutenant General de cette ville d'Orleans, & le Docteur de Sorbonne possedent vne bonne Bibliotheque, qu'ils ont faits auec vn grand soin.

Des Capucins. Quant à la Bibliotheque des Peres Capucins, ie treuue qu'elle est en estime entre les belles Bibliotheques d'Orleans.

De M. Mesmin. M. Mesmin Conseiller au Baillage, a esté curieux de rechercher les bons liures pour garnir sa Bibliotheque.

De M. Destap. De pareille curiosité a esté porté M. Destap, pour faire sa bonne Bibliotheque, qui est fort notable pour auoir vne partie de ses liures en grand papier.

De M. Meusnier M. Meusnier, Docteur en Theologie de la Maison de Sorbone, Chanoine & Archidiacre de l'Eglise d'Orleans, grand Vicaire & Official de M. l'Euesque d'Orleans, a fait aussi vne Bibliotheque de consideration.

De M. Boucher. M. Boucher sous Doyen de saincte Croix, a erigé vne Bibliotheque, qui n'est pas des moindres de cette ville.

About the Editor / Translator

Professor John Warwick Montgomery served in the Reference Department of the Library of the University of California at Berkeley before becoming Head Librarian of the Swift Library of Divinity and Philosophy at the University of Chicago. He holds three degrees in library science and bibliographical history: the B.L.S. and M.A. from the University of California, Berkeley, and the Ph.D. from the University of Chicago. He is the editor/translator of *A Seventeenth Century View of European Libraries: Lomeier's* De Bibliothecis, *Chapter X* (University of California Press).

Dr Montgomery's parallel careers in theology and law are represented by his doctorates in Protestant Theology from the University of Strasbourg, France and his LL.D. from the University of Cardiff, Wales, and by his extensive publications in those fields. He is an *avocat à la cour, barreau de Paris*, an English barrister, and a member of the bar of the Supreme Court of the United States. He is Professor Emeritus of Law and Humanities, University of Bedfordshire, England, and Distinguished Research Professor of Philosophy at Concordia University Wisconsin, U.S.A.

www.ingramcontent.com/pod-product-compliance
Lightning Source LLC
Chambersburg PA
CBHW052108010526
44111CB00036B/1573